The Book
of Not Knowing

The Book
of Not Knowing

Exploring the True Nature
of Self, Mind, and Consciousness

Peter Ralston

Edited by Laura Ralston

North Atlantic Books
Berkeley, California

Published by
North Atlantic Books
P.O. Box 12327   Cover and book design by Mike Kane
Berkeley, California 94712   Printed in the United States of America

The Book of Not Knowing: Exploring the True Nature of Self, Mind, and Consciousness is sponsored by the Society for the Study of Native Arts and Sciences, a nonprofit educational corporation whose goals are to develop an educational and cross-cultural perspective linking various scientific, social, and artistic fields; to nurture a holistic view of arts, sciences, humanities, and healing; and to publish and distribute literature on the relationship of mind, body, and nature.

North Atlantic Books' publications are available through most bookstores. For further information, call 800-733-3000 or visit our Web site at www.northatlanticbooks.com.

Library of Congress Cataloging-in-Publication Data
Ralston, Peter, 1949–
    The book of not knowing : the true nature of self, mind, and consciousness
/ by Peter Ralston.
        p. cm.
    ISBN 978-1-55643-857-8
    1. Consciousness. 2. Self-consciousness (Awareness) I. Title.
    B808.9.R34 2010
    126—dc22
2009015610

1 2 3 4 5 6 7 8 9 SHERIDAN 14 13 12 11 10

TABLE OF CONTENTS

PART III: In Search of Real Being

PART IV: Creating Self

PART V: Penetrating Experience

INTRODUCTION
Grounded Enlightenment

Just as suddenly as a bubble bursting, my mind opened up to a new level of consciousness and I felt my sense of self completely dissolve.... In that instant, I became clearly and absolutely conscious of who and what I am....
  —Peter Ralston

1   For forty years I've had the good fortune of being able to make a living teaching in two extraordinary fields: martial arts and ontology—the investigation of the nature of being. My reputation as a martial artist is what draws most people to study with me—in 1978 I was the first non-Asian to win the full-contact World Championships held in China, and I am considered to be among the best in the world. I might be better than most at fighting, but as every new student of mine quickly discovers, the heart of my work has always been "consciousness."

2   While it was increased consciousness that transformed my skills to the level of mastery, some people are still a bit surprised to learn that everything I teach in the physical domain—from effective body-being to the Art of Effortless Power—relies heavily on mind work as a foundation. In Japan, the samurai began to practice Zen contemplation because it made them better warriors, but this connection was discovered much earlier, almost by accident,

in the Zen monasteries of ancient China. Long hours of stillness in contemplation can be detrimental to the body, so the monks began to incorporate calisthenics, and over time this practice evolved into martial arts.

3   The study of consciousness itself can stand entirely on its own and does not require any physical activity. For me the fluid, ever-changing action of fighting provided an excellent way to investigate all aspects of "being," allowing access to areas of the mind that remain obscure to most people. Both my physical training and my contemplation work were always driven by a fascination with uncovering the truth behind the human condition. I was relentless in my pursuit of understanding every facet of being human, including the nature of perception, relationships, and even reality itself. An essential contribution to this effort was a breakthrough in consciousness, which Zen people call an "enlightenment."

4   There is a lot of misunderstanding about enlightenment in our culture, and such an experience is too often shrouded in mystery and fantasy. It is a life-altering leap in consciousness, but one enlightenment doesn't necessarily turn you into some wizened old sage, and practically everyone is capable of having such an experience. For me, it was a beginning, an entrance into a completely new and inconceivable consciousness. It is impossible to accurately convey such an experience, but I'll try to give you some idea what my first enlightenment was like:

> I'd just finished several days of intense contemplation. I'd never worked harder at anything in my life, and yet I hadn't become conscious of the nature of my own self. I was still at the meditation hall the following morning, sitting contentedly against the wall in a sunlit loft, when I had the most remarkable expe-

rience. Just as suddenly as a bubble bursting, my mind opened up to a new level of consciousness, and I felt my familiar sense of self completely dissolve. It seemed like my awareness both expanded and merged with what had always been true: the very essence of "being." It was unlike anything I'd ever known, and no description could do justice to the experience. In that instant, I was clearly and absolutely conscious of who and what I am.

A deep sense of peace washed over me, and also an unexpected feeling of freedom. No joy I had ever experienced even remotely compared to this awakening. My mind was freed of burdens that I didn't know I had. Assumptions about reality and limitations in my awareness just disappeared. My sense of self was . . . open and without location. A sense of calm, lightness, and ease saturated my being, and I felt I had at last become one with my real self. All inner turmoil evaporated. All doubt and struggle fell away. It was the most extraordinary moment of my life.

5   Such an awakening is completely outside of conventional human experience. The normal operating principle that used to *be* and *live* as my "self" was no longer there. I didn't even speak about this enlightenment for several days since there was no "self" left to desire to communicate it. I wasn't freed of self completely, but it simply wasn't a feature at the time, and has never regained the same importance. It turns out that consciousness is not dependent on the self as we might assume, but the significance of this reality can only become clear through personal insight.

6   The realization in that one instant permeated every part of my awareness — my whole sense of *being* changed. Having so much

assumption fall away in one moment had the effect of re-creating my consciousness as a blank slate. I was opened up as never before. Suddenly I had room to experience new insights that would previously have been overwhelmed by my lifelong accumulation of beliefs and conclusions. I could see that I had been trapped within my own perceptions, my own logic, my own knowledge and experience.

7   In such an open state, my ability to learn was completely transformed. Discovery became a real possibility — not something to be left to other people, but a joyful exercise to be taken on for myself. I investigated my intellect, my awareness, my perceptions, beliefs and assumptions. I explored my body, movement, interaction, and relationships. I discovered that the more I learned, the more I *could* learn. From such investigation, many more insights arose, and my continued contemplation led to further, even deeper, enlightenment experiences.

8   Over time, I developed new abilities and ways of thinking. Because my experience was authentically based, issues of self-esteem and self-image had become irrelevant, and without effort I gained a natural sense of authenticity. I didn't have to pretend anything or doubt myself. Limitations of self-doubt gave way to self-acceptance and an openness to whatever is true. Relationships turned from acting out patterns of behavior to seeking out an honest and real expression from myself and others. I was empowered to investigate and clearly see aspects of being human that had previously seemed beyond reach, except as hearsay or belief. I came to understand the nature of belief itself and discovered that the very foundation of my sense of reality and life was but a collection of assumptions and misconceptions.

9   Becoming unconditionally open to the truth regardless of personal preferences showed me that consciousness is also the key to being truly effective. In time, my body became attuned to principles that facilitated my discovery of effortless power. For the first time, I felt truly comfortable within my whole body. It became soft and relaxed, unified and integrated, full of energy and sensitivity. I could feel every cell of my body all at once, as well as the ground beneath my feet and the space all around me. I developed a powerful ability to feel the presence of other people, and from there made great leaps in skill. Such magical possibilities continued to spring up, and these are what led me to mastery. If I'd been a surgeon or pianist, I'm certain the changes and leaps in ability would have manifested there instead.

10   While I get excited about the possibilities available through this work, I urge you to consider that enlightenment is not a matter to be pursued as an abstract concept or some fantasy on a mountaintop. Taking on the work in this book means a real and personal commitment to experience the truth of your own being and reality, *whatever that may turn out to be.* I can help you with this, but it will do you no good just to believe what I say. In fact, as any Zen master knows, students need to cast aside *all* beliefs and make the trip for themselves.

11   Zen masters are notoriously reticent, and with good reason: matters of consciousness and enlightenment are impossible to convey. Nevertheless, since I myself am notoriously talkative, I'm about to spend twenty-six chapters trying to help you personally discover the truth about yourself — beyond belief, hearsay, or conjecture. Although the truth is already so and is profoundly simple, it is not accessible within the world as we know it. What's

needed is a new kind of "communicating" and "listening," so please keep that in mind as you read.

12   This book contains real issues about human existence. It has been painstakingly crafted to help you transform your life from the ground up — including your experience of self, perception, mind, and consciousness. A foundational shift of this magnitude requires your participation and commitment. I promise that if you delve deeply into what's being said, create the insights you're invited to create, and work hard to truly grasp this communication in your own experience, your entire outlook and experience of life and self will be transformed in ways that you cannot yet comprehend. This book is about penetrating to the very source and nature of the human condition. In other words, it is about *you*.

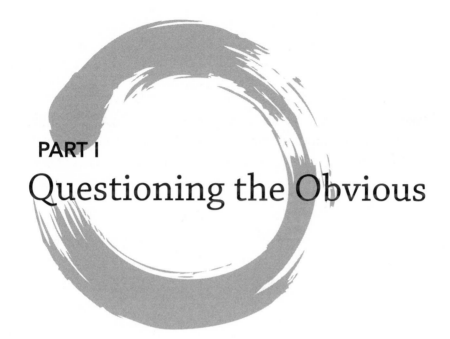

PART I
Questioning the Obvious

CHAPTER ONE
A Powerful Openness

We question not for an answer,
but to experience whatever is true.

Beginning to Wonder

1:1   The heart of the matter is this: to move toward enlightenment, you must begin with not-knowing. Genuine not-knowing is a completely open state of mind that always precedes the leap into a direct consciousness of Being. If you can make that leap right now — become directly conscious of the nature of self and reality — then close the book and go for it. There's nothing left but for me to begin speaking on and on about self and mind, perception and consciousness.

1:2   If I were to say to you that in this moment your own mind and perceptions keep you from an experience of your true nature and the nature of reality, you may well wonder what I'm talking about. That's OK. Simply be open to the possibility that there may be something about yourself and reality that is "hidden in plain sight." Not-knowing certainly isn't the sole topic of this book, but rather the best state from which to read it. The real topic of this book is *you.*

1:3   If you're interested in what "you" are all about, I might be able to help you with your efforts. But why would you care to take me up on that? Why would someone question his or her experience of self and reality? It certainly seems there are more pressing matters to deal with in life.

Chop wood, carry water.

1:4   Some Zen sayings appear to be reminders for the monks to tend to earthly tasks. Perhaps this is to help keep their consciousness grounded in objective reality.

After ecstasy, the laundry.

1:5   The monks might question deep matters of consciousness and being, but clearly life must go on. Maybe, like ours, the monks' life is just laundry after laundry as well, but doesn't it seem they're more content with mundane chores than many of us are with all our acquisitions and entertainments?

1:6   Consider for a moment that the human condition is exactly the same in or out of a monastery — a condition of discomforting uncertainty. Wondering about the meaning of self and life seems to be universal, but outside the monastery, we generally let others provide the explanations for us. We don't recognize how much we have to gain by looking into these matters for ourselves.

Beyond the Self Mind

1:7 People seldom look for answers when they don't have any questions. When reality is perceived as solidly "known," it engenders no investigation — why would it? We seem to live our lives at face value and rarely look beneath the surface of our daily existence. We move through different circumstances — engaging in events, interacting with others, judging, perceiving, reacting — all within our taken-for-granted worlds. We act as if we know what it's all about. But something at the core of our being remains apprehensive about the possibility that our sense of reality and sense of self are somehow fabrications.

1:8 Well, it's true — they are.

1:9 From infancy, the human mind struggles for certainty, continually drawing conclusions in an attempt to discern the meaning of everything we perceive. Many such skills are needed for self-preservation. We learn to recognize a relationship between hand and mouth, and pick out the sound of our mother's voice, then quickly move on to essentials like "Will it eat me?" or "Can I eat it?"

1:10 As we grow, we assimilate and develop very basic beliefs and conclusions, not only about the world but also about ourselves. These core beliefs fall into the background as permanent organizing factors for all new information. As a survival mechanism it's quite efficient, but one of the major drawbacks is that all future encounters will be biased by these previous conclusions. This is no small matter. Anything we perceive — even whether or not we perceive it — is subject to the filter of our beliefs and assumptions. What we don't realize is that we are so deeply entrenched in these convictions and beliefs that they are unrecognizable. Our core beliefs simply appear to us as reality.

We don't know who discovered water,
but we're certain it wasn't a fish.
—John Culkin

1:11   It's not hard to discern when other people's beliefs and assumptions are self-serving or mistaken, but recognizing this dynamic in ourselves is another story. Just as an eye cannot see itself, the awareness from which we perceive the world has no ability to perceive itself. This makes recognizing and questioning our own beliefs a uniquely difficult undertaking. As with an eye, we are constantly aware of the view, while giving little or no thought to what is providing it. We don't notice the set of assumptions from which we comprehend the world, and yet it determines our reality in every moment.

1:12   Our "knowing" is like a closed circuit that limits possibilities in our thinking, our relating, and in our way of being in the world. To step outside of it is very freeing, but it takes effort, and questioning ourselves in this way can be uncomfortably open-ended. We have to be willing to let go of familiar "landmarks" like our self-identity and cherished beliefs. Whether these ideas are based on truth or untruth is insignificant here. Our job in this book is not to decide which beliefs are most accurate—what we want instead is to personally experience what's true. For that, we need to loosen our grip on what we already hold as the truth.

1:13   The alternative is simply to continue operating as we always have: rather blind to the mechanisms that run us, and living at the mercy of our own predetermined reactions. People often accept this as inevitable, but it need not be. Making even a small shift away from this "programming," we find that our experience of life and self are altered significantly, and a new kind of freedom becomes possible. "Knowing" can be useful, but learning *not* to know creates a powerful openness that is inconceivable until it is experienced.

1:14   One of the first objectives here is to assist you in looking at knowing and not-knowing in a different way. You'll come to see how the cultural attitudes we share regarding both knowledge and self can sentence us to a lifetime of low-grade desperation and superficiality. Start to think about this for yourself. For instance, note that I use the negative term "*not*-knowing" out of necessity. In our culture, we name what interests us, and apparently we have little interest in the state of consciousness that is prior to comprehension. We denigrate not-knowing as "stupidity" or, more kindly, as ignorance. Obviously, we've all experienced not knowing something, but we disregard the fact that such a state always exists before achieving any kind of insight.

1:15   If you are honestly willing to look into these considerations, this work will engage you in a process of becoming increasingly conscious of the real nature of self, and the true nature of being. If you happen to discover some handy tips for better living here, fine, but that is not the purpose of this communication. To get anything truly useful, you're going to have to get it in the form of a *conscious experience*. You're probably not sure what I mean by that, which is one of the reasons we're going to proceed with this whole endeavor as though we're ascending a steep mountain. Like traversing a switchback trail, we will encounter the same views again and again, but always from a slightly higher vantage point.

Knowing and Not-Knowing

*Genius, in truth, means little more than the faculty
of perceiving in an unhabitual way.*
—William James

1:16   Certain names are synonymous with genius. Names like Albert Einstein, Isaac Newton, and Galileo live on in our culture because of the remarkable discoveries these people made. Although their fields of expertise were different from one another, each of their impressive contributions began with one simple principle. People like Gautama Buddha, Solomon, and Aristotle are known as sages, people with extraordinary insight and wisdom. Their insights were founded on the very same principle that made scientific innovations possible. What all these remarkable people had in common is that they went beyond their beliefs and assumptions to a state of not-knowing.

1:17   But not-knowing sounds like ignorance, and in just about any culture ignorance is a bad thing. We certainly don't make the connection between this state of openness and the wonder it generates, which is so necessary for learning. From early in life, we're often praised for knowing and frowned on for not knowing. We grow up being afraid of our own ignorance and terrified that our ignorance may show. Over time, we're conditioned to appear as "knowledgeable" as we can, while carefully concealing the limits of our understanding.

1:18   Consider the overused phrase, "think outside the box," which suggests that a person look beyond any conventional views and come up with some useful new insight. The term's popularity likely stems from the way it implies a creative approach to thinking without emphasizing the "undesirable" prerequisite for that leap, which is a state of not-knowing.

1:19   We all experience the dawning of a realization or grasp a new idea now and then, but insight doesn't seem to be something a person can just tap into at will. To access genius, we need to be able to step outside our familiar self-mind and resist the urge to hastily fill in the blank spaces with our *knowing*. Being willing to not-know means having the courage to surrender all that we think we know, and all that we believe is true. When we open up in this way, we create a space to experience what is actually true. From there, anything can come to light.

We must know, if only in order to learn not to know.
The supreme lesson of human consciousness is to learn
how not to know.
That is, how not to interfere.
—D. H. Lawrence

1:20   Knowledge has great value for us, both in the biological and social domains. We admire and cling so much to *knowing* because humanity has advanced by virtue of its growing body of knowledge. Since prehistory, our basic physical survival has demanded that we swiftly categorize all incoming information. Knowing how to avoid danger or defeat an enemy, where to obtain food or material for tools, and how to construct a dwelling or heal a sickness were all necessary for staying alive.

1:21   Although the dangers associated with physical survival may have eased a bit over time, our increasingly more complicated social structures demand an ever-expanding range of knowledge. The stakes are high in our social survival. What we "know"—or appear to know—not only creates our sense of identity, it also establishes our place in the community, which determines the degree of access we have to all that we need in order to survive, both socially and physically.

1:22   It's not surprising that we frequently hear the phrase "knowledge is power." In fact, that is one of many culturally accepted truisms that so often obscure the larger truth. We unquestioningly assume that if knowing is power then *not* knowing must signify weakness.

1:23   Let's set that one aside for a moment and look at another such truism, which also applies to our current consideration. We've heard many times the assertion that "everyone is unique." It's true that the culture we live in provides us with a seemingly limitless range of possibilities from which to create our personal self-identities, beliefs, and behavior. But a closer look reveals that our cultural assumptions act as a kind of filter through which certain ideas simply do not pass.

1:24   While each one of us can claim to be unique in some way, we must keep in mind that we all fashion ourselves in relation to the culture in which we live and develop. The "lone wolf" may scorn the "sheep" of society, but the lone wolf is a much more common identity symbol than the sheep. Both notions clearly exist "inside the box" of our cultural framework, and neither is unique. Every aspect of a person's individuality—indeed, his entire experience of self, life, and reality—is largely a product of the culture in which he lives. And of course, everything he knows to be true, and all the knowledge that he can access, is also based on this unrecognized cultural framework. Becoming aware of this framework creates the possibility of freedom from it, and freedom from it empowers our ability to discover the truth for ourselves.

1:25   Knowledge may be powerful, but holding it as "the truth" greatly narrows the prospect of any further discovery. Consider people who cling to a belief system or dogma as though it could possibly embody the truth, failing to make a distinction between believing these things and having an experience of whatever is really true. This dogma may derive from someone's profound grasp of the truth, but believing and memorizing what someone else says are not the same as experiencing the truth for oneself.

1:26   Not-knowing allows an open and authentic experience of this moment right now, and it's this kind of genuine experience that allows for great leaps in awareness and creativity. Few spiritual practices will admit that believing in something can only provide us with an idea, a possibility. Merely believing the idea is easier because it seems to relieve us of any responsibility, but it also diminishes our curiosity for looking into the truth of the matter for ourselves. Pursuing an ancient art or spiritual practice is perhaps a positive direction, but only insofar as we use it for furthering a sincere inquiry of our own.

Seek not to follow in the footsteps of men of old;
seek what they sought.
—Matsuo Basho

1:27   How genuinely we experience life is determined by the level of our conscious awareness. Unless we're open and willing to directly experience the truth of something for ourselves, there is no way for such an experience to take place. If we rely on hearsay, or fill in all the blanks with beliefs, no genuine experience is likely to occur. Any time that we can open up and *not* know, we clear a space for understanding something beyond our habits of thinking. This is how someone like Picasso might suddenly be able to see the world in a new way. And evidence of gravity was there all along for Newton, but it took a certain transcendence of his own "knowledge" before he could conceive of it.

1:28 From a state of not-knowing, people like Galileo and Einstein were able to undertake the open questioning that allowed them to discover and invent new ways of thinking about the universe. Take note that their discoveries weren't just new ideas — anyone can come up with new ideas. What each of these people had was an insight, which is a sudden awakening in the mind or consciousness, a personal encounter with real possibilities. Their insights were grounded in reality — the result of something actually experienced — and they changed the way we relate to the physical universe. Although it might be harder to recognize, the same kind of openness that fostered those insights was also the source of Rumi's poetry and Gautama Buddha's massive enlightenment.

1:29 Humanity advances through the contributions of individuals. Before any contribution, there is insight, and before insight, there must be openness. The opening power of not-knowing is found wherever creativity is active. Whether they're aware of it or not, artists abide in not-knowing when they create, athletes need it to get into the "zone," lovers use it to allow total communion with another, and scientists must continually return to it before they can make any new discovery. This key to the very source of creativity is available to every human being in every circumstance, and we can all use it to help find our way to a deeper and more genuine experience of ourselves.

No problem can be solved from the same level
of consciousness that created it.
—Albert Einstein

Self and Being

1:30   Consider the possibility that there are two distinct aspects of your-self. One is what you are originally or naturally. It is your "being," who you really are without pretense, affectation, programming, or any supplementary process. The other aspect is what you have come to *know* as yourself—a self-identity that is created and main-tained through all the beliefs, assumptions, and knowledge you've acquired in life. Since it's all you know, it's not easy to see that this identification of your self is strictly a secondary process. Your self-identity is conceptual; your real being exists *prior to* concept.

Self "knows."
Being just is.

1:31   Our ability to transcend the conceptual aspect of self isn't some mystical journey to be undertaken with lots of chanting and incense. It requires no rituals or ceremony, no spiritual doctrine, and no beliefs at all. Such efforts can only supply us with addi-tional concepts, which often merely feed our fantasies, or at least distract us from our goal of an authentic experience. Transcend-ing the self does not involve making "additions" to yourself or to your knowledge, or increasing your activities, but rather the oppo-site. It is simply the ability to locate and become deeply conscious of a genuine experience of "being."

1:32   We probably all get a glimpse of our own "being" at one time or another, so it's safe to say that everything needed to accomplish this is already with us. What's also true is that just about everyone experiences some form of resistance to the work of becoming more conscious of self and being, and this resistance is often hard to recognize at first. Remaining open and honest without ignoring whatever we experience can help us face any challenges that may arise. The deep self-honesty required for pursuing such insight can seem daunting at times, especially to someone who doesn't yet understand how much he or she has to gain through this work.

1:33   Whether participating in a group effort or studying on their own, most people who pursue consciousness work soon gain access to new levels of honesty and insight. They often experience an increase in creativity, and they notice a greater capacity for intimacy with others. In all different facets of their lives, new possibilities spring up that were previously unimaginable. It's a powerful and sometimes dramatic shift, but there's nothing artificial or particularly mysterious about it. Becoming open to discovering the truth for oneself has a way of making us responsible for and more present within our own lives. We discover that the richness of life isn't all created by people, events, and acquisitions, but by our ability to open up and fully *be* with whatever is occurring—present in heart, body, mind, and connecting fully with others and with life.

1:34   Making a distinction between our real selves—what we might call "being"—and our conceptual selves can sound simple enough on paper, and essentially it is. But in practice we find that we continually bump into obstacles that arise from our habitual thinking and familiar emotions, and from assumptions that we unknowingly share as a culture. That's why one aspect of this work involves learning to recognize how cultural assumptions and habitual beliefs can stand in the way of any genuine experience.

The most profound experiences arise from questioning the obvious.

1:35   In our culture, we spend most of our time looking outward in search of some satisfying experience. We focus on the circumstances of life — attaining our desires and avoiding our fears — yet, when all is said and done, we still find little satisfaction. When conventional methods don't work, we take on the unconventional. In the hope of "finding" ourselves, we might explore yoga or extreme sports, practice meditation, study an art form, join a spiritual movement, or read books on philosophy. We might not find our real selves, but we do keep busy!

1:36   Everyone has had a moment or two when he or she experienced just being themselves, and it probably had some element of surprise to it, as well as a certain familiarity. How this happens, and how often, seems as varied as there are people in the world. In a flash, someone might recognize that she's been living within an act, a pretense. Dropping the facade for even a moment allows her a glimpse of her more honest self. Someone else may be in great distress, but then break free of the pain to have an experience of himself as an entity independent of his own suffering — somehow free and yet more real. Perhaps another person hides behind subtle artifice spurred by the desire to be liked, approved of, valued in some way, but in a courageous moment braves his vulnerability and bounds forward with what's real in his heart. Maybe another gets a good look at herself through the eyes of others, seeing in this reflection something repugnant to her own heart, and in this moment she opens up to a more genuine sense of her self.

1:37 No matter how it occurs, it's as if an invisible mist parts to reveal a glimpse of a simpler and more genuine self, uncluttered with complications and affectations. This moment is self-validating, since in that instant an undeniably real experience of ourselves is awakened—is "remembered." Whether it comes as an inkling or a full blown awakening, the direction is the same—it is toward what is real.

1:38 But the moment passes. Although this experience of ourselves is clearly more genuine, it slips once again from view, and does so without our noticing. We slide right back into what is familiar, and the realness is rarely missed since it is once again buried so that no contrast remains to remind us of our inauthenticity. Why does this happen? Why is such an obviously more real experience of ourselves replaced by what is clearly—at least within the moment of insight—less true to ourselves?

1:39 It seems that an honest and clear perception of oneself is "incompatible" with any familiar and habitual self-identity. Rather than dwell in the uncertain realm of the real, it's much easier for us to revert to an already established and acceptable sense of self. Wary of uncharted territory, our awareness falls quickly and easily back into the habits and routines that serve our many self-concerns. What we don't realize is that anything we do, think, or feel from here simply adds more layers to the self-identity, further burying what is real. We substitute information for wisdom and confuse fantasizing about something with having a genuine experience. So immersed are we in our cultural setting that we are unable to recognize how the very methods we use to try to fill the void actually make an authentic experience nearly impossible.

1:40   This way of perceiving ourselves and the world around us greatly hampers our ability to discover new possibilities outside of our familiar experience. Since our experience is dominated by assumptions and beliefs, we're limited to pursuing a self that is more conceptual than real. But there are other ways to be. Instead of holding our thoughts, feelings, and beliefs as "reality," we can open up beyond the world of our beliefs and honestly investigate what's true. It's not so much a way to live as a way to wake up.

Try being alone, without any form of distraction, and you will see how quickly you want to get away from yourself and forget what you are. That is why this enormous structure of professional amusement . . . is so prominent a part of what we call civilization. If you observe, you will see that people the world over are becoming more and more distracted, increasingly sophisticated and worldly. . . . Because we are inwardly empty, dull, mediocre, we use our relationships and our social reforms as a means of escaping ourselves. I wonder if you have noticed how lonely most people are. And to escape from loneliness we run to temples, churches, or mosques, we dress up and attend social functions, read, and so on. . . . If you inquire a little into boredom you will find that the cause of it is loneliness. It is in order to escape from loneliness that we want to be together, we want to be entertained, to have distractions of every kind, gurus, religious ceremonies, prayers, or the latest novel. Being inwardly lonely we become mere spectators in life; and we can be the players only when we understand loneliness and go beyond it.
  . . . because beyond it lies the real treasure.
                              —J. Krishnamurti

1:41 Consider once again the two aspects of your self: the one that you know as self, which is founded on a collection of overlooked assumptions and beliefs; and the other, which is who you really are prior to the layers of conceptual identity that presently obscure your authentic experience of being. What if you could learn to live your life from this more genuine self? Would it make you rich, sexy, lovable? Maybe not, but it would be the truth.

CHAPTER TWO
Moving Beyond Belief

The Delphic Oracle said that I was the wisest of all the Greeks.
It is because I alone of all the Greeks know that I know nothing.
—Socrates

Learning to Not-Know

2:1   One of my apprentices, let's call her Susan, was a math student who liked to share this story about an experience she had in drawing class: In the first class they practiced a few shading techniques and then sketched some fruit from a basket on the table. At the end of class, even her best drawings looked like circles and ovals rather than oranges or grapes. In the second class they sketched some pots. Susan drew cylindrical forms all right, but they didn't look much like pots. Discouraged, she went to the instructor to drop the class, explaining that a math mind was obviously not equipped for drawing. The instructor listened and said that she should attend one more class before giving up. Susan agreed.

2:2   In the next class, a still life arrangement was there as usual, but was completely covered by a sheet of white muslin. Susan suspected the instructor was having some fun at her expense, but she took out her pencils and did her best to depict what was laid out before her. Afterward, she again asked permission to drop, but the instructor wanted to see her drawings.

2:3   Susan showed him, and the instructor told her she had greatly improved. Susan was confused. She looked from sketchpad to table and back again. It was true! Although the drawing was not very attractive, the forms depicted on the paper were very close to those on the table. Some of the folds of muslin in her drawing actually had the character of fabric, and there was an almost photographic realism to the shading on the mysterious shapes. When Susan expressed her surprise, the instructor told her that whether she realized it or not, she had been drawing the familiar objects from memory and association rather than from sight. The unfamiliar shapes made her have to see what was really there.

2:4   When we know something intellectually, but fail to experience what's right in front of us, we are only fractionally engaged with the world around us. On the other hand, allowing ourselves to know "about" something, and at the same time "not-know" what it really is, provides a new relationship to our knowledge — including what we know, but giving it a backseat to our present experience.

2:5   The same is true in any instance of learning. In any sport, art, or craft, the techniques can only give us a direction. At some point we must diverge from our reliance on intellectual data, let go of assumptions, associations, emotional considerations, and "knowing." Once we open up to engage with what is truly real in this instant, genuine insight becomes possible, and we reach our greatest levels of creativity.

2:6   What Susan's drawing instructor did was force her to come from not-knowing. While Susan sketched fruit or pots, her "knowing" provided the "idea" of what was before her eyes. She was not drawing an apple, but rather her concept of an apple. When this familiar pattern of interpretation was interrupted, she was able to observe things with "fresh" eyes. Rather than seeing familiar objects, she saw what was present, and she saw it in terms of space, shadow, and light — all necessary distinctions for translating a visual image to paper. She had discovered for herself the difference between "knowing" what's there and "perceiving" what's there.

> *Everyone takes the limits of his own vision*
> *for the limits of the world.*
> —Arthur Schopenhauer

Natural Contemplation

2:7   Any valid inquiry begins with not-knowing, or else it merely serves to confirm what is already known. Making a shift from knowing to not-knowing opens up a space for new understanding to arise. Clearly this shift is necessary for creativity, but many people don't realize that it is also the basis for contemplation.

2:8   Contemplation as a meditative discipline is looking into some matter for oneself with the intent to discover what's true about it. To some degree, we all contemplate throughout our lives, but serious contemplation requires great discipline, great curiosity, or great stubbornness. As a child I possessed two of those three qualities in abundance. I would frequently set my attention on some puzzling matter and wonder about it steadfastly until something more was revealed. Around the age of six, for example, I became fascinated with the idea of time, and began to investigate it.

2:9 Like most children, I lived in a pretty simple and yet continually emerging world so it wasn't unusual for me to start wondering how it could be that "now" changed, and became "later," but was still always now. I had to check this out. I sat on the edge of my bed and imagined a future of standing up, knowing that once I stood, the experience would be as real as sitting. Then I would stand, and find myself in the world that I had only imagined. Although I knew I was only imagining the future, the future kept coming to pass.

2:10 I remained fascinated by this puzzle for some time. Standing and sitting, I repeated my little experiment over and over. Eventually something strange began to sink in. I realized that my whole life was somehow already happening now. It was *all* now, even though I could only perceive what seemed to be occurring one piece at a time. Then I suddenly got something rather startling to me. Just like moving from sitting to standing, I would move from life into death, and experience dying *as* the present moment. I felt like there was no separation between my present experience of being a child standing in my bedroom, and being an old man dying in my bed. This had a profound effect on my experience of life. Aside from being somewhat unnerving, it was probably the time when I first began to grasp what could be revealed through a persistent kind of wondering.

It's not that I'm so smart,
it's just that I stay with problems longer.
—Albert Einstein

2:11 Some of my questions led to insights, but most only led to more questioning. By the time I was a teenager studying martial arts, it was natural that I would spend as much time "contemplating" Judo as I did practicing it. Unable to train as much as I wanted, I'd spend hours working out the throws in my mind. One day, I suddenly realized what the "essence" of Judo was, and my skill took a giant leap forward. Virtually overnight, I became good at it, whereas before this insight I was no better than any other beginner in my class. From this experience, I became convinced of the power of contemplation to bring about insight. I wanted more, and naturally continued to investigate things on my own, but then at age twenty I took up the study of Zen.

Zen Influence

2:12   The word *Zen* means "to sit" and refers to a practice of meditation. The purpose for this meditation is to reach what Zen people call "enlightenment"—a leap in consciousness to a sudden awareness of the essential nature of "being." Since such an experience cannot be achieved through the use of the intellect, it lies outside of what we know. It is literally "unthinkable," which is why Zen has a reputation for being puzzling or nonsensical. Through prolonged meditation, the austerity of having no distractions, and the Zen master's unanswerable questions, the practitioner is pushed beyond his "knowing." At this point, if he lets go of his mind, he is ripe for life-altering insight. Not-knowing is an essential part of making such a leap in awareness.

2:13   Perhaps because Zen was simply a formalized continuation of the contemplation I'd been doing for so long, in a relatively short time I had my first full-blown enlightenment experience. Over the years, I continued to have many other breakthroughs and enlightenment experiences. All of these contributed to my investigation into the nature of being human by providing recurring access to an awareness that is beyond knowledge or even thought. It may seem strange, but being able to experience "no-mind" greatly increased the clarity and depth of my ability to investigate both consciousness and "mind."

2:14   Throughout all of this study, contemplation, and research, one of the more significant discoveries came as I worked to discern the difference between what I personally experienced to be true and what I only believed to be true. It was here — beyond beliefs, dogma, and wishful thinking — that I discovered the awakening power of not-knowing. Since it exists in a place that few think to look, it isn't common or popular, but venturing into this domain produces a freedom and provides new possibilities with each step. Everyone has access to this same facility, but the "place" we need to come from is buried under countless layers of beliefs.

2:15   It's true that beliefs are very powerful. It's not a new idea that to change anything about ourselves, we must change the beliefs from which our emotions and behavior are created. Several popular self-help trainings involve consciously exchanging one set of beliefs for another. For example, a person who lacks faith in himself might try to override his negative self-image by deliberately formulating a belief that he is intelligent and capable. If he can maintain this new perspective, he will begin to interpret events differently, and his more positive interpretations will support an increasingly positive view of himself. Although this kind of work can have a positive effect, it does nothing to increase our understanding of the real nature of mind or the self.

Relating Differently to Beliefs

2:16 If manipulating our beliefs is this powerful—if we can alter our sense of self in the world simply by switching to a different set of beliefs—imagine how powerful it might be to get free of our beliefs entirely. It never occurs to us that this is possible. In the desperate scramble to feel better about ourselves, it's easy to forget that whether we act from a belief that we're worthless or important, neither viewpoint is the truth—it's a *belief*. In fact, most of what we think of as our *selves* is simply an amassed collection of beliefs and assumptions. Fabricating a few more optimistic beliefs might help alter some aspect of our behavior, but it does not, and cannot, lead to a more genuine sense of self.

2:17 The good news is that we don't have to live exclusively in relation to our beliefs. Rather than manipulating ourselves into exchanging one set of beliefs for another, we can look into what beliefs *are*. At this point, it may be hard to understand what is meant by this. Don't worry—a large part of our work here is learning new ways to think about some very ordinary things. In fact, the more familiar they are, the harder it can be to see them in a different way.

2:18 Here's an analogy that's useful for approaching this belief business: if all you've ever done with your car is put gas in it and drive around, it would mean a huge shift in both focus and effort if you decided to start learning how cars work. Each of these activities concerns a car, but understanding the mechanics involved is very different from using one for transportation. Being driven by your beliefs is a very different matter than consciously understanding how it is your beliefs are created and what purpose they serve.

2:19   If all you've ever done with your beliefs is just believe them, taking a look "under the hood" at what you hold as true can be a radical shift. It's an investigation that takes place within your self, so while it may sound strange, it's not inaccurate to call this direction more "intimate" than blindly following your beliefs. If you've been reading mindfully, you've probably noticed something of this already. Such "self-intimacy" on an immediate experiential level can be exhilarating, as well as uncomfortable at times — something like getting a glimpse of the unexplored frontier of your own consciousness. So, while it's wise to be prepared for some sort of reaction, all you need to recognize for now is that it's possible to make a shift regarding your beliefs, and open up to a genuine experience of this moment.

2:20   Once we truly experience the nature of beliefs, we can decide to keep those that we consider empowering or otherwise useful, or take steps to detach ourselves from all of them if we choose. And while "detachment" from something can sound cold or emotionless, it also aptly describes an experience of freedom, of unencumbrance, and that is what I mean here. I'm talking about opening up to the possibility of experiencing what's true rather than believing whatever comes to mind based on the same old presumptions.

2:21   Shifting from belief to experience is like the difference between, say, trying to eat the picture on the menu rather than the food itself. Or the difference between memorizing some knowledge instead of grasping the truth of what's being said. However you can imagine it, the point is that not-knowing allows access to what's real. Making this shift, your personal experience becomes new and fresh, taking on an immediacy and authenticity rarely felt by most people. And perhaps more important, no matter what becomes known or unknown, you remain secure in your honesty and realness, and this affects you in a deep way that is not easy to convey—it needs to be experienced for oneself. A prerequisite for this transformation is the ability to embrace a state of not-knowing.

Only when we realize that beliefs are not the truth will the door of possibility open so that we can experience what "is" true.

Creating a New Perspective

2:22 We're told that once upon a time people thought the earth was flat. Now we know better and so we look back at those people as ignorant, even silly. Pretty arrogant of us when you think about it. What makes us so certain that everything we know today is true? Any reasonable person will admit to the possibility that some of what is currently known, even taken for granted, is likely incorrect. If we consider the matter with care, we will conclude that fallacy is inevitable and some of what we confidently hold as true now will eventually prove false. But how can we discern what this is? Within all that is known, how do we separate our mistaken assumptions from what is factual?

2:23 Imagine you lived long ago and that you are one of the people who think the earth is flat. Don't blame yourself too much—it's a culturally accepted assumption of the time. Remember, you do not imagine it could be any other way, and the earth's flatness is quite observable: when you stand on high ground and look out, you can see the landscape going on into the distance quite horizontally. Yep, it's flat all right. When someone leaves your village and travels as far as anyone you've known, they come back pretty much by the same route. Things have always been this way, and it all makes sense to you and everyone you know.

2:24   Actually, the idea of a flat world fits pretty well with what we can personally observe about up and down, here and there. In fact, it fits better than a round one. If I drop a ball to the ground from the upper window of my house, and you drop a ball from the upper window of your house across the valley, and John drops a ball from his house in a faraway town, there is no reason to suspect that the ground each ball hits is not on the same general plane or level. We could easily assume that this ground is the same flat piece of dirt (with bumps) all across the earth. This flat earth also translates well to a flat piece of paper — much better than trying to make a global map flat.

2:25   And consider this: although we all "know" it's true, who among us takes the time to even imagine that we are currently spinning around at roughly 25,000 miles per hour? Or that in space "up" and "down" don't exist? Even though we believe it's a fact that the earth is round and spinning, we generally live every day as if the sun rises and sets, moving from one side of our flat piece of terrain to the other. Even in the face of our current beliefs on these matters, our daily view actually ignores them and functions instead within the same perceptual "reality" that was so for people in times past. The idea of a flat, stationary world is not as far-fetched as we make it seem. It is only our cultural arrogance and fear of being seen as ignorant that compels us to place such notions in the category of foolish old misconceptions.

2:26   Now once again, pretend that you live in an era in which everyone assumes the world is flat, but this time, try to imagine that you yourself aren't so certain that it is flat. Since we live in a time in which we are told the earth is round, it's pretty easy to imagine that we don't know the earth is flat. But take the time and use your imagination to pretend in earnest and make it real. Rather than just thinking about it, really get it as if it's an experience you're having in this moment. Try to feel as if everyone around you knows the world is flat. No one ever really had to sit you down and explain it; you just know it along with everyone else. But for some reason, you no longer feel certain. You refuse to unquestioningly believe the current cultural presumptions, choosing instead to admit that you don't really know what shape the earth is.

2:27   What are you left with? What occurs in your mind and perspective? Probably the possibility of the earth's roundness arises, even if you wouldn't think of it at the time. As a matter of fact, all sorts of possibilities can arise. Maybe it's a cube, or a half-sphere, or maybe it has a different nature from anything conceivable. It's wide open. This is the nature and power of not-knowing.

2:28   To investigate further, it's important to use a current assumption about which you feel certain, and yet not something you'd find too hard to let go. You can try not-knowing anything you like, but a round planet serves well. Explore your own direct understanding of the earth. Without using hearsay or secondhand images, experience that you do not actually perceive the shape of the earth. When you do this, what do you get? If you don't notice a shift in your awareness of some sort, work on it until you do. Get that in this moment you personally do not actually know what shape the planet is.

I refuse to be intimidated by reality anymore. What is reality?
Nothing but a collective hunch.
—Lily Tomlin

Empty Your Cup

2:29   At the root of every true inquiry from Zen Buddhism to the cutting edge of science is openness and not-knowing. Within these endeavors there is always a possibility that something true or profound can be discovered, but what frequently stands in the way of even the most sincere and honest investigation is our tendency to grab too quickly for answers and beliefs. Reaching the edge of our own understanding, we confuse not-knowing with ignorance and quickly grow uncomfortable. We desire a hasty departure from the state of "nonunderstanding" that is our real experience. The usual way out is to retreat to our familiar beliefs or adopt some aspect of hearsay or common opinion, but of course this rules out discovering anything new.

2:30   In more "spiritual" pursuits, a peaceful clear-mindedness is considered laudable and, to the newcomer, somewhat mysterious. If we look closely at this state of mind, we find that at its base is simply openness, a willingness to not-know. This aspect of wisdom's clarity usually goes unrecognized, since what followers most often seek is knowledge and answers. They don't realize that these cannot produce an experience of the truth. Instead, they suspect that the sage is in possession of some vast body of knowledge that he could impart to any worthy person of his choosing. Independent of any knowledge or understanding he may have, the truth of his wisdom is more likely based on the "nothing" that not-knowing provides. Since this is impossible to understand, for most people such wisdom will always seem mysterious.

2:31 True understanding demands experiential investigation. In undertaking this work, your job must be to consciously experience whatever is true regarding your own self and life. As you read, be aware that the "answers" may not be immediately intelligible, but your ability to look into your own experience is always available. With this disposition, our work proceeds authentically toward a direct personal experience, and not from hearsay or hasty conclusions. This can be a painstaking endeavor, but in the end it is real. Without direct and firsthand insight, we remain unable to validate the ideas proposed by any method of inquiry, including this one.

A university professor went to a master to inquire about Zen. The master served tea.

He poured the professor's cup full and then kept on pouring.

The professor watched and then finally exclaimed, "Stop! the cup is full."

"Like this cup," the Zen master said, "you are full of your own opinions and speculations. How can I show you Zen unless you first empty your cup?"

2:32 As you start to look into the issue of knowing, and carefully observe your own mind, perceptions, and experiences, you'll probably find it surprising and a bit unnerving to realize that much of what you think you know is actually just a belief. It may be true or it may be untrue—don't worry about that for now. The issue is you take for granted that many ideas are true when you really have no personal experience that this is the case. There is a new kind of freedom that comes from separating the truth from what's believed. This action allows you to let go of your own knowledge and open up to freshly experience this moment without presumption.

2:33   Start making a distinction between what you merely believe to be true because you've been told it's true — by whatever source: family, friends, religion, science, culture, books, teachers, and so on — and what you have personally experienced as true. If you haven't had a firsthand encounter with whatever it is you say is true, then call it a belief. This encounter could be in the form of personally undergoing an experience with something, personally having an insight or grasping that a thing is true, or having perceived for yourself the fact of something occurring. Other than merely concluding something in your own mind, or using your intellect to logically assume it must be so, if you've experientially validated the truth of something, then call it an experience. If not, it is a belief.

Emptying Your Cup Exercise

2:34   Go through everything you believe or hold to be true. As best you can, bring to mind all that you know. Everything that comes up for you that you consider true, or assume is true, ask yourself whether you have actually experienced it or if you just believe it. Certainly this will take some time, and you may often be unclear whether something counts as a belief or as an experience. Take all the time you need, and if you still aren't clear, set it aside for later contemplation. The vast majority of what you "know" will turn out to be beliefs.

2:35 Try to come to grips with the fact that the truth of these beliefs is actually unknown. Allow this unknown experience to sink in. The more you can free yourself of countless beliefs — instead staying with a sense of not-knowing — the stronger your sense of the present moment will become. Although the beliefs might be numerous and varied, the not-knowing will always be the same. It is only one experience, and it is always now and always true. Use this to open up and wonder about the nature of your awareness of this very moment.

2:36 The above exercise is not something that needs to be accomplished all at once. The point is for you to start opening up to seeing the ways that beliefs affect your life, and to begin not only to question their validity, but to open up beyond any belief, valid or not, to experience this moment as it is. In the next chapter, we'll be looking into this matter on a less personal level: our shared inheritance of cultural beliefs and assumptions.

CHAPTER THREE

The Cultural Matrix

We often applaud an imitation and hiss the real thing.
—Aesop

We Are Culture

3:1   On some deep level almost everyone feels insecure, afraid, separate, isolated, and unsure of his or her own authenticity and value.
We rarely openly confess and share these feelings with each other
without attributing it to some specific cause or incident. Sometimes our anguish shows up in works of art or drama, or when it
has built up to a point of crisis that can no longer be kept hidden.
But about this personal suffering as a constant background condition, we generally keep our mouths shut and our gaze elsewhere.

3:2   To cover up this raw state, we obtain knowledge and adopt beliefs.
From these, we fabricate a particular sense of self from which we
deal with life. We might feel more "valuable" in the eyes of our
community, but this does nothing to change our base condition.
The only difference is that we've added yet another layer to our
sense of "self." It's here that we step into an unending struggle
with life. We suffer a nagging sense of fragmentation and dissatisfaction, and we lose our sense of real being—the source of our

genuineness and innocence. Seeking relief, and unaware of any alternatives, we obtain new goals and possessions or adopt new character traits to bolster our self-identity. With each new attribute or acquisition, we further lose touch with the source of our own power, creativity, and inner peace — the very qualities we desire most, and also the only means to repair our situation.

3:3 How did we end up in such a pickle? The main source of this buried condition is the profound effect that our culture has on our entire frame of mind. Our culture is, in fact, what *constructs* our frame of mind. We all operate from a set of shared taken-for-granted beliefs — the matrix of our culture. This "consensus reality" may unite us in a shared domain of thought and perception, but many of the inherited assumptions behind it actually foster a sense of uncertainty and isolation. Various perspectives of our culture seem to offer solutions to our individual doubts and insecurities, but since these remedies arise from the same assumptions that cause the difficulty, they do not and cannot resolve our deep sense of personal inauthenticity and disquiet.

3:4 For example, we might feel a gain in status when we achieve a personal goal or acquire something we desire, but this is merely an embellishment of our self-sense, and as such it is both superficial and temporary. One of the first steps toward *real being* is learning to recognize our cultural beliefs and how they lead us into the very struggles, dissatisfaction, and inauthenticity that we want to avoid. In this chapter we'll look into two of our most damaging core cultural assumptions, and some of the inevitable consequences of assimilating them. Since culture is something we take for granted, let's first take some time to consider the nature of culture.

3:5   To be "cultured" originally referred to having a refined appreciation for the arts. Over time the word "culture" has come to indicate the collective viewpoint and customs of any group of people. Although we now acknowledge that there are many different kinds of culture, the word can still carry connotations of particular esthetic refinement. So, hearing the phrase "cultural assumptions," you might have the impression that you could find these down at the museum or opera house. Certainly you will find evidence there — our cultural values are expressed in every piece of artwork, architecture, or anything else that any of us creates. But where exactly is our culture?

3:6   We tend to overlook the fact that a culture exists only within the people who make it up. Instead, we live as though individuals and cultures are separate events, as though somehow we exist apart from our culture. This is a bit like thinking a forest exists independently from the trees. When we look at it impartially, it's plain that culture is purely conceptual — there is no culture outside the minds of the people who comprise one. Our culture is made up of our collective temperament and values, our assumptions and beliefs, our methods of thinking and our cosmologies. Our culture is found in every building, every word, every idea, every routine, every ritual, every method, every book, every mind, every emotion, every value, every action, every bias — in short, it's made up of everything we do and are.

3:7   Since we're born into a culture, we can no more avoid being shaped by it and passing it along to our children than we can avoid being the product of a gene pool. The assumptions of our culture exist in our minds and perception, in our feelings and beliefs. Although they are "merely" conceptual, they live within each of us, as a very basic part of our experience, and they manifest in every activity we undertake and in every place we live. Our culture, our community, our society *is* you and I—and everyone else. Culture exists in us. It is one of the most basic factors in the framework from which we perceive the world around us.

3:8 Cultural assumptions are part of the foundation for our perceptions. We can't help but take them for granted. We look out *from* them, which makes it difficult to look *at* them. No matter what we encounter, much of our interpretation of the event or object or person is predetermined by the assumptions that unconsciously shape our perceptions. One obvious example is gender stereotype. The bias, beliefs, and programming that exist in a given culture will be superimposed on an individual's perception of every male and female. Core cultural assumptions bind us all and are as common and natural to us as the air we breathe. These assumptions are shared beliefs adopted not from personal choice but simply as a result of being part of a community.

3:9 Even various subcultures, regardless of their differences, are founded on the same basic assumptions. It may sound as though these assumptions are somehow force-fed into our thoughts and perceptions, but our indoctrination comes about quite naturally in the process of growing up within our culture. These background beliefs are reinforced at every turn and simply fall into place like basic "truths" that dictate the nature of our experience by shaping our interpretation of whatever's perceived. Since these assumptions are shared by everyone around us, we don't recognize their considerable influence.

3:10 Since the birth of humanity, people have created many phantom worlds in which to live. In fact, our most powerful inventions are not technological at all; they are conceptual. Every culture needs structure and values in order to function as a cooperative effort, and commonly held beliefs and assumptions provide a central unifying force. In response to the questions of existence, such as "Who are we, and why are we here?" a staggering number of belief systems, values, religions, cosmologies, and worldviews have been invented, lived, and taken very, very, seriously. For the most part these "inventions" occurred organically or collectively over a period of time, but despite their unpremeditated beginnings, they are inventions nevertheless.

3:11   By design, the modern human mind craves knowledge, especially in places where we can find none. When faced with an absence of information, we'll make something up — we will believe and assume. This tendency appears to be universal — in every culture, some form of beliefs arises to fill in for the lack of absolute "knowledge." Every subculture with a set of beliefs clamors to have the last word on the subject, claiming themselves guardians of the Truth. Many of the different factions are willing to war over their inventions, but no one is willing to confess that they simply don't know what the truth is.

We delude ourselves that we want to implant honesty in our children: what we really want is to imbue them with our particular kind of dishonesty, with our culture's dishonesty.
—Sidney Harris

3:12   Everything we invent in this way and live as if it were real or true will have repercussions. While we might understand and accept that there are consequences to the actions we take, it's difficult to grasp that our beliefs and assumptions also have a cost. To recognize this, one would first have to forego attachment to his or her own personal opinions and admit that the ideas at issue are beliefs rather than the truth. Acknowledging this point is scary for anyone. It opens the door to doubts, and few people can tolerate the possibility of their whole belief system unraveling before their eyes.

3:13   Keeping that in mind, it becomes easier to understand how difficult it is for us to question any of our beliefs, no matter how subtle or seemingly inconsequential they may be. We're quite willing instead to accept the consequences. We'll shoulder all the woes of the world so long as they fit in with our way of holding reality. But what if a great deal of our suffering is based on assumptions that are false? The resulting consequences would be completely unnecessary.

3:14   As you can imagine, there are many kinds of beliefs and assumptions that warrant scrutiny. In working our way toward understanding, however, we need to proceed in layers. At this point we will focus our inquiry on the following two categories of cultural assumption:

> 1. Our views regarding not-knowing:
>   Which result in the veneration of knowledge, an aversion to ignorance, and the adoption of beliefs in place of experiencing the truth.

> 2. Our assumptions regarding "self":
>   Which result in the adoption and preservation of a fallacious "conceptual" self.

Not-Knowing in Our Culture

3:15   Before the earth was completely explored and charted, one feature of many world maps was this phrase at the edge of what was
known:

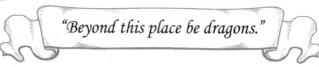

"Beyond this place be dragons."

Although it's not something we normally consider as a culture —
especially in the United States, where a "pioneer spirit" is high on
our list of values — we still harbor fear and mistrust concerning
the unknown, and especially the unknowable.

3:16   One largely unquestioned cultural assumption I've already mentioned is that not-knowing is bad. Look into evidence of this in
your own life. Have you ever felt embarrassment regarding ignorance, as though it is something to be avoided or denied, like a
rash or being caught with your pants down? Most people have.
The understanding is that a good or smart person "knows" —
knows how to behave, knows the right answers, knows what "it"
is all about, knows how to make it in the world, knows how to
please the opposite sex, knows what's funny, knows what's in and
what's out, and any number of other specifics depending on the
group in which he or she lives. Knowing is always preferred over
not knowing. At best, the absence of knowing is looked on as a
temporary state of the uninitiated, and at worst, as a flaw or defect.
We abhor being ignorant and fear being stupid, and we work hard
to ensure that no one finds out that we're either one.

3:17   The issue here isn't whether not-knowing should be allowed to
occur — it already does. Our challenge is the ineffective relationship

we have to its occurrence. Even using the term "*not*-knowing," we are drawn to hold it as a negative. Although we have no appropriate term for this state, this tendency of language indicates our cultural values and is not necessarily an adequate expression of what's there.

3:18 Not-knowing is *itself*. It is primary. Before knowing can happen, there must first be a space for it, a state of *non*-knowing. In our culture that doesn't matter — we avoid not-knowing. We avoid the appearance of it, the awareness of it, the existence of it as a primary state of being. You and I continually experience not-knowing, but our attention is on what we know and perceive, so we don't discern — and don't *want* to discern — the not-knowing. Although not-knowing is the "source" of knowing and is indispensable for creativity, it remains a virtually unrecognized principle in our culture.

3:19 Not-knowing isn't just acceptable, it is "so"; it is true. In every moment of every day there is much that is unknown to us. The very act and nature of knowing means that there must be not-knowing. It is a basic and natural part of our awareness, or consciousness. Not-knowing is a constant, ever-present aspect of "being." Knowing some answers doesn't change that or diminish it in any way. For us it may appear as an emptiness, as ignorance, or as a sense of disconnectedness from the source and absolute nature of life and being. It may appear as what's yet to be grasped, as openness, or as room for understanding and wisdom. Not-knowing appears to people in different forms, and while many of these may seem negative, none of them is a defect.

3:20 Consider for a moment the experience of not-knowing as a state in itself, rather than as the absence of something we value. What if you perceived it as a harmless, even beneficial condition, such as being calm? Without reference to knowing, and so without a "not," it would just be that fundamental experience, perhaps something akin to openness, or nothing, or freedom. It would be like a clear space or a blank canvas: the basis for what is to come.

3:21 Held in this way, it becomes easier to see how such a state would provide a wider perspective. Without the clutter of opinions and beliefs, we are free of bias, and free to look in any direction. We are no longer stuck in beliefs or conventions, or limited by our cultural histories or individual past experiences. We might even approach real wisdom, since rather than the usual sophisticated juggling of facts and opinions that frequently passes for intelligence, we are now receptive to genuine insight. At the heart of this state we also discover a freedom of being. Here is our primary self, the one that is original, unformed and open, creative but without mental chatter filling in all the blanks. This is the nature of the *real-self.*

3:22 The state of not-knowing is the mother of openness, questioning, authenticity, and freedom. Its nature is consciousness without form, possibility without limit, honesty without distortion. Not-knowing is a natural and healthy aspect of being alive, but in our culture we have no foundation upon which to understand it. Placing ourselves in a negative relationship to something that is fundamentally true in our own daily experience is a very silly and damaging thing to do. To go through life as though not-knowing is bad — when, in every moment of our experience, not-knowing is true and always present — what does that leave us with? It leaves us with a constant struggle. It leaves us with an aberrant relationship to our own condition. And isn't that what we've got?

3:23 As we begin to recognize and challenge the many assumptions we live by, we uncover a new freedom and open possibilities. It becomes clear that we need no longer take any of our assumptions as reality. At any time, we can set them aside, open up to not-knowing, and seek out a more genuine experience.

There is no freedom of thought without doubt.
—Bergen Baldwin Evans

The Self in Our Culture

3:24 So what does a knowledge-oriented culture such as ours do about our inherent inability to answer a question so important to us as "What is a self?" We invent things, of course. Since we could first form the question, we've been devising theories about what it means to be a self, where a self comes from, where it resides in the body, and where it goes when the body expires. All manner of beliefs have been created, but the fact remains that no one actually knows some of the most essential aspects of life and existence.

3:25 In our culture we've long assumed that our "being" is somehow related to our "knowing." From ancient religions to the growth of philosophy, psychology, and cognitive sciences, we've launched a multitude of differing campaigns aimed at comprehending our own selfhood. But what if the *idea* of being and the *experience* of being are mutually exclusive? What if we simply don't know what self is? That idea doesn't sit well in our culture. With a bit of a shrug, we're willing to call certain matters "ineffable" for now, but we're certain it's only a matter of time before someone discovers what our existence is really all about. In the meantime, we tend to embrace some belief or other and live life according to its dictates.

3:26   Although some beliefs can offer helpful guidelines for living, neither religion or psychology—not even philosophy—is appropriate here. Whether or not these embody any truth is beside the point. For us, the ideas behind them will always remain hearsay and so cannot affect the depth of our being. Instead, what we're after here is a direct no-frills personal experience. Our task is to grasp what something *is*, not just what we think or feel or hope about it. We could say we need to look "beyond the limits" of our beliefs and knowledge. But "beyond" sounds even further away, and what we want is in a different direction, *closer* to us somehow. In order to experience what is so, what we need to comprehend is what's *prior to* all of our beliefs and knowledge.

3:27   Think about it; what do you get from your knowing, anyway? Is the experience of "being you" made complete by what you know? Perhaps you get answers, a personal history, some cohesive operating parameters, an identity, clear social status, etc., but is any of that deeply satisfying? Is it you? Knowledge, answers, and identity are all external to you. They are "viewed" by you, perceived and received by you, adopted by you, and maintained by you all day long, but they are *not you*. From these, you get to be something knowable, fathomable. You get to have a structure and be filled with your own unique set of answers and beliefs. In short, you get to live as a conceptual-self. Is that all there is? In our cultural environment it is just about the only possibility. But do you feel complete and whole?

Why are you unhappy? Because 99.9 percent of everything you do is for yourself—and there isn't one.
—Wei Wu Wei

The Cost of Our Assumptions

3:28   Our two main cultural assumptions regarding not-knowing and self play off each other and create a powerful interplay of consequences. In our culture, not-knowing is bad, and one of the main things we don't know is who or what we are—what a self is. Since we feel we *have* to know what a self is in order to be one, we rely on our cultural perspectives to tell us what a self is or should be. From this mental-emotional blueprint we proceed to construct a self using programs, beliefs, assumptions, and conclusions. What we invariably end up with is a sense of self that is isolated and conceptually oriented. With no discernible alternative, we just assume that this is simply an inevitable part of being human. In our culture, these two "facts of life" work subtly in tandem so that we are completely dissociated from an experience of real-being.

3:29   Operating from these core cultural assumptions fosters a number of negative conditions that we each mistakenly suppose are a result of some flaw within ourselves, or simply a part of life that we have to put up with. The conditions are so pervasive, so familiar, and so distressing that we rarely allow ourselves more than an occasional glimpse of their existence. Although they influence entire domains of our experience, these conditions are so elusive that our first challenge is simply to locate them. In an attempt to simplify the nature and scope of these consequences, they are identified here as five general effects:

Emptiness

Self-Doubt

Feeling Trapped

Suffering

Struggling

3:30 Essentially everyone has these issues to a greater or lesser degree. Some people are more sensitive to one or two of these effects, while others may relate more readily to a different set. Yet if we look deep enough, and through all of the disguises that frequently cover up their presence, everyone will discover all of these dispositions operating in some form within themselves. Freedom from these effects will only come about through discovering the assumptions from which they arise. This will be part of our work throughout the book, but for now a brief look will assist us in realizing the profound influence they have on the way we live.

Emptiness

3:31 From time to time, most people run into a core feeling that might be described as emptiness or meaninglessness. It is the sense that something is missing in one's self or in life. It sometimes arises as a feeling of being personally incomplete, as if there is a void that needs to be filled, and that obtaining whatever is missing would make one feel whole. The feeling may appear in different forms, but in each it comes as a raw and simple sense, even though what's behind it is not so simple. Frequently people experience these effects as almost physical: an ache in the heart, or in the pit of the stomach, or as a hole deep within the core of themselves, and always as something uncomfortable. I'm referring to this rather complex condition as "emptiness." Do you know what I'm talking about? Can you find it in yourself?

3:32 Accompanying this sense, or included in it, is almost always a feeling of isolation and separation — the sense that you are alone, even in a crowd. Most of us are not happy being alone, but neither are we completely happy in our relationships with others. Both seem to hold a "promise" that remains unfulfilled. We find some sense of hope in the beginnings of fulfillment — in either being alone or in relationships — but this almost always degrades into vague feelings of disappointment because it never goes all the way. We then tend to assume that real fulfillment is simply out of reach, either temporarily or permanently depending on our personal history and programming. But none of us questions the foundation of our relationship to this matter. We don't notice that overlooked cultural assumptions may be the source of both our desire for happiness and our failure to achieve it.

Self-Doubt

3:33 Some people are surprised to hear that everyone has feelings of self-doubt. The seemingly most powerful and confident people doubt themselves from time to time. But the sense of self-doubt that we're discussing here goes deeper than merely doubting one's actions or capabilities. The deliberate pursuit of the issue of self-doubt invariably leads us to discover a deep inner embarrassment, a very personal sense of inauthenticity. I have never met a person who was free of this feeling, nor one who could easily address it. It might be buried deeply, but once they understand what I'm referring to, virtually everyone admits to experiencing this sense of inauthenticity. It's the feeling that you may be the only one who doesn't really know who you are or what life is about, or the uneasy feeling that you may have been left out of some privileged "cosmic" information loop.

3:34 One result of this sense of insecurity and uncertainty is an inclination to "improve" our self-image. Here we pretend, misrepresent, embellish, fake, and so on. No matter how sophisticated or subtle the artifice, deep down we're aware it is fraudulent, and as such it further contributes to a sense of inauthenticity. The sense of self becomes even more tangled as we add such distortions as phoniness, insincere sincerity, affectations, adulterating or withholding expressions of our "inner self," and many other patterns and activities too subtle to identify. In simple terms, we doubt our selves. We have a deep and often unacknowledged sense of self-doubt.

Feeling Trapped

3:35 Feeling "trapped" is a commonly shared experience within our culture, and it covers a wide range of feelings and circumstances. We might feel stuck, powerless, ensnared, restricted, limited, dominated, imprisoned, incapable, helpless, or ineffectual. We can feel trapped by outward circumstances such as a marriage or job, a city or family. We can also feel pushed around by obscure forces within us, unable to free ourselves from our own weaknesses or history, or from the influence of someone. We may feel stuck in patterns of behavior or reactions, such as flying off the handle with little provocation or feeling intimidated by others. We seem trapped by the limits of our own ability. Even a sense of having to dominate others can be understood as a trap and be difficult to stop.

3:36 The issue referred to as "trapped" can take many forms. It is found in our inability to change something, or to get free of things we don't want. It can refer to our own abilities, perceptions, feelings, or beliefs, or it can be about any number of situations or circumstances. It is the entire domain of feeling incapable or "stuck" in some way.

Suffering

3:37 No one will deny that a certain amount of pain, even some form of suffering, seems to be a part of life. Yet when we look a bit closer we see that many forms of personal suffering may not be necessary. Of course, if we knew they weren't necessary, we wouldn't endure them. Or would we? We might have to allow some embarrassment to emerge before we're ready to confess that we have more say in our distress than we're willing to admit. The embarrassment is itself one form of suffering, even if it's relatively insignificant and manageable. The point here is that most of our fears, reactions, upsets, longing, thwarted desires, anger, stress, anxiety, doubt, worry, embarrassments, and other painful experiences are very often an unnecessary consequence of personal and cultural assumptions.

Between grief and nothing, I will take grief.
—William Faulkner

Struggling

3:38 Given our experience of emptiness, self-doubt, feeling trapped, and suffering, we naturally have a desire to "solve" these problems or make them disappear, replacing the painful experiences with more pleasant, self-affirming ones. This whole endeavor could be called struggle. Especially in our culture, competition is common on many levels, and in many subtle as well as obvious forms. Even when all is well, if you look beneath the surface of anyone's daily life, you will likely find a background unease, a muted sense of some inner struggle going on continuously. This inner struggle often manifests as our individual attempts to achieve something in the world, or to become fulfilled in some way.

3:39 Struggling to survive the demands of life is a constant activity. Worrying and trying to avoid the bad things of life are a struggle. Trying to overcome personal defects or resolve unwanted inner feelings always occurs as a struggle. We see obvious and sometimes unacknowledged power struggles emerging in our relationships, both intimate and casual. Trying to learn something new is often felt as a struggle. Struggle can even be found in many innocuous acts such as choosing what to wear to work or trying to sound smart at a party. This constant effort to persist in our culture is most often a struggle for "social survival." If we scrutinize our every thought, feeling, and action in terms of effort, we will find a great deal that we might call struggle.

Your Own Experience of These Consequences

3:40 Some aspects of these five consequences will be apparent to you right away. A deeper and more encompassing recognition will take daily observation and contemplation. I invite you to look into it. The following meditations will assist you in identifying and questioning the nature of these consequences as they occur in your personal experience. Whether hidden in the background or clearly visible to you, some combination of these feelings is part of the experience that you identify as "being yourself" or "knowing who you are." Even a quick look into these consequences will suffice for now, but you can take it further if you choose.

Consequence Meditation Exercise

3:41 *Emptiness*

Put your attention on your most intimate sense of yourself. Can you find any feeling within your "internal state" that you might call empty or meaningless? What is that like for you? When you run into feelings like this, what do you usually call them? How do you explain them or deal with them? Do they feel located within your body somewhere? If so, where? When you isolate one of these feelings of emptiness, does it seem to have a specific cause, or is it always there? If it has a specific cause, something that happened recently, can you recall whether it was absent before that cause? Is it possible that the feeling was present already, and that you felt some relief when the apparent cause arose and could be identified? What, if anything, seems to "fill" this emptiness? Look into the issue of emptiness and see what you can find in your own experience and life. Don't stop on the surface. Look deeper and ask yourself what's at the heart of this feeling. Sit for a while with this meditation on emptiness and then come back to the book to continue.

3:42 *Self-Doubt*

Now put your attention on any sense of self-doubt that you might have. Dig into it some. Is there anything about you that you feel is not fully genuine? Do you have any doubts about yourself? Are you the same on the inside as you appear to be to others? What would it feel like for you — good or bad — if suddenly everyone could see inside your heart and mind? Would they be surprised? What does that mean about you? Would you say that some aspects of yourself are fake? If so, is that all right for you, or would you feel better if your inside and outside matched more closely? Do you feel certain that you fully and deeply understand what life is all about, or what you are supposed to be? Can you find in your experience a background sense of uncertainty? What is that about? Focus your attention on this experience of doubt or uncertainty and see what you can discover about it. Once again, don't stop on the surface. Look deeper and ask yourself what's at the heart of this feeling. Sit for a while with this meditation and then come back to the book to continue.

3:43 *Feeling Trapped*

How many forms of feeling trapped can you identify? If you like, you can begin by writing these down. Jot down what comes to mind without thinking about it too much. Afterward, look over what you've written and consider the nature of these "constraints" that you feel. Consider each separately at first, and see if you can get to the bottom of what these are. Then consider them altogether. What is at the source of these feelings? Look into any feelings of helplessness, powerlessness, and even feelings of being stuck with your own behavior or reactivity. What do you think might happen if you moved from one of the positions that you feel stuck in? Would you be afraid, embarrassed, a failure? Would someone get hurt? Would you lose something? What seems to keep you feeling trapped? Take some quiet time and focus on any feelings you can find that relate to being trapped or incapable. Once again, don't stop on the surface; plunge into the heart of these feelings. Sit for a while with this meditation and then come back to the book to continue.

3:44   *Suffering*

Suffering isn't hard to locate. What forms of suffering have you experienced in your life? Is there any sense of suffering that seems to drag on continuously or repeatedly — hanging in the background like a cloud, or in the forefront as in some crises currently being endured? How do you meet this suffering, and what do you do about it? Beyond the obvious suffering, can you sense subtler forms of this activity? As you locate these feelings, continue to ask yourself what generates them; what is at the core of your experience of emotional pain? Why does it exist? Notice suffering that you may have overlooked, that you don't usually call suffering but is still putting up with some unwanted experience. Why do you endure it? Does it always seem inevitable, or do you sometimes find that you may be generating some of it? Do you get anything out of maintaining this suffering? Dwell on any sense of suffering you can find in your life, dig into it, and see if you can discover its source. When you've spent some time on this, then come back to do the next meditation.

3:45   *Struggling*

Finally, focus on any sense that life is a struggle, that some form of turmoil, either within or as an outward activity, seems inevitable. Why can't things just work out? Do you experience a deep inner peace all the time? If not, what's there that's not peaceful? Would you call that a struggle? What are you struggling with? Locate any inner struggle and meditate it. Observe your relationships with others and see any struggle, perhaps "power struggles," going on. What are you trying to accomplish with these? In contrast to having no conflict or resistance or worry at all, what can you find that has some element of struggle to it? Concentrate on any sense of personal struggle you experience and see if you can become clear on what this activity is and what it's for. Why do you do it? Spend some time meditating this before you come back to the book.

3:46   Learning to recognize these consequences can help lead us to the source of them — the assumptions that govern our experience of life and of self. Whatever we believe about ourselves will be perceived as part of us. Since we are already programmed to believe in our assumptions and to regard their presence and effects as an aspect of ourselves, our inclination will be to excuse and defend them. In order to approach their dissolution with the necessary intent, we must clearly experience that the pain of these consequences is caused by our own assumptions. Only then will we be able to regard these beliefs and reactions as separate from us, and as unnecessary. Once it becomes clear that our assumptions and their consequences are indeed not our real-selves, our resistance begins to subside and we become empowered to let them go.

What really raises one's indignation against suffering is not suffering intrinsically, but the senselessness of suffering.
—Friedrich Nietzsche

3:47   Understanding begins with recognition, but real wisdom arises through insight. To help us open up and attain the insight we need to unearth our core assumptions, we will turn our attention to achieving a genuine experience of not-knowing. Chapters Four and Five give us the tools we need to discover and understand these personal and cultural assumptions, as well as help bring consciousness to our entire subject matter of self and being. Once we learn to adopt the principles of real questioning and genuine experience, we can approach these seemingly impenetrable issues in a distinctly new and powerful way. While our work thus far might seem rather mundane and even homely, we have already set foot on the path to greater consciousness and even enlightenment.

CHAPTER FOUR

An Experience of Not-Knowing

My own habitual feeling is that the world is so extremely odd,
and everything in it so surprising.
Why should there be green grass and liquid water,
and why have I got hands and feet?
—Don John Chapman

Learning versus Knowing

4:1 If I were to ask, "Which is more important: inhaling or exhaling?" you might see the question as nonsense. Grasping, as you do, the need to exhale before you can take in more oxygen, you are not likely to keep sucking air trying to expand your lungs beyond their capacity. Instead, you will blow out stale air and breathe in again.

4:2 Obviously you have to do this to stay alive, but maybe you do it poorly and with resistance, making your breathing difficult and certainly not what it could be. If you investigate, you'll realize that even something so taken-for-granted as breathing can be fine-tuned and improved. You'll learn that blowing air out is just as important and necessary as drawing air in. You might even discover that using different muscles and intention will pull the breath deeper into your belly, affecting your physiology in several beneficial ways. In time, you'll learn to breathe more naturally and with greater capacity.

4:3 It's the same with knowing and not-knowing. To be efficient, there has to be a balance. Whenever you or I learn anything, "not-knowing" has occurred — whether we intend it, or we haven't a clue that it is taking place. Even when we try sliding quickly through not-knowing to get to knowing, somewhere in there not-knowing has occurred or learning didn't happen — just as exhaling occurs, or inhaling doesn't happen. In either case, this interchange can proceed with different levels of efficiency. If we resist not-knowing at any stage, our learning capacity is impeded and we'll have more difficulty acquiring new skills or understanding.

4:4 As we saw in the last chapter, cultural assumptions strongly influence our view of reality. What we collectively know and don't know, and how we regard knowing and not-knowing, are both founded on cultural presumptions. For instance, the "Western mind" might find it difficult to accept that something intellectually ungraspable can still be true and even accessible to consciousness, just not to the intellect. None of us avoids assimilating our culture's foundation beliefs, and disengaging from these even temporarily can be tricky. We assume that whatever *we* do as "thinking" is the way thinking has to be done. Powerful learning is open to what has not been thought previously, and so it must begin outside the confines of any personal patterns.

4:5 So from our usual cultural vantage point, the first step in such learning would appear to be a step in the wrong direction. We generally ignore the not-knowing part since we prefer to think of learning as something like gathering valuable nuggets of information, preferably ones that fit in with and support what we already believe. Instead, I'm suggesting we look in a direction other than the one that follows from what is known. The shift required to do this is both subtle and open-ended, and it may take some effort at first. The main thing to grasp at this point is that it's simply not possible to wonder, to truly question, unless we acknowledge that what we already know is not what we want to learn. In short, by definition, we want something unfamiliar to us, something new.

4:6   I once taught two professional ballerinas to become more conscious of basic body principles. Since a ballerina's career is spent trying to be "up" most of the time — up on her toes, or leaping into the air — my main task was to draw the dancers' attention toward the ground. After a few weeks of grounding work, both dancers came back exclaiming that they could jump much higher than ever before. Establishing a more conscious relationship to the downward aspects of body movement had enabled them to create a more powerful relationship to jumping up. Probably the greatest difficulty had been to persuade them to get past their predisposition about "up." Before they could make any real advancement in this area, they simply had to let go of their "knowing."

4:7   People might hear "let go of knowing" in one of two ways. Someone could simply follow the suggestion, and focus on the "letting go" part, seeing it as a kind of meditative practice that might free the mind of stress and distractions. On the other hand, a person might reflexively tap into our cultural disposition toward knowledge and hear such a suggestion as rather worthless, or an excuse for ignorance, perhaps even threatening, and not such a good idea at all. Neither of these reactions is what I am intending, and each represents an obstacle to this work.

4:8   We've already talked about our cultural attitude toward not-knowing, which is reflected in the negative stance toward the suggestion of letting go. But what's wrong with taking the "positive" view, seeing not-knowing as a relaxing meditation? Because, as with any cultural assumption, a personal assumption — whether positive or negative — is not the same as an experience of the truth. It can only stand in the way of such an experience. Any presumption at all is a way of "knowing," and as such it limits our ability to learn anything outside of our usual experience.

Thinking without a Net

4:9   If you did the exercise a few chapters back where you played with your personal experience of the shape of the earth, then to some degree you have had an experience of not-knowing. Don't underestimate these exercises; truly experiencing even such a relatively trivial game can provide an "earth shattering" insight. As satisfying as it is to question *something in particular,* right now what we're looking into is the state of wonder itself. The entrance to this state — and even this questioning — is a particular one. Once you manage to get a glimpse, however, the experience of not-knowing opens your mind to a whole new relationship with life.

4:10   It's helpful to remember that when I say *knowing,* it includes all that is available in the vast domain of knowledge, even if it is not coming to mind in this moment. It also includes the idea that somewhere out there is an answer that can be read in a book, heard from another, or deciphered from some wisdom or facts already known. So, although you might say you don't know something at present, this is not the same as experiencing a state of not-knowing. Simply having the idea that you don't know will not allow powerful wondering to arise. The idea itself is a form of knowing because it takes place as a thought that something know-able is temporarily unknown by you. Unless we experience a real and open state of not-knowing, our wondering will be limited to our familiar ways of searching for an answer among what's known or knowable.

4:11   I facilitate lengthy contemplation intensives in which I guide the efforts of participants trying to become directly conscious of their own true nature. For days on end, they'll struggle to get past their own "knowing" about "who" they are. Try as they might, their minds continue to serve up "knowing" in the form of ideas, images, desires, associations, feelings, intuition, and other mental activities both subtle and obvious. I repeatedly advise them to get that they really *don't* know, and that real openness will not be possible unless they genuinely get not-knowing as an experience.

4:12   Of course, repeatedly hearing this instruction in no way endows them with a sudden experience of not-knowing. It just helps them keep looking in that direction. When someone does actually grasp it, the understanding comes almost as a bodily sensation that no matter what knowledge they possess or what their mind generates for them to view, at the root bottom they in fact *do not know*. Such a genuine experience of not-knowing profoundly deepens their contemplation because it opens their awareness to the immediate presence of the real possibility of having an insight into the very nature of being.

4:13   That's an example of some pretty intense contemplation in a work-shop setting, but the principle is the same for any true inquiry. What you're moving toward here is the possibility of *experiencing* this work rather than just reading about it and intellectualizing through the same old patterns of thought. I am attempting to streamline the communication between author and reader by speaking *from* experience *about* experience *to* experience. This is very important, because the more you can "experience" for yourself what's being communicated, the greater the impact it will have on your consciousness. What you're probably used to — living within "knowing," as we all generally do — is intellectually "surfing" what's presented to make some quick conclusions that support your own belief systems. What really matters, and what really changes anything, is found only in your experience of what's being said.

4:14 Think about it. Why are you reading this? Whatever your specific reasons, it's likely that you want some experience beyond what you've got right now. Doesn't it make sense then that in order for that to happen, something different would have to occur within your experience? Acquiring more nuggets of information is great, but you don't really need to change your knowledge. What you need to change is your experience. There is plenty of useful information in here. But your job is not to make sense of it all and commit it to memory. When you read about not-knowing, or assumptions, or consequences, or whatever, don't take my word for it. Your job is to use this work to honestly encounter what's true within your own experience.

The great difficulty in education is to get experience out of ideas.
—George Santayana

4:15 Any information that you read here is like a one-way ladder. I want you to climb up the ladder and get off. You may have to climb the ladder many times, but the goal is to be able to throw the ladder away. If I asked you to use the ladder, climb up on the roof, and describe the view to me, you'd have to get off the ladder, right? You can't just carry the ladder around. If you say, "I understand the ladder" and just walk around with it, that may be great, but your view stays the same, doesn't it? So this isn't about collecting ladders. It isn't about merely figuring something out. You can intellectualize about it until your brain breaks — and right there would be a good place to start — but real progress begins when you set out to *experience* what's being communicated.

4:16   Our inclination to jump to conclusions and our desire to grab onto an answer precludes the openness necessary to experience the truth. I once saw this Zen cartoon: Two monks — one old, one young — are sitting in meditation. The old monk is turning to the novice saying, "Nothing's next, this is it!"

4:17   OK, so maybe you had to be there. I like it because it hints at the tendency in our contemplation to wait for some punch line, or the next step, as if those are somehow going to "do it" for us. We forget that what needs to occur can occur right now, without further explanation or any outside occurrence, and without a punch line. This is it. This is you and your experience. What is it for real? Who are you, actually? What is the nature of *your* existence?

What Is an Experience?

4:18   Take a moment and notice your experience right now. What does it consist of? The physical pressure of sitting on a chair, the temperature of the room, looking at this book, your mood and attitudes — whatever is so for you right now. Maybe you're flattered by the attentions of a cat purring on your lap, or maybe the neighbor's mowing is a background irritation. Perhaps you're still smarting from an argument with your mate, or you might be bored with what you're reading. All that you're aware of right now is your present experience.

4:19   Experience is always taking place right here and now, and it's always the only thing we've got going on. But what is it? It's surprisingly difficult to address the real nature of our own experience. There's a lot in the way of discerning this nature, and what is in the way is difficult to see. As is often useful in making new distinctions, we'll begin by looking into what we hold as "the obvious."

Some basic definitions of the word *experience:*

1. The apprehension of an object, a thought, or an emotion through the senses or mind.

2. To personally undergo.

4:20   Within our awareness, we experience or perceive many things on many levels at once. We see a telephone in the room, but we also wonder if Jill is going to call. We are aware of both of these perceptions, and, although it's usually overlooked, we can notice the difference between perceiving an object (the phone) and perceiving a thought that someone might call. When the phone actually rings we experience an activity, full of sensation and sound. Simply imagining the call, however, we have to say there exists no activity except in our own thinking.

4:21   Yet even when we experience an actual phone call, many concepts fill much of the space in that experience. We may react to something, such as being surprised at what the caller says. This reaction isn't the same as the information received, nor is it the sound we're hearing. The feeling of surprise is a separate mental-emotional activity. Is this an experience of the phone call? Ordinarily, we would say yes, we experienced a surprising phone call. We combine our reaction with the activity of hearing what's said, and we lump it all together as the "experience." Normally this just doesn't matter to us, but it's useful to recognize that there are a few things going on.

4:22   Notice that the perception of our reaction is different in "kind" from the perception of an activity or an object. Generally, we experience a thought just as we experience, for example, a rock. What we refer to with the word *experience* usually means "to perceive"— we perceive thoughts and emotions arising, and we perceive objects and movement. But I want to propose a new possibility here that suggests we can *experience* the thought versus just thinking it, or *experience* the rock versus just seeing it. The difference between perceiving something and experiencing it can perhaps be found within our level of participation in the encounter.

4:23   When we experience something, we "personally undergo" an encounter with it. The difference between a thought and an object is pretty easy to see. A rock is clearly outside of our imagination. It seems not of our own making and provides consistent information that we seem to have no choice but to receive. The rock is hard every time it hits us in the head, and we can see its shape and color, which also tend to remain consistent. We perceive these things as independent of our imagination. We say we experience the rock when we are clear there is a rock present and we perceive it or personally undergo an encounter with it. It's not difficult for us to discern the difference between concepts, such as our fascination with the rock or our anger at the rock, and the rock itself. When we do that, and put our awareness on the rock independent of any notions or reactions about it, then we are "experiencing" the rock. But what about experiencing a concept, like an idea or belief?

4:24 We do seem to "personally undergo" our thoughts and feelings, which is why we often state that we're experiencing them. Our emotions, ideas, impressions, and memories enter our awareness in much the same way as anything we see and hear. So how do we distinguish between experiencing an idea and just having an idea? Beyond the presence of the idea as a mere figment of our imagination — like all ideas — how would we "experience" something that is itself a concept?

4:25 Adhering to a specific definition of the word *experience* provides us with some solid ground on which to begin sorting this out. If we define experience as "whatever we personally encounter as real and not merely imagined," an idea becomes an experience for us when we have an immediate personal encounter with the reality of the idea itself or what the idea represents. We're not having a thought about the idea, nor are we merely choosing to believe in it.

4:26 As with the rock, first we need to get the idea as itself, as conceptual, and not anything else. Then we must put our attention on the "truth" or presence of what's there. In the case of an idea, it is whatever is real in that matter. What's real might be that the idea is false or made up, and then that is what we must encounter. It could be that the idea itself is an abstraction — meaning that the idea refers to no objective reality but instead the reality of the idea exists within a nonphysical domain — and yet still may be true. In this case, in order to experience the idea, we need to encounter what's real about this abstract construct. Most of the ideas we have are relatively lightweight notions or conjecture "about" something other than the ideas themselves. It is rare indeed to discover the source of a profound idea, to directly and personally "experience" the reality from which the idea is conceived.

4:27 So on the one hand we have an experience of some matter, and on the other hand we have thoughts *about* the matter. Whenever we confuse our knowledge, associations, beliefs, and fantasies with something we encounter — whether it's a rock or an idea — we're not having an experience of what's actually there. We're having our thoughts and beliefs about it, and this is in a completely different domain from experience. In this work we will need to experience what's true about ourselves and about being, not add to our thoughts and fantasies about what's true. Do you get the difference?

4:28 It might be easier to see this distinction more clearly by using an example of something present but nonobjective, like our awareness. We are quite certain that we are aware. Yet awareness is not an object, and when we look more carefully we also see that awareness is not even perceived. We perceive many things, but it's that very act of perceiving that we call awareness. That we are aware of something implies that there is something called "awareness" present. But simply taking this for granted is different from experiencing awareness. We can make the distinction between having thoughts and assumptions *about* awareness, and consciously *experiencing* awareness in this moment.

4:29 Try it. Notice that you are aware. Usually this is taken for granted, and your attention is on the *object* of your awareness. Now see if you can experience awareness itself, rather than thinking about it, or assuming it, or imagining what it is. When you experience this awareness clearly and presently without conceptualizations, then you'll have a better understanding of what I mean by "experience."

A perceiving is in itself pure, i.e., impersonal and real.
—Wei Wu Wei

What Is an Experience of Not-Knowing?

4:30 Some powerful communication is taking place here, but the work of understanding must be done by you, the reader. You've got to delve into your own experience. It doesn't become real merely by reading about it. Having an insight into your experience is not something you do on a whim, or merely by obtaining a chunk of knowledge. It takes looking into your inner workings, and as you began in Chapter Two, starts with admitting that much of what you seem to know is only stuff you believe — perhaps have always believed — but have not personally experienced. Sometimes it takes the courage to say, "I've been pretending to know what everyone else seems to know, but I don't." It takes the courage to embrace not-knowing as a real and present experience. This takes repeated efforts, which may be why Zen masters keep talking about emptying your cup.

4:31 The main challenge of getting to a state of not-knowing is that we always look for *something* to be there. When you ask yourself, "What is the state of not-knowing?" you'll search for something that is that state. Try it, and see what occurs. Although there really is a state of not-knowing, it isn't filled with anything, so there's nothing there. It's not that one's experience vanishes, or that all perception stops, but whatever is perceived or known in this moment is recognized as distinct from the state of not-knowing.

4:32　Not-knowing is what is not known. It's what is *not* perceived or experienced in any way, so attention on this state finds nothing. It is open, unfilled; empty, in a sense. A true experience of this state, however, is more dramatic than you would think. Outside of an experience, all we have of not-knowing is the concept of a state devoid of knowing, or the idea that something is not known. These are ideas, thoughts *about* it, which are not the same as the actual experience of not knowing. Such an experience frequently comes as an awakening. You may feel vulnerable or have various reactions to it, but when you look closely you'll see that the reactions aren't the state; they are reactions. Not-knowing is simply a lot of nothing, but this can be a very powerful experience.

It is the emptiness within the cup that makes it useful.
—Lao-tzu

4:33　The fact that the above quotation shows up most often as a philosophical cuteness at a coffeehouse suggests that our culture has difficulty absorbing what's being said. When it comes to cups, our attention falls to what is there or about to be there. The use and value of the cup is found in filling it. When we look at a cup we see the shape, the handle, the design, and what the cup is made of. These are important in the world of cups, no doubt about it. Yet without what "isn't" the cup, without the space that we say is "not" cup, the cup would not exist, and so would certainly be useless as a cup. Of course, we don't really care all that much about cups. The point is, what fills our awareness is primarily what is known, the "things" that are perceived. When we shift our perspective to include what's overlooked—what isn't there but is essential to what is—we move into a more alive, present, and real encounter with the thing.

4:34   The moment we encounter anything—some feeling, thought, conversation, object, activity—it is immediately perceived to "be" some way. It is reflexively interpreted as a particular something in relation to one's self, and becomes endowed with meaning, history, identity, association, emotional charge, etc. This all takes place at about the speed of light.

4:35   Applying not-knowing to this "known" perception suddenly begins to pull the thing out of its taken-for-granted state into a more fresh and present encounter. The thing becomes more real and clear. Our attention is drawn to what is present rather than our presumptions about what it is and what it means. Our interpretation of what's there doesn't necessarily disappear, but we shift into a more present and keen perception of what is consciously encountered in this moment.

4:36   Think back to the drawing class at the beginning of Chapter Two. Like Susan, when you look at an object, you immediately know what it is. But beyond this information, what is it? What is it really, as itself, for itself, without having any use or meaning for you? Looking without knowing what something is can momentarily lift the veil of your taken-for-granted presumptions and interpretations. Such an open encounter keeps you from quickly filing the perception away as usual. Instead, you are drawn to look afresh at what is there.

4:37   Right now, look at some object in this manner—a chair, this book, a tree, the cat. See it as whatever you think it is, but also not-know what it is as you gaze at it. While you look in this way, more perceptions about the object may become apparent. You may get a deeper, and yet more subtle sense of its "thereness," its presence. A sense of wonder about it might begin to emerge. What happens as you try more fully to perceive what is in front of you, not taking what's there for granted?

4:38   At first you may not have a knack for perceiving in this way. As you work at it, however, and begin to experience not-knowing as a reality rather than as a thought, you will become more adept and powerful in your encounters. Remember, you're not trying to "pretend" anything. It is a fact that you don't actually know what anything is. Simply get in touch with that fact, and wonder, *What is it?* As you do, you should notice an increase in the quality and depth of the object or being. Before your eyes it will become more present and somehow more "real." This shift in the fullness and aliveness of your perceptions will begin to change how you relate to what you encounter. You will come to understand that not-knowing isn't just a subject of our inquiry, it is also the first step of *any* true inquiry.

4:39   Once you recognize within your own experience that you in fact really don't know, then you can start to openly wonder. Once you wonder, real questioning can begin. Answers may come and go — these are possibilities — with true questioning, however, nothing will suffice but a genuine personal insight into the matter.

What Is an Insight?

4:40   Remember that guy in school who really seemed to understand the math or physics when you didn't? Aggravating, wasn't it? He seemed to be able to do so much more with the subject than anyone else. The whole class worked hard memorizing formulas, but it was obviously easy for that one guy. Why is that? Probably he understood the actual principles that founded the subject. He experienced the "reality" of the subject—even though the subject matter might have existed primarily in the domain of abstraction. Yet we were never taught that such a thing was possible or desirable. Instead, we were led down the path of rote learning in order to pass tests. No one mentioned there were actually powerful and real *experiences* to be had. And the most powerful of these are called insights.

4:41   An insight is not simply having a good idea. It's not believing something. An insight is an experience. You don't have to "believe" your experience of an insight any more than you have to believe you are reading right now. You're right there! When you set out to have an insight, you must participate in the effort. You must do the experiments, make the connections, follow the bouncing ball. You're the one going after genuine understanding. When insight arrives, *you* are the one who makes the breakthrough. Whether it concerns your self, your world, or any aspect therein, an insight is when you "experientially" become conscious of what's true about something. This is what makes life joyful, happy, and fulfilled. The thrill is not so much about *what* happens to be there; it's that *you* happen to be there.

4:42   An insight can be defined as the sudden awakening in our consciousness when we realize something that is true and authentic. It could be about anything: how something really works, what something actually is—anything about life that was unseen, unknown, or unnoticed that becomes clearly understood. The depth and quality of insights can vary greatly, but each will have some things in common:

- An insight is "true," or it is not really an insight.

- An insight is not simply an opinion or a guess.

- An insight is an authentic experience.

- An insight is beyond any belief — it is instead something personally encountered and understood.

- An insight is self-validating, since the truth or validity of the realization lies inherent in the thing realized.

- An insight is authentic, and a person who has one will speak with authority since no guesswork is involved. With insight, a clear and personal grasping of the subject matter is the authority.

4:43   When Archimedes discovered how to calculate the amount of metal in King Hiero's crown, did he jump out of his bath and run through the streets of Syracuse exclaiming, "Perhaps I've got it figured out!"? No, he'd had an insight, an awakening to something self-evident, and what he said was "Eureka!" which means "I have found it." There was absolute certainty in his declaration because he had personally experienced the principle behind measuring an object using water displacement. Insight is not merely an encounter with a new thought or the dispelling of a doubt, or becoming convinced about a good idea. An insight arrives with such depth of perception that it suddenly turns what might have been only a good idea into a living experience. Insight arrives as present and complete. And it always arises from a state of not-knowing.

4:44   There are a lot of people out there who haven't really grasped that they can have a profound realization or an insight for themselves. This is an important point, so look into your own position on this matter. Maybe you've read up on psychology or philosophy, or you're a skeptic, or a commonsense kind of person. Maybe you're reading this to affirm your beliefs, or because you want to argue, or agree, or you want to validate what you've already gotten out of your experience of life. Throw it all out! Whatever it is that you "are" or "know" is just fine. But if you really want to get something new here, you've got to step off every one of your taken-for-granted positions, at least for now. You can come back to them later — trust me, they won't go far.

4:45   It is to be hoped that you're reading this because you want to awaken in some way, to encounter something new, or discover what's true in your own experience. If you're unwilling to set aside what you already know, this material can't really take you anywhere. You can read it like any other book and come away with an intellectual grasp of the work, but subtle distinctions will escape you as you read further and encounter what appears to be mere repetition. I want you to *use* this book — to get everything out of it that you can, and make it your own personal inquiry into the truth. If you haven't begun to do so, the principles offered in Chapter Five will help get you on track.

The Principles of Discovery

*Discovery consists of seeing what everybody has seen
and thinking what nobody has thought.*
—Albert Szent-Gyorgyi

Four Cornerstones of Discovery

5:1 Insight is exhilarating. Having a previously inconceivable reality suddenly illuminated by conscious understanding has to be one of the most satisfying mind states we can achieve. Gaining insight into the nature of one's own being may be the most exhilarating of all, since it holds the promise of personal transformation. Because profound insight can alter so much of our perceived "reality" all at once, it can seem as though we have somehow stepped into a different world. We've leapt beyond our own limits to a clear understanding we previously hadn't recognized. We feel alive, aware, and powerfully engaged with what's *real*.

5:2 As we learned in the last chapter, insight is an authoritative experience that begins with a state of not-knowing. While the mind habitually clings to knowledge, associations, and beliefs, these are in fact obstacles to awakening insight. In other words, when we hold things to be a certain way, we restrict our openness to all other possibilities. If the first key to insight is to let go of "knowing" what's so, the second key is to undertake an investigation of what's actually so. This chapter is about four principles that will empower our investigation into what's true about anything.

5:3 In Chapter Three we began to explore some of the consequences of living predominantly within a conceptual self. You may have gotten a sense of the relationship between your self and your suffering, but that doesn't mean you can just step aside from this whole dynamic and experience simply "being." What we want to do is make steady progress in the direction of discovering whatever is true about real being — regardless of how it affects our lives. As we do so, we become aware of new distinctions in our way of being that allow us to make powerful choices that were previously unavailable within our normal life pursuits.

5:4 If it were possible to strip away everything that you "know" as yourself, it might leave you on the threshold of an experience of being, but reality would be quite different from what's normally experienced. So much would seem to be missing, and yet such a shift would probably give you a sense of being closer to the real you. Any valid inquiry begins with not-knowing, or else it merely serves to confirm what is already known. To investigate your self, however — since you are the one doing the investigating — you have little choice but to begin with whatever you presently experience as your self, and work from there.

5:5 We'll look deeply into self later on, but for now just try to imagine what it might be like to experience an authentic, genuine you, free of all your ideas about yourself. With your awareness cleared of all the conceptualizing that usually dominates your experience — your beliefs, history, education, assumptions, drives, emotions, etc. —

you might have a sense of being present even without really knowing what it is that's *being* present. You might simply have an immediate and genuine experience, unobstructed by self-image, personal history, or any other self-oriented activities. Imagine the freedom of experiencing life, others, and self from such an open position.

5:6   This kind of "alive" direct awareness—happening only in the present, and free from conceptual tinkering—is where we want to go. You may have gotten a glimpse of this direction in some of the exercises we've already done. It's a good beginning, but there is still much we need to work on in our approach to real being. We need to look more deeply into what a self is, and how a self is created and maintained. We want to investigate the nature of concept and the mechanisms of perception. In short, we want to get to the bottom of what it means to be a self. All this will be addressed as we move ahead, but for right now it's fine if "real-being" is just a hazy possibility. What we need now is a way to personally investigate self and being, one that compels us to experience these things for ourselves.

5:7   There are a few fundamental principles that encourage real discovery. They empower our investigations of self, life, reality, or anything else, for that matter. In fact, if these principles are active in our pursuits, real discovery is inevitable. Although they are actually four distinctions within the same basic pursuit—and it is the spirit of this pursuit that we wish to adopt—they act as cornerstone principles for this endeavor by setting the stage for true inquiry. These four principles are neither moral nor arbitrary. Adhering to them will push us toward what is so. Without them, we go nowhere. We've looked at these possibilities from a few different angles already. Now it's time to adopt them as our tools for proceeding with this endeavor.

her, these four principles embody our underlying method

ing an experience of being:

...hentic Experience

Honesty

Grounded Openness

Questioning

Authentic Experience

5:8   The principle of authentic experience indicates where we want to go and also provides the direction we need to take to get there. As an operating principle, it pushes us to become more and more adept at experiencing things as they are. This begins by being as straightforward and as truthful as we can in relation to our ordinary experience of things. It is noticing what's what and not trying to pretend something is true that isn't, or that something is some other way than it is. It is removing fantasy and personal beliefs and desires from our encounter with the presence of reality. It is being increasingly conscious of whatever is true to the best of our ability in each moment.

5:9   At the same time, the words *authentic experience* can refer to having a direct conscious experience of being, the pinnacle of which is a rare and sought-after awakening, or enlightenment. It doesn't matter that these words are inadequate to the task of representing this kind of realization—any words would be. We just need to keep moving in that direction, whether it leads to a profound awakening or just a solid personal encounter with the truth of something. What we want is to become personally conscious of what's true.

5:10   When it comes to knowledge, we basically have two options in our culture. We can either be convinced by conclusions that were arrived at through observation and experimentation, or we can simply believe whatever sounds right when we hear it from others. These two schools of thought are generally divided into science and spiritual or philosophical pursuits. Both of these approaches may have merit, yet neither is a direct experience of the truth. One of them relies on logical conclusions, the other on faith or intuition, but neither acknowledges the possibility of having a direct personal encounter with the truth itself.

5:11   The point isn't whether science or spiritual doctrine is right or wrong. Our basis for believing one or the other depends on the merit and value that they have for us as individuals. Still, they are indirect methods used for *making conclusions* about what's true. We don't want a conclusion, not even our own. Instead we're looking for some way to experience for ourselves what's true.

5:12   Obviously a direct method would have to be personally attended; hearsay just won't do. And we would have to acknowledge that the truth is inherent in the thing itself — in whatever we are investigating — rather than being determined by our beliefs, decisions, conclusions, or any other applied activity. But how can we become directly conscious of the true nature of anything? Most people would say it is not possible, and they would have a very strong case. Any such claim or assertion, however, is just that, and does not come from direct experience.

5:13   I am asking you to entertain the possibility that we can, independent of our self-serving agendas and perceptions, directly encounter the truth for ourselves. Did you catch that? I said "independent of our perceptions," and I mean just that. We can —

without belief, knowledge, conjecture, interpretation, or hearsay— experience the truth of something, or the thing itself, beyond subjectivity. I'm not asking you to accept this as true, for therein lies the danger that the idea of a direct conscious experience will become nothing more than a "belief" and so be lost to the domain of fantasy. Rather, I'm asking you to create a space for the possibility that somehow you can become directly conscious of the truth or nature of reality.

If you cannot find the truth right where you are,
where else do you expect to find it?
—Dogen

5:14 This experience has been sought after for thousands of years in contemplative practices like Zen. Over the course of more than two millennia, many claim to have achieved it, but there is no way to validate such claims. There is not even a way to accurately convey the experience to another person. Even if I communicate that direct experiences have occurred for me, it will never be more than hearsay for anyone else. It can only be confirmed in one's own experience. There is no other way.

5:15 Now I'd like you to sit quietly for a moment and let it sink in that it's all right not to know what is true regarding this principle. Whenever we have no genuine personal experience, the truth is that we don't know what the truth is, and all the hearsay and fantasies in the world won't change that. All you need to understand for now is that the principle of authentic experience provides the direction we need to take in order to carry on with this work of becoming more authentic. As I said earlier, the direction is the same whether we're talking about living within the most honest and authentic experience we can have in this moment, or an extreme possibility such as direct insight into the nature of reality. Committing ourselves to the possibility of having a direct encounter with what's true changes our perspective. It points the way toward a more truthful and genuine experience and also helps us learn to gauge the veracity of our experiences.

Honesty

The dictionary defines *honest* as

1. Not deceptive or fraudulent; genuine.

2. Characterized by truth; not false. Sincere; open, candid, frank.

3. Without affectation.

5:16   We immediately see how honesty relates to the principle of authentic experience. The more honestly we relate to something, the better equipped we are to set out to experience it. Of course we all know what honesty is, and no one really needed to review the definition, right? Maybe so, but we have to keep in mind that words can only represent, and that we frequently mistake our response to the word for the experience that the word represents. In this endeavor, we must look into *experiencing* what is represented, not the thoughts and associations that spring up as a result of hearing the word.

5:17   Honesty is telling the truth, not only to others but to ourselves as well. Here, this distinction goes beyond the conventional use of the word to a profound and real experience of an activity that is as "rock-bottom" honest as we can manage. Our normal tendency is not one of such powerful honesty. We manipulate our own thinking and feelings, and our experience is so influenced by our beliefs, fears, and desires that we cannot trust it without challenge. We must maintain a diligent probing into the truth of anything that arises — from our ideas on how something works to the nature of relationship or reality. This is not honesty as a moral issue, and it's not looking for some fantasy called "Truth." We're seeking only to *align ourselves with what is already true.* Yet, we don't begin to participate in this until we are honest with ourselves and others.

5:18   Remember, understanding this work through experience is a different matter than merely hearing about it. Since an authentic experience occurs as real and true, we don't need to memorize the information any more than we need to memorize what we're doing right now. When we come to this work through honest experience, we find we have no need to fit it all together intellectually, or to make a decision whether we believe it. It is either so for us or it is not.

Anything more than the truth would be too much.
—Robert Frost

5:19   We all have some activity that we call "telling the truth." Sometimes telling the truth to others is different from telling the truth to ourselves. In either case, because of our desire to be seen a certain way — by others and by ourselves — it can be hard to admit what is simply there. We might look for negative things to confess, or we might emphasize aspects that present us in a good light. Any bias will alter our perception of what's there, refashioning the plain truth into a likeness that serves our needs, but this is not the truth. What is actually so? If we just start with being open to that question and then resist offering up any of our usual reflexive answers, we are already on a much better footing for telling the truth.

5:20 After an intense four-day live-in workshop I facilitated many years ago, a young man approached me and said, "When I came here I considered myself an honest person. Now I see that I lie all the time." A bystander might've been puzzled by his bright smile as he said it, but the two of us understood that his words represented a valuable realization in this work. Generally, it is assumed that discovering something positive within ourselves is a useful event, while discovering something mistaken or negative is unwanted. This assumption is neither correct nor appropriate. We find as much value in discovering what's wrong as what's right — as long as it's the truth. Given the task in front of us, the above assumption is an attitude we can't afford.

5:21 Recognizing a personal limitation or false belief is a powerful experience. Being able to face unwanted personal attributes clearly and without avoidance — not overdramatizing them, or sugarcoating them, but earnestly trying to observe what's there — is a necessary skill for discovering what's true. Consider viewing personal patterns of behavior, emotion, or thinking as a scientist might, trying to discover their real nature and origin. Our goal is to discover what is true regardless of how we feel about it or what we believe. Therefore, it is wise to look on the discovery of even negative aspects of ourselves as a very useful and valuable event.

5:22 Honesty is an essential principle for experiencing the truth. Think about it. Without total honesty, how could we approach what's true? To be honest implies perceiving and representing what is actually here as it is, without alteration, misrepresentation, bias, adulteration, preference, aversion, or any other distortion. There is a relationship between what "is" and honesty. Without honesty there is no possibility of experiencing the truth. It is essential that honesty be an ongoing principle in our investigations.

Grounded Openness

5:23   The Chinese have a saying: Paradox and Confusion are guardians of the truth. Why would they say that? Because what is true, especially what is Absolutely True, is not restricted to what's intellectually comprehensible or logical. It is only restricted to being what it is. Since what's true exists as its own nature and not that of our minds or our intellect, we may well be stopped by an apparent paradox, or be confused by what we encounter. To experience the truth, we must be willing to experience whatever is so, whether or not it fits within the bounds of our logic or our beliefs. The truth often lies in unexpected places. How can we approach the truth if we are not completely open?

5:24   A collection of definitions for the word *open* is quite revealing.

   Open:

   Adjectives:

   1a. Affording unobstructed entrance and exit; not shut or closed.

   1b. Affording unobstructed passage or view.

   2a. Having no protecting or concealing cover.

   2b. Completely obvious.

   2c. Carried on in full view.

3a. Accessible to all; unrestricted.

3b. Free from limitations, boundaries, or restrictions.

4a. Susceptible; vulnerable.

4b. Willing to consider.

5. Available; obtainable.

6. Not engaged or filled.

7. Not yet decided; subject to further thought.

8a. Characterized by lack of pretense or reserve; candid.

8b. Free of prejudice; receptive to new ideas and arguments.

Verbs:

1. To release from a closed or fastened position.

2. To remove obstructions from; clear.

3. To remove the cover, cork, or lid from; undo.

4. To unfold so that the inner parts are displayed; spread out.

5. To make more responsive or understanding.

6. To reveal the secrets of; bare.

7. To come into view; become revealed.

8. To become receptive to understanding.

Openness without Groundedness

5:25   Merely reading the list and considering the freedom implied with the word *open,* one might well feel inspired to go forth and adopt a position of openness. "Yes, that sounds right, that's for me. I'm going to be a more open person." Obviously that's not a terrible idea, but it is only that, an idea. As an idea, "openness" remains stuck in the intellect. There, it might be entertained, approved of, or fantasized about—and sometimes conveniently rearranged whenever the reality gets a bit scary—but since it isn't grounded in one's experience, this conceptual-openness eventually reveals itself as hollow and pretentious. People who adopt only a belief in openness tend to become superficial. They may have a broad-minded philosophical stance, but this open-mindedness floats in the abstract world of beliefs. This is openness without ground-edness.

"Openness" Gone Sour

5:26   People who try to operate from the mere belief that they are open will eventually discover that it has somehow become false or pre-tentious. That is, if they're honest. Because the openness is not grounded in experience, they have no real understanding of what they're talking about, and any assertions they make will begin to have a hollow ring—even to their own ears. To become grounded from here usually requires a fall from their lofty world of make-believe. The whole idea suddenly looks like bullshit. What a crock! Now they see that their "openness" was a fantasy, and that fantasy has gone sour. They may entrench themselves in a negative disposition for awhile, stuck in rejecting any form of openness as pretentious and insubstantial—as airy-fairy.

Openness as an Experience

5:27   From that closed position, it will probably take a while for them to realize that openness as an experience is a different matter. It is both natural and real, and much more present than thinking about or pretending to be open, a bit like the difference between eating food and eating a picture of food. An open person might waver in his degree of openness, but when he's open, his mental and emotional states and his perception and sensitivities will all be strongly influenced by this openness. He will be operating *from* openness rather than trying to *appear* to be open.

Groundedness without Openness

5:28 On the other hand, there is groundedness without openness. When people are grounded but not open, it shows up as being "closed-minded." They have a position that works for them, and they don't plan to budge from it. They cannot have breakthroughs or transform because they are unwilling to challenge their own opinions and unable to detect their own dishonesty. "This is the way it is. I know the way the world works." They may be closed-minded, but they're very grounded. That's groundedness without openness.

Balance

5:29 Once the negativity and isolation of being grounded but closed become overwhelming, we might be drawn to open up. And if this openness is merely an affectation without groundedness, we may well close down again. But such a roller-coaster ride may be unnecessary. Instead, we could stop to notice that these two extremes are simply complementary dynamics that need balancing, especially in our investigation of what's true. We can guard against being intellectually abstract or airy-fairy, and also avoid being closed-minded or stuck. We can go for a real experience, and be open to whatever is true.

An Experience of Grounded Openness

5:30   An experience of openness has a quality of uncertainty to it. If we're used to a frozen and predictable idea of openness, then by contrast the experience of openness will seem indeterminate, indefinable, and perhaps a bit scary. This is because experience is alive and exists only in the present. As an experience, openness is whatever it "is," and we don't know exactly what will arise.

5:31   To counteract the tendency to float in abstract worlds or to ignore what's real in our experience, we need to be grounded—which is to be real, committed to something, clearly standing on authentic insights and effective distinctions. Maintaining the balance of grounded openness allows us to explore, to be creative, to make breakthroughs, and entertain radical possibilities without becoming pretentious, abstract, or lightweight.

5:32   The tendency to be open without being grounded, or to be grounded without being open, is present for all of us. Some people may engage more dramatically in one or the other, but each of us needs to remain sensitive and attentive to the dynamics involved. The tendencies will continue far past any clarity we achieve in this matter, and past any resolutions we might make about it. Like walking a tightrope, one can't simply put a foot down and that's the end of it. Balancing is a constant activity within any changing circumstance. Life and learning are always changing circumstances.

5:33   The issue of balancing groundedness with openness comes up in many aspects of life, and at every turn of our investigations. When the two are in balance, we find that we can attain our most genuine experience. Any growth or change is dictated by a conscious experience of what's true, rather than by intellectual fabrications. Our growth is genuine, and our experience deepens. In this way, our investigations are empowered to become as real and as far-reaching as possible.

Questioning

5:34 As a result of the way our culture holds not-knowing, we're inclined to think of questioning as simply a request for information, asking for the answer. "What time is it?" or "Where is Tobago?" Such questions can be expressed just as well in statement form: "Tell me what time it is." Or "Point to Tobago on the map." No real wondering is needed. Accessing a stockpile of information to find an answer is not true questioning; it is a data search.

5:35 We have in our culture a sort of caricature of a wise man who is frequently the subject of cartoons. This "sage" is immediately identifiable and is most often pictured alone on a barren and rocky mountaintop, a bearded old man sitting cross-legged in a robe. There is usually an exhausted pilgrim making his way to the peak to ask some profound question about the meaning of life. The sage character juxtaposed with an ordinary person makes for some ironic and humorous captions. But did you ever wonder what he was doing up there on the mountaintop? Is he just so enlightened that he need not come down from the clouds? Is he sitting there for the view, or because it feels good? What's he doing up there? Where did we get this guy?

5:36 The image is derived from the monastic tradition of contemplation. Cartoons notwithstanding, the "sage" isn't sitting there to act as some kind of drive-through window of wisdom. He's not there for the view — the cliff just helps him stay awake and alert. He's there to get free of the distractions of his culture, and he's contemplating because he wants to experience something beyond what he's already got. He's sitting up there questioning. He's not trying to figure something out or piece together some information. He's intending to become deeply conscious of the truth of some matter.

The only Zen you find on mountaintops
is the Zen you bring up there.
—Robert M. Pirsig

5:37   Simply wanting to know an answer or requesting information is not a true question. Questioning as a genuine and powerful activity is real wondering — dwelling on and wondering about a subject, and being open to the possibility of realizing something about it that you do not now know. Such profound questioning remains unattached to any answer or outcome. Without the power of questioning, there is only knowing. With only knowing, there is no question and so no discovery, no insight, no learning, no mystery, and no experience of the authenticity of simply "being." Questioning demands real wondering, and wondering demands not-knowing.

5:38   Now, put your attention on the principle of questioning with as much honesty and grounded-openness as you can, with the goal of having an authentic experience of questioning itself. Come from your own present experience of not-knowing what is meant by "questioning," so that you really wonder: *What is this activity?* Tackle it freshly, as if you really don't know what questioning is, but are ready in this moment to find out. Ask yourself: *What is the act of questioning?*

This is questioning.

The moment one gives close attention to anything, even a blade of grass, it becomes a magnificent world in itself.
—Henry Miller

5:39   Learning to question isn't complicated; in fact the difficulty lies in its very simplicity. When we speak of questioning, we're not talking about going into nature to ponder the meaning of life, or mentally sailing off into abstract notions of the cosmos seeking some answer. We're talking about being right here. That sage on the mountaintop may be questioning to understand something beyond himself, but he begins by looking into the truth of his own present experience.

5:40   Our everyday experience is so familiar that we assume we know everything there is to know about it. Let's use this way of holding experience to practice some real questioning.

> **Questioning Exercise Part I**
>
> Put your attention on a specific sensation that you perceive right now—the feeling of pressure on your fingers as you hold the book. Focus on this sensation for a moment. Where is it located? Exactly where does the sensation begin, and where does it end? Concentrate on this task for a while. What comes up as a result of trying to more clearly pinpoint this sensation?

Remember, real questioning comes from a state of not-knowing, and with no attachment to an answer, just a commitment that it be the truth.

This simple exercise already provides an unusually sensitive probe into a taken-for-granted phenomenon, but let's go a bit further with it and try to distinguish more clearly where this perception is located, and where it isn't.

> Once again, focus on the sensation of holding the book. Can you notice all the subtle beliefs and interpretations, meanings and associations, assumptions and conclusions that get added to the pure perception? See if you can separate out your ideas and beliefs and history regarding the perception, and become more presently aware of the immediate experience: the pressure on your fingers.

5:41 We need to practice telling the truth even at times when "honesty" seems not to apply, such as in this exercise. Here, by learning to discern what is and is not our immediate perception, we are actually exercising our ability to be honest. To take this ability further, however, you must be open to discovering any subtle, or not so subtle, assumptions that you might be harboring and might have had for most of your life. This is difficult at first because our assumptions are habitually absorbed into our perceptions, and so they're normally received as part of the whole experience.

5:42 **Questioning Exercise Part II**
> Now return to the sensation in your fingers, and ask yourself whether the sensation is really that, or that way, or do you just take for granted that it is? For example, is the sensation in your fingers the same as touching the book, or is it merely a sensation that you interpret as a book, mostly

because you're looking at your hands touching it? When you explore the sensation, you will find that it is separate from your concepts of books, and separate from your visual feedback regarding holding one.

Once you've gotten to the simplest and most immediate, no-frills perception you can get at this time, continue to focus on it. Now that you have a present sense of and attention on a specific perception, begin to ask: "What is it? What is the perception itself?" Since your brain will quickly supply a ready-made answer to that question, which is "holding a book," you will need to consider past the answer. Ask yourself, "What is the perception beyond my ideas of it? Am I holding a book?" See if you can generate enough openness that even such a ridiculous-seeming question can be considered in earnest. What happens when you entertain such questions?

"Am I touching a book?" Of course you are touching a book. You can see it, feel it, and you know what a book is. This is fine, but is there something missed because you are so certain of the experience? What is the present sensation without this certainty? Do you begin to become aware of the perception itself? Then what is that? What is the essence or nature of this sensation or awareness? Can you experience it directly without thought, without interpretation, without meaning, but grasping what it is at its most fundamental level?

5:43 **Questioning Exercise Part III**

Now do this whole exercise again without rereading above. Instead of using the sensation in your fingers, use your awareness of your environment—being in a room or being outdoors. Concentrate on this awareness, and try to move through all the points we just covered with the finger sensation exercise. See what you remember, and what you have gotten just from the spirit of the exercise. Ask: What is this awareness?

Once you've done that, go through it again while rereading Parts I and II—substituting "awareness of your environment" for "sensation in your fingers." See if you missed something the first time you questioned awareness, and whether it makes a difference or deepens your contemplation. As you move toward the end of the exercise, if you are aware of being in a room, for example, ask such questions as: *Where does this awareness reside? Is it in my head, in the room, both, or neither?* Further ask: *Am I in a room?* See if you can generate enough not-knowing that these questions can be genuinely asked.

5:44 If you threw yourself into the exercises above, you should notice that your relationship to and awareness of your perception has changed. You may not have grasped the absolute nature of perception, but what did happen? Did you notice anything that you'd overlooked before you began questioning? Did you make a new distinction in your experience?

5:45 Did you grasp, for example, that the actual sensation or awareness is itself distinct from whatever you are feeling or aware of, and that it is also distinct from your ideas and knowledge regarding what it means or what it "is" in any conventional sense? Did you become more presently aware, more sensitive to what's happening now? Did you create an openness that changed how you were perceiving something, how you related to it? How far did you go?

5:46 It doesn't matter that you reached any conclusion. What's important is that you opened up to the most honest and direct experience, and questioned beyond the ready-made answers. As you do this repeatedly, it becomes obvious how inherent and necessary not-knowing is to such questioning. Without genuine not-knowing, true questioning cannot take place. Do not underestimate the significance of this principle. This kind of questioning is a powerful ability, one absolutely necessary for the task of delving into the nature of your own real being.

I respect faith, but doubt is what gets you an education.
—Wilson Mizner

Embracing Paradox

5:47 I want you to keep in mind that none of the four principles is presented as truth or facts to be believed, and that the directions and possibilities offered in this communication are for your own exploration and investigation. The point is not *what* you discover, it's that you learn to engage in an ongoing process of questioning to discover for yourself what is actually so in any matter. As you read onward, return often to these principles. As your experience deepens, so will your grasp of what's being said. Continually look into whether you can be *more* honest, *more* grounded, *more* open in your questioning.

5:48   Although authentic experience was the first principle, it is also the last. Since our ultimate goal is to have an authentic, direct consciousness of being, it can be said that authentic experience is where honesty, grounded openness, and questioning lead. In other words, it is both active within and the end result of these other principles. We begin and end with authentic experience because, besides being our goal, it sets the stage for the work ahead and points us in the proper direction. Without our intent to be authentic, none of the other three principles will be valid or useful.

5:49   You may begin to see how these principles are intertwined, really four parts of a single endeavor. Honesty, grounded openness, authentic experience, and questioning are the main activities through which anyone can make progress toward uncovering an experience of real-being. Paradoxically, they're also the abilities needed for grasping and using the principles of honesty, grounded openness, authentic experience, and questioning.

5:50   So to begin this work requires having already begun it. I hope that some of this conundrum is sorting itself out as you apply yourself to getting an experience of the communication. Although we must keep looking back and ahead, back and ahead, trust that we have already begun the work. In a way, we're always beginning the work.

5:51   Trying to study one's own awareness can be like looking at an Escher drawing, where ordinary things often don't line up the way we're accustomed to seeing them. Our knowing tells us this isn't logical, and we may feel discomfort, which is how Paradox and Confusion so effectively guard the truth. As we embrace a willingness to not-know, however, we see the discomfort for what it is, and our confusion becomes acceptable. We're free to explore in any direction we choose, and we find that committing ourselves to these simple principles will guide our efforts as far as we want to go.

5:52 Our honesty helps us align with what's true. Grounded openness is a balanced position that allows us to experience real possibilities in unfamiliar territory. With our commitment to honesty and grounded openness, the stage is set to pursue through questioning what we're really after: authentic experience, a direct encounter with what's true, whether it's the truth of our present experience, our way of being in the world, or of reality itself.

5:53 Armed with these principles and the desire to know the truth, we can begin to tackle the nature and composition of our self-experience as we live it. What we hold to be true, or what we assume is so, may not actually be true. If we apply ourselves and listen carefully to each step and each consideration as the book unfolds, we can begin to sift through all that comprises our view of self and world, and discover what is fact and what is fabrication. As the dynamics of human experience become illuminated, we create a powerful springboard to leap beyond our current ignorance into an enlightened consciousness of the true nature of being.

PART II
Our Self Experience

CHAPTER SIX
Conceptual Dominance

Creating a Conceptual World

6:1 When we watch little kittens we're bound to notice that their most common activity is play, which consists largely of mock fighting and hunting. Their early attempts are like slapstick comedy, but soon they begin to demonstrate exceptional grace in their movements and great skill in their physical interactions with the world. By the time a kitten becomes an adult cat, what is she good at? Fighting and hunting, of course. And while her activity can still resemble play, survival is a serious game, and the results are most often deadly for her prey.

6:2 When we watch young children, we notice that their most frequent activity is also play. There's a healthy measure of physical activity as they learn to use their bodies effectively, but even more notable is their propensity for creating and inhabiting fantasy worlds — what we call "make-believe." They'll push an eraser around and call it a race car while making revving sounds, act out relationships between dolls, or battle pirates on a make-believe ship that in reality is just a few chairs pushed together. They'll defend the house against aliens, have tea with a bear, or cast magical spells on their siblings. Children spend a great deal of time making up situations and acting out imaginary roles. Just like kittens becoming cats, what are adult humans good at? Conceptualizing!

6:3   Even at an early age, humans have an astounding capacity for creating concepts and a natural ability to make up entire "worlds" in which to be and act. We think of it as merely playing, but make-believe is more than just an imaginative way for children to amuse themselves. What such activities really do is train their ability to conceptualize.

6:4   The phrase *make-believe* correctly suggests that a belief is "made." As children we spend countless hours constructing fictitious roles, story lines, and circumstances, inventing the necessary sets, props, and partners to act them out. All these are created as a "reality" so that we can act in accord with the pretense. As with kittens, the motivation to play appears to be simply that it's fun, but without such skills we could not function as intelligent creatures capable of perceiving a great deal more than what is in front of us.

6:5   Of course, interwoven with any child's play is a constant learning process in which, piece by piece, certain observations and beliefs are made real. Some of these serve the practical purpose of survival—"hot" or "sharp" objects are not to be touched, and it's dangerous to play in the street or talk to strangers. Also, from a very early age, children pick up subtle instruction in views and values. They might learn that knowledge, talent, and possessions are evidence of a "deserving" person (and the lack of these indicates an "unworthy" person), that the beliefs of the family and community are correct while all other beliefs are incorrect.

6:6   Being predisposed to internalize these lessons, children often reinforce them in their play. They enjoy escaping from imaginary dangers, caring for stuffed animals or dolls, imitating figures who seem powerful to them like a queen or superhero, or acting as if a pretend fire is hot. They invent roles and situations in which they can demonstrate the personal qualities, skills, and knowledge that are admired in their family and community. Make-believe can be a lot like making real.

Fur comes from fir trees.
—Sally, in *Peanuts*

6:7 It's not difficult to think of a child's imaginative play as a conceptual activity, but we don't usually consider that everything we perceive as adults is subject to a similar if more sophisticated system of conceptualization. In fact, one difference between adult and child is that the child is more likely to recognize that he's the author of his fantasies. He might get annoyed when his world of make-believe is interrupted, not wanting to admit that he isn't really Superman, or that his magical energy beams may indeed not be all powerful, but when called to dinner he knows it's time to return to the "real" world. As adults we are far less likely to do so. By the time we reach adulthood, much of what we "know" actually falls into the category of "make-believe" but we don't recognize it as such. Having thought this way for as long as we can remember, we take it for granted that our beliefs are real.

6:8 The mere act of "having dinner," for example, is not a fact of the universe but an event and custom learned most likely from our families. In the simple act of "coming to dinner" we have specific ways in which to behave and a small "reality" in which to step. As we join in the ritual, the mood often shifts a little and the conversation may take a turn appropriate to dining. Whatever our particular relationship to having dinner may be, without inspection we don't notice that a fabricated reality—albeit a rather minor one—adds to our experience of this event. It may be pleasant or inconsequential, but it's made-up nevertheless.

6:9 When we start considering all that we have adopted and made into our reality and view, we begin to discover a great deal that is seen as "reality" when it really isn't. We have beliefs that we recognize as beliefs—I believe in God, or I believe in the tooth fairy—and yet we have many more beliefs that we just assume rather than recognize. We hold many notions that are taken for granted as a part of life or reality. We may assume that children are innocent, humankind is becoming more advanced, thinking is what "I" do that I call thinking, emotions are what we suppose they are and are necessary aspects of being human, love is universal, disease can be cured, all "good" religions are based on valid truths, contrary belief systems are ignorant at best, animals have emotions, something written in a book is likely true, my self is unique and meaningful, not to know is bad. These and countless other "truths" like them are only beliefs, but still we live as if they are correct.

6:10 So many ideas have been instilled in us for so long that it can be a challenge just to recognize our beliefs, much less disengage from them. This is not necessarily an easy thing to grasp, even when you want to. You might take on faith or figure out intellectually that a great deal of your perceived world is purely conceptual, but that does very little to provide you with the means to challenge or transcend it. You need to have experience after experience, and insight after insight that this is actually the case. You need to do the work of recognizing the true nature of your own perceptions. Even if you've made such observations in the past, the work isn't done until it's done.

Exercises in Recognizing Your Beliefs

6:11 Now take a moment and look into your personal conceptual domain. What do you believe? Whatever comes to your mind with that question is something you can begin to investigate. The beliefs themselves are not so important — we're looking at how you hold them as true. Can you uncover some assumptions that you live with but don't notice they're only an assumed frame of mind? For instance, what do you believe about your life? Is it an exciting adventure or a woeful sentence to be served until death? What do you think is true about life in general?

Notice that no matter what you come up with, it's conceptual. It's an idea within a web of ideas that makes up your sense of life and reality.

6:12 Continue the exercise by seeing what comes to mind when you consider what's true about your family. Think about your relationship with different family members, your family's values, and what you think and feel about your family — whatever comes up. Just check out any ideas and beliefs you have regarding your family.

After a few minutes with that, do the same thing with your country. What arises when you think about your country?

Notice that with each of these issues there are a multitude of taken-for-granted ideas, feelings, associations, and judgments that constitute a perception of that whole matter for you. Take a moment and see if you can pick out what you actually feel and think about those two things: your family and your country.

Regardless of the specifics that came up, the amount of thoughts and feelings is quite significant, isn't it? And it's all conceptual.

6:13 Now do the same for yourself. What do you believe is true of you? Who are you? Are you sure? Can you uncover every judgment and assumption you take for granted about yourself? What comes to mind when you think of yourself? Do you notice there are a multitude of taken-for-granted ideas, feelings, associations, and judgments that constitute a perception of yourself?

If not, work on it, because every modern individual has a very complex and multilayered conceptual matrix that comprises the simple perception called "self." It is highly useful to be in touch with what that is for you. You will run into a conceptual sense of yourself everywhere you turn because your experience is actually dominated by concepts and beliefs.

What Is a Concept?

6:14 But what actually is a concept? There is some confusion about what is meant by concept, so let's look into it by starting with a definition or two:

Concept:

1. A general idea derived or inferred from specific instances or occurrences.

2. Something formed in the mind; a thought or notion.

3. A scheme; a plan.

Conceptual:

1. Of, pertaining to, or relating to mental conceptions.

6:15 We often think of a concept as a general idea, or a vaguely organized mental image: *I've never been to a barn raising, but I get the concept.* But anything that is fabricated in the mind is conceptual. A concept is unreal in the objective sense, meaning nothing substantial exists. Some people might call it a "conceptual object" since it appears to us as some "thing," but a concept has no mass, no location, occupies no space — it exists solely within our mental perceptions or imagination. This does not make it any less powerful, simply less objective. What we need to grasp at this juncture is that concept is not something that exists of its own accord, but is the summation of a mental process. It *refers* to something; it is never the thing itself.

6:16 Concepts are ways of knowing, and everything we know is conceptual. Some examples of concepts are interpretation, memory, beliefs, ideas, notions, dreams, imagination, thoughts, fantasies, visualizations, assumptions, and anything else that is a product of the mind. We could even say that emotions are conceptual in nature since they are produced through conceptualization. Concepts are not limited to one aspect of mental activity; they comprise the entire field of mind and as such they influence almost everything of which we are aware.

6:17 Abstractions, such as a mathematical formula, a daydream, or a decorating idea, are easily recognized as concepts because they are different from our normal experience and perceptions. But one of the main jobs of concept is to mimic our everyday perceptions and experiences. This means that a perception such as the sight of a bus can be somehow "known" when there is no bus around. We can "see" the bus in our minds, so to speak. It is the same with sounds — like remembering a song — as well as smells, tastes, and touch. Anything we've perceived, and even things we haven't, can be conceptually perceived in the mind. Whenever we remember something, we are "reperceiving" past events. Given we are conscious that these events have passed, we know them as memories, but they are conceptual nonetheless. Concept not only *mimics* reality, however, it serves to help *create* reality.

6:18   When we look at a tree, we imagine that we are merely perceiving the tree when in actuality we are interpreting or "knowing" it as a tree. We may see some object there, but when we interpret it as a tree something more is now perceived that wasn't there previously. This is a conceptual superimposition placed upon what is perceived, without which we would not see a "tree." We don't recognize that we live entirely within a conceptual reality any more than a fish recognizes that water has always surrounded him.

6:19   Everything we perceive, whether it's an object or mental image, is subject to interpretation — making sense of incoming data so we can recognize and categorize it. Interpretation allows us to order our world, which requires mental processes that are all conceptual. It is also true that much of what is "experienced" as oneself is really a concept rather than an experience. And as I've suggested already, there is a distinction we need to make between the *experience* of being and the *concept* of self.

Concepts Dominate Our Perceptions

6:20   In simple terms, every perception we have is understood in relation to the concepts we have about what is being perceived. Once
we learn to glimpse perception *prior to* our conceptual additions,
we begin to understand the nature of concept and how it can limit
us in our ability to experience. I'm not suggesting that we attempt
to live without concept, but that we need to be aware of how concept dominates our perceptions and experience. We've already
touched on this notion, but now let's look into it in more detail
and depth.

6:21   Pure perception is incomprehensible to us. What we commonly
call perception is really the interpretation of a meaningless phenomenon into a specific and useful "cognition." Fundamentally,
a perception is simply a sensory encounter with some object or
occurrence, and is without association or emotional charge.

6:22   There are two major conceptual contributors that dominate all of
our experience: "interpretation" and "meaning." Since perception
as itself is meaningless, what we perceive is useless without interpretation. The mere fact of seeing an object, hearing a sound, or
feeling a sensation means nothing unless we know what it *is* and
how it relates to *us*. To make sense of what we perceive, we automatically associate, classify, and interpret the meaningless data
that is available. First, everything perceived is quickly interpreted
so as to determine what it is — a flower, a squeak, a dog, a chair,
soft, fast, a person. Having conceptually identified what something is, we then immediately relate it to ourselves.

6:23   No matter what we perceive, once we interpret it in some basic way, we will go on to assess its value or threat to us by associating it with an array of past experiences and beliefs, and so supply it with meaning. This meaning renders the thing ugly, expensive, mine, hers, sacred, too big, useful, ridiculous, friendly, dangerous, or what have you. Once meaning is attached, our minds will immediately infuse the thing with some "emotional" charge, subtle or gross, to indicate in a feeling-sense how we should relate to it. This charge is based on the value or threat that a thing or notion has relative to us, and so this feeling-reaction contains information suggesting particular behavior — should we run or feed it a biscuit? Such feeling-charge manifests as attraction, fear, disinterest, annoyance, desire, boredom, importance, repulsion, and so on, as well as many such feelings far too subtle to warrant a name. The application of interpretation, meaning, and emotional-charge occurs so fast and automatically that we do not distinguish any of these as separate activities within our whole experience.

6:24   This mechanism is a remarkable feature of the human mind — a rapid means of converting all perceptions into a self-relating form which enables us to take the necessary actions to insure our safety and survival. It's wise to remember, however, that everything we think we "know" is an interpretation. Every bit of information we take in is influenced and altered by our particular set of beliefs, assumptions, and associations. These alterations are conceptual "add-ons" that strongly influence our experience of whatever is perceived. What we react to is not the object itself but rather the interpretation and meaning that we ourselves apply to the object.

There is nothing either good or bad, but thinking makes it so.
—William Shakespeare

6:25   The same process that we apply to objects of perception also works the same way on our own thoughts, emotions, and sensations. We associate them with the past, we assess their meaning and value — just about any reaction we can have to physical objects will also arise in relation to our own mental processes. Our ideas and beliefs and, in a way, our entire history are applied to everything that comes into our awareness — whether it's people and objects, or our own thoughts and feelings.

6:26   What we know as reality is influenced by the concepts with which we interpret it. From "tree" to "hot" to "disgusting," what something means to us predetermines how we will perceive it. Yet this relationship between concept and reality is so seamless it is undetectable. The car "is" beautiful in our eyes, the apple "is" delightful in our mouths. Our reactions to an ugly and dangerous monster are pretty much the same thing to us as the experience of the monster itself.

6:27   Unless we make the distinction between our additions and what's there, we can't become conscious of what's actually there. Our whole experience of self and life is conceptually dominated. This means that we are not simply experiencing life and who we are; we're also constantly "imagining" life and who we are. Since it doesn't seem like it's our imagination we're perceiving, we don't know the difference between what we are adding and what is there. Let's see if we can recognize the way this conceptual influence acts on our personal experience.

There's More to Perception than Meets the Eye

6:28 Boiling down what I said above: any perception we have is only understood through concept. This is a very dominant aspect of experience. Seeing an object doesn't give us much until we recognize it as a chair that we can sit on, or a dog that might bite our leg, or a rotten apple that is best thrown away. Along with every perception is an automatic mental association with many concepts.

6:29 But don't take my word for it; take some time to look around you.

> Gaze at different objects and try to ascertain what each object means to you. What do you believe about it? What feelings come up immediately when you look at it? What is the object called? Do you like it or not, or don't you really care either way?

6:30 For example when you look at a red sports car, a certain lifestyle association immediately pops up along with commensurate feelings and attitudes. Glancing over at a minivan reveals through contrast the many reflexive associations made with the sports car, since very different meaning is placed on the van. A rock may have a rather lackluster set of mental connections, unless you need one to throw at the dog who wants to bite your legs. A bar of pure gold usually conjures up associations that evoke much more exciting reactions, while an old rocking chair might elicit many fond and comforting memories.

6:31 Once you've done a few of these, try another practice.

Just as you did in the exercise in Chapter Four, look at an object and try to see it without knowing what it is. Knowing is automatic and immediate and difficult to stop, so you'll need to put some real effort into it. Keep your attention on whatever you perceive and try to not-know anything about it — like what it's used for, what it can or can't do. Attempt to throw out any and all reactions, associations, and feelings you have about it. Don't know what it "is" for a moment — not even what it's called. Focus on the object until everything familiar about it has dropped away from your awareness, until you can see it without all the normal mental applications in attendance.

6:32 What happened when you did this? Among other things, you should have noticed that what you perceive has many concepts attached to it, without which the perception falls into a very different category of awareness. Apply this technique to other objects or people. With this simple exercise, you become more apt to recognize how much concept influences your entire experience.

6:33 This kind of conceptual influence is equally present in the experience of one's self. Our experience and perception of ourselves are found within and dominated by concepts — thoughts, feelings, beliefs, images, memories, assumptions, and programming. Yet this entire conceptual makeup cannot, as a matter of fact, bring us to, or even represent, an experience of our real being. Why this is so will unfold more clearly as we go.

6:34 Examining the relationship between concept and experience may not seem very important except for one frequently overlooked fact. The very concepts that dominate our experience, attention, and awareness are strongly influenced, if not outright determined by, unconscious personal and cultural beliefs and assumptions. This in itself perhaps wouldn't be a problem either, except for another overlooked but very important point: many of these are wrong.

The Solidification of Concepts

6:35   When something is held to be true or real—existing outside of our imagination—we hold it in a different category than something that's known to be just a concept. In the hierarchy of perceptions, we relegate abstract ideas to a lower rung of importance than objective reality. We may not like what the bus driver thinks about us, but we'll be sure to get out of the way of the bus. Experience tells us we need to take that solid objectivity seriously. Even if we had the belief or fantasy that we could fly, when the bus bears down and flying isn't an option, we will jump aside instead. We respect the uncompromising aspects of objective reality, yet often blur the line of distinction between it and our mental activities. In so doing, each of us frequently perceives an idea as if it were a self-evident truth.

6:36   For example, someone might imagine that sex is somehow evil, or that his political party embodies the only correct view of human relations, or that her religion defines the nature of reality, or that science has the only real description of the universe, or any number of notions, many of which are far too subtle or ingrained to recognize easily. But all of these are simply concepts that are believed to be representative of what's true.

6:37   We stand just as firmly on many assumptions about ourselves. When someone says that he is worthless, we may know clearly that he is not, but for him, this self-description is a fact of his existence. The assumptions surrounding this "truth" are so ingrained in him that he can't see it as merely a powerful concept that influences his every thought and action. This trap makes what is only imagined in our minds seem like something objectively so.

6:38   Such a distinction is significant because what we can and can't do in relation to objects is different from what we can and can't do in relation to concepts. For example, if you have no legs, there is little you can do to change it. Pretending you have legs doesn't improve your running skills. If you think you are bad or stupid, clumsy or worthless, and that these assessments exist in the same category as having no legs, then you are just as stuck with them as you would be with a wheelchair. Although they are only assumptions that you've adopted, or have been trained to believe, they are deeply programmed and are perceived as if they are permanent traits. On the other hand, if you realize that these attributes are conceptual in nature, immediately you will experience the possibility that you can change them, or get free of them altogether.

6:39   Shifting your self-concept in some way does indeed change your perception of yourself, but if this is something you desire, it's ineffective to rush ahead without a proper foundation. Such a change is rarely easy because our presumptions run deep, not just personally but culturally. Our self-views are based on conceptual fabrications that are deeply rooted in the values, beliefs, and assumptions of our culture and personal history. We observe that cultures don't seem to change overnight, and we observe the same thing about individuals.

6:40   The beliefs upon which self and culture stand are not easily recognized, nor are they easily discarded once we identify them.
Remember that both culture and self are created in much the same
way — they're the products of many foundation assumptions.
These assumptions — accepting particular ideas to such a degree
that they become taken-for-granted realities — give structure to
our lives. They are the backdrop for our sense of self and reality,
and they offer what seems like solid ground in a world of uncertainty. We may benefit from such structure, but we need to recognize that our assumptions are also responsible for most of the
limitations and suffering that we experience. What generally goes
unnoticed is that they are not facts but merely beliefs, and since
they are conceptual in nature, they are not necessary in and of
themselves.

Challenging Conceptual Dominance

6:41   To create the possibility of recognizing things unseen, we begin
by more clearly noticing what's there. If we can't see that our experience is largely made up of concepts, how can we address this
condition intelligently or effectively? When something exists as one
thing but is perceived to be something else, our ability to interact with it or change it is extremely limited. Yet our experience
just seems to be our experience. There's a reason that people look
everywhere *except* into their own experience when they want to
change. They assume their perceptions are simply an accurate
reflection of reality, not noticing that there is a difference between
what is experienced and what is true. To adjust this mistaken
impression, we need to fully perceive and acknowledge the dominating influence that concepts have on our moment-to-moment
experience.

6:42   Have you ever tried to stop your thinking for even a minute? Try it now. (Even if you have, try again, and try to keep it up longer than normal.)

> Sit for a few minutes (set a timer if you like) and stop all thinking of any kind. Keep a vigil on your experience from moment to moment. You may seem to have shut off your thinking, but begin to notice a subtle background kind of thinking, a sort of "talking quietly to yourself." See if you can shut that off too. Perhaps you notice that your mind continues to work even when you perceive no internal speaking or chatter; see if you can shut that down also. Don't even form mental images or engage in any other conceptual activity. Can you do this for a few minutes? Try. I'll wait here while you do.

6:43   Couldn't do it, could you? If you indeed tried to stop all thinking for several minutes at a time, you experienced an inability to do so. If you didn't attempt it, then please do. Experiencing this inability is far more valuable than taking my word for it. It won't become clear, however, unless you attempt it in earnest.

The composer Stravinsky had written a new piece with a difficult violin passage. After it had been in rehearsal for several weeks, the solo violinist came to Stravinsky and said he was sorry, he had tried his best, the passage was too difficult, no violinist could play it. Stravinsky said, "I understand that. What I am after is the sound of someone trying to play it."
  —Thomas Powers

6:44   Why do you think it's so difficult for us to suspend our thinking? I propose it's because something needs to happen that can't occur without constant mental activity. (It might have something to do with the creation and maintenance of a conceptual-self and the management of that self in relation to everything perceived, but we'll look into that possibility later.) What's important to recognize right now within your own experience is the power and dominance of concepts. The ceaselessness of our thinking is one place we can clearly see the drive to conceptualize.

6:45   Another area where we find conceptual dominance is a place few people would expect. Our culture's way of holding thought as distinctly separate from emotion sets up the assumption that they are of two completely different natures, or at least that they are independent activities. There is certainly something about a thought that is very different from a feeling, no doubt about it. But there is also something quite similar in how they each arise, and this we overlook. Emotions and thoughts are both produced through mental activity. It's easy to recognize the conceptual nature of thinking, but we prefer not to acknowledge that emotions—and the many feeling-reactions and impulses too subtle or obscure to be labeled as emotions—also occur within the mind.

6:46   Now, the moment I say that emotions are concepts, I suspect more than one reader will object. Clearly emotions have a charge to them; our feelings have gusto and passion. They aren't "dry" like intellect, or mere thought. We're moved by our emotions. It seems as if we're in charge of our thoughts, but emotions seem to arise without our bidding. If we recall our attempt to stop thinking, however, we might hesitate to conclude so boldly that we indeed control our thinking.

6:47   The activity of thinking appears to be less than completely under our control. Conversely, we must admit that we do have some say in our emotions. We've all experienced being a little angrier than was called for — found ourselves actually pumping it up a bit because we liked the effect it was having on ourselves or on others. We might pout or fan the flames of our hurt so as to elicit more sympathy, or perhaps nurture feelings of love even though we perceive that the circumstances don't really warrant such romantic feelings. So we have to admit, even if only to ourselves, that we influence our emotions also.

6:48   What most of us don't realize, however, is that the basic nature of all emotions is conceptual. A feeling-reaction occurs as a result of a complex mental stimulus that is conceptual in nature. This is what we experience as an emotion. A fuller explanation of the phenomenon of emotion will emerge as we proceed, but for now I'd like you to take my word for it that emotion is conceptually based. It's important for you to recognize the full scope of our conceptualizing so that you can see just how dominated we are by it. Usually, the strong influence that our feelings have on us is more readily apparent and acceptable than the fact that we're dominated by our own thinking.

6:49   It's not difficult for us to look back and recall the many emotions we've had over our lifetime, including those that were painful or undesirable. Even in our more recent past we can count a large number and variety of emotional feelings that have passed through our experience. More difficult perhaps is to be aware of the ever-present activity of feeling-states that pulse through the body and mind as steadily as a heartbeat. If you take a moment to check out your feelings right now, you can probably identify some mood or emotional feeling that occupies your background awareness.

Unless you are particularly moved by what you're reading or your sister has just poured cold water down your shirt, you may not have a clear and "loud" emotional experience at present. But you do have feelings, right now and always.

6:50   Begin to increase sensitivity to your current feeling activity by doing the following exercise:

> Put your attention on the sensations and feelings in your body and mind in this moment, and see how many you can identify as not physically produced. In other words, what feelings can you find that aren't something like an itch on your foot, or a sense of the room temperature? How you feel *about* the itchy foot or in reaction to the warm room are not in themselves physiological sensations. Perhaps the itching bothers you, or maybe you enjoy scratching it. The warm room might feel cozy and safe to you, or perhaps it's uncomfortably stuffy. These background reactions may not occur to you as clearly as some emotions, but they are emotional in nature.
>
> Other feelings you have are not even that clear. If you pay close attention, you can begin to pick up more subtle moods and feelings, some of which would normally pass for sensations. Upon inspection, they turn out not to be physically based, but rather subtle emotional reactions to certain background ideas and mind states. You might notice that feeling energized is really an underlying excitement, or discover that the slight discomfort of wearing a tie is actually impatience making you a bit hot under the collar. Feelings like these remain obscured in the background. Either they're so familiar that we take them for granted, or so subtle or insignificant that we fail to become conscious of them.

See how many feelings and varieties of feeling you can identify just as you sit there. Over time, watch them shift and change. Merely putting your attention on them and increasing your sensitivity will create a marked change in the feelings that you have. Regardless what you do with them, notice that these subtle and not so subtle emotional feelings are a constant activity.

6:51   Having noticed that feelings — various moods and attitudes, reactions and emotions, impulses and urges, dispositions and mind states — are constantly a part of your overall experience, it is time to acknowledge their influence.

Just as you did with your thinking, take a few minutes, perhaps a few more than you did with thinking, and attempt to suspend all feeling of any kind. Stop feeling any emotion or even having an attitude toward anything. This means you must give up all dispositions and judgments because all judgments are emotionally charged. Try to have no impulse, no desires, fears, drives, or urges of any kind. Be completely free of any possible reaction or upset, no matter what may occur. Know that suppressing or ignoring what you feel is not being free of it. Try to remain aware and receptive but without a hint of feeling for several minutes. Do this now.

6:52   Difficult, isn't it? Actually you'll find that it is as difficult as suspending your thinking. This is because thinking has an interrelationship with feelings, and vice versa — they evoke and provoke one another. There is a reason for this, which, once again, you'll look at later. For now, focus on increasing your awareness of the influence that concept has on your experience and perception. If all thinking and all emotional feelings are conceptual in nature, consider how much of your experience is dominated by these activities.

6:53   The task of directly experiencing the real nature of Being requires that we recognize and free ourselves of any and every concept we have — even the subtle and hidden ones — about who we are. This can be as immense and difficult a task as it is a worthy one. In the next chapter we're going to take this notion of conceptual domination and apply a more grounded look at how it operates in our daily lives. Proceeding in steps and stages, we can begin to uncover and detach ourselves from the dominance and confusion of the conceptual domain and take steps to return our consciousness to a more genuine sense of self.

CHAPTER SEVEN
You Don't Have to Rehearse to Be Yourself

Being Yourself

7:1 How can we begin to return to a more genuine sense of self? We don't have to experience the absolute nature of existence in order to make huge leaps in becoming more authentic. Some people focus so hard on some sort of "spiritual" attainment that they forget to work with what's right in front of them. To create the requisite foundation for discovering the "absolute" truth, we simply need to be more real, honest, and genuine in every way we can. But how can we begin such work? Here's an idea: We could stop pretending to be something we're not.

7:2 In the introduction I spoke of just "being ourselves." Yet how do we know when we *are* being ourselves? Everyone has met people who seemed phony. We've all seen someone pretending to be something he is not, either faking it or trying to con us into believing some fabrication about himself. Often the person he seems to be trying to convince the most is himself. We've also met people who seem to live within fantasy worlds, or who adopt ideas or affectations that we see as superficial and unreal. When we see these things, we have immediately made a distinction between the "real" person and what they'd have us believe.

7:3 It might irritate us that they hide behind such obvious pretense, but our irritation suggests we recognize that a real person is there doing the hiding or pretending. We would prefer for them to simply come out and "be themselves" rather than pretend something that isn't genuine. Yet they must harbor a fairly strong belief that the opposite is true — that people want them to be some other way than what's real — otherwise why would they venture down such an unhappy road?

7:4 Although this tendency is easier to see in others, the very same dynamic applies to ourselves. From time to time we find ourselves guilty of pretense, or trying to be something we're not. Perhaps we adopt mannerisms that indicate a way we'd like to be seen, or alter the representation of some aspect of ourselves or our history. Most of us can find examples of some sort of personal misrepresentation, yet what if this tendency goes deeper than we know or are willing to confess?

7:5 When we perceive a person being false in some way, we immediately sense what it would be like for him to be real — otherwise we wouldn't know he is being false. Yet what if we didn't perceive such falsehood? Someone or some thing may be false, but if the inauthenticity isn't perceived, we won't know it's not real, nor could we sense what is real. This is also true of ourselves. If something unreal exists within us, in order to eliminate it our first task would be to discover what it is. We can't do that unless we learn to recognize what is real and what is not. Discovering what's real is dependent on recognizing what's false.

He who would distinguish the true from the false
must have an adequate idea of what is true and false.
—Baruch Spinoza

The Real and the False

7:6 To investigate what is genuine, it is essential to clarify what *real* and what *false* are. Since our work is primarily focused on ourselves, this distinction must be grounded in the experience of ourselves, so consider the following definitions in that light.

Real:

1. Genuine and authentic; not artificial or spurious.

2. Free of pretense, falsehood, or affectation.

3. Having an existence in fact and not merely in appearance, thought, or language.

False:

1. Arising from mistaken ideas.

2. Not genuine or real.

3. Erected temporarily.

4. Resembling but not accurately or properly designated as such.

Unreal:

1. Not real or substantial; illusory.

7:7   When it comes to yourself, what is real and what is false? If you find
       something that is in any way not genuine, or is erected temporarily,
       then you must call it false, or at least not call it your "self." If you
       discover that something you've called yourself is illusory and
       insubstantial, created to "mimic" or resemble yourself but is not
       in fact yourself, then this too needs to be recognized as false.
       Whatever is born of mistaken ideas must also be called false.

7:8   Without any other practice, simply devoting ourselves to strip-
       ping away all pretense is an incredibly powerful and transforma-
       tive thing to do. Engaging in such a practice brings us quickly to
       consider: *What could I be pretending or affecting that has gone unno-
       ticed?* We begin to search for subtle ways in which our presentation,
       communication, even thoughts and feelings have been less than
       straightforward. We discover many expressions that in our hearts
       we know aren't as genuine as they could be. This practice brings
       immediate and ongoing changes in our personal presentation and
       also in how we think of ourselves. It begins to make searching for
       what's true easier, and makes what's false in ourselves and oth-
       ers more visible. As much as you can, freeing yourself from pre-
       tense, falsehood, or affectation will go a long way towards helping
       you discover what is real.

7:9   Beyond our practice of being as genuine as we can, we should con-
       tinue to bring to light all that isn't really us, whether it is pur-
       posefully false or not. We will begin to discover much that isn't
       real, and much that is in subtle ways false, that previously we
       accepted as simply a part of ourselves. Just because we're used to
       being a certain way—believing in the things we believe, acting in
       the ways that we do, having the opinions we have, expressing the
       character traits we've adopted, and reacting in familiar patterns—
       doesn't make these things true, and it doesn't make them us. Of

course, there is a lot of pressure not only to develop these personal attributes, but also to maintain them and to improve upon them.

7:10   Your real self can only be genuine and authentic. It cannot be artificial, false, or merely a thought. According to the definitions it cannot even be the product of language. Do you grasp some of the implications of that? Can you see how much the experience of yourself lives within your internal dialogue? Now imagine an experience of "being" without any language at all — without any speaking, not even to yourself. Since thinking is very much tied up in language, what can you experience as you without confusing yourself with your thoughts? Concept is a tool and an abstraction, and is always erected temporarily, so consider experiencing "being" without any concept at all. Identifying everything about yourself that exists as a concept — an idea, image, belief, or any other mental activity — is necessary in order to distinguish your real self from what is not-you. But why would anyone confuse attributes, ideas, and behavior patterns with themselves if these aren't really themselves?

Masks and Hats

7:11   It's true that in our culture we are rarely accepted for who we actually are as a being. Instead, we are appreciated, valued, and loved primarily for what we do, how we look and act, and what we say — in other words, from the impressions made on others and how people feel about those impressions. Clearly, in order to secure a sense of being valued, we are moved to adopt a persona — to develop and display an assumed social image or personality. We may or may not be successful at getting what we want through these means, but our motive is clear—we want to be accepted, be approved of, and be a part of our particular community. Yet this is not the only motive that drives our behavior, thinking, and feelings.

7:12   An infusion of programming from various sources throughout our growing up has molded us into a complex structure of shoulds and shouldn'ts, values and fears, needs and methods for fulfilling our needs. Trying to fulfill our many needs—be they emotional, financial, personal, or professional—leads us to try out, invent, and adopt many perspectives and forms of expression. To get what we want out of life we use various tools. Over time we become more and more permanently attached to particular expressions, attitudes, mannerisms, reactions, and moods, and this is then seen as our character or personality. When we dissect anyone's habits of character and methods for trying to fulfill needs, we find many adopted attributes—in short: many "masks and hats."

7:13   For example, we feel and act differently in various surroundings. We wear a different "hat" at work than we do at home or in our other relationships. A person can be quite different as an employee or boss than he is as a spouse or sibling. This adjustment to our various roles is not simply a matter of altering expression. It involves feeling differently, thinking differently, having a different self-image and perhaps even a different worldview. Remember that in our definition of false we find, "erected temporarily." Anything created to serve some end is not what is already and genuinely ourselves.

7:14   Accommodating our changing roles by adopting different "hats" is only one area in which our self-concepts reveal traits and experiences that are clearly adopted to serve a purpose. Another such arena is seen in the various "faces" that we put on to encounter different situations. We might smile and act friendly when asking a favor of someone, or put on an air of bravado in times when we desire to be seen as brave or aloof. We may adopt movements and expressions that make us appear harmless when we need someone to be unafraid of us, or we might put on the face and voice of anger to cow a child into safe behavior. These "masks" have become familiar additions to our repertoire of ways to get what we want, serving some need or fear. They seem to arise automatically, but they're adopted purposefully as the circumstances warrant. Many of our expressions are not actually reflective of how we feel at the time, or of our more fundamental experience of ourselves, but we've used them so often and the habit is so strong we've forgotten they are masks, and instead they become indicators of "the way we are."

7:15   If we study ourselves carefully, it becomes increasingly clear that most of our habitual behavior and character traits, as well as our ever-shifting and purposely crafted expressions, exist solely to fulfill needs — they are conceptually produced reactions to external stimuli that come to be known as aspects of ourselves. All together these comprise most of what we know *as* our selves. Yet in some sense this is a "false" self. It is false or unreal in the sense that it is secondary. It is founded on external programming and created to serve external goals. It is not based on what simply exists as the being that we are "as-is." "Doing" something is not the same as "being" something.

7:16   The activity of *expressing* is preceded by the activities of *feeling* or *thinking* that motivate your expression. All of these activities are doing something rather than being something. The idea that you exist as an internal entity that is then expressed or communicated outwardly in various ways is not the end of the story about masks and hats. Collectively, these adopted internal traits and outward expressions not only help compose your sense of self, they tend to preclude any further discovery of your original sense of being. Being attached to and confused with all sorts of artifice places an impenetrable barrier between your consciousness and genuine being. Through recognizing, and perhaps eliminating, all that is secondary, you should have better access to an original sense of yourself.

7:17   In Chapter One, I suggested that you are comprised of two aspects of "being"—who you really are (without pretense, affectation, programming, or any additional process), and what you have come to identify or "know" as your self. Broadly speaking, the self is known through the adoption of beliefs, ideas, and traits that pass for who one is. In our culture we acknowledge the conceptual contribution to our sense of self whenever we refer to our self-image, self-concept, self-identity, and self-esteem. These activities of "imagining," "conceptualizing," "identifying," and assessing one's "worth" are always conceptual. They are phenomena we use to identify, know, and define ourselves.

7:18   Because we don't make a clear distinction between a built-up conceptual identity and our own being, this conceptual-self dominates our perceptions, thinking, and feeling. We are burdened with the immense job of maintaining this "adopted-self" and have become thoroughly confused and identified with it. Therefore, almost everything we do is done in service of this self.

7:19   To get free from the culturally mandated destiny of a life spent trying to fulfill the needs of something unreal and unnecessary, we need to make a distinction between what is real or original within ourselves and what is secondary and conceptual. When we begin to relate to and from what is secondary as if it is actually ourselves, rather than something added on to serve some purpose, we run into problems (recall the consequences outlined in Chapter Three: emptiness, self-doubt, feeling trapped, suffering, and struggle).

7:20 By making a distinction between being and self, we realize that most of what we identify as our selves is conceptual. This distinction and realization then enable us to work with our conceptual-selves more consciously. Concepts can change. Therefore it is possible to change anything that is conceptual about ourselves. Yet if we don't understand the forces that motivated us to adopt these abstractions to begin with, we will be unable to free ourselves from their return even if we are successful for a time.

Superficial Remedies

7:21 It's not uncommon for someone to feel upset with a life or self that seems meaningless, or without true worth — and everyone seems to wrestle with this challenge at least on occasion. From this underlying condition many attempts are made to remedy our sense of inauthenticity and bewilderment. Some of these "solutions" come from the community, such as religions, spiritual movements, or other shared belief systems. Some are found within the individual as a collection of beliefs, opinions, assumptions, and fantasies. These remedies might serve to provide some dignity and a sense of worth — for a person or for a life. Yet all are only additions, something placed on top of what's inherently present. They do nothing to clarify the experience of the being that is there.

This whole dynamic represents the tip of an iceberg, as we'll see in the following chapters. By engaging in such "solutions" we only further reinforce the creation of a conceptual "self" from which to relate. This self is always in some way artificial.

7:22   We need to realize that these solutions we've adopted — as individuals and as a culture — are based on mistaken assumptions, and therefore do not and cannot resolve our deep sense of personal inauthenticity and disquiet. The only way to do that is to experience directly what's real and authentic, which is who we really are. Adding beliefs and convictions, or going through the rituals of life that promise redemption but can't deliver, are futile activities. This is like someone trapped in a burning building piling papers up all around to save himself. It ain't going to work.

7:23   The more we have failed in our attempts to overcome our sense of inauthenticity, the more it adds to our sense of incapacity. We've all heard the phrase "I'm only human" and other such statements that accept as fact that we are all flawed. Perhaps we've decided that being human is inherently less than perfect. On one level this may be so, and we should acknowledge this possibility in our attempt to experience what is actually true and real about "being."

7:24   Although it may turn out to fly in the face of our belief in our own limitations, our purpose is to experience what is true even if we discover that we are not flawed in any way. Directly experiencing what's already so is a very simple act. Yet so much seems to stand in the way — distracting our eye and demanding our attention — that it becomes a complex task. The complexity lies in our conceptual identity; our "being" is already simply so. If we could toss out all that isn't genuine, perhaps we'd be left with an experience of who we really are.

Looking for Self in All the Wrong Places

7:25   The vast majority of remedies for our sense of inauthenticity or disquiet can be found in our beliefs. Our consciously adopted beliefs — used to patch up our incomplete sense of self — only add a superficial layering, of which we may be aware. Our subliminally held beliefs, which are more deeply believed or assumed about ourselves, form the parameters of our actual "self sense." Since many of these assumptions are not known for what they are, we see them as real aspects of ourselves and so, try as we might, we find them hard to dismiss.

7:26   As a culture, each of us share in the notion of improving ourselves, and so from time to time consider changing some self trait for another. Yet of all that we experience as characteristic of ourselves, we might ask: What should we toss, and what should we keep? We tend to agree that whatever provides the most benefits in health and well-being, success and growth, are probably keepers. Conversely, anything that creates unnecessary limitations, ineffectiveness, and pain should go. Making this decision isn't the hard part. Our challenge lies in knowing which is which.

7:27   Yet before we can successfully sort out the genuine and beneficial from the false and unnecessary, we need to be able to identify what it is that we believe, and uncover all that we assume. Looking at definitions of beliefs and assumptions might help us better recognize these activities as they are occurring within our own experience.

Belief:

1. Mental acceptance of and conviction in the truth, actuality, or validity of something.

2. Something believed or accepted as true, especially a particular tenet or a body of tenets accepted by a group of persons.

7:28 We see that by definition the nature of belief is conceptual. Given that every belief is a concept, it must be separate from whatever the belief is about — in other words, it is not a direct firsthand experience of the truth. It is the "belief" that something is true. Since it is a concept, and in most cases not even based on something perceived, it is only a mental fabrication.

7:29 The key here is not so much to find the "right" beliefs, but to adopt a more healthy relationship to all beliefs, to return belief to its true status: a concept, and not the truth. Without allowing "the truth" to be unknown, we are unlikely to embark on such an enterprise.

7:30 It is the same with assumptions. An assumption is basically a core belief that goes unnoticed and is taken for granted as an aspect of reality. Assumptions most often operate beneath the surface of our consciousness. These overlooked core beliefs exist both as deeply ingrained cultural assumptions and as something individually assumed. Let's consider a bit more carefully what an assumption is and how it permeates our experience.

Assumption:

1. The act of taking upon oneself.

2. The act of taking for granted.

3. Something taken for granted or accepted as true without proof; a supposition.

4. Presumption; arrogance.

7:31   Any assumption, whether cultural or personal, is absorbed into our consciousness throughout the process of our upbringing. Whenever there is an assertion made — be it a family belief, a community superstition, a religious dogma, or a scientific postulation — the moment we adopt this view, we also take on the assumptions that go with it. Of necessity we learn from our parents, our community, our educational systems, and so forth. Some of this takes place in a conscious way, but much more occurs as a matter of absorption or programming. In either case, the assumptions that exist within any kind of thinking or knowledge will be passed on along with the rest of the information. Much like when a computer virus infests a particular application, both the application and the virus will be downloaded into the computer. Perhaps more accurately, it is like a computer program that has inherent flaws: when you accept the program, you accept the flaws.

7:32   Beliefs and assumptions show up within our thoughts and feelings. Sometimes they show up *as* a thought — I believe we should love one another; I believe high cholesterol causes heart problems. Sometimes they are buried within a feeling-reaction — being angry at someone for teasing you, assuming that people's motives are always suspect. And sometimes they show up as core foundations for our thinking and feelings — believing in personal superiority, assuming self is always correct in its assessments, or perhaps feeling incapable of handling life in general. We will tackle beliefs and assumptions repeatedly and in greater depth later in the book. For now, as we continue to challenge what we think is true, remain open to discovering something you assume that has yet to be perceived.

7:33 How can we better recognize assumptions buried within the mass of taken-for-granted information that comprises our selves and our knowledge? We begin by creating the ability to do so. This requires a number of skills, such as a deeper honesty than our cultural norm, a new level of self-discovery, and a degree of openness that will enable us to think outside of our programming. As I mentioned earlier, one of our key ingredients must be telling the truth. This involves more than what usually passes for honesty. It requires an ability to discover and admit what we unconsciously (and consciously) tend to keep hidden. In our effort to clear up all that we believe or assume, the main drawback is that these are not always available for our scrutiny. Far too much of this domain is hidden from view.

CHAPTER EIGHT
Unknown Origins

Our "Need to Know" Level of Consciousness

8:1   We find our beliefs and assumptions revealed in the particular thoughts and feelings that fill our minds every day. Since our characteristic behavior is motivated by these thoughts and feelings, they determine the roles and expressions we will adopt to meet any given circumstance. No doubt about it, what we think and how we feel are keystones to our self-experience. Yet in more than one way, we are impressively blank about the source of this cognized mind.

8:2   Our thoughts and feelings seem to determine almost everything we do and "are," but where do our thoughts and feelings come from? We assume it is our "real self" that generates them, but even if this is so, we don't personally experience this source, nor what's involved in creating what we recognize as an idea or emotion. Although the complexities of this process will unfold in later chapters, we need to consider the possibility that an unseen dynamic takes place every time we think or feel something.

8:3   The simple version of what's taking place is this: what we experience as ourselves — what we believe, value, and assume, as well as our memory, programming, self-image, and so on — is related to and weighed against the currently perceived circumstance or issue. From this assessment, the "internal state" deemed most appropriate for relating to those conditions is summarized in a feeling or thought. Yet all we're aware of is the resulting feeling or thought.

8:4 It seems our conscious awareness provides too narrow a focus to grasp and hold large complex processes within our daily lives and activities. Like a low-ranking member of a spy operation, our personal awareness seems to come into view on a "need to know" basis. Which is to say, much goes on within our minds that remains unknown. What we obtain in the way of thought, impulse, emotion, or whatnot is the end product of a complex activity, but apparently it has been predetermined that we don't really need to know all that much.

8:5 In order to consider the matter more deeply, we must look past our existing relationship to our cognitive functions, and we can't do that unless we first recognize where we stop short. As an analogy: if the only access you had to food during your entire life was a refrigerator that was stocked by someone else while you slept, you might well assume that food originated in that refrigerator. If I asked you where food came from, you'd say: "the refrigerator." If I pressed on, you would simply have to insist that food comes from the refrigerator and that's the end of the story. Since you and I really know that food comes from the store—OK, from the farm—we see that it's silly for someone to think that food comes from a refrigerator. But we don't know where food comes from prior to "farm," do we? We aren't at all clear about how food gets to "be" at the farm, how things come to live and grow; we only know that they do. At some point our knowledge stops.

8:6   In most matters, we know nothing more than our given answers or assumptions. When it comes to our perceptions and experiences, we assume we know what they are all about, but this belief is actually based on cultural assumptions — not unlike "the farm." With closer scrutiny we begin to realize that we don't really know where our thoughts and feelings come from, or how they come to pass, or what they really *are*. We can only recognize this limitation, however, if we consider beyond our usual inclination to accept our ready-made answers.

8:7   Like food coming from the refrigerator, we assume that a certain thought is valid without knowing why we think so, or that a belief is true without having personal experience of the matter, or that every feeling we have means what we assume it to mean. This is like "stopping at the refrigerator" and not ever wondering how those items got in there. We think we know what an emotion "is" simply because we have emotions and can identify them. We assume that fear is what we assume fear to be, or that anger is simply our experience of anger, and that that's the end of the story, without really knowing what makes up fear or anger. This condition persists because of a lack of introspection and conscious sensitivity, but it begins as a result of what might be considered a necessary convenience.

8:8   Our conscious assessments and linear thinking are processes that are much too slow to handle the amount of data needed for and stored within one simple feeling or emotion, or what pops out as a ready-to-use conviction or judgment. In contrast to all that goes on within the convoluted decision-making and reaction-producing aspects of our minds, the information we consciously receive is quite limited. Our thoughts and feelings are primarily the conclusions of complex processes. This conclusion or "summary" tells us what something means to us and how we should relate to it. Most of this data is stuffed into a feeling, or it stimulates a conclusion or idea, revealed in the act of having a thought.

8:9 As a simplistic example, I might feel anger when I discover Daniel has been deceiving me about something. When I look into all that constitutes my anger in this case, I discover memories of my past relationship with Daniel and concepts of similar circumstances with others. I perceive a sense of the danger to myself inherent in being deceived, and a sense of hurt at having been lied to — which includes the reasons why someone would deceive another. I will also discover personal values that I have, as well as the shared values and agreements of my society. I notice an overlooked feeling that Daniel must not love me or respect me (threatening to interfere with any need I might have for love and respect), a sense of impotence, an impulse to protect myself by destroying this present threat, and much more. All of these connections are made rapidly, and pop into my consciousness as a feeling of anger. It arises as anger since the conclusion of this process is that anger will create the proper disposition from which to relate to Daniel, protect myself, and manage all that is involved with this turn of events. It is quite simple, but also very complex.

8:10 This single feeling-experience carries with it a great deal of information and provides the impulses for whatever action or disposition I will take on. The conclusion, and so the feelings that spring from the conclusion, can change at any time as circumstances change. If I were to discover that Daniel indeed hadn't deceived me, that I was mistaken, instantly my feeling would change. This change would also be the result of associations and implications, reasoning and meaning, but it would occur in my "conscious" mind as a simple change in experience. All that I would really be aware of is a feeling of relief or some such. In either case, what is "given" to me in my awareness is one basic feeling, and some accompanying thoughts. This is what my mind decides I need to know in order to go about the business of life in this moment.

8:11 Pretty much all of the conceptual-emotional orientations we experience about ourselves and life fall into the same domain as "food comes from the refrigerator." In other words, we live within many unchallenged assumptions about ourselves and about life, and this is where our consciousness stops — we don't know how our mental-emotional activities get into the "refrigerator" of our minds. One reason we don't consider questioning this is that everyone around us seems to live with the same condition. We accept it as commonplace.

What one dog barks incorrectly,
a thousand other dogs bark as correct.
—Japanese saying

Mistaking the Uncognized Mind for the Real Self

8:12 Not recognizing the source of our mental-emotional activities is commonplace in part because of an overlooked assumption that exists within all of us. This assumption isn't easy to see since it forms a central part of the experience of yourself. Only a personal insight will do you any good in this matter. To get at this assumption, consider the following.

8:13 You recognize that somehow you have thoughts and feelings. Sometimes it seems that these experiences come *to* you, that you are the recipient of a thought or an emotion. If someone "makes you angry," then it seems as if this anger was caused to arise in you by that person, and so the emotion appears to come to you. It is the same whenever a thought seems to arise as if from somewhere unknown, like a muse providing inspiration for a piece of music. In these cases our cognized mental activities seem to "arrive" as if caused by something outside ourselves.

8:14 Yet, this isn't the whole story, is it? At other times it seems like thoughts or emotions come *from* you. That somewhere inside "you" have generated the thought or emotion—like when you say, "I just had a great idea," or "I love you." In this case, you experience your "self" as the source of these activities. It appears as if thoughts and feelings both come *to* you or are somehow caused to occur in your experience, as well as come *from* you or are generated by you. But what we are trying to get at here is the *you* that either generates or is affected by these activities. What is that?

8:15 Sometimes we refer to ourselves as our collection of thoughts, emotions, behavior, and so on. When that's the case it seems as if self *is* those things, and so that's the end of the story. But from time to time we also refer to our self as the one having thoughts or producing emotions, or as the one being affected by whatever we encounter. This self is then held as if somehow "behind the scenes," since the self itself is not apparent; only the thoughts and emotions it produces are perceived. We take for granted that this "me" is the source of my thinking, etc. We rarely notice that we are not directly perceiving this source. We are not directly perceiving this me—it is suspected or "intuited" but not "seen." It falls into the same domain as uncognized mind—or food coming from a refrigerator—but this fact is overlooked.

8:16   Having a thought about "the me that is having the thought" is still not perceiving me. It is assuming that this very thought arises from the one being thought about, but that one is actually unrecognized. Because the source of the thought is held to be you, it is also held to be the "real" you—as opposed to the you that's a collection of thoughts and emotions. In this case, it is much like the Wizard of Oz running the show from behind the curtain. We don't see the Wizard, we only see the show; and in our case we simply suspect that there is a Wizard or real-self back there generating and perceiving these thoughts and emotions.

8:17   In your experience right now I suspect there is an unquestionable sense of *you* presently existing, as if behind your awareness. This sense feels real and solid, doesn't it? Yet what if this very sense of "real-me" is simply a collection of uncognized mind, rather than your true nature? You could be assuming that the domain of mind that you don't cognize is the "real" you. Think about it. We accept that the thoughts and feelings provided to our consciousness arise from the self, and since we aren't conscious of the complex processes that provide this activity, we assume this uncognized aspect of mind is the "real self."

8:18   What if the very sense of your "self behind the curtain" is actually not you? Consider the possibility that this self-sense is founded on an assumption that you must be the one generating thoughts and reacting to stimuli, so whatever does generate these activities would be thought to be you. If what does generate thoughts and emotion is a complex domain of mind that isn't recognized, then this would be held to be your real self, wouldn't it? This assumption, combined or confused with a background perception of an overall bodily sensation, could provide that "feeling-sense" that you assume is you. Imagine that all together these form that sense of your "real self" existing just behind your awareness. If this is true, then the real source that you *are* could easily be missed, couldn't it? It's possible that your ignorance of the workings of your own mind makes it appear as though the complex processes of the uncognized mind that produce your thoughts and feelings are the real-self. Such an assumption would play a central role in any conclusion you might make about yourself, and would tend to stand in the way of the openness necessary to ask: if this uncognized mind isn't me, then what is?

8:19   The beliefs and assumptions that both comprise and arise from these uncognized activities remain the arbiter of our perceptions. What stirs us to take action, draw conclusions, or create a perspective are activities of mind that remain unknown to us. As such the domain of uncognized mind seems to be the source of our awareness, thinking, and reactions. Since this domain of conceptual activity is unknown to us, it is generally held as unchangeable and as one thing—ergo a "self"—and so appears all the more as the solid and consistent root of our self-experience. These unconscious mechanisms are a part of a basic human condition that people have rarely understood. Given all this, it seems inevitable that we become distant from our original sense of being, that we should become highly conceptual, and on the surface at least, in some ways false.

The real voyage of discovery consists not in seeking new landscapes but in having new eyes.
—Marcel Proust

The Origins of Your Self

8:20 In the last chapter, we addressed the phenomenon of becoming confused with many character traits and beliefs. This confusion goes much deeper than any superficial facial expressions we might use, the particular personas we adopt for various occasions, or the internal chatter that constantly fills our heads. That brings us to our current observation where we see how unaware we are of what's behind our constant flow of thoughts and emotions, and that this domain of uncognized mind could well be the focal point of the sense that our real selves exist somehow behind the scenes.

8:21 We locate ourselves in our thoughts and emotions. We also suspect ourselves to be some entity generating thoughts and feeling emotions. But where did this conceptual-self and sense-of-self come from? Delving into the origins of our own self-experience requires that we dip into the abstract a little bit. We can't consider our world as we normally would. Instead, we must consider how our world came to be the way it is. To do this requires that we think differently, as if our experience of the "world" as we know it hasn't been created yet, and we are searching for its beginnings.

8:22 Let's start with the observation that most of what we call ourselves is conceptual. Consider: Even if we are naturally drawn to use and adopt these conceptual attributes to manage life, why would we mistake them for our selves? When we look into the *overlooked obvious* we discover a fact that has been ignored and misunderstood from the beginning of our lives. To experience this fact personally, take a moment to do the following guided meditation.

8:23   **The Origins of Your Existence Guided Meditation**

> I want you to look into your memory as far back as you can, and recall a time in your life when life and self were just starting out for you — back to the beginning.
>
> At some point in life you became self-aware — "you" came to exist. Try to recall what it was like for you in the earliest part of your life.
>
> When you remember back as far as you can, eventually your memories of yourself end — your memory of "being" goes no farther back. Go back to where you personally can't remember life or yourself existing before that point. Even if it's rather vague or unclear, concentrate on any sense of yourself as far back as you can remember.
>
> Now, fully observe that you do not experience yourself existing prior to that time.
>
> Seriously consider: did this self-awareness exist prior to your memory? How did it come to pass? Where did you, as an awareness, as a conscious entity, come from?

8:24   You don't know. You can't remember. Probably you never knew. This is a very important matter, but it is most often overlooked and ignored. You don't know the true nature of self-awareness, although you "are" self-aware. You don't know the true nature of "being" even though you do exist. This is not a flaw or mistake. It's what's true. You don't know how it is "you" came to be.

8:25   Take a serious look: you do not have a firsthand experience or consciousness of the most essential aspects of your own being and reality. You have no personal experience of how "you" came to exist, or what life is, nor do you consciously experience the essential nature of reality. You haven't consciously experienced for yourself the most fundamental and deepest aspects of "being" or reality. You don't know, and yet you pretend like you do.

8:26   Think about it: if you have no access to the truth of the matter, you can't authentically say what that truth is. Everything is then conjecture, hearsay, belief — it is not actually a direct personal experience of what's true. You simply don't know — that's a fact. Yet this is a very important thing not to know. This is how you came to exist, to "be," and you must confess you don't know. Most people completely ignore this fact.

8:27   Perhaps in the beginning your self-sense was rather simple and nonspecific, but over time it has been built into a highly complex multifaceted mechanism. Yet no matter how complex your self-identity becomes, the fact remains that at your core you still don't know what you, life, and reality really are. Not-knowing these essential aspects of your own existence invites you to invent or make things up to fill in this gap in your consciousness. Since you fundamentally don't know how you came to exist, you are living deep inside of a central and constant not-knowing. This must have some effect on you.

8:28   Grasping the deep impact that this condition has on your core sense of self is best experienced rather than merely heard. You must experience for yourself that you don't know what you are or how you came to be. Yet the most intimate and personal experience you have in life at this moment is of yourself. It is the place you reside; it is where you exist and are aware. And yet, in this most immediate and intimate place, you are completely devoid of an experience of your own creation. Don't think this has gone entirely unnoticed by you. It may have been buried, but my guess is it has been noted — and that it bothers you.

8:29 This means that the self you've created and "become" is not founded on an experience of creating it, or even on knowing what your existence really is. Somehow you simply came into existence. But since you don't know how that happened, you also don't know how to keep your life from going away, or what no longer existing is all about, or how you could recreate your existence if you happened to cease to exist. Don't you think such a primary condition in consciousness would have a significant impact on our primal psychology?

8:30 From this condition such impulses as pretending, taking on beliefs, asserting convictions, accumulating knowledge, or remaining ignorant seem to be the only options. They are not, and coming to grips with the fact and presence of "not-knowing" — that it is a universal and natural function of being a self — frees us from the many damaging dynamics set in motion by misunderstanding the true nature of not-knowing.

8:31 What is life? What is the real nature of existence, of reality? What really occurs when we die? Does God exist or not? What is the nature of "being," of existing? We don't genuinely know any of these — which is to say, we do not have a direct personal experience of them. The most fundamental questions cannot be answered authentically by us. We really don't know. This fact is hidden, overlooked, buried, or ignored, but is nevertheless true, and deep down everyone knows that they don't know.

We are here, and it is now. Further than that,
all human knowledge is moonshine.
—H. L. Mencken

8:32   Discovering our own depths of not-knowing begins to reveal to what degree, and why, a conceptual-self has displaced our real sense of being. Feeling truly complete and whole, authentic, and alive only becomes possible if we recognize this fabricated self-identity for what it is, and seek out an authentic experience of real-being.

8:33   Now that we are on the threshold of deep and genuine not-knowing, we can begin the real work of setting out to experience what self and being really are. As we go forward, it may seem in some ways that we are going backward or repeating some of the basic communications already addressed. We are not. We are going forward. Take each step as an invitation into a deeper experience. Contemplate what's said and delve into the overlooked obviousness. Starting once again from the ground up, let's look into how a self is constructed and what a self is. In the next chapters we will work through how our experience of self and life has been shaped—touching on the essential elements, components, and motivations that create our experience of self and reality.

PART III
In Search of Real Being

CHAPTER NINE
What Am I?

Our Experience of "Being"

9:1   All day long you walk around in your skin. You look out of your eyes, and hear with your ears. Although the sights and sounds are what grab your attention, the fact that it is "you" doing the looking and hearing is always tacitly in the background. Throughout the entire day "you" are there. Without thinking, you are the one looking. You're the one who delights in an ice-cream cone. You're the one dodging cars as you cross the street. You're the one sharing a joke with coworkers. You're the one rubbing an achy shoulder. A constant stream of perceptions, thoughts, and feelings flows endlessly to and from you all day long. The centralizing factor to all these perceptions is "you." That's taken for granted.

Yet, what are you?

9:2   When we think of ourselves, a certain set of images, thoughts, and feelings will consistently come to mind. "I am this person right here. I have certain characteristics —I'm smart, strong, gentle, fat, persistent, intense, timid, educated, black, Asian, funny, a good Christian, or whatever. This person is me. Who else would I be? What else? I'm just me, always have been." But are these sets of attributes actually our selves? We suppose they are; otherwise why would they come to mind when asked to consider one's self?

159

9:3 Frequently, when we look into such matters, we are stopped by our first impression. Often this is a taken-for-granted identification of what's there and why it's there. When it comes to ourselves, much of what we experience falls into the domain of subjective psychological activity—emotions, internal chatter, reactions, and thinking. This is an important arena in which to look, but it is not the primary issue that we need to address right now. If asked to consider outside our normal mode of personal assessments, we often search for a more philosophical response—religious, metaphysical, scientific. But neither the psychological nor philosophical domains are appropriate to our task here. If we want to experience something beyond the limits of our beliefs and knowledge, then we need to grasp what something is, not just what we think or feel about it.

9:4 In our culture we just assume that what we are is what we identify as ourselves. This is a reasonable assumption, but it is mistaken. In fact, as we touched on in Chapters Three and Seven, the purpose for some of our most basic cultural assumptions is to cover up our inherent inability to grasp what a self really is. The high value we place on knowing creates discomfort whenever we encounter what we don't know. Mostly we avoid this problem by holding "self" as either too obvious to question or too inaccessible to grasp. If pressed to consider beyond our everyday position that "I am this," we simply refer to our favorite beliefs—usually philosophical or religious—which declare something about self or being. We don't really give it enough consideration, which is why even within the supposed obviousness of being ourselves, misleading cultural assumptions can operate unnoticed.

9:5 In the previous chapter we confronted the fact that we don't personally experience how we came to exist. This ignorance alone is the source of quite a bit of mischief, and the creation of more than a few beliefs and assumptions that generally go unchallenged — religious assertions, scientific assumptions, psychological paradigms. But what about our *experience* of self? What *is* all this that is experienced as ourselves, or as anything else, for that matter?

9:6 If I point to a chair and ask, "What is that?" you'll probably say, "It's a chair." Now I know what to call it, but I could still ask, "What is a chair?" You might respond with, "It's something to sit on." This informs me about its use, and so its relationship to me and my needs, yet I could still ask, "But what is it actually?" At this point, you're likely to throw it at me, or resort to searching your mind for some philosophical response that will shut me up.

9:7 Such a reaction indicates that in truth we don't know what a chair *is*—or what anything else is — beyond label and use. We perceive shape and substance and then relate to that object — we search our minds for its name and how we can use it; in short, we "identify" it. This is certainly enough for our needs, and we go no further with it. Risking reader irritation, however, I do want to point out that what we have confessed here is that we are not fully experiencing the chair. We do not perceive the nature of the chair, only the form and name. We freely admit we do not, since it is clear that the chair is a separate object, distinct from our own minds and perceptive faculties, and we cannot perceive its nature from here. In other words, we are not the chair and so don't perceive anything more than its external qualities — we don't experience "inside" of it so to speak, or even from its "point of view."

9:8 This is not so strange. What is strange, however, is that we experience much the same problem with our "selves." Unlike with the chair, we can't claim that the cause of our ignorance stems from the fact that we are not it — after all, we "are" ourselves. But if we're honest about it, we must confess that we're not aware of our own nature either. We perceive ourselves essentially the same way we perceive the chair; we simply have much more content. We identify characteristics, sensations, emotions, images, judgments, body, history, and the like, and are satisfied that they are "us." As a culture, what we fail to notice is that every one of these identifiable attributes, with the exception of our bodies, is conceptual — it's an idea, an abstraction. And we don't experience them any more directly than we do a chair, since, like the chair, they are not us — the very one who is perceiving them.

9:9 When it comes to the body, we still know little more about it than we do the chair. We appear to "reside within" or "be" the body, but this doesn't bring us any closer to being made aware of its nature any more than our perception of the chair gives us the chair's nature. Residing within or "as" something, then, doesn't seem to provide us with a direct awareness of the nature of the thing any more than our perception of external objects does. Some people claim to be nothing but a body, and some claim to be an entity within a body; either way it makes no difference. Although we feel the sensations of our bodies, and enjoy the various perceptions provided by the perceptive organs, the component we call awareness or consciousness has not been granted insight into the very nature or even the inner workings of our bodies. Most importantly, the aspect that we call our conscious self is still not fully understood or directly and completely experienced — much remains unknown. We have questions regarding our selves and the nature of being and life. That pretty much says it all.

9:10 It's fine that we don't know what a self is. We don't really know what anything is. What's important is to *recognize* that we don't know. We ourselves do not directly and fully—without reference to hearsay, knowledge, or belief—consciously experience the nature of existence. Overlooking this simple condition allows the charlatans to flourish—within and without. All sorts of beliefs can be bandied about, asserted and refuted, or readily accepted and even died for, simply because we fail to acknowledge the truth—we don't know, and others don't know either. The truth is that we find ourselves in a condition of ignorance, a blank slate in this matter, and no amount of debate or number of ideas changes that in the least.

The mystery is not "how" the world is, but "that" it is.
—Ludwig Wittgenstein

9:11　Once again, a resolution to this condition is not necessary here. Nor is it even necessary that our ignorance be true in the end. What's important for us to realize is that it is in fact a foundation relationship of self to life that permeates humanity. This foundation is that we do not know what existence really is. We do not experience the true or ultimate nature of reality, including ourselves, and yet we ignore this condition. In so many ways and on so many levels, we pretend to know. We insist that some knowledge held by one or another segment of our human community—religious, scientific, philosophical, common sense, personal opinion, or what have you—must have the answers (or soon will) to this unknown aspect of being. The unknown aspect we are talking about, by the way, is the most essential aspect of being. It is the essence and nature of existence itself.

9:12　But who cares? I mean really, who cares? What we care about is more immediate and useful. What's for dinner? Did the project go well at work? Are the kids safe? Where shall we go on our vacation? These are legitimate concerns, and actually far more important to us than our ignorance of the essence of being. We don't know, so what? When somebody finds out, they'll tell us. Now let's get on with life.

9:13 Quite right. There seems to be nothing we can do about it, so what's all the fuss? I'm not suggesting that attending a lecture at the university regarding philosophical arguments about the nature of existence has any more value than having a beer and watching *Gilligan's Island*. Both are entertainment, and when they're over, they've changed very little in the course of our lives (except sometimes). It is not the *idea* that "we don't know" to which we are invited here, it is the *fact*. And this fact will again quickly disappear from view once our fascination with it is over. That's the point. We have an assumed relationship to this fact that makes it very slippery and hard to hold onto, and yet it has far more impact than we realize.

Identifying Ourselves

9:14 Getting back to the experience of ourselves: we live every day with what we identify and assume to be ourselves, but this self-sense is built upon presumptions that have distorted our identity from the beginning. The embarrassment that we don't really know who we are compels us to hide this fact away, and we've done that so well we can even forget that it's true. In general, we live within an experience in which we both know and don't know who we are in the same moment. How is this possible?

9:15 Our assumption that what we identify as the self is indeed the self provides an experience of "knowing" who we are, and so we act and react accordingly. It is an experience of self that exists within the same domain as an experience of a chair, and isn't any deeper really than "food comes from the refrigerator." As we've seen, we don't actually know how we came to exist, or the nature of our own existence. This is a central limitation in our consciousness, but it isn't the only limitation.

9:16 In a more psychological vein, can any of us say straight-faced that their inner workings are perfectly clear to them? We all seem to have some concern about what may be true of us deep down in hidden places; we don't know what may lurk beneath the surface of our consciousness. Sometimes we're afraid to discover that something bad may turn out to be true of us. Or we fear others may discover something within us that we'd rather keep hidden. If we're honest about it and not blinded by some dogma or other, isn't uncertainty about who we really are a shared human phenomenon? There seems much unknown. People have doubts regarding themselves, both existentially and psychologically. So we can see that although we claim to know who we are, we must also confess that in many ways we do not.

9:17 If we do not perceive something, we cannot identify it, nor identify with it. This is so because we don't know of the existence of whatever is not perceived, and so cannot recognize it or consider it to be ourselves. If we perceive something, we can then identify it. Still we may not identify *with* it. We can identify a rock as a rock, but we don't call the rock ourselves because we don't identify with the rock—we don't recognize the rock as the self. Whatever we perceive and identify as the self is what we will *experience* as ourselves.

Identity:

1. The collective aspect of the set of characteristics by which a thing is definitively recognizable or known.

2. The set of behavioral or personal characteristics by which an individual is recognizable. . . .

3. The distinct personality of an individual regarded as a persisting entity; individuality.

9:18   What we know of ourselves is what we identify within our field of awareness as ourselves. How is this done? Our eyes can look at a chair, but cannot "be" the chair. Just so, we can look down at our own foot and recognize it as a foot, and more importantly as "our" foot. But the recognition itself is not what we behold — we behold the object "foot" — the recognition is a concept generated by the beholder. The one doing the recognizing is what we consider to be ourselves. So how do we identify this beholder?

9:19   When you think of yourself, what is there? Certainly a general sense of your body, and an awareness of the body's perceptions. Yet much of what is identified as your self, as a unique conscious entity, is not found there. Most of your sense of self is found in self-images, self-concepts, a self-awareness, and the specific and general sense you have of your self. Take a look. How do you recognize your self? What do you perceive that you call self? Since there may be a difference between what you call yourself and what you experience as yourself, what do you "live" as yourself even when you don't think about it?

9:20   It is generally accepted in our culture that there exists a "person" within the body, an awareness that "is" one's self. The sense of self that is manifested as this "person" is constructed from the perception of various notions, images, associations, activities, memories, and such. From these perceived aspects, we identify the person that we are. We've seen that collectively, all that is perceived and identified as oneself appears to refer to a source from which these attributes come — existing within or behind our awareness — that we infer is the true entity that we are.

9:21   I know this may sound a bit like Philosophy 101, and for those of us not interested in abstract philosophical pursuits, this line of questioning may seem irrelevant and headache-producing. But it is important to grasp the foundations upon which we stand as a self and as a culture. The explanation is more difficult than the matter itself. The matter is quite simple, yet we tend to overlook it or just believe what someone else has said. We need to look into it for ourselves and discern what's what. There is a reason for reading all this, so bear with me.

9:22   When we look out of our eyes, they see what is in front of us. We may see a chair, or Bob, or a glass of water. We know these things because we can perceive and identify them. This power is provided through the organ of the eye. If, however, the eye tries to look at itself, it cannot do so directly. The best it can come up with is a reflection. So it is with our selves. When we look out, it is the self's awareness that is looking out. When we consider ourselves, we experience strong feelings, beliefs, notions, history, and other familiar perceptions. Do we perceive the self, or do we perceive what the self perceives? As a matter of cognitive mechanics, it's possible that we do not perceive ourselves, but only what comes into our field of perception. Just as the eye doesn't see itself, we may not be perceiving ourselves. Then what is this stuff that we "know" as our self? Good question.

There ain't no way to find out why a snorer can't hear himself snore.
—Mark Twain

9:23   We've seen that in recognizing something—identifying it—the first order of business is that we must perceive it. If we do not in fact "perceive" ourselves directly, then we can't be expected to identify the true being that we are. In this way it remains an unacknowledged unknown. No matter how many notions we have about ourselves or how many attributes and characteristics we can "perceive" about ourselves, we are still not directly perceiving the one that is doing all of this thinking and perceiving. We simply imagine or take on faith that these two are the same—that the stuff we think about ourselves and the stuff that we perceive and attribute to ourselves is the same as ourselves. This may not be true. Interesting thought, isn't it? Whatever the case may be, there is one fact that should not be denied. All of these "perceptions" of ourselves are dependent on concept.

Our Conceptual Self Experience

9:24   The assertion that our self experience is really just conceptual doesn't sit well, does it? This is why we must address this phenomenon repeatedly. It may not be hard to hear, but it is actually quite difficult to "experience" and even harder to "live." Remember, what's most important to know about concept in this case is that a concept of something is not the thing itself. I cannot sit on the thought of a chair. I won't get to the store very fast driving my memory of a car. I needn't wear a spacesuit while imagining I'm on the moon. These are all concepts, and although useful, we must distinguish them from the real objects or activities they are conceiving.

9:25   A concept is a representation, an "abstraction." Concepts, being the content of what we call the "mind," do not exist as physical objects but as mental formations. They are not considered "real" in the physical or objective sense. The conceptualizing itself — or whatever activity produces concepts — may be objectively occurring, but that activity isn't what's perceived as the concept in question. Considerations like this can quickly become overwhelmingly circular, but again, all we need to get a handle on here is that a concept of ourselves is not the same thing *as* ourselves.

9:26   Did you follow that? When we consider ourselves — and even when we don't, since this self-concept remains constantly in the background — what comes to the forefront are the currently perceived concepts of our self-identity. For example, the sense of being a good-but-vulnerable person might arise in one particular moment of relating with an intimate partner. Perhaps the thought of being inferior to others, combined with a feeling of doubt about one's ability to communicate clearly, might come to the forefront at another time or circumstance. Even reflecting on the sentiment that this is "my life," or dwelling on the sense that I am "over here," are concepts contextualizing a self. Any number of thoughts, feelings, and images can emerge. But no matter how strong, familiar, or important they are, they exist solely within the conceptual domain.

9:27   Within our experience, and helping comprise our experience of ourselves, reside many taken-for-granted notions of self-concept, self-image, and self-identity. Take a moment and reflect on what some of these are for you personally:

When you put your attention on your self, what comes to mind? You may conjure up thoughts you have about yourself, such as "I am a smart person," or "I'm someone to be reckoned with," or you may recognize an infusion of family history and values that have molded you into a unique collection of beliefs and reactions. Everything that comes to mind when you consider yourself or think about yourself will reflect your self-concept. Altogether, every concept, idea, notion, belief, assumption, suspicion, or judgment you have of yourself makes up your self-concept. So consider: what's there for you?

Intertwined with these conclusions about yourself is how you "view" yourself. What do you view as yourself? As with any image, a great deal of data and detail can be conveyed within one picture — and I'm sure you have more than one picture of yourself. When you call to mind your self-image(s), what is included in the image? For example, if someone saw themselves as a beautiful and noble woman, disdainful of the common folk, we can imagine many behavior patterns, attitudes, preferences, values, and a philosophy that would be consistent with such an image. What is piled into your self-image?

Tackling all that comprises your identity can get very involved. One's identity includes such assessments as character traits and personality, values and beliefs, habits of behavior, frequented emotions, overall disposition, recurring attitudes, worldviews, opinions, and so on. What is your character? What do you repeat as behavior patterns, or emotional reactions? What values, opinions, and attitudes do you have? How do you view yourself and the world?

You might recoil at the thought of having to list in detail every aspect of your self-identity, yet with some serious and honest contemplation, you may be able to discern its scope and content.

9:28   Beyond any specific self-assessment that we might entertain at any given time, what dominates our experience overall is the concept we have of ourselves as a whole. Remember, concept mimics reality. A well-done full-fledged multidimensional conceptual composition regarding ourselves will look, feel, and seem for all the world very, very real—*as if objectively occurring.* Take a look. Right now, pause and get a sense of yourself. Now imagine that the sense and perception you are having of yourself in this moment is largely, possibly even completely, conceptual. It seems very real and solid, doesn't it? If it's a concept, then who is having this concept? How can you experience the one who is conceptualizing whatever you are perceiving as yourself?

9:29   Just as it seems obvious that we exist, and our proof is the experience we are having in this very moment, it is also undeniable that there is something quite unknown about our own existence—also in this very moment. This latter sense may show up in various ways—such as self-doubt, inauthenticity, confusion, a nagging sense that something is wrong or missing within—but in the end what is actually true is that we simply don't know. Like I've said several times (and will say again several more), we don't directly experience the nature of existence, and so we do not directly experience the nature of our own existence. We don't know, and that's a fact—but not a disease.

9:30   When we identify something as ourselves within the field of our awareness, we assume it must be what we are. Yet we fail to notice that what we recognize in this way is a conceptually constructed identity, and that this is separate from who we really are. When we ask what something is, we are asking, what is it "being?" or, what does it exist "as"? In the case of ourselves, we would say: what is being is "me," or "I." So if we consider "what am I being?" or "where am I being?" we naturally assume this is the same thing as what is identified as ourselves. Yet in so doing we fail to acknowledge the difference between the thought of something and the thing it is as itself. We don't make a distinction between the process of identifying something, and the experience of the thing itself independent of our notions or viewpoint. In setting out to experience real being we need to make that distinction.

9:31   In this very moment our experience of not knowing what we are is overwhelmed by what is perceived and "identified" as ourselves. If indeed we are not what we perceive, what is all this stuff that we know and love and call ourselves? It seems two questions need to be answered. One: what are we really? And two: if we aren't what we think we are, what is it that we have been living and "being" as far back as we can remember? Working this out will take lots of back and forth. We'll need to work to make a distinction between what is perceived and identified as oneself and the actual experience of "being" oneself. If we can get a clear view of the one then perhaps we will be better equipped to approach the other.

CHAPTER TEN
Self and Being

*What is troubling us is the tendency to believe
that the mind is like a little man within.*
—Ludwig Wittgenstein

10:1   That we experience ourselves is not in question—it is obvious. In every moment we experience the perception called "me." It is not hard to find. What is a bit more difficult to discern, however, is the actual nature of this perception. You may anticipate that I'm about to say this very experience and perception are largely conceptual—and, of course, you are right. But why do I harp on this fact? The thing is, we can hear it but still not experience it. One of the hardest things to get is that I am referring to the very experience of self that you are having right now.

10:2   Whenever we speak of concept, we tend to immediately associate this notion with an image of dry intellect or abstract thought. But our experience of ourselves is not dry or abstract. It has sensation, feeling, emotion, a sense of presence, and is clearly familiar and intimate. So what's all this nonsense about concept? What is important to grasp, and rarely understood, is that even this very intimate feeling-experience is conceptual by nature. How this comes to pass is complex, but in our time and culture it is inevitable.

173

To get a handle on this we must repeatedly step into the experience of what we live and breathe as ourselves. What we don't notice is how much of our very "sense" and perception of ourselves is a product of mind, even though it appears to be an observation or direct experience of what's there. To more fully set the stage for our continued work on the conceptual nature of our self "experience," we need to make a clearer distinction between the nature of self and the nature of being. If we could clarify and put into a big pile all that is our self-concept, self-image, and self-identity, what would be left over? We certainly insist that we are more than these concepts, and I'm not challenging that assumption. But can you clearly distinguish what is your self, independent of any of these conceptual components? Try. It's an ability that most people of our culture don't possess.

What Is a Self?

10:4 Self is a concept. This doesn't seem like a new assertion. I've been saying our experience is conceptually dominated throughout the book, so what's new? Here I'm asserting not that our "experience" of self is conceptual, but that "self" itself is a concept. For most of us this is rather hard to grasp, and even harder to accept. After all, we appear as a body full of movement and animation, and a body obviously isn't a concept. Yet a body is not a self; it's a body.

10:5 We don't call the chair a self. It is simply an object that we identify as a chair. The body isn't a self until it is identified as oneself. Without such recognition within your perception it would not be yourself, it would simply be an object among objects. We may identify one body as "me" or "mine," and others as "not-me" or "not-mine," but what we're identifying here is simply self being attributed to an object. Just as a "tree" only exists as an interpretation applied to an object, we perceive bodies as having "selves" or being "selves."

10:6 Yet our idea of the self that a body "is" or "has" is not a perception of something that exists on its own; it is an interpretation that we apply to a perception of what's there. Without the concept of self, we would not recognize a self. We refer to a dead person in the past tense—"he *was* a good guy"—and so it's clear that in this case we hold the self as elsewhere. The body may be present, but we place the self in "heaven," or nowhere, or at least not in the body. This certainly indicates that we believe a self to be other than an object, and perhaps even an independent entity. Although we might think that, recognized or not, the self would still exist without our interpretation or perception, we have to admit that without such faculties, we would have no self-consciousness, and so no self-image, no self-esteem, no self-importance, etc. Is this in any way like our current experience of self? Not at all.

10:7 We say self is composed of a mind and a personality, that we have an "ego," and even an unconscious. We are full of emotions and almost always behave in ways typical of ourselves. One might be honorable or a liar, brave or cowardly, friendly and kind, or cold and cruel. We say these are "attributes" of a person, and hold that the person is the self to which the traits are attributed. When someone behaves otherwise, we say the person is not "being himself." Remember, we are speaking of a cultural viewpoint from which we generally experience ourselves. At this point in our investigations, the truth is unknown.

10:8 We hold ourselves to be at least more than a body, and perhaps not even a body. In fact, we are apt to refer to our bodies as "my body" rather than "me," and this suggests ownership, which certainly separates the body from the "me" who's doing the owning. In general, we hold "self" to be some indistinct and yet specific "me-ness" that somehow includes every trait that we identify with. We may consider these aspects to be our selves, or at least be attributable to whatever is really ourselves, yet actually "self" is a concept that we *apply* to what we perceive.

This "being" of mine, whatever it really is, consists of a little flesh, a little breath, and the part which governs.
—Marcus Aurelius

10:9 A "self" is perceived through differentiating an individual entity from any other thing or entity. In our culture, each self is held as unique. This unique self is considered to be "me," and can be located through a set of specific characteristics. But this still doesn't tell us what a self is. So what is a self? Let's start sorting this out by looking at a few definitions of self.

Definition of *self* from the *Oxford Universal Dictionary:*

1. That which in a person is really and intrinsically he — in contradistinction to what is of the nature of an addition from without; ego — often identified with soul or mind as opposed to body; a permanent subject of successive and varying states of consciousness.

2a. What one is at a particular time or in a particular aspect or relation; one's nature, character, or appearance, considered as different at different times.

2b. An assemblage of characteristics and dispositions which may be conceived as constituting one of various conflicting personalities within a human being.

Definition of *self* from the *American Heritage Dictionary:*

1. The total, essential, or particular being of a person; the individual.

2. The essential qualities distinguishing one person from another; individuality.

3. One's consciousness of one's own being or identity; the ego.

For our purposes we might boil down these definitions of self into the following:

An assemblage of characteristics, dispositions, and qualities distinguishing one person from another; individuality. One's consciousness of one's own identity.

10:10   We imagine that self, as we know it, has always been an aspect of human existence. This may not be true. The thought that somehow a "self" did not exist for humans or within the human experience in our distant prehistory is rather unthinkable. It is difficult to imagine because self is such a strongly rooted assumption within our culture. As a matter of fact, in our culture, most people project the notion of self onto all creatures. We imagine that every entity has a self—and that their actions and awareness are sourced by this self. Actually we imagine that each entity "is" a self. This is so taken-for-granted that trying to picture the existence of an entity that does not have a "self," or is not being a self, is very difficult for us to do. Self, however, may have only been born within humanity as an offshoot of the development of abstract thought. Since we have confused this notion of self with the perception of existence or "being," we think of them as one and the same. In order to recognize self as distinct from being we need to separate the two.

10:11 We say that a chair exists, that it is "being" there. Yet most of us don't say the chair has a self, or "is" a self. Something "being," such as an object existing, doesn't mean a self must also exist. Understanding this starts us down the road to making a distinction between "being" and "self." Yet it can be difficult to discern what simply "is" or is "being there" from the added aspect we call self. Even when the chair has the added quality of being "mine," it has something it doesn't have when it is just a chair. Whether something perceived is possessed by a self or possesses a self, the concept of self is always added to what's there.

10:12 For instance, when it comes to projecting the idea of a self-notion onto all creatures, some people imagine that trees have a self. If we sit contemplating a tree, the character of a tree-self can be hard to imagine. Trees seem so patient, quiet, and "selfless." We could imagine an unseen activity taking place within the tree that is somehow equivalent to our mental processes, yet, since this is not expressed or demonstrated to us by the tree, we must confess it seems more a function of our imagination than of observation. If we don't project onto the tree the attributes of a human mind, the "tree-self" appears vastly different from our own. Since trees don't harm us, and give themselves without a whimper to our needs, the common consensus is that they are benign. So we might imagine a rather benevolent selfless creature, infinitely patient and merely growing to fulfill its destiny of life. We could also consider that the tree is very directly filling life functions without the existence of a self acting as intermediary. But life without self is not a popular notion within our culture.

10:13   It seems that we are aware of ourselves, but more accurately we could say we identify our "selves" within our awareness. This identifying process is a result of accumulated convictions that form the parameters that define our selves. This formation provides that "sense" of self that we call "me" or "I." The specifics of these parameters allow us to create the measuring stick we use to determine whether we will accept or reject whatever we encounter. Because both accumulation and formulation are so ingrained and centered within our perceptive faculties, the resultant experience appears as an objective reality. But it is not.

10:14   I know what I just said may take a few readings to grasp, but the short version is: "you," as you know your self, are a concept. And as we've seen, the possibilities and consequences of this fact are different from the possibilities and consequences of something that exists objectively. The distinction of self is made within what is perceived to be. In this way, self is created, and yet perceived as if it exists on its own. Without the "creation" of self, there is no self to be perceived. Once self is created and identified, however, it becomes the central aspect of our awareness, and we fail to notice that it is in fact not an experience of being.

The true value of a human being can be found in the degree to which he has attained liberation from the self.
—Albert Einstein

What Is Being?

10:15 Being is what we really are. It's what is simply so, what is most true. Being is what "is" as itself. Yet, how could anything be other than itself? It can't, except in our mind or perceptions. It is our experience of things, our perception of things, that determines what anything is for us and so how we will relate to it. It is here that the thing exists *for us,* not *for itself.* If it is perceived as anything other than the thing it is as itself, we're not actually experiencing what is "being" there. This means that in taking the first step toward perceiving "being," our awareness of something cannot be influenced by personal bias, beliefs, opinions, judgments, assumptions, reactions, or any other activity that alters an accurate perception of what is simply true.

10:16 For example, we know a rock to be a rock, but we don't actually perceive the rock itself; we perceive the external qualities — hard, gray, jagged, four ounces. When it comes to rocks, that's enough for us, since all we need to know are its qualities so we can determine what value it has for us — I could throw it, I could ignore it, I could use it as a paperweight. When it comes to our selves, knowing what use or value we have for ourselves is not enough — nor really relevant. As we've seen, we don't actually know what we are, and so don't perceive what our own being is "as itself." The impact of not experiencing or perceiving who we really are is felt in many ways and is the source of many inner and outer problems, and yet this isn't understood or acknowledged in our culture.

10:17 In addition to not perceiving the rock *as* itself, we may not even recognize the rock *is* itself. How can we do this? Easily. If we are angry at the rock one day and see it as ugly and evil, and then love it the next and see it as beautiful and magnificent, we might ask: has the rock changed? We don't think so. Its nature is the same. Yet the rock-as-itself is a different experience than is the rock-for-us. When we fail to recognize this in our dealings with things, we are not actually relating to what is there, but to our own concepts about and reactions to what is there. In this way we really don't perceive the thing, and we don't acknowledge that something is not perceived. If pressed, we might intellectually say we understand the difference between what we perceive and what is there, but this doesn't show up in our daily experience. This can be far more subtle than we normally think, and more important than we give credit. It doesn't seem to matter, but it does.

10:18 In our case, when we speak of being, it is who we really are. If we want to experience who we really are, we need to make a distinction between self-as-we-know-it and being. Making a distinction means learning to recognize two clearly different things within one habitually muddy experience. Here, we are trying to differentiate our "real-self" (being) from our conceptual-self (the identity and image we have come to think of as a self). Since we've looked at definitions of "self," let's now look at some definitions of "being."

Being (from the *American Heritage Dictionary*):

1. The state or quality of having existence.

2a. A person.

2b. All the qualities constituting one that exists; the essence.

2c. One's basic or essential nature; personality.

3. To exist in actuality; have life or reality.

Being (from the *Oxford Universal Dictionary*):

1. Existing, present.

4. That which exists or is conceived of as existing.

10:19 What within ourselves is "being" and what is "self?" We see similarities in the definitions of *self* and *being* because normally we make no distinction between the two. This means we experience them as the same thing—our self is our being and vice versa. This is a mistake. To understand the nature of this mistake, we must be able to perceive these two as distinct from each other. If we were to use the given definitions of self and being to sort this out, we might come up with the following:

Within the distinction of *self* we would place:
(From the definitions of *self—Oxford Universal Dictionary*):

1. Ego—often identified with mind as opposed to body.

2a. What one is at a particular time or in a particular aspect or relation; one's character, or appearance, considered as different at different times.

2b. An assemblage of characteristics and dispositions which may be conceived as constituting one of various conflicting personalities within a human being.

(From the definition of *self—American Heritage Dictionary*):

1. The individual.

2. The essential qualities distinguishing one person from another; individuality.

3. One's consciousness of one's own identity; the ego.

(From the definitions of *being—American Heritage Dictionary*):

2b. All the qualities constituting one that exists;

2c. Personality.

(From the definitions of *being—Oxford Universal Dictionary*):

4. That which ... is conceived of as existing.

Within the distinction of *being* we would place:
(From the definitions of *self—Oxford Universal Dictionary*):

1. That which in a person is really and intrinsically he (in contradistinction to what is of the nature of an addition from without); a permanent subject of successive and varying states of consciousness.

(From the definition of *self—American Heritage Dictionary*):

1. The total, essential being of a person.

(From the definitions of *being—American Heritage Dictionary*):

1. The state or quality of having existence.

2b. The essence.

2c. One's basic or essential nature.

3. To exist in actuality.

(From the definitions of *being—Oxford Universal Dictionary*):

1. Existing, present.

4. That which exists.

10:20 Noting the placements above, we may begin to sense this distinction. In our culture much confusion results from an overlap of these distinctions, but perhaps the key is found in our failure to draw a line between what is actually so and what is only conceived to be true. Notice how Oxford's definition of being includes "That which exists or is conceived of as existing." Being is given as an either/or possibility! It can actually exist, or it can be conceived of as existing. Within this definition both are considered "being." But there is a great difference between what is actually present and what is only a concept. In one sense we can say both "exist," yet we cannot say that they share the same nature.

10:21   In this distinction we can see the obvious difference between what exists as a tangible object and what exists only as a thought, but we should not fall into the trap of assuming that "objectively so" or "present and real" refer only to objects or things. What we are considering here is what "you" really are, which may or may not be an object. We want to uncover what is real versus what is merely imagined or believed—in other words, conceptual—but this does not mean that only objects are objective. For example, we do not perceive awareness as an object. It can't be found anywhere having mass, weight, location, shape, etc., and yet we can experience awareness as objectively so. In other words, awareness itself is not a concept. It is something real and present rather than something thought or imagined. Certainly we can confuse many thoughts and beliefs with awareness, or confuse awareness with what we are aware *of,* and perhaps fail to make the distinction in our field of perception between actual awareness and what we've added to it. Yet by making this distinction, we can contemplate what awareness is as itself, and begin to sort out what is real and what is not.

10:22   When we make a distinction between "what *is* as itself," and what is only conceived, we see that every quality, characteristic, assessment, judgment, and identification is a concept. "Being," on the other hand, must be what is actually there, prior to concept or opinion. With regard to a human being, it is what the being "is" as distinct from what is thought about him, said about him, judged, or identified as him — even by himself. After all, something *does* exist. Making the distinction between being and self demands that we perceive the difference between what is actually present and what is only thought or imagined.

What Is Your Self and What Is Being?

10:23   Remember the assertion of Chapter Six, that our experience and perceptions are conceptually dominated? Given that this is so, it's only natural that our experience of ourselves is also conceptually dominated. What we experience as ourselves is primarily concept. Yet a concept of ourselves is not the real deal. If I believe I'm stupid, or even simply that I'm an entity behind my eyes, these notions will dominate my reality and determine my experience of myself, but neither may actually be true. It is essential that we learn to tell the difference between what is real and what is not. Recalling the definition of *concept* from Chapter Six and revisiting our definitions of *being* and *self* above, let's reconsider these by boiling them down further.

Definition of *being:*

That which in a person is really and intrinsically he — in contradistinction to what is of the nature of an addition from without. The essential being of a person. One's true nature.

Definition of *self:*

An assemblage of characteristics and dispositions. Ego (identified as mind [by mind]). What one is at a particular time or in a particular aspect or relation. Character or appearance. The essential qualities distinguishing one person from another; individuality; identity.

10:24 Both of these descriptions seem applicable to ourselves, don't they? Why would one be real and the other not? In simple terms: one is actually oneself; the other is a complex of ideas called oneself. Still this may not seem enough to sway us in any way to experience as "unreal" that which our character and identity represent and provide, since we are very attached to these notions and attributes. The fact that they are conceptual may not be enough to warrant our challenging their realness, but three more observations are.

10:25 One: these concepts of ourselves are not known and perceived as concepts. This places them in a domain where they do not belong, and from which much mischief arises. Our way of holding them is very similar to presuming that a belief is the truth. Once the belief is held to be "so" it is no longer simply an idea and obtains a status it does not deserve. Any belief masquerading as the truth will effectively eliminate the possibility of discovering what's really true, since the belief is displacing the truth. If we don't grasp or even suspect that what we perceive as the self is not what we are, we won't set out to experience what's true.

10:26 Two: these self-qualities are, in many cases, misrepresentations. These concepts exist to serve as representations — to represent and express the one we are — and yet because of cultural demands and personal ambition they are very prone to turning into inaccurate representations, or deliberate misrepresentations. In short: we lie about ourselves. In Chapter Seven, we confronted the fact that many of our personal attributes — character traits, behavioral

habits, expressions, moods, and emotional reactions — are misrepresentations. They serve a purpose other than accurately representing the one we experience ourselves to be, even if that self
is only a concept. We misrepresent what we experience as ourselves in order to appear more interesting, escape repercussions,
get what we want, appear as we'd like to be seen, avoid what we
fear, or fulfill any number of agendas and needs, and to promote
what seems like our social or personal effectiveness. Our motives
aside, if we identify with misrepresentations, we can't possibly
grasp what is true.

10:27   And three: the tendency for these concepts to become misrepresentations is not a whimsical possibility; it is built into our culture. Since we are genetically programmed to survive, we are
powerfully motivated to pursue any available means to do that.
Whatever we are conceptually identified with obtains citizenship
within this same motivation and purpose. Therefore, in our culture, misrepresentation becomes a viable avenue to pursue the
survival of our "social" self and self-image. Misrepresentation is
purposefully done — and will continue to be purposefully done
until the elements that comprise this operational dynamic are
clearly exposed and understood. This dynamic will be detailed
and clarified as our consideration unfolds. At this time, however,
our efforts are best directed toward learning to distinguish between
what is real and what only mimics reality.

10:28   These three observations properly understood should raise the
motivation level for challenging our deeply rooted assumptions
about the self. Not only do we confuse ourselves with so many
concepts that we displace any genuine experience of being, but
our tendency to misrepresent ourselves is built in — unless we
somehow derail this dynamic, it will take place. If we cannot detach

ourselves from the world of self-concepts, how can we set out to experience what is real about our own existence? An experience of satisfaction, authenticity, and aliveness depends on being clear about what is real and what is not. Living life as someone who is "real" is the only way to feel authentic. Moving through life unknowingly dragging along and expressing yourself as a conceptual conglomerate can only lead to dissatisfaction. Being ill at ease with one's self and life, feeling like something is missing or not right, or having a sense of being inauthentic in some way, are all directly related to our inability to distinguish between our real beings and our conceptual selves.

10:29   Having made this distinction, you need to turn your attention onto yourself. What are you as a self, and what is an experience of "being?" Your sense of self is rather evident, with a multitude of self-concepts always close at hand, but what is an experience of the being that you are? In other words, without thinking, imagining, identifying, reacting, judging, or any other conceptual activity, who are you for real? This question is asked, in one form or another and with varying degrees of determination, by almost everyone. What arises as an answer may differ, but frequently it is at least secretly confessed that the answer is "I don't know." Still, we are fairly certain that we do exist and are real — that somewhere we are not merely a figment of imagination.

10:30   As hard as it may be, asking this question is more easily done than realizing the answer. Experiencing our own true nature is not something that usually takes place on a whim. Our entire sense of self and life has been (and is) dominated so thoroughly by so many conceptual components — so many assumptions, beliefs, convictions, and identifications — that we find virtually nothing that is not of this domain. And whatever we find that seems most real and present is still subject to suspicion. But don't despair; this is a good state to be in. It is open and not-knowing, and empowers the possibility of an insight breaking through at any moment. As we continue working on this distinction — separating out all that we can experience that is unreal, or at least not "being," and letting it be "not-us"— we start to develop more and more clarity in the matter, and our sense of self begins to change.

The most profound experiences arise from questioning the obvious.

10:31   Using the distinction we are developing here between self and being, we can turn our attention toward our most genuine and real sense of ourselves — who we are as a present, aware entity. As we do, however, we constantly run into what we can now see is a conceptual image of ourselves. One might recognize himself as a gentle person born in Wyoming whose name is Harry and who believes in spirituality. These may be true descriptive statements about himself, but are they who he really is? What was he being before he was named? Who is there that could have been born anywhere, or have different beliefs, or characterize himself with any number of emotional-behavioral qualities? Doesn't he exist when he is angry or aggressive? Would he cease to be if he learned that he was actually born in California and that his name was originally Mike? We can see that the descriptive assessments and labels through which we identify and characterize ourselves are not the same thing as ourselves, and yet such data abounds within our experience, supplanting what is simply there.

10:32   Since we identify so strongly with our "selves," and this identity exists as a collection of concepts, it is natural that we would cling to what are really fabrications as though they're objective truths.

After all, we've got nothing else to represent ourselves with, and self is the most precious commodity to us. It seems to be the only real thing that we have, and we are clear that no matter whatever else is lost, self must persist. Without self we wouldn't exist. But this is another one of those assumptions made within our culture. In fact, it may be the biggest or most influential assumption we make.

10:33 Clearly I've just implied that we can exist without ourselves. It sounds rather stupid, doesn't it? Yet when we make this distinction of self and being, we begin to see that perhaps an experience of our real existence can only occur when we are not caught up in or confused with the mind. Throughout this book, I will continue to demonstrate how this is so, as well as why it is so important. Remember, many of our problems and difficulties, including deeply rooted unwanted feelings, originate from unnecessary cultural assumptions that dictate our sense of self. In order to address this, we must lay an experiential groundwork, something on which to stand that is free of these assumptions.

You are eight years old. It is Sunday evening.
You have been granted an extra hour before bed.
The family is playing Monopoly.
You have been told that you are big enough to join them.
You lose. You are losing continuously. Your stomach cramps with fear.
Nearly all your possessions are gone. The money pile in front of you is almost gone.
Your brothers are snatching all the houses from your streets.
The last street is being sold. You have to give in. You have lost.
And suddenly you know it is only a game.

You jump up with joy and you knock the big lamp over.
It falls on the floor and drags the teapot with it.
The others are angry with you, but you laugh when you go
upstairs.
You know you are nothing and know you have nothing.
And you know that not-to-be and not-to-have give an immeas-
urable freedom.

—Janwillem van de Wetering

10:34   To contradict a lifetime of old assumptions, you must be able to experience deeply new perceptions regarding what's true. From time to time this work may seem to collide with common sense. Hang in there. My intent isn't to present a philosophical argument that is only intellectually convincing. That would leave your more fundamental sense of self out in the cold, or leave you treading the same old circular paths. Instead, I intend to facilitate a very real and bold movement within the very core of your being. This includes a shift that affects every aspect of yourself from emotions, common sense, and intellect to gut feelings and instinct.

10:35   Now that we've started to clarify the domain of "being," and have carved out a space distinguishing being from self, we've established a better footing from which to look more deeply into the self. So far, our best sense of "being" seems to reside within an unknown. We may not be able to put our finger on it, but this open state of not-knowing is sufficient to hold the place of our sense of being. Let that be for now while we turn our attention to systematically uncovering the assumptions and dynamics inherent in our experience of self as we've been living it.

10:36 We need to proceed slowly and in stages, peeling back layer after layer of the individual that we seem to be. This can't be done all at once or be understood fully with one simple explanation. What's important is for you to inspect all that you relate to and identify as your self. Thinking about it once or twice is insufficient for the job. Hearing about it is not enough. Even personally observing the multifaceted conceptual nature of your "self"—which you need to continue to do as we proceed through the book—is only the beginning. In the next few chapters we will examine in more detail the composition of self, the motivations of self, and the founding principle from which self operates and exists.

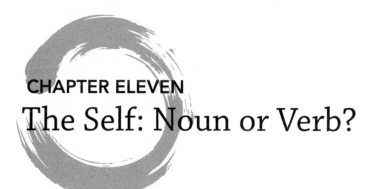

CHAPTER ELEVEN
The Self: Noun or Verb?

How are you?
Perfect, thank you. I'm traveling incognito.
Oh? As what are you disguised?
I am disguised as myself.
Don't be silly. That's no disguise. That's what you are.
On the contrary, it must be a very good disguise,
for I see it has fooled you completely.
—Sufi Mullah Nasrudin

11:1   If we were to open up your skull and look into your brain to search
for the number four, do you think we would find a "4" in there?
No, we would find a lot of tissue and blood. Just so, if we were to
look for your "self," what do you think we would find? We have
difficulty knowing exactly where to look for the self. As we've considered, we can look at the body and claim self is that, but then
what about all that is nonphysical? We can look at concepts and
claim a conceptual composition as ourselves, but then must confess that we are merely a fabrication and representation — simply a complex figment of mind. We can look at awareness and
consider that to be the self, but have difficulty locating the source
and substance of this awareness. Yet, when all is said and done,
isn't our awareness or consciousness what we most relate to as
our selves?

11:2   We consider the self to be the source of our awareness, where awareness originates. It might be true instead that self originates from awareness, rather than the other way around. In either case, the mere act of being aware is as close to an experience of "being" as we seem to get.

11:3   Without trying to determine whether our awareness is a product of mind, body, or something else, we can still assert that we sense the presence of this awareness. Since awareness, or "consciousness," is not conceptual, it is not a representation but the very "thing itself." Don't confuse awareness with "mind," or with mental activities taking place, because these are also activities of which we are aware. All of our thoughts and conjectures about awareness are no more "it" than a thought about an apple is the apple. Awareness may or may not be physically produced, but we don't need to know that. The true nature of awareness can remain unknown while we proceed on our mission to recognize the difference between real self-awareness and mere self-concept.

11:4   We might begin with the recognition that *what* we are aware "of" is not the same as the awareness itself. Consider the way an eye is unable to see itself. No matter what is seen, it will never be the eye. If the eye in this example is analogous to awareness, this suggests that whatever we are aware of cannot be the awareness itself. Unlike the eye, however, which can see itself as a reflection, we can find no such reflection for awareness. This indicates that everything, every single thing that we are aware of—every thought, sight, sound, sense, etc.—is not an awareness of our awareness. It is only an awareness of something other than the "awareness that is *being* aware." If we consider that our awareness itself is as close to an experience of "being" as we can come to at this point, this implies that everything we are aware of is not our real being.

11:5   This immediately creates a new domain of possibilities in considering our own nature, since awareness is rather open-ended and not restricted to whatever notion, feeling, or perception enters our field of cognition. We find that we cannot discover any certain location, although we assume this location to be some organ of perception by which we are able to be aware. Since we can't perceive awareness-itself, it is difficult to assign it any specific characteristics or identifying markers. Yet we seem to be able to notice the *act* of awareness and so sense the presence of awareness-itself without knowing what it is. We can put our attention on the act of being aware, and separate that sense from the conceptual amalgam that has built itself up as the self, and perhaps bring us closer to a genuine sense of "being." Take a moment to experience the presence of your own awareness. Notice how it is always and only occurring in the present moment. But don't confuse this sense of awareness with anything you are aware of, even though this awareness-sense occurs only through the activity of being aware. This may further help clarify what the conceptual-self is and isn't.

11:6   Let's postulate that awareness arises directly from one's being, as a natural expression of being alive. The conceptual-self, on the other hand, arises from the conceptual identity, and so is a function of representation and misrepresentation. It is a conceptual fabrication that has been confused with one's being. The nature of one's real-self is different from the nature of one's conceptual-self, just as an object is different in nature from a thought. But this conceptual-self does not only include concepts. If everything that is perceived is *not* the perceiver, then even such objective perceptions as the body, sensations, and physiological activities are also not the perceiver. These "objective perceptions" are part of the conceptual-self in that they are claimed to be oneself. This claim is a conceptual assertion.

11:7 When we allow that awareness is necessarily different from what we are aware of, this shifts our attention away from all that is commonly recognized as the self. Shifting away from an attachment to what is conceptual and toward what is simply present but unknown creates a completely new set of possibilities for us. Leaving these possibilities open-ended, we can use the space it provides to continue to sort out the muddle that constitutes our experience of being.

Am I a Noun or a Verb?

11:8 As humankind developed the ability to conceptualize — to fabricate or represent things that aren't actually present — we started down a path that is both powerful and slippery. Once a concept can be created to represent something real, it can be used to replace what is real. For example, we are able to think of our house when we're not at home. This means we can imagine what color might look good on the house while we are at the paint store, saving us a great deal of time and effort running back and forth. Yet when we bring the paint home, we might find that the house of our imagination doesn't exactly match the house in which we live, and so neither does the color. When it comes to painting houses, this is just an accepted flaw. If we can't personally manage this conceptual discipline, we can hire a decorator to manage it for us. The mistake of confusing an image with the real thing becomes much more dangerous, however, when it comes to immaterial phenomena, such as our self-awareness. This confusion creeps into the root of the self-identity and provides the opening that allows for a "false" self to eclipse our sense of real being.

The Dancing Rock

11:9   The door being opened for concept to be confused with ourselves unfolds in more than one way. As we consider what we are "being" we run into an overlooked entanglement. When we speak of "being" we could be referring to either a noun or a verb. In other words, we could be saying: "a being"—as in an entity—or we could be saying: "being performed"—as in an activity that is taking place. For example, a rock might "be"; it exists, and it exists as a rock. It "be"s a rock. So we say it "is" a rock. Yet the rock might also dance, and then we say it "is" dancing, and so the rock "is" a dancer. In this way we could say the rock is "being" a dancer. Because there is an activity taking place, we say that the activity "exists" or is happening, and we refer to this occurrence as "being" a dancer.

11:10   In the case of "being a dancer," however, the activity isn't the act of dancing; it is the act of *identifying* a primary characteristic of the behavior of the rock, which happens to be dancing. We see that dancing doesn't always occur—sometimes the rock just sits there. But what is occurring is that the rock "thinks" it is a dancer. When asked, it might say "I *am* a dancer." Yet we can see that this mental verb is different from the actual noun. The rock "is" a rock. This is what the rock is being—like a noun. The rock may identify with all sorts of things, and so say it is "being" a dancer, a bad stone, a fireman, a king, a bum, a mind, or body, but none of these things are what it is as a noun. Since we don't identify much with rocks, we can more easily recognize that a rock isn't really a dancer or anything else mentioned above. The point is, neither are we. We might pause at the reference to being a body or mind, saying,

"But that 'is' what we are—a mind and/or body—just like the rock is a rock." But is it really?

11:11 Isn't what's actually going on an activity in which we are conceptually claiming to be the mind or body or both? Just as the rock claims to be a dancer, we assert that self is one thing or another. Remember, the activity taking place that makes the rock a dancer isn't the fact that it dances; it is the act of identifying a characteristic or repeated activity, and claiming that to be what the rock *is*. Mind and body are also what's perceived and claimed as oneself, and it is this activity—this claim—that makes it us, not the mere observation that a mind or body exist.

11:12 In the case of the rock it seems pretty clear that it is just that, a rock, an object. It doesn't think, it is not self-aware, and it doesn't dance. As far as we can tell, the only thing the rock is is a rock. But this is not so of ourselves. We appear multifaceted, full of complex characteristics and qualities, activities, and aspects. We assume that these are us, or at least aspects of ourselves. We also assert that we are the one who's doing the perceiving of all these qualities. Although this claim assumes we are referring to ourselves as a noun, our assertion gets its authority from the observation that we are *being* aware, and once again this—observation and activity—is a verb. So we can't ultimately say whether what we observe, or are aware "of," is us or not. We identify with processes and activities and so can say that we are "being that way." But it gets tricky to sort out what we are being like a rock and what we are being like a dancer.

11:13 The rock can dance its heart out and claim to "be" a dancer, but it must know it is a rock "being" a dancer. It doesn't exist "as" a dancer; it exists as a rock—and it happens to dance. This is a slippery distinction that we lose all too easily. In the analogy of a dancing rock it is easier to see, but within the complications and buried assumptions that root us in a conceptual-self, it can be quite a bit more difficult.

To Noun or to Verb?

11:14　All our beliefs and assumptions relate to the self. The conceptual nature of beliefs and assumptions places them in a category of conjecture and representation. No matter how significant they are, they are not ourselves, but are instead "comments" on ourselves. The comment may or may not be accurate, but regardless of accuracy it is still not ourselves. If I say I am a dancer, I've made an assertion about a commitment of much of my life's activity, yet if I never dance, am I a dancer? Only in my mind. This is also true of being a dancer if I dance all the time. Coexisting with my self-existence, there may or may not be an activity called dancing.

11:15　So it is with any activity, assessment, or judgment. Being stupid, being worthless, being a politician, being cute, being frustrated, gentle, or a genius are all assessments of activities that may occur for us, but they are not our selves. They are activities or assessments that we may or may not engage. Remember, since concept is not the same as the thing conceived, no self-concept we have can be our real selves. Spend some time and try to notice how conceptual acts like beliefs, judgments, assumptions, identifications, images, emotions, reactions, memories, values, opinions, assessments, and so on fill in the day for you. These are all aspects of the self. Taking notice of them will begin to illustrate that, while a conceptual self is very intricate and complex, constant and dominant, it is still not real in and of itself.

11:16 Clearly we might think that the above assessments are "true" of us. Being a dancer could be something observed and attributed to someone, but this doesn't make it him. For instance, if a dancer were in a car accident and could no longer dance, would she cease to exist? Of course she would exist, because in fact she is not a dancer, she is a person who dances. She exists independent of dancing. Dancing can come or go, but that doesn't determine whether the person comes or goes. If one thinks he "is" a dancer but can no longer dance, this could well become as if a life-threatening crisis. It might produce much suffering, but it won't make him disappear as a person, only as a dancer.

11:17 If one were to think that she "should be" a dancer even though she doesn't possess the physical talent to accomplish this ideal, a lifetime of suffering is likely to accompany her like a dark cloud trailing all she attempts. If one were to believe that he is the only great dancer to exist, he is likely to suffer an extreme sense of isolation, feelings of being unappreciated or misunderstood, feelings of frustration and irritation regarding others, and many other consequences of this belief. Although we might think all of these various assessments are "true" or valid, none of them are actually the person having them, or to whom they are assigned. Not being able to separate the two always leads to unnecessary suffering.

11:18 If I were to strap a huge rock tightly to your body and force you to live with it, your experience of life would change. Add to that a porcupine, a glass of water, and a number 2 Mongol pencil and your perceptions will change some more. If you identify these things in your perception as your self, then you will assess that you have changed a great deal. Yet the perceiving hasn't changed, just what's perceived. Just so, if you are a dancer who loses her legs, have you changed? What you identify as yourself might undergo a dramatic alteration, but you can see that your self as a being hasn't changed one iota. No matter what is added or subtracted in your experience, it is not who is being aware of these changes. The awareness that perceives these changes is not itself changed by them any more than an eye is altered by what it perceives. But if the eye were to somehow identify the view of the landscape as its "self," imagine the unnecessary suffering that might occur around witnessing, say, a grass fire or strip mining.

11:19   There is no inherent problem in *having* concepts, but we must not trap ourselves into *being* concepts. Since we already confuse ourselves with them, however, much distress seems inherent in simply being human. Such conceptual activities are not likely to fade away simply because we begin to entertain the notion that they are not us. We depend on many of these assessments and reactions daily to cope with a highly social and conceptual world. It is an ability we are not likely to lose and, for most of us, not one we care to lose. The problem is not that they occur, but that we create unnecessary suffering when we perceive them as our "selves." Like the rock, we are free to dance our hearts out, but shouldn't confuse our selves with the dancing. And when we find ourselves trapped in some unwanted mental program or activity, we should be free to drop it. This is unlikely if we think we "are" it.

11:20   We can imagine or believe that we are any number of things, yet once we realize that every one of these things is merely made up, even our most concrete identifications are recognized as unnecessary activities rather than objective realities. I might claim to "be" a hard worker. It may be true that I am one who believes in values consistent with working hard, and this is a reflection of what I am willing to take on. This may seem like it must be a reflection of "me" somehow, and in a social context it absolutely is, but this association rarely stops there. Because of my belief, I'm also likely to think I am a good person, and perhaps identify with values and images that, in our culture, are associated with people who have a strong work ethic. This is likely to influence how I dress, what music I listen to, where I hang out, who I associate with, and many other characteristics I could adopt. I may well begin to resent those who don't work hard, or produce what I consider a worthwhile product. I might also feel burdened by my own self-image in the knowledge that I must keep working hard in order to support my self-view, and resent having to do so.

11:21 We can see that a simple, apparently noble identification and expression of laudable values can turn into an attachment to much more than a simple commitment. It becomes an identification with a particular lifestyle and various forms of self-image, all of which are unnecessary, and can even be a means of suffering, and none of which are actually the person who adopts them. As a matter of fact, most of it has little to do with the simple and original commitment to a value. My real self is my real self, on top of which I may commit to something such as working hard. This, however, doesn't make the activity of working hard the *same* as my self, and it certainly doesn't make all the trappings of such a commitment my self, or even reflective of my self. I can easily adopt all these trappings just to gain approval, or even entirely as a pretense. Either way, none of it is my self.

11:22 If observable characteristics are not my self, then something made up or pretended or believed or assumed is certainly not me either. These fabricated self-assessments are even more apt to be distorted. They're likely to be further from a true representation of my original nature, since they are easily created to be whatever way is desired, having no relation to the truth or to anything observed. Adopted characteristics can be any way I want them to be, but the truth can only be what's true.

11:23   If I represent myself as an honest person and I act, speak, and think accordingly, I could say that honesty is part of my character. Yet this doesn't necessarily make me honest, nor is honesty an experience of my real self, but merely a commitment that I've taken on. On the other hand, I could well *say* that I am an honest person and not be one at all. I could pretend to be honest, but in fact be full of concealed deceit. This would be a misrepresentation — and also a commitment that I've taken on. Just like other such commitments, it will come with many associations and activities I need to uphold in order to maintain the pretense. If I know that I am lying, then I am misrepresenting myself on purpose. But even if such distortion occurs unknown to me, it will still be purposeful nevertheless. We will see how this is so in later chapters. Regardless of our degree of awareness in the matter, if representations are not myself, misrepresentations certainly aren't, and misrepresentations cause an even greater sense of inauthenticity, isolation, and negative consequences.

11:24   Our sense of self is so thoroughly dominated by these activities of mind that they determine our life experiences and personal abilities and inclinations. Getting clear on what these mind-formations are is the first step in beginning to change them. Yet all too often we simply end up exchanging one set of beliefs and concepts for another. If we wish to bring about a significant transformation in our experience, it is imperative that we become able to free ourselves from captivation by any activity of mind. Toward this end, we would do well to discover the underlying assumptions that govern our beliefs and clearly recognize the shared human dynamics that determine our perceptions. A deep sense of fulfillment and genuine freedom can only come from having an experience of being real. Nowhere within our framework of mind is this likely to happen.

"Doing" versus "Being"

11:25 Whatever we "are" exists in the present — it is what we are "being," and that is a *current* condition. This means that what is not presently existing cannot be ourselves. Therefore our memories of the past and our desires and fears for the future are not who we are as a being. Certainly a memory, desire, or fear could be described as existing presently, but the subject of the memory, desire, or fear cannot. These functions are activities that may occur now, but are not directed toward the experience of what exists now, nor are they even about now. We need to be able to make this distinction between what exists, and the activity of imagining what might exist or did exist. We seem to get a bit stuck viewing the what-isn't rather than the what-is. It's sort of like shining a flashlight at night in the forest: we can see the distant trees but can't see the flashlight right here in our hand that illuminates them.

11:26 We have confused self with the complex conceptual activity ("being" like a verb) that we call mind. We must remember that this is an activity of representation and imagination. It is not the source of the activity itself. Whatever produces this activity can more rightly be called Being (like a noun). The activity is what we are "doing"; it's not what we "are."

11:27 Our "doing" is so constant that this activity is easily confused with "being." A great deal of our sense of self has been built up over time. We identify "self-traits" by recognizing repeated patterns of behavior. Through sheer repetition these can take on a very solid and forceful presence, since we have so much historical "evidence" that suggests they reflect inherent aspects of ourselves.

11:28   The truth is, our personal traits are all based on the conceptual activity that we call memory. There are three problems with that. One: This activity is not an experience of our current existence. Two: Our memories are likely to be biased, and to distort even more over time. And three: these character traits are predisposed to relate to some "story" we've made up, or that we have heard repeated time and again by us, family members, or others, and will be consistent in meaning and significance with the kinds of stories told by our culture. Such stories paint a picture of a character (you) interacting with circumstances.

11:29   For example, when you recall your childhood, what comes to mind? You may remember enjoying a vacation up at the lake, or being bitten by the neighbor's nasty little dog. These represent a self interacting with events, and contribute to your "life story." What really impacts your sense of self — far more than isolated memories of events — are the repeated ways you were treated, and your recurring reactions and behavior. Your mother may have habitually slapped your face when she was angry, your father could have repeatedly admonished you for your lack of athletic skill or chided you for your laziness. Perhaps you were expected to achieve great things, become the president or a great artist, or maybe you were ignored and disregarded. All of these factors helped mold your self-image and view of life.

11:30   Of course, in reality, there are far more influences at work, the details of which are too numerous and complex to describe in general terms. It isn't only the dramatic or even the remembered events that are influential. Frequently the subtle and mundane incidents collectively outweigh more obvious events, and can imprint even deeper belief patterns. Each person encounters a particular string of circumstances and environmental factors, and his characteristic methods for interacting with these events are determined by the beliefs he's adopted from family and culture. This represents much of what emerges as a self.

11:31   How you reacted to circumstances throughout your life shaped your personal temperament and helped establish many of your personal characteristics. You may have pouted with regularity, or thrown tantrums when you didn't get your way. Perhaps you sought revenge for ill treatment and plotted ways get back at your antagonists. You could have lovingly cared for your pet ducks, or hid away for many hours reading adventure stories. Whatever it is you experienced and did, and how you viewed what you experienced and did, became known over time as "the way you are." This seems obvious because it represents what you indeed did, and so reveals the "ways" in which you interact with life. But were they actually you?

11:32   By no means does this interplay between circumstance and self end, or even diminish, after childhood. As an impressionable child, newly forming and developing a sense of self, this time of life is important and tends to set the stage for what is to come. As we grow, however, patterns and beliefs only increase. The kinds of interactions we must engage in and the demands made on us become more complex. In order to deal with life as it unfolds, we establish new sets of personal patterns and traits. These eventually tend to overwhelm our childhood traits — which may disappear beneath the surface, but never go away entirely, and usually simply find alternative ways of expressing themselves. As an adult one might still pout, throw tantrums, and seek revenge, but the methods for doing so will have become more sophisticated, and likely more effective. Over a lifetime, so many beliefs and methods are accrued and attended that naturally they come to be seen as indicative of one's self. Yet, if they weren't founded on an experience of real-self to begin with, no amount of repetition or complexity can make them so.

11:33   It is within our behavior and memory that patterns are recognized and traits established. When we study our memory of life, both early and recent, it becomes clear that much of it exists as stories — which are what we say to others and ourselves indicating our view about the way things were and are. These stories serve a purpose, which is to encapsulate, reorganize, and oftentimes alter past events so that these events make sense and are consistent with the beliefs from which they are viewed.

11:34   Patterns emerge in our behavior because our behavior is a reaction to circumstances that we consistently view from a set of personal and cultural assumptions. Given that these assumptions and beliefs are conceptual to begin with, such an interaction with circumstances primarily takes place between a conceptual-self and the perceived circumstances. This creates a nonrandom expectation of personal behavior and so is called a character trait. After awhile, we could say that an individual's personality is reproducing itself by interacting from this set view, and creating more of the same patterns.

11:35   For example, if a central aspect of my self is that I am a stupid person, this "stupid person" will be the one who interacts with circumstances. Since I think I'm stupid, I am likely to view life as difficult and a bit beyond me, while others seem privy to more knowledge and ability than I possess. These two elements, my self-view and my perception of life, will continually interact — a "stupid person" will relate to "difficult circumstances."

11:36 We can see that by feeling disadvantaged in the first place, and lacking confidence, I'm likely to experience failure in dealing with these difficult and confusing events of life. Unless I'm Forrest Gump, the outcome will probably be consistent with the input. Even if it is not, I'm likely to interpret that it is, and view any success as an exception. My self-concepts and life perceptions will be self-fulfilling. This means that over time the patterns that are discerned to be characteristic of my self will be more and more about how these conceptually produced patterns (and their foundation beliefs and assumptions) interact with my perceived environment.

11:37 Do you see the loop here? In simple terms, I'm saying that certain concepts are adopted as oneself, and these concepts determine the behavior that will be taken. As patterns emerge — which is likely, since the same set of assumptions and beliefs will continue to produce the same interpretations, reactions, and outcomes — these are identified as traits. These traits will be thought of as a part of the self and so will also be influential in the next set of encounters. And so on. Our "life history" will show consistency if for no other reason than it is a conceptual-self telling a story largely created by the concepts adopted by this self as it interacted with life.

11:38 I know that is hard to follow, but it is exceptionally easy to do. When we start thinking of ourselves as particular concepts, these concepts dominate our behavior and our perceptions. This means we will produce patterns of behavior and thought, and view these patterns from the same assumptions and beliefs that generated them. As this cycle feeds on itself, it grows so large as to block out the light of our authentic and simple sense of being.

11:39 The point here is that our conventional sense of self is not real, but is confused with a complex activity that resides within the domain of concept and belief. Our "real selves," or the actual beings that we are, are buried beneath this conceptual-self, and so the real-self resides, hidden, as it were, within an unknown aspect of our experience of "being."

11:40 We must continue to layer into these many dynamics. Addressing them is one thing, but our real job is to experience them in place. In other words, we need to pound at this complex of conceptual-identity from many angles and learn to recognize the many subtle traps that have gotten us into and keep us in this condition. This takes time, observation, and contemplation. Our focus throughout this section and the next is on what we live and experience that is not our real being. Remember, if something you read sounds like it's been covered already, intend to experience it at a deeper level and discover something new previously overlooked.

PART IV
Creating Self

CHAPTER TWELVE
Inventing Self and World

12:1 At some point in human development we acquired the ability to do more than see an object. We could "see" something that was not present, like having a mental image of the sky while we were deep inside the cave. This was a leap beyond the power of the creatures around us, and eventually led to our domination of the planet. With this ability, we became far more creative, but as we saw in the last chapter, we also ran the risk of mistaking concepts for reality.

12:2 The first and foremost job of conceptualizing is to represent an experience with a thought. This takes the form of imagining something that isn't present — like remembering what Sally yelled at you as you walked out the door this morning, picturing that new car you want to buy, or longing for the warmth of your fireplace as you jog home through the snow. Since Sally's voice, a new car, and the warm fireplace don't actually exist for you at the time you "perceive" them, they must be concepts.

12:3 Concepts that represent objective reality create a "mock" perception within our field of awareness. Because we cannot personally locate the particular field in which mock-perceptions take place, we just call this field "the mind." Current Western thought concludes that the mind is a function of the human brain. Whether this is true or not makes no difference to our work here since we're dealing with our experience, not theory or hearsay. We don't know where these mock-perceptions take place except to say that they somehow occur for us — that we become conscious of them — and this we call "mind."

12:4 Being able to mentally represent objects that are not currently perceived has certain advantages that we don't often consider. One example is that it allows us to have a constant mental representation of our bodies, which aids us in using them more accurately. For instance, look into it right now and you'll find that you have an "image-sense" of your head even though you can't see it. As you move your head around, or make various facial expressions, you don't just feel the movement, but you also have an idea of what your head movement looks like. Since this representation mimics perception — in other words it seems like you are *seeing* your head in some way and this arises as an "image" — it's easy to forget that it's a representation (a translation of the feeling into a sight) and not an objectively perceived reality. In the same way, we "hear" our internal dialogue though no sound is actually being made or heard.

12:5 When we put attention on our bodies, we find it's not hard to tell the difference between a "perceptual mimic" and an actual sense perception of our physical selves. It's clear that these conceptual representations take place in the mind. But what about the less tangible aspects of self — the nonphysical "self?" How could this self be represented? Before we could conceptually represent a self in our minds, we'd first have to locate something objective or real that is our self. Is this what we do? Or do we begin by creating the self through concept alone, with nothing real or objective found that is then represented? If that's so, then we aren't representing an existing self, we're creating one.

12:6　Whatever is conceptually created in this way can then be "represented" through expression to another by communicating some thought, image, belief, or feeling that we say is an aspect of ourselves. But what exactly is it that's expressed? When we speak of "expression," we're referring to some internal impulse or feeling or thought that we externalize in some objective form as a symbol of this internal activity. We might *speak* about our emotional state, *gesture* with our hands, *write* a letter to a friend, or even *wear* a particular style of clothing. Any physical action that represents some aspect of our internal state is called an "expression." But it isn't actually the self that's being expressed, is it? Since we can find no actual self within our experience, how could we possibly express it? If this is the case, then what are we doing?

12:7　Obviously there is some confusion regarding self: we believe we are indeed expressing our selves, and yet find no real self to express. It seems that what we're really doing is identifying with some specific internal state or personal characteristic. Our identification with this activity of mind and emotion remains private unless we share it with others through some perceptible form, through some expression. Because the experience we're externalizing is ours alone, and refers to a quality we possess, we say we are expressing *ourselves*.

12:8　Since it is highly possible that this self is created in the act of conceptualizing it, then no actual self is being represented or expressed. Our self-experience may inherently be a fabrication rather than something that we *are*. So what we are expressing would not be a representation of ourselves, but an act of reinforcing t has been created and identified with. What we believe to be true of ourselves, then, goes a long way toward becoming the experience we call our selves. How this plays out in our lives can be complex and obscure.

The Self-Identity Reinforces Itself

12:9 It's not hard to see that a negative belief about one's self or life could produce negative experiences, but such beliefs are sometimes hard to locate or confess, and usually very difficult to drop. Once we get past habitually clinging to our negative beliefs, however, we clearly recognize a desire to be free of them. We have no such desire with our many positive beliefs because we assume these produce only positive experiences.

12:10 In an example mentioned previously, it's easy to see that if I believe I'm stupid, then I will probably experience myself as a stupid man dealing with a difficult life. I'll also likely live with a constant sense of shame as I compare myself to others, and feel extremely limited in what I can do, and this will influence what I will even attempt. I may well cut myself off from learning or entertaining new ways of thinking, since I've already accepted that I am incapable. We can imagine the many social and personal consequences that will result from this negative belief, but the same is true with what seem to be positive beliefs.

12:11 I might think I'm smarter than everyone else, or a great person. These seem positive and yet, as with believing I'm stupid, I'm likely to feel isolated and separate from others, misunderstood, and underappreciated. I may well become protective of my "status," which could be the only value I feel I have as a person and the only characteristic through which I can relate to people. I would become less and less willing to look the fool, or risk revealing myself as "normal" or fallible, and so cut myself off from any real and honest interactions or self-expressions. We can see how this will feed upon itself and how the condition could easily become more and more intolerable as it grows.

12:12   Certainly we can also have personal dispositions that lead to positive consequences. Being open-minded, for example, can lead us to look into new ideas and challenge old ones. But we should note the difference between the fact or principle of open-mindedness and the identification of being an open-minded person. These are not the same. Being open-minded is being open-minded, and it can occur for anyone at any time. Someone known as an open-minded person may well be open-minded from time to time. They may also rarely be open-minded, but instead merely think and behave in a way consistent with their image of an open-minded person. If you think about someone living this way, you can see how it is very different from actually being open, and you see that the personal consequences are also very different.

12:13   Positive or negative, the beliefs we identify with will result in any number of effects that will dominate and shape our lives. In order to be free of these effects, we must free ourselves from our identification with such beliefs. Still, you might respond: "But these so-called 'beliefs' are really just assessments, things I've actually witnessed in my self. They're not something I just made up." Which illustrates my point. We continue to think and act within these patterns — further reinforcing the conviction that they are genuine aspects of ourselves — because we believe they *are* us. We see them as natural expressions of the way we are, and will defend our right to act them out. Even if we attempt to get free, we're likely to fall again into being "stupid," or "superior," or what have you, since that is what appears to us as true.

12:14 Once a conceptual identity occupies the place of "self," this is what we think we are "being." Continually thinking of oneself as a bum, a mean old man, a strapping youth, a mothering person, a hot business exec, a cute young thing, a man on the go, a rebel, smarter than most, a refined sort, a dark soul, a victim of circumstance, special and unique, and on and on, will cause us to become very attached to these images and roles. We tend to think they are simply assessments of what is so, but they're not. They are fabrications within one's mind and they exist to serve some end.

12:15 Whatever we experience as ourselves was first conceptually created. Once it is experienced, it is identified as being *of* the self— either representing the self, coming from the self, or as a quality of the self. The thoughts and behavior one identifies with are repeated to create patterns that will appear as character traits. Acting from these beliefs will reinforce their presence and provide the "proof" that they are indeed indicative of oneself. With recurring observation by oneself and others, these traits not only become familiar, they stand as *convictions*, which adds yet another layer of substance to their apparent validity. This dynamic unfolds in various ways, one of the more obvious of which occurs through the stories we tell ourselves.

To set up what you like against what you dislike
—this is the disease of the mind.
—Seng-T'san

The Never-Ending Story of Me

12:16 From moment to moment a drama unfolds within our own minds. We think and feel and tell ourselves stories. We reflect on and react to the world around us and, perhaps more importantly, to the world within us. An inner dialogue runs pretty much unceasingly though our minds. Sometimes we listen; sometimes we barely notice. The commands and assessments of this story line are there all the same, even if the depth of their influence goes unnoticed. But the most dangerous fictions aren't those we recognize as stories. Of more concern to us here are the ones we assume to be real.

12:17 If I were to say that this inner dialogue, as well as your thinking and emotions, are running their course purposefully — that it's no mistake what you think and feel — this might sound plausible. After all, it does seem reasonable that your mental activity should be consistent with your desires and self-interests. If I went on to say that this activity is far more *creative* than is commonly recognized, you might start to wonder what I'm talking about. Normally, when you're aware of your own internal states, such activities as observation, assessment, and reaction don't appear to be creative but simply ongoing responses to what is so. We don't consider that the stories we tell ourselves and the emotions that these evoke create a perception of reality that doesn't exist without this activity. These actions of mind are not merely observing a world; they are also creating a world.

12:18 For example, most of us fail to acknowledge the degree to which we live in fantasies, although with a little honesty and self-inspection they're not so difficult to recognize. Some of these are rather obvious — pretending to be like the hero in a movie just seen, acting the "tough" so as to impress your buddies, nostalgically indulging old self-images that pop up when we hear music from the past, or adopting affectations at a social occasion. Some are harder to discern — the collective fantasy shared inside the opera house or a baseball game, the notions one has about his country, every religious or spiritual pursuit, images of the future, views of the cosmos or what life is all about and one's place within it. Regardless of the specifics, these fantasies thrive within the many stories we tell ourselves — in which the central character is usually oneself.

12:19   Personal fantasies abound within the mind of every individual, but unless we're willing to recognize them as such, they'll merely seem like observations and ideas about reality. These stories or fantasies portray some aspect of what is thought to be true, as well as what is wished or feared to be true, about oneself, others, and life. They are consistent with our beliefs and revealing of our desires and fears. We rely on our stories to position us in relation to every person, idea, and thing that we encounter.

12:20   Probably we've all had some experience where we caught ourselves "playing the victim," or generating an internal scenario in which we were the hero, or the martyr, or some such. Our stories help shape our self-image even when we're aware that it's often just an indulgence on our part. If we pay attention to our inner dialogue, we can begin to recognize just how many stories roll through our minds — from tiny story fragments to full-blown scenarios that we play out in our internal dialogue and imagination. Once again, the existence of the stories isn't so much a problem as our inability to recognize them as fabrications.

12:21 Clearly we make up and tell an endless stream of stories, and we use them to motivate ourselves and help make sense of our place in the world. In some ways, our stories and beliefs are like wrapping bandages around an invisible "self" so as to make it visible, give it shape, and provide us something solid to relate to. But we should remember, the idea that there is a self being clothed is also something we've invented. Our life of mental fabrication isn't limited to our surface chatter and the complex imaginings that we use to establish our sense of self. We live *in* and *as* a complex web of invented worlds that adds to—and in many ways "creates"—our whole sense of self and reality.

It's like trying to unravel a sweater that
someone keeps knitting and knitting and knitting. . . .
—Peewee Herman

Inventions

12:22 In Chapter Three we addressed the idea that humans invent conceptual worlds in which to live. These conceptual worlds exist in the form of belief systems, values, religions, cosmologies, self-images, fantasies, moralities, and many others. Why is it important to know this? Because we're after a conscious experience of the way we make up the reality in which we live every day. Unless we grasp that our "observations" are actually something made up, we will have a wrong relationship to what we perceive, and no possibility of freedom from this whole affair. Freedom from these dominating conceptual activities begins by going beyond merely hearing that they are inventions to actually experiencing them *as* inventions. To help us gain a foothold in this overlooked and elusive domain, let's take a look into the nature of invention.

12:23   An invention is a tool, a formula, a mechanism, an idea, or way of thinking that is made up by humans. The principles of inventions are basically the same no matter what kind of invention we look at. Inventions begin in the mind. By its very nature, an invention serves a particular purpose. Although this purpose might be accomplished in many different ways, an invention has to be *some* way. At some point we must put our foot down and choose a design that will get the job done. Once this choice is made, however, we are restricted to the strengths and weaknesses of our design. For example, inventing a means of travel faster than walking, we might design a car with wheels to travel from place to place. Now we can move more quickly, but we are confined to roads. What's also true is that any invention could have a completely different design as long as it served the purpose intended, and from one invention, many more can follow. These are the basic "rules" of invention, and they apply to every invention, whether mechanical or conceptual in nature.

12:24   Remember, though, our most powerful inventions are not technological at all; they are conceptual. Every single belief that every human has, or has ever had, is an invention. It is something conceptually made up, by one or more of us. As an invention, each of our beliefs must be specific and serve a particular purpose, although it could also be some other way. For example, if a young man requires some degree of reassurance that he will survive the ordeal of asking a girl out, he may create the idea that she is a kind person who won't cruelly reject him. But he has the power to represent her in any number of ways. He could instead create the belief that her response will reflect the sort of person she is — in other words, a rejection would mean something about her, not about him. Both of these perspectives serve the purpose of helping the young man summon the courage to approach the girl. They are specific, but different.

12:25 Any culture is built upon an invented set of agreements. Most of these are useful, like rules of conduct that address issues of living as a community. But what does a culture do with the fact that no one actually knows the answers to some of the most essential aspects of life and existence? Because we crave knowledge in places where we can't find any, we tend to just make something up to fill in the blanks—we believe and assume. While not necessarily relevant to our discussion here, it's interesting to note that the more dependent a cultural invention is on belief rather than practical experience, the more defensive about it we seem to become.

12:26 A culture is made up of individuals with shared beliefs. No one ever had to sit you down and teach you all of the beliefs of your culture, but you likely hold certain ideas the way you do because of the environment in which you learned them. I'm not merely talking about opinions here when I say "beliefs"—it goes much deeper than that, which we'll continue to explore as we progress. A few analogies to get us in the ballpark: If your mind was a computer, your cultural assumptions could be like your "operating system." We might also say your cultural assumptions are like the clay from which you construct reality. To help you recognize cultural worldviews, I want you to look at the following list, which consists of a random sampling of rather well-known names of various groups, genres, cultures, and subcultures.

12:27 Simply watch what "world" comes to mind the moment you see each name. If you have no knowledge of a particular group, just pass on it, since it probably has little to do with your consciously held personal beliefs. See what comes up for you as you pause a moment at each name on the list, and consider what perspective or "worldview"—which includes beliefs, attitudes, self-view, cosmology, cultural bias, outlook, mood, and other ways of perceiving reality and humanity—might be held by each one of these. Just take whatever comes up—whatever is stimulated, or whatever images pop up as you think of each category. Also observe whatever emotions, resistance, or attraction arise, as you automatically relate each to your own worldview, values, and beliefs.

12:28 **Worldview Exercise**

> Bring to mind: fascists, hippies, African bushmen, pagans, politicians, Hindus, scientists, Buddhists, witches, Christians, astrologers, environmentalists, Muslims, swingers, cowboys, rockers, psychics, Jews, feminists, jocks, liberals, rednecks, Californians, Aztecs, Samurai, intellectuals, American Indians, Western medicine, opera buffs, hookers, conservatives, rebels, nerds, yogis, evangelists, the military, holistic medicine, upper class, monks, rappers, pacifists, capitalists, ancient Greeks, Taoists, Americans, poets, communists, WASPs, white trash, Mafia, artists, college graduates, vegetarians.

12:29 Which do you identify with? Which do you reject? What comes to mind with each word? Of course, we could name many, many more. Notice the complexity of images and reactions one word can elicit. This is because each of these represent a possible worldview or worldview fragment. Can you name one person that you know who actually created their view of any of the above rather than received it as a cultural hand-me-down? It's difficult to consider the origins of these inventions when we and everyone we know have grown up into a world where most of them have always been available, and our views and beliefs about them were probably programmed early on. Even the actual founders or creators are usually relegated to hearsay and belief, and in many cases their identities are lost in the obscurity of the past.

12:30 Rarely do we recognize that these views are all *inventions*. If we consider the matter at all, we regard some of them as discoveries, or something passed on through tradition, perhaps from a divine source or at least from some authority on the matter. Some represent newer beliefs or subsets of beliefs, and membership in these indicates the particular way in which adherents hope to be special, or are simply identified and classified. I invite you to seriously consider that they are all inventions of the mind, conceived of by human beings. Perhaps genuine insight or inspiration sourced some of these inventions. But over time, as with all human activities, it is the mechanical ritual and dogma that are remembered, and distortion frequently replaces the original intent.

12:31 In our consideration here, we're looking for what is essential to "being." We need to weed out what is not essential and yet is experienced as though it is. For that, we need to recognize the real purpose of the stories and other inventions that make up our reality, both cultural and personal. We must come to understand the true nature of the beliefs that constitute our self-view and worldview. Challenging these is no easy task.

12:32 Part of our resistance might be due to the fact that our stories and beliefs seem to help us verify our place in the world. We say, "knowledge is power." Knowing what everything is and how to behave and what it all means is important to us — such certainty has a calming effect. But admitting that our assumptions about reality actually *are* only beliefs? "Whoa, beyond this place be dragons!" We get scared. Not-knowing can feel like we're adrift in something like a disturbingly undefined reality. Unaccustomed as we are to not-knowing, we don't understand the freedom that awaits us when we experience life beyond our beliefs.

12:33   To move in the direction of authentic being, we need to engage in an ongoing process of locating our every assumption and belief, observing the nature of our inventions, and unraveling these fictions one by one. The more we do this, the more likely we are to have a breakthrough where all at once the whole dynamic can be grasped and recognized for what it is.

> *People seem not to see that their opinion of the world*
> *is also a confession of character.*
> —Ralph Waldo Emerson

Inventing Personalized Worlds

12:34   Discovering our buried assumptions first requires the will to do so. Most of us have our hands full just dealing with our various needs and life activities, and testing the validity of our belief system is something we find hard to "get around to." It might seem to be rather superfluous, a distraction from "real life." In any case, life happens. What we might not realize is that the life demands with which our hands are full actually stem from these unconscious assumptions. The "self-perpetuating" nature of our belief systems actually creates the very issues that threaten to overwhelm us. Once we grasp that this is in fact true, our will for discovery, and so freedom, strengthens. Whatever we believe or assume — whether it comes from our culture or is unique — will dominate our experience of both self and life.

12:35   It takes a lot of work to begin to force the brain to take on and realize the immensity and true nature of our self-inventions. This domain includes all that we identify with, and all that we identify as the self. We are slow to challenge the validity of our wants and needs, our fears and aversions, because we are too busy fulfilling them. As a clear example of this, when our physical survival is threatened, our attention is completely devoted to handling that threat, and other considerations fall by the wayside. It is the same when any part of our identity is at risk. Considering whether the threat, or even what we are defending, is real or not is a luxury we reserve for a time of safe reflection.

12:36   In our rush to take care of ourselves, instead of simply *being* ourselves, we are unknowingly caught up in a struggle to maintain self-concepts, beliefs, childhood programming, and whatever else we happen to perceive as aspects of ourselves. This burdens us with a great number of self-attributes and also the complex strategies needed to manage them. We struggle to preserve our self-identity in many areas — in our relationships, social encounters, at work, and in relation to life as a whole. When we feel something lacking, we tend to embellish our identity further. By adopting more attributes, however, we are just adding to what is identified as self and so creating even more limitations and boundaries, and so more to defend, validate, and promote. The work of looking into our assumptions may begin to sound like a daunting task. As a whole, it may be, but it's less like fighting a tiger than it is like climbing a mountain at your own pace.

12:37 Let's scratch at the surface of this mountain of mind by taking a look at one rather benign example with which your "self" has probably identified. Consider: What music do you like — country, rock, Beethoven sonatas? No matter what music you lean toward, we could ask: is it real? But the question itself is stupid. So what are we asking? We wouldn't insist that the music we prefer somehow sprang up from the physics of reality, since we understand music to be a human invention. And yet what does it say about you and me that we like one form of music over another?

12:38 Frequently people find themselves identifying with a "kind" of music. Certainly it isn't merely the sounds that attract them, it is the shared perspective or "world view" that has been attached to such sounds. We imagine that the opera goer might see himself as rather clean, educated, and refined, much of which is associated with the well-to-do, whereas the country-western view might be more rugged, outdoorsy, and down-home. Whatever goes along with the image attached to a musical form — and everyone knows that in our culture each form of music identifies with some particular image — is what frequently determines one's preference for it. It fits a desired facet of one's self-image in some way.

12:39 Besides music, try to grasp how much more there is to a self's entire identity. Bring to mind some of the other things that you identify with — particular ways of dressing, the car or truck that you drive, your hairstyle, your decor, the style of sunglasses you wear, the type of friends you seek out, kinds of ornamentation your put on your body, what you read, your sexual preferences, your religion, morality, values, politics, your racial and ethnic background, the kinds of recreation or sports you like, and so on. As you bring these to mind, see how much you "find" yourself within them or in relation to them. There are many areas and relationships in which we identify ourselves as being one kind of person and not another, as having particular character traits, self-concepts, and beliefs. Altogether these are perceived as the reality in which we live. In actuality they are the inventions in which we live.

12:40   Two reasons these mental fictions are seen as reality rather than invention are that we don't experience their true nature, and we are apparently unable to change them at will. We live with them as if they are accurate reflections of the way things are. We remain unaware that we tend to distort incoming data to conform to what we believe and that this separates us from the truth.

12:41   Although our belief-dominated experience remains self-consistent and seems benign, we are actively suffering the consequences of such conceptual dominance. We just confuse this distress for an inherent condition of life or reality, which it is not. Even rather innocuous dispositions, such as being bothered by the presence of something you dislike, can produce unnecessary suffering. A rock fan might hate country music or a country fan may loathe Beethoven to such a degree that when music antithetical to his self-image is heard, he actually suffers. Perhaps not a great deal, but it is painful nevertheless. Why is that? It's not one's preferred music, but why suffer in its presence?

12:42   Some people are capable of enjoying country, rock, and classical music equally. Some who prefer one are still not pained by the others. Yet many people are actually uncomfortable when forced to listen to music that represents a "reality" felt to be antithetical to their own. They are actually threatened by it, but are slow to admit the threat. This reaction usually surfaces simply as a "distaste" that causes some level of discomfort — maybe the conceptual equivalent of eating something too sour or of hearing the sound of fingernails screeching on a chalkboard. Although it is hard to see, a strong reaction to rejected music is a result of one's self-identity. It is completely made up and produces unnecessary pain.

12:43 We're not trying to resolve anything about musical taste here. Rather we're using this example to indicate and draw out the overlooked consequences of identification. Individually they may not amount to much, but we should remember that our storytelling and invented worlds exist in abundance within our experience of self and life. We may not be conscious of all that we assume and believe. Nevertheless, this foundation for our experience shows up not only in the "stories" we tell ourselves and the "inventions" we adopt, but also as the consequences that result from viewing things in this way.

Manipulating Circumstances

12:44 Earlier we talked about the underlying sense of self-doubt, inauthenticity, and emptiness that surfaces in all of us from time to time. As a culture we simply attribute these things to life, and presume that our discomfort is caused by the current circumstances. Our way of dealing with these painful experiences is to try to manipulate the circumstances and so free ourselves from the pain. What we tend to ignore, but what continues to present itself anyway, is that it's not working.

12:45 Still, we foster the notion that if we work harder or get better, or life would just give us a break, we could somehow make everything work out and at long last feel happy and fulfilled. This may not be possible. If for some reason we were stuck in assumptions, or methods of thinking and acting, that prevented such an outcome, then obviously it couldn't work out. Guess what? We are all stuck in such a cycle.

12:46   Aside from circumstances, there is one other place that we blame for our failure to make everything work out — ourselves. We can, and often do, blame ourselves for not being smart enough or capable enough to make life turn out the way we want. We entertain the notion that it is our fault. If we can attribute our failures to others or circumstance, we prefer to do so — we might have to suffer the same hardships as if inflicted, but at least it's not our fault and so we feel better about ourselves. Yet even when we attribute the circumstances as the cause for our suffering, we'll still tend to blame ourselves for not being able to manipulate the circumstances effectively.

12:47   For the most part, we either successfully manipulate circumstances or we blame ourselves for our failure to do so. Of course, we hear about unconventional possibilities outside our usual way of operating. We hear about meditation to bring inner peace, or contemplation to attain enlightened liberation. We hear of surrendering to God, of returning to one's natural organic state, or undergoing decades of psychotherapy. There are methods that promise relief from our ongoing or repeated suffering, and just like every other manipulation, they work sometimes. Unfortunately, for most of us most of the time, they don't work well enough.

12:48   When we pursue such practices, even though they may do some good for a time, often we come to find that our relationship to these pursuits is something of a fantasy. We indulge in them, however, to superimpose a perspective on life that feels good and hopeful. Living within such an imagined world can provide a more positive experience. Pretending to be the "spiritual" seeker provides a sense of self-worth and a transcendent worldview. Casting ourselves as the struggling patient of therapy provides hope for a better future. Becoming a member of a religious order lets us be the "child" guided by the knowing "parent," and to hold a view of ourselves as having a special and correct relationship with God.

12:49   The difficulty in all such belief-powered constructs is that the basic self-concerns that drive us in life will also be driving us in these imagined worlds. Accustomed as we are to living through beliefs, we will adopt a perspective and fill in the blanks according to our new worldview, trying to adhere to its precepts. But the same patterns that brought disturbance into our ordinary lives will emerge in our "fantasy" lives — in whatever kind of life we construct. What we perceive will still be a function of our already formed self-concerns, but we will also filter whatever we experience so that it is consistent with our newly adopted worldview. Any negative experiences we encounter are simply labeled with different names, seen as failures, or ignored completely. What we fail to do, however, is truly understand what gets us into these cycles in the first place, and what keeps us there.

12:50   A simplistic answer to something so elaborately constructed as our self and reality cannot provide any insight about what's really going on. The ability to conceptually represent objects, people, and abstractions is quite useful, but we can get muddled very quickly if we remain unaware that such invention and belief, assumption and superimposition actually "create" the parameters and the experience of self and reality. This is true even when we're doing our best to be clear and honest. In the next chapter, we turn our attention to an even more inventive aspect of this dynamic.

CHAPTER THIRTEEN

Lost in Translation

What Is Not and Never Was

13:1   Curiously, the very same phenomenon that gives us so much power as human beings is also responsible for most of our pain. The ability to perceive "what is not"—conceptualization—creates whole new realms of possibility and power, but it also has consequences that are frequently overlooked.

13:2   In the last few chapters we've discussed some of the possible dangers of mistaking concepts for reality. For instance, being able to "see" the sky while we're inside the cave might have been confusing for the minds of early man if they couldn't make the distinction between concept and reality, but perhaps no less confusing than supposing a mental activity is somehow a "self."

13:3   In this light, it seems possible that human conceptual ability could be the point of the Garden of Eden story. According to legend, obtaining the "apple of knowledge" somehow produced destructive results for humankind. The benefits and power of this ability may appear enticing, but it's also true that the capacity to reason opens the door to all sorts of abstract woes. In fact, our conceptual ability is the very source of the legend of its own evil.

13:4 Concepts that "reproduce" objective reality are representations. These ideas and images "stand for" what's there. They serve as a conceptual placeholder for the reality that we've perceived. But as we discussed in the last chapter, our conceptual ability doesn't stop at forming mental images of objects that are no longer there. We also have the ability to be creative, inventing something that not only isn't present, but never was present.

13:5 At first this could be quite simple. Instead of just reproducing an image of the gray rock seen outside the cave, we can imagine a blue rock that we've never seen before. We've seen blue in the sky and a rock on the ground, so we simply combine these two qualities to get a blue rock. This ability seems innocuous enough, and can be extremely helpful when it comes to being inventive. But the ability to represent and then to mess around with our representations inevitably leads to the ability to misrepresent. In short: concurrent with the ability to conceptualize—which is the ability to "perceive" what is not present—comes the ability to lie.

The ability to represent is also the ability to misrepresent.

13:6 Since it's possible for us to represent ourselves, it is also possible for us to misrepresent ourselves. We practice this as children playing games of make-believe, and as adults we continue to fall into making up "characters" in which to "be." In fact, by adulthood we're so good at make-believe that we can live it nonstop, and there's no one to call us in for dinner and back to reality.

13:7 Not only might I confuse a repeated activity for myself and so believe that I "am" a dancer, I can believe that I am a dancer when I've never danced a day in my life. I can represent myself as all sorts of things, both to myself and to others, but in so doing I am actually misrepresenting myself. This may seem creative and fun sometimes, but most often it gets us into a lot of trouble.

13:8 Because we're conceptual creatures, we represent and interpret everything that we encounter. We also misrepresent — sometimes deliberately, but mostly without realizing it. Since any representation of what we perceive is never "the thing itself," we have to admit that we only "know" a thing in a different form than it is as itself. As a matter of fact, our representations are almost always misrepresentations in that they never exactly duplicate what-is. We might be the biggest liar in the world or the most honest person; either way, we can't *not* misrepresent to some degree. When we forget that *all* our representations, however "accurate," are simply made up, we get stuck in our own fabrications, both negative and positive. The place where real and false get all tangled up and confused is in the process of interpretation.

Somebody was saying to Picasso that he ought to make pictures of things the way they are—objective pictures. He mumbled he wasn't quite sure what that would be. The person who was bullying him produced a photograph of his wife from his wallet and said, "There, you see, that is a picture of how she really is." Picasso looked at it and said, "She is rather small, isn't she? And flat?"

—Gregory Bateson

Interpretation Revisited

13:9   Once again, remember that the foremost job of the mind is to relate all incoming information and perceptions to the needs of the self. The mind is driven to *know,* to discern the meaning of everything encountered. "What is it? What does it mean to me? How should I relate to it? Is it dangerous or is it valuable?" These questions need to be answered immediately in order to make sense and respond appropriately to what we see, hear, think, or feel. In this way, I can kick a stone off my path, eat an apple, avoid a snarling dog, or pursue an attractive female. This information needs to be available quickly and reflexively, and each person's intricate interpretation process tries to ensure that it is. When you think about it, our ability to sort and prioritize data is amazing. It's even possible to *simultaneously* kick the stone and avoid the dog while enjoying the apple and catching the woman's eye.

13:10   It's reasonable to say that snarling animals and tasty fruit may evoke pretty much the same responses in just about anyone, but much that we encounter is more ambiguous, and everything is subject to a great deal of individual perspective. I not only view the world from my personal core beliefs but at any given time, my current needs and fears, moods and states, will color whatever I perceive.

13:11   Maybe I love fruit, but I just ate an entire watermelon, so an apple is not appealing. When I'm tired, a chair is a welcome sight. I immediately know I can rest on it, and recognizing this potential I see the chair as a good and valuable thing. On the other hand, when I'm ready to exercise or practice tai chi, the chair becomes an obstacle in the space I need for my movement. Clearly the chair itself is neither good nor a problem, but relating it to myself and my needs creates the bias in which I perceive it.

13:12 Aside from influencing how we interpret data, our self-minds also suppress or omit information that has no significance to us. Much is resisted, either because it lies outside our interests or because awareness of it contains some element of threat. Exactly *what* is threatened is an issue that we'll explore more later. Meanwhile, it's useful to look into our own experience of perception to understand just how much we distort, ignore, select, and essentially "personalize" all the information that comes to us.

13:13 Recognizing one's own interpretive process can be tricky. For a more grounded look at the particular way in which you receive data, you might want to carefully observe your way of being in the world. Try to grasp all that is involved within your mind and perceptions to successfully manage an interaction. For example, participating in any kind of competition requires juggling a great deal of perceptual information very quickly. For me, decades of martial arts proved an excellent means to further my investigation of how we process and respond to incoming data. When someone distorts or omits vital information during a fighting contest, the results are pretty clear — they get hit. One of the first things my students learn is that effective interaction means responding to what is occurring rather than any thoughts or beliefs about what is occurring. Adhering to this principle always improves any action or interaction, physical or otherwise.

13:14 Responding to what's occurring seems like a "no-brainer," but just how difficult it is in practice helps illustrate how much we unknowingly disconnect from reality. Without interpretation to add meaning, incoming information would remain too abstract to be useful, but the self-serving agenda of the interpretive process leaves little room for experiencing what's actually true. The mind's goal is not to get at the truth but to fulfill our needs, and like a computer with very specific programming, the mind's interpretations are based on what's already known or believed.

13:15 We're marvelously equipped to recognize useful distinctions and associations within our environment and culture, but naturally self-limited to that particular way of perceiving reality. And, if the "programming" (our beliefs) is flawed or the data is incorrect, then false conclusions will show up in place of what's true. Perceptions will be biased, but will appear to simply reflect reality.

13:16 When we put attention on where our attention goes, it's possible to discern that our awareness gravitates toward what we think is useful. If we're honest about it and open to detecting what is really going on, we can also recognize how the interpretation process takes what is perceived and tries to fit it to the beliefs that we already have. This is especially true if we have any investment in how the perceived data turns out. Whatever is interpreted as threatening or contradictory to self's desires tends to be distorted, considered bad, or just plain ignored. To put a square peg into a round hole, much has to be omitted.

13:17 All our perceptions and experiences are shaped by interpretation. This process is necessary or the world would make no sense whatsoever. Without it, the information would remain outside our ability to conceptualize and we wouldn't recognize anything. In other words, what we perceive is always an interpretation and never "the thing itself." We are completely dependent on interpretation and yet the very nature of the process is so subject to self's needs that we can easily misrepresent reality to ourselves.

We can add details, omit facts, or even invent perceptions that are not at all true. Although we don't realize it, the interpretative process is quite causative — meaning that something is created that doesn't exist without this process. Yet since we are so grounded in personal and cultural programs, beliefs, and assumptions, this creativity doesn't exist as a choice. It is purposefully creating our world to be "self" consistent.

Reconstructive Interpretation

13:18   We alter our interpretations in many different ways and to varying degrees. At the root of this activity are the personal and cultural assumptions we've been talking so much about. But there are layers and layers of different kinds of "knowing" that interfere with our experience of the truth. Aside from all the personal and cultural programming that dominates the tenor and flow of our perceptions, we are also compelled to add our own creative flair to the mix. I'm not just saying that we embellish our view of reality — it goes deeper than that. What we do could even be called "reconstructive interpretation," which is an unconscious automatic patterning that reorients our experiences and perceptions to make them particularly useful to us.

13:19   If you've taken time to put attention on where your attention goes, you may have gotten a glimpse of how those things that register as "meaningless" are automatically filtered out. With any interpretation that seems important, we will pile on self-referential revisions to make the information more personally "useful." One distortion that can be difficult to detect is what we're going to look at now: the way we change or "reinterpret" events — what someone says, what happened, what something means, etc.—to reflect what we assume, believe, fear, or want to be true. Whether we act consciously or not, what we're doing is misrepresenting to ourselves or others what we originally perceive by creating an alternate version of what is or was.

13:20 While we do it in "real-time" as well, a more easily discernible "reconstruction" of our experience can be seen in our memories. Of course, a memory is always and only a concept. The event we're recalling doesn't actually exist in present time; we are simply reproducing what we think is a fairly accurate image of what was. What we remember is what we "perceive" as personal history, but a memory is strictly a representation. As such, it is even easier for it to be a misrepresentation than is a current perception. At any time after an actual event, our memory of the event can be distorted or altered, replacing a more accurate representation. As we discussed in Chapter Twelve, each of us is the central character in the "never-ending story of me." Especially when the consequences of a factual recollection are undesirable, our memory-stories tend to become distorted. This may be difficult to catch, but if we are honest and careful we can detect it.

13:21 For example, when confronted with a social circumstance the outcome of which is that we look foolish or wrong, we might well go away feeling awful. At first we may feel bad—embarrassed or shamed—but this can feel intolerable. No one wants a self-image that includes being inept, cowardly, or an idiot. Over time, most human minds will begin to retell the events and circumstances until finally the story is bearable.

13:22 One of the most common "re-creations" of such memories shifts the blame for our negative experiences to the others involved. Once this has happened, we immediately feel much better. Our self-image is intact, and although the unpleasant ordeal is still distasteful in our memory, our part in it isn't nearly as bad as it once was — even to the point where we become the "hero" of the story, or at worst a victim of other people or unavoidable circumstances. In this case, and in this way, it is clear that the memory of past events is distorted and biased.

13:23 Who can say in all honesty that they have never done such a thing? When we study this and similar phenomena, we find that it occurs far more frequently than anyone is able to admit. The reason it's so hard to see is that the very nature of the distortion demands that we remain unconscious of what we're doing. Since the goal is to get our memory squared with our self-concept, we must "believe" that the memory is accurate. We need to convince ourselves that things happened one way and not the other or our new version of reality will have no power. When a memory revision like this works well, we merely "observe" that we are who we want to be, and that our behavior, expressions, and internal states were all consistent with this self image.

13:24 It's not hard to understand how the pain of identifying with traits such as being worthless, stupid, weak, and so on can inspire a round of personal whitewashing. When we feel foolish or ashamed, most of us just set about the task of reconstructing our interpretation of events, usually without even thinking about it. Perhaps one reason we refrain from questioning our own interpretations is that whenever we start to look into how we hold reality, the terrain can start to feel rather slippery. Approaching these matters through our experience rather than just intellectually can greatly simplify our task, but a new challenge arises. The deeper we go in our questioning, the closer we get to confronting the core assumptions that run our lives. Keep in mind that confusion, upset, and other personal resistance are likely to arise as our questioning threatens the very basis of our self image.

13:25 Every one of us feels better when we "like" ourselves, but as humans, we inevitably engage in behavior that we don't feel good about later. When we reconstruct our self-image to correct this, it doesn't just add a layer of inauthenticity to our sense of self, it also has the effect of masking the core assumption that we are somehow inherently flawed. This is one of the cultural assumptions that we addressed way back in Chapter Three, but the damaging implications of this nearly universal mistaken belief should be more apparent now.

13:26 I'm saying that the original premise that compels us to distort our memory may well be rooted in a hidden false assumption. This means that our distress over the undesirable self-image is triggered by a belief that is no more real than our new and improved misrepresentation of self. Not only is all this image-doctoring unnecessary, our preoccupation with it keeps us from recognizing the possibility that this whole strategy is based on something unreal. It's a mistake on top of a mistake on top of a mistake. The question now is why would we engage in such a fruitless cycle of conceptual shenanigans?

We know ourselves chiefly by hearsay.
—Eric Hoffer

Self as We Know It

13:27 Within our culture, "self" and "mind" are held as one and the same. It's an easy assumption to make—what else would we suppose? In our awareness, we make an important distinction between what is "me" and what is "not-me." Within the "me" distinction, we observe an endless stream of mental content that is exclusive to our particular self—our memories, perceptions, fantasies, thoughts, character traits, emotions, sensations, and our very sense of awareness. All this activity is held together, given continuity, and made usable in large measure through the ongoing stories we tell ourselves—in which each of us is the central character. We live our lives inside its plot, and this endless internal narrative simultaneously frames, reflects, and creates the reality in which we live.

13:28 Where does all this come from? Our selves, obviously. But what and where is the self that generates all this mind activity? We're not very clear on the subject, but we have got some entertaining notions about it. It's not hard to imagine that in some hallowed chamber of unconscious mind there resides the genuine and pure root that is our "real" self. We might suppose that, simply through existential mechanics, this real self must remain "backstage"— always out of sight, but still managing the whole show like some Wizard of Oz. Although some of this may seem to be self-evident, it's really all assumption and conjecture; we don't actually experience what's true about ourselves.

13:29 The original function of mind is to do a job, the essence of which is to keep you alive and successfully being you. Toward this end, it creates your story lines and maintains the continuity of your character and identity. It works pretty well, doesn't it? You don't get your self mixed up with any other self. Of course, the mind must also protect, maintain, and perpetuate itself—if it gets lost or damaged, it can't do its job. The mind unceasingly promotes the interests of the one who "possesses" it, and all its mental/emotional activity is calculated to get this one body-mind through every moment of life in the most secure manner it can conceive.

13:30   This is all well and good, but for reasons we'll look into later, it seems that the conceptual activity that is created to serve the self has *become* the self. We become attached to our beliefs, to our roles and traits, and also to the strategies needed for maintaining all this. We rarely acknowledge that all our mental, emotional, and perceptual activities are *processes,* and that they're there to serve a specific purpose. We're so busy identifying with mind's conceptual mechanisms that we lose touch with what's real. It is not hard to see, then, how self becomes confused with the mind.

13:31   Inevitably, the presence of mental activity is identified within one's awareness *as* the self. We consider our thoughts and emotions to be aspects of ourselves, and we hold our awareness and intellect as though they *are* ourselves. In this case, when the mind serves "the self" it is actually serving something of its own making—a conceptual self.

Life in the Loop

13:32   Whatever we think of as "self" we will protect and maintain. If it's a conceptual self, and likely it is, then we end up with mind protecting mind. This produces a rather "introverted" self-mind creating thoughts and perceptions in its own image. When self becomes confused with mind, and mind becomes seen as the self, the mind's self-serving activities end up creating an experience of reality that is entirely self-referential.

13:33 Remember, mind has no interest in what's true—its job is to keep you alive while maintaining an identifiable sense of self. To do this, it not only creates and identifies with physical and mental-emotional activities, it also builds on past experience and any previously established conceptual identity. You're still alive and you're still you, so mind will naturally protect and promote all the beliefs behind the activities that keep you that way. Unless you think to question the validity of the assumptions behind all this, they will simply appear to you as reality.

13:34 We've all come up against people whose minds are obviously closed to any fragment of an idea that does not fit their beliefs about the truth. Against all logic, they will protect this "reality" with everything they've got, even when doing otherwise might make life better for them. If the image of such a person is distasteful to you, you're going to like it even less when I say that you do the same thing. You might happen to be more open and reasonable, but you protect your own conceptual self with the same zeal as the close-minded person.

13:35 For example, if being reasonable is an important part of your self-image, it's possible that your need to see yourself in this way is a reaction to some deep core assumption that you are really *not* a rational being. The truth of the matter is probably that you are capable of being both reasonable and unreasonable, but early in life you may have come to view yourself as an irrational person, and so now your self-mind works to hide, misrepresent, or contradict that "fact."

13:36 Because their roots are buried deep within our convictions about reality, and so remain hidden from view, we each suspect that our negative traits — our personal "defects" — may well *be* us, that perhaps they represent "self" more authentically than our carefully maintained self-image. By altering our behavior in daily life, we can make-believe that we have successfully changed what seems to be an inherent aspect of our conceptual identity. To validate this belief and give it enough power to counter the core assumptions that conflict with our image, we must always act in accord with our adopted identity.

13:37 If, for example, one of your adopted traits is to be "the voice of reason," you might surround yourself with like-minded people who will not challenge your identity or what you hold as the correct way to be. When you behave outside your typical reasonableness — as you inevitably will — your mind will set to work correcting your self-image in some way. Maybe it will find a reasonable excuse for the behavior while you were "not being yourself," or it might simply begin to reconstruct your interpretation of events. Depending on the amount of personal suffering you're experiencing at the time, you might be motivated to turn to one of your like-minded friends and misrepresent the whole incident in such a way that they will respond by completely absolving you: "Any reasonable person would've blown up long before that," or some such. You might even come out looking better than you did before.

13:38 We don't just try to maintain our conceptual self as-is, we also put a lot of time and energy (and sometimes money) into making it appear better in our own eyes and the eyes of others. Why? Because we're in pain, feeling empty and inauthentic, and struggling with self-doubt. One of the main reasons we feel this way is that we misrepresent and distort and sometimes lie. Why? Because we're in pain, feeling empty and inauthentic, and struggling with self-doubt.

13:39   The general cultural prescription for feeling better about ourselves is often in the direction of more misrepresentation, distortion, or lies — although it is never seen as that. We attempt to appear as all sorts of things — reasonable, spiritual, tough, harmless, honorable, intelligent, one of the guys, enlightened, or whatever fits our desired self-image. Yet even with all of our efforts we are often left feeling like we're simply acting out a movie script, or going through the motions. This is because we are. No amount of alterations to our appearance, mind, or behavior will change the fact that we don't know who we are.

13:40   Trying to improve this condition while living as a conceptual self is an exercise in futility, but we keep trying. We revise our memory and our self-story, add onto our flagging self-image by making life changes, and if we can afford it, maybe we get plastic surgery or a new car. There's nothing inherently wrong with doing any of these things as long as we're clear about who we really are, and that it has nothing to do with what we appear to be, either to ourselves or others. This kind of clarity is not easy to come by — we need to be ruthlessly honest in our self-assessment just to begin the process. But not only do we neglect to challenge our beliefs, assumptions, and less-than-authentic "selves," we defend and promote them all the more when someone else challenges them.

13:41   As long as something is identified *as* the self or *of* the self, our minds will nurture and defend it. It's not exactly a life-and-death struggle to maintain our character traits, and yet the drive to *continue thus* is so strong that it may as well be. Perhaps it's because the stories we tell and the traits we insist on acting out are part of what makes a self itself. This brings us back to our question about why we engage in all these conceptual shenanigans: we do it to maintain a recognizable self identity.

The Great Way is not difficult
for those who have no preferences.
When love and hate are both absent
everything becomes clear and undisguised.
Make the smallest distinction however
and heaven and earth are set infinitely apart.
—Seng-T'san

13:42 You might be accustomed to recognizing only the "conceptual-self" aspect of your existence, but that doesn't mean that's all there is. All theological, philosophical, and scientific theory aside, we don't actually know what a self *is*. If you — your real self or real being — are separate from the processes of intellect, emotion, and cognition, then what are you? If not in those conceptual activities, where do you find your self? You can't. You don't.

13:43 This doesn't necessarily mean you're not there, just that you may be looking in the wrong place. Looking in any other way would require some kind of unimaginable mode of apprehending your own existence, something outside, or beyond, or perhaps *before* perception. People have been pondering this for millennia, so don't worry if this is confusing. All you need to understand is that the moment you pin "self" down into a perception, it's not you anymore — it's something "you" perceive.

13:44   Living entirely within a loop of self-serving concepts doesn't do much for our sense of authenticity. When we truly enjoy ourselves, we often say that we "lose ourselves" in some activity. Our focus is entirely in the moment. We're not fantasizing or fretting or thinking strategically — in fact, often we're not really thinking much at all unless it is entirely about the matter at hand. That is when we're simply "being ourselves," and it's a refreshing and calming break from the usual "self-referencing" activities of the self-mind. It's still conceptual, of course, but it is not so "self-conscious" — instead, awareness is directed *outward*. The intellect is engaged in the task at hand while self simply remains in the background directing the activity. It's not necessarily an experience of *being* — all our usual conceptual shenanigans are just on hold — but it's a step in the right direction.

CHAPTER FOURTEEN
Creating an Experience of Self

The Myth of Real Self

14:1   In one form or another, we've been looking into self for most of this book. This questioning isn't easy for anyone, and unless the matter is approached on a purely intellectual level, each person must wrestle with it alone in their own experience (theories only lead to more concepts about self). As we approach the matter from direction after direction, you've probably had some insights about it by now, or at least you suspect on some level that you don't find anything clearly recognizable as your "true" self, although you suppose it's there *some*where.

14:2   In our "switchback" trail up the side of this very steep inquiry, we find ourselves passing the same views again and again from slightly different perspectives. Now we're nearing a view that I'd like to point out for you as we begin to wrap up Part IV, "Creating Self." In fact, because hammering away at the same issue time and again is essential to real questioning, much of this chapter will be a sort of "overview" of what we've already addressed. I want you to start by thinking back to Chapter Three. To save some time, let's just review a bit to see how your understanding may have shifted.

    We were talking about the following two categories of cultural assumption:

1. Our views regarding Not-Knowing:
Which result in the veneration of knowledge, an aversion to not-knowing, and the adoption of beliefs in place of experiencing the truth.

2. Our assumptions regarding "self":
Which result in the adoption and preservation of a fallacious "conceptual" self.

14:3 We hold not knowing as bad, and yet we don't know who or what we are. One question asked was, "What does a knowledge-oriented culture such as ours do about our inherent inability to answer a question so important to us as 'What is a self?'" The answer was that we invent things.

14:4 Such an answer so early in our investigation couldn't really have much impact, since it's just an idea and not part of our experience. Some readers probably looked upon it as a sort of Socratic game that would somehow end in the revelation of a meaningful answer to the question-within-the-question: "What is a self?" But in truth, we just weren't ready for the sheer mass of "invention" that we were going to uncover. Its scope would have been unrecognizable from where we stood, which was (and is) *within* it.

14:5 After addressing some of the consequences of our cultural assumptions in Chapter Three, we identified the principles we'd need for genuine questioning and then started looking for self in Part II. Mostly we learned that our concepts of self are not the same as the "real self" that we so want to meet up with. The closest we've come is some slippery distinction between "conceptual-self," as a set of qualities based on beliefs, and "Being," as simply and only what is actually *there*—what is as itself.

14:6   In Part IV we've looked quite a bit at what we *hold* as self, and the creative capacity of our minds to contribute to that self. We've seen how we invent whole worlds and "stories" in which to live, and how we invent and reinvent parts of our self-image, memory, and reality.

14:7   In the event that any of you are still holding your breath about "What is a self?" I'd like to tell you clearly that the "answer" can only exist within your own direct consciousness. No explanation or concept will suffice and would only amount to hearsay. The leap into direct consciousness is a mysterious paradox. It is unassailable by intellectual means, but understanding the fabrications that are identified and experienced as oneself can provide a powerful springboard.

14:8   In this chapter, we'll further view the dynamic of the conceptual self through metaphor and examples, and in the next chapter we'll confront the fundamental motive and principle that drives our creation of self and our every effort in life. Chances are, however, that none of this is what you had in mind. Maybe you want to locate and commune with your own real genuine self. That's understandable, commendable even, and it sounds great, but it's impossible to get there from here. Self as we know it is purely conceptual.

14:9   But you got that already, right? At least as a notion. It is my hope that at some point in our investigation you'll get that fact as an experience, on a level that the Apprentices used to call "butt-clenching." True insight doesn't necessarily take place at the end of a series of propositions. It occurs at any time. For example, truly grasping the nature of your conceptual self requires in the same moment becoming conscious of the nature of your real self. This can happen anywhere in the process of looking into this stuff.

It's like a cartoon we kept up on a board at the center showing a man talking to his dog, Ginger. What the dog heard was "blah, blah, blah, Ginger, blah, blah, blah." This is sort of what happens with this work. You read and understand what is being said, contemplating it as you go, but still it is rather "blah, blah," until suddenly a "Ginger" pops in there. "Ginger" here represents an insight. So, Ginger away.

14:10 One of the things we are attempting to grasp presently is that your familiar self is "conceptual," and this is a hard thing to grasp, much less hang onto. But the truth is, the "real self" that we hope to discover — that we hope to "perceive" and therefore interpret and "know" — does not exist. Being does not "perceive" itself. The perceiver perceived becomes a perception. Self as we *know* it is a fancy paint job on the invisible man. It's a balloon skin of concepts. Without the skin, there's nothing there. As you can see, metaphor is irresistible in the face of trying to convey the nonsensical news that there is no "graspable" or accurately representable "real self."

Whenever you get there, there's no there there.
—Gertrude Stein

Apples and Oranges

14:11 An apple is an apple, but the thought of an apple is a thought, and the image of an apple is an image. Take away all thoughts and images and the apple still exists. So, thoughts and images are not the same as real apples. At best, they can represent or refer to those objects. The same is true of something intangible like a principle. The thought of gravity is not the same as gravity. And the same is true of a self. The thought of a self is not the same as a self—or is it? Much of what we call "self" turns out to be conceptual in nature.

14:12 Self itself is always a conceptual event—having one, living as one, sharing one with others. Here I'm not referring to what we think about self, or what we imagine as the self, although those are certainly included. I'm saying that the presence and awareness of a self is a conceptual activity. Even your most honest self, and even your most immediate and present sense of "self-in-this-moment" are conceptual events.

14:13 In the consciousness workshops I do, people frequently have a breakthrough in which they move from a habitual assumption of self to another, more real and present experience of themselves. Maybe someone simply realizes how much they've been dishonest or "asleep," or someone else becomes suddenly "aware of being aware." They experience some insight into their own nature beyond intellect, a shift in "consciousness" that "shakes up their world," or at least their way of viewing it. But this is only a beginning, since from here they are more able to see the many levels and layers attainable within the conceptual event of selfhood, which further opens them up to the possibility of an experience of Being.

14:14 You'd think that the clarity achieved in such an event would forever prevent a person from reverting to "dishonesty" or "falling back asleep," but this is not so. Unless someone has a major enlightenment experience on the nature of their own being (and even then ...) they might become more open and honest, but will soon return to living as the already established habitual self. The demands of life require that we operate as a consistent and identifiable self, with "the truth" and "an experience of Being" as extremely low priorities.

14:15 Say there's a scale on which we can examine the honesty, awareness, and general accuracy of our conceptual representations of self. It includes all that constitutes our self for us, from self-image to our most real and secret inner self. Say the scale is from one to ten, with one being equal to complete pretending and misrepresentation, and ten being as real and honest as you can manage — a veritable mirror of how you truly feel, act, and are.

14:16 Now, with this scale in mind, consider that there is still no room to include the absolute "accuracy" of Being. Being isn't something represented, or even experienced or perceived — it is what *is*. Even if we made the scale more complex, it would make no difference. If Being can't be represented, it certainly can't be quantified. The clarity that you can achieve by moving from misrepresentation to true representation is one kind of honesty. It is "realness" on a conceptual, conceivable scale, and work here is certainly as useful as it is difficult. But you need to understand that even such honesty is relative, and it takes place in a different domain than what we're calling "Being."

14:17 Being doesn't need to be honest; it can't be anything else. True Consciousness is already what it is, and there is no possibility of misrepresentation. Being is so thoroughly just and only *itself* that it is not accurately representable by concept. Being just *is*. When we get tangled up in our web of beliefs and misrepresentations, and we lose our sense of authenticity, the direction we need to go is toward what is genuine. But Being is not a better web of beliefs, or an untangling of misconceptions. Being is an absolute — there is nothing there to tangle.

Believing in Your Self

14:18 Whenever we believe in something, who is it that believes? Obviously it is we who believe, but since we've made a distinction between self and being, which of these is responsible for the believing? To investigate this question, let's start with what we find in our self-experience. We find our particular identity, our familiar perceived qualities, a sense of awareness, and the assumption that a self is behind this awareness. With the possible exception of our present awareness, all this is conceptual. None of this "mind activity" can relate to our real being because, in our experience, we find no real being. Our beliefs and assumptions relate to the self, not to being.

14:19 Since this self is necessarily created from concept, and is composed primarily of the numerous assumptions and beliefs that we hold, it becomes clear that all of our beliefs and assumptions must relate directly to the self. They are self-referential — both forming the self and referring to the self. The relationship between belief and self is automatic and ongoing. Even all of the information and ideas that we *don't* believe will be related to the self. This is necessary in order to compare what's encountered with what we *do* believe so that we can "know" that we don't believe it. What we don't believe defines us as much as what we believe. This process usually takes place so quickly and automatically that it merely surfaces as a knee-jerk opinion.

14:20 Try to catch this in operation right now. Bring to mind something you believe. For example, maybe you believe the earth is round. When you dwell on that notion for a moment, what happens? It comes to you as a "yes," doesn't it? In other words, you perceive the thought and image as true, a correct perception, and it sits well with you. It is something "you" believe. Consider something else that you believe, something about yourself. It could be you believe you are a smart person or a good person; perhaps you believe you are special or maybe cowardly. Whatever you believe about yourself, isolate one notion and dwell on it for a moment. Observe what happens and how quickly it happens. This belief not only sits as true for you, it is *about* you, and so feels like you are perceiving into your self, doesn't it?

14:21   Now consider something that you don't believe. Perhaps you don't believe the earth is flat. When you peer at this image, this notion, what occurs? It is a "no," isn't it? Without delay it is slipped into the category of rejected, not so, wrong. Notice how "you" don't identify with it, how it is not correct, and represents something "other" than your beliefs, and so in some way not where "you" will go.

14:22   This all happens in a heartbeat, and so the significance of it could easily be missed. But if you seriously watch what occurs for you as you believe and disbelieve, and how these beliefs relate to your self, it should become clear that something nonrandom and quite complex is taking place. Because concepts are not the reality they represent, and are produced and shaped by the mind, beliefs are free to be tailor-made to suit oneself. This dynamic leaves the door open for a conceptual self to recreate data in any way that serves it.

Mandatory Misrepresentation

14:23   The way I keep contrasting the conceptual-self with both real-self and "being" implies that the conceptual-self is not real. Why would I suggest that our self-experience could in some way be false? For two reasons: representation and misrepresentation.

14:24   We believe that every trait and characteristic we observe in our particular self actually defines who and what we *are*. But how could they *be* us when everything we perceive — including ourselves and our attributes — are representations in our minds? Since a representation is at least once removed from reality, and never the thing-itself, it is technically also a misrepresentation. As with all interpretation, the interpretation known as "who we are" is both completely created and entirely self-referential. No matter how much is represented or misrepresented, it is still not "the thing itself," and so not who we really are.

14:25   If I have no genuine experience of who I am, then what am I going to present as who I am? I must either believe something I've been told or make something up. As I do these things, I am not presenting who I really am, I'm presenting whatever "takes place" and serves the function of who I am. In this way I am presenting something false. This act of replacing the unknown with something known will soon be forgotten or ignored, since there appears to be no alternative.

14:26   Everyone and everything around me seems to be specific and particular — this is what defines their existence. So I need to be specific and particular too. But uh-oh, there is no graspable real self available. I really have no more insight into my true nature than I do into the nature of that chair.

14:27 In our culture, we seem to be set up to handle this dilemma by assuming and accepting that defining a specific and particular self is the same as what we are. This demand to present ourselves as "known" requires a sort of mandatory misrepresentation. "Of course I've got a self; I *am* a self. I'm just not totally clear on the matter . . . yet. So I'll fudge it for now. Perhaps I'll 'find myself' later and get free of this nagging feeling that I am inauthentic. Maybe a religion would help clear things up. Meanwhile, I'll present whatever comes into view as 'my self.'" The need to identify with something specific appears like an honest mistake — it seems there's just nothing else to do. But most of us don't stop there; we go on to consciously produce something even less straightforward.

Know thyself? If I knew myself, I'd run away.
—Goethe

Living as a False-Self

14:28 Frequently we desire to be something better or somehow different than what we experience as ourselves, or what we think others experience as us. For whatever reason, we don't always want to "be ourselves" and we are drawn to alter our presentation or expressions a bit. In an attempt to give a better impression, we misrepresent ourselves, often with little or no acknowledgement that these affectations are false. They are misrepresentations of our experience and character, and so are not even a concept of what is there, but are a concept of what is "not there." By design and intent they are false. To the degree that a self is built up of these altered or invented attributes, it is a false-self.

14:29   Self as we know it is not necessarily false. It is what it is — a conceptual fabrication. But if a representation is not a real self, a misrepresentation certainly isn't. Deep and shallow, active and passive, much that we identify with as our self is false. It is a conceptual invention of some kind, some quality or way of appearing or acting that is *not* aligned with what's actually experienced as us in this moment.

14:30   Some of this is immediately visible as false — we ourselves don't even think it is real. Some is more difficult to admit because it is motivated by the strong impulse to manipulate oneself and other people for the purpose of fulfilling one's needs. It is also so familiar that we're hard-pressed to recognize it as something put on. And there is an even deeper falseness that operates on such an obscure or barely cognizable level beneath our normal consciousness that we don't seem to be consciously "doing" it but rather we're unconsciously "being" it. This too can be called false.

14:31   Conceptually altering or changing what's interpreted or expressed regarding a self is easily done — in contrast to, say, altering or decorating an objective reality like a chair, which takes more process and is harder to hide. Taking artistic license with our representation of self is not just hard to pass up, it is exactly what the false-self is founded on and needs in order to exist.

14:32   A false self is what is adopted or pretended to be oneself, to others and to yourself. It includes what you misrepresent yourself to be to serve some purpose, what you want to be, or are trying to be, even what you fear you are. It is in all the manipulations that you engage to convince yourself and others that you are some way that isn't authentically experienced. It is in what you hide away fearing you might be. It is even found infecting the very presence of your most immediate sense of self.

14:33   Normally we do not address this fact of a falsified self. It's just part of the human experience and may be of no interest to those satisfied with life and self as they are. But not everyone is. Some people want to be authentic and want to get beyond their current self-experience — which doesn't seem like the whole story somehow. Some want to know the truth simply because it is what's true. It takes a certain amount of courage to honestly question the self. In contemplation work especially, as we strive to experience whatever is true, it's possible to encounter a deep sense of falseness that seems like a malignant growth that has permeated our very sense of awareness. Such a recognition can be distressing at first, but it affords us freedom from having to be "this particular way" for a lifetime.

Monkeys are superior to men in this:
when a monkey looks into a mirror, he sees a monkey.
—Malcolm De Chazal

The Snowball Effect

14:34   No matter what we perceive as an aspect of ourselves, it will be subject to an irresistible series of events that defines self and life. Whenever we observe some attribute, idea, trait, belief, conclusion, reaction, behavior, or emotion as an expression of ourselves, we naturally see it as manifesting the self that we *are*. The moment we identify with it this way, a mere observation of something turns into a perception of "ourselves." We are then immediately called to protect and defend what's observed.

14:35 For example, I may conclude that my hand is a part of me. The moment this occurs, I will not only claim the hand as mine, I will be drawn to protect it from harm and promote its well-being. This is not a real problem when it comes to hands. If someone attacks me and tries to cut off my hand, I will move it or otherwise take action. This all seems natural and straightforward. It becomes a little more sticky, however, when someone says, "Your hand is ugly." Now my feelings are hurt, and I feel that my hand is under a different form of attack. How do I defend "my self" against this attack?

14:36 If the hand was just "a" hand, someone's comment on it wouldn't mean very much to me. I might agree or disagree, depending on what beliefs I held, but the hand would lie outside the jurisdiction of things that I need to defend, or at least defend with gusto. The fact that it is "my" hand changes everything. If someone calls *my* hand ugly, they are calling *me* ugly. Now "I" am being criticized, not just the hand.

14:37 This verbal "attack" may not be overly threatening, but I will be affected by the pain it causes and so react in a protective way. To defend against further criticism, I'll feel compelled to hide my hand. This same impulse leads to keeping many aspects of my internal state hidden, or misrepresented, so that no one can judge them as ugly. Since in this case I'm already exposed, I might imply their words are powerless to hurt me by saying "Sticks and stones . . ." or I might say their hand is ugly too, or I may sit down and cry pitifully, trying to make them feel guilty and so take back their statement. I could do any number of things in reaction to their comment, but as long as I hold the hand as an aspect of myself, all my actions will be directed toward defense.

14:38   The hand itself is an object, but my hurt feelings and other internal reactions to negative comments are not objects. They exist instead within the conceptual domain, which is why we call them "internal reactions." It is within this domain that our *self* exists, and within which arise the majority of our personal problems and distress. It is also here that a matter of personal identification can proliferate into such an unwieldy mass that it becomes difficult to manage.

14:39   Imagine a snowball. It's just a small collection of snow at first, but then picture it rolling down a snowy slope, gathering layer after layer of snow as it goes until it reaches a size many times larger than the original snowball. Our self-identities follow a similar dynamic. In fact, one of the reasons this matter is so difficult to understand is that our self-identity has "snowballed" into something so large and complex that it is impossible to grasp with the intellect alone.

14:40   Personally identifying or attaching ourselves to any idea, trait, disposition, characteristic, or what have you, is the beginning — the formation of snow into a ball. It could be *any* handful of "snow" to begin with. Consider the openness and vulnerability of a young child's mind and it makes sense that our deepest core assumptions took hold because of something we experienced or were told very early in life. But throughout our lives this dynamic is occurring. All that's needed is a belief in some idea of what or who we are, or about our personal worth in the world. It doesn't have to be at all true—anything "believed" will do—the conceptual self will make it seem real.

14:41 As we absorb this new belief about ourselves, we begin to adopt new forms of behavior and thinking that relate *to* it and *from* it, giving it even more substance—the beginning of the snowball. What was at first seen as merely an aspect of our identity will come to be perceived as a "genuine" personal attribute. As we continue to defend and promote this attribute, we will also begin to create and then identify with the new behavior and thinking as well—a bigger snowball. These newest attributes will require their own defense and promotion, creating even more patterns of behavior and thought, adding more and more layers—a growing snowball.

14:42 Are you following this? On and on we go, amassing a huge and complex matrix of self and self-serving traits. Like a snowball, we add layer upon layer of qualities and traits, attributes and reactions. None of which, by the way, are actually us.

14:43 The sense of self is one thing; the activity that arises to serve and preserve this self is another. When we begin with something that's not real, everything that builds upon it will also be inauthentic. If the first patterns or traits were never actually true, or at least not the real-self, then reactions to them cannot be called real either. Such traits create themselves through an endless conceptual process of identifying and protecting—in other words, assuming things about ourselves (or anything else, for that matter) and then defending these beliefs. This cycle generates more and more characteristics and attributes, beliefs and assumptions, forming a unique and complex sense of self.

14:44   In the case of my "ugly" hand, for example, I may wear a glove all the time to hide the hand from ridicule. Soon I might be known as a strange guy who wears one glove. This will undoubtedly lead to behavior consistent in reaction to being seen as a strange guy. Perhaps I associate as little as possible with others because I don't want them to see me as strange or discover my embarrassing secret. This could easily lead to being seen as a "shy" guy, which of course, will tend to make me actually become shy.

14:45   Commensurate with this accumulation of characterizations, whenever "strange" or "shy" is attacked or even a matter of discussion, I will orient defensively around these attributes since they are now mine. Depending on the environment, I might adopt a "proud to be strange" attitude, or I might sulk about being shy. Now two more attributes join the fold of what I see as my self. I become both proud and a sulker. These in turn will be defended when attacked, and accepted when praised.

14:46   When dealing with others, and within my own thoughts and feelings, I will relate both to and from an "ugly-handed, strange, shy, proud, sulking guy." Whatever new behavior, reactions, or thinking might emerge to "manage" these attributes will also become identified over time as my self. On and on this will go. I will certainly begin to recognize patterns and traits that seem to be true of my particular self. A cycle is created and maintained as I defend concepts of myself that were themselves originally created to defend the self. And the "snowball effect" is under way. Fascinating, isn't it?

Your duty is to be; and not to be this or that.
—Ramana Maharshi

Assembling a Particular Self

14:47 Begin to discern within your own experience what you have come to know as your "self," or more accurately, as the "way that you are"—what you are like, qualities you attribute to yourself, emotional reactions that you frequent. Notice what you think is true of you—both negative and positive attributes. Consider the experience of yourself in light of our most recent discussion. Start to recognize the astonishing number of effects your "self" traits have on your experience of self, others, and life.

14:48 Since these concepts about self are accumulated over time, they are representations (or misrepresentations) of what *was,* not what *is.* They are largely a collection of memories, personal decisions, beliefs, assumptions, programming, and patterns of thought, emotion, and behavior. Added to this ever-increasing compilation are the many reactions and patterns of behavior and thought that arise to relate to and protect what's already been adopted. This complex accumulation congeals into the self-image and self-concept that you experience presently.

14:49 Constructing a self in this way sounds too big to miss, but it takes place every day, all day, in our every thought and gesture. It seems odd that so much could be involved in the simple self-sense we experience in this moment. It might be a bit like our experience of an object. We see the object and make a few distinctions about it and this seems rather simple and graspable. What we don't see are the billions of atoms and molecules whizzing around forming a complex web of activity that creates that object. Our rather busy but unconscious self-mind formulates what seem on the surface to be commonplace experiences.

14:50   Perhaps our taken-for-granted strategies of self-manipulation are most clearly visible in the emotional patterns that arise as we attempt to fulfill our many needs. Consider a child pouting because he fails to get his way. His original impulse might be desire, which is then thwarted by his mother. The child's reaction to his frustrated desire manifests as pain — a feeling of hurt. The hurt alone doesn't help fulfill his needs, so he generates a strategy of action. He makes his pain visible with an expression of pouting and thus more effectively manipulates his mother to give him what he wants.

14:51   We can see that his reaction of emotional pain and his expression of pouting arise in relationship to his thwarted desire, but we might not realize that both are secondary activities. The child may well *feel* hurt, but the emotion itself arises as a manipulation to get what he wants, as does the more obvious expression of pouting. This suggests that he is the author of his own pain, although it is not always a conscious choice. Unless our pouter creates an experience of emotional pain, it will be difficult for him to generate a convincing pout.

14:52   If successful, over time the child is likely to repeat this behavior whenever his desires are thwarted and eventually may adopt some form of automatic pouting — a skill that will become increasingly more subtle and sophisticated as he grows up. This rather familiar example of the manipulative process frequently adopted by children helps illustrate the possible origins of a particular characteristic. Whatever works has a chance of becoming a pattern, which will then be adopted as part of the identity. Once the boy identifies with being a pouter, or whatever he may call it (most likely he will graduate to thinking of himself as a "victim," or as frequently treated unfairly, or as a sensitive person misunderstood) he will in turn develop more traits and attributes to serve and defend his "miserable" disposition. As you can see, the potential for spin-off characteristics is enormous, and this is just one of countless facets of his personality.

14:53   In simple terms, once we think we are some way, this thought will become confused with ourselves, and so must be preserved. Some behavior or reaction will arise to provide this service, and this in turn will become a characteristic of ourselves, and so on. The first thing is served by a second thing, which becomes thought of as self and so must be served by a third thing, which needs to be justified by a fourth thing, and so on. This is the snowball effect.

14:54   So it appears that the self exists in accumulated layers, and maybe the solution to our inauthenticity is to strip away the layers and get down to the core. This won't actually work, however, since at the core there was no real self to begin with. The layering began as a "mistake" and continued that way.

14:55   I remember an image I saw as a child watching *The Little Rascals*. One child is given an artichoke. Having never seen one before, he assumes the edible part must lie inside, so he begins to pull off the leaves looking for the real vegetable. When he gets to the center he is left with nothing, and is rather mystified about where the artichoke went. For us, however, layering into our core is a very valuable experience for getting to know what it is we've called "self" all these years, and to understand on what all these attachments and personal reactions are based. It's difficult to free ourselves from what binds us without becoming conscious of the bindings.

*Things are entirely what they appear to be and behind them
... there is nothing.*
—Sartre

The Way You Are in Particular

14:56   Recall *The Never-Ending Story of Me* from Chapter Twelve and that you are constantly telling yourself a "story" about yourself and your life. What is this story? Exactly what are all of the characteristics and levels that compose the story of "you"? In a minute I'm going to ask you to contemplate this. I would like you to take some time and actually contemplate what it's like to be you, to live and think and feel as you do. Not just the story you tell yourself on the surface, but all that you "live" that is true of you.

14:57   To make this more interesting and to help keep you on track I'd like you to imagine that you are getting this experience across to an "unformed entity," a blank slate of open possibility, one who knows nothing of what it's like to exist in the world like you do. Pretend that this "entity" is available to become you and take over that job, so you can be freed of the burden of having to be you. By forming a sort of "Vulcan mind meld" all you have to do is experience yourself, and they will experience it also. But you need to become fully conscious of everything that is true of you, every facet exactly the way that it is for you, otherwise they can't get it and you would still be stuck with the burden of having to carry on the way that you are.

14:58   Contemplate to be conscious of the one you are being in particular, not what it is to be human in general, or even what it is simply to "be," but what it is like to be *you*. Do it in such a way that this unformed entity can experience what you experience, so that they could actually be you if they decided to take the job. This means that it's very personal, intimate, honest, and true. You can't give them the way that it's not or alter it in any way, since then they would not experience self and life as you do. If you only tell them the story you tell yourself to make yourself look better in your own eyes, for example, then what they would be is that story, not you or the way it really is for you. Honesty is a factor. Your job is to recognize fully and acknowledge the entire scope and reality of you as an individual, positive and negative, to consciously come to grips with the way you are simply because it is the truth.

> **Self-Contemplation Exercise**
>
> Now, contemplate what it's like to be you, as if "open possibility" were applying for the job. (Do that first; then when you've done that, come back to the book.)

14:59   OK, take a look at what you came up with. Did you get it all? Could you admit and fully experience the truth of you regardless whether you like it or not, or whether it fit all of your ideals? Did you experience the multilayered nature of your internal workings? Did you become conscious of everything that you are up to in being a self? Did you include but get beyond the internal chatter that frames up so much? Did you experience yourself being exactly the way that you always be, in all the ways that you be that way? If not, try the contemplation again, and be as ruthlessly honest as you can be.

> **Mirror Exercise**
>
> Now go and look in a mirror. Look into your own eyes, and with that look recognize anything and everything else you didn't notice in your contemplation. Simply recognize the entire truth of the individual self that you are.

14:60 There not only seems to be a lot of stuff there, but it also seems quite consistent and firmly bound together, doesn't it? Day after day you can do this contemplation, and although you might discover new depths unnoticed before, the "you" that you contemplate will still be the same one, and the way that you are is likely to remain rather familiar. On and on you go, "being" you, persisting as you, acting the way you do. Why would you do this? What drives you to create and cling to *this* self in *this* way? It's a deep universal human drive. For now, we'll call it "The Self Principle," which is the title of our next chapter.

CHAPTER FIFTEEN

The Self Principle

All about You

15:1   When you get rock-bottom honest, you can probably admit that the most important thing in the universe is your self. You may love others and cherish your ideals and principles, but how could these sentiments exist without you to create them? When you get down to it, your self is the only real thing you have. It certainly seems to be the only means you have to experience love, or to realize your ideals. Self appears to be the very core of your existence.

15:2   Culturally, we believe that awareness comes from the self, and that self is where perceptions are received. We're pretty certain that each self is unique and essential for our existence, and yet to acknowledge the primary importance of our own self is considered impolite. Being "self-centered" is held as a negative activity, but where else would you be centered? Go ahead and drop your manners and really delve into your experience. Admit it. "Yes, as a matter of fact, the universe *does* revolve around me." Your self is the central aspect of existence. It is *you*, and that is the only totally indispensable item there is. Even if all is lost, you still have your self.

15:3   This brings us to what could be called self's operating principle: You *must* continue to exist. If "do unto others" is the Golden Rule, then the Platinum Rule is this: "Survive!" A deep and powerful part of you abhors danger, and you don't want to die. The unparalleled strength of this primal force is pressing you to persist. Even if you just hold your breath for awhile, you begin to feel an increasingly urgent desire to breathe. Confronted by a serious physical threat, notice the emergence of extremely strong feelings and reactions, which will remain to color your awareness long after the threat is past. Chances are, you yourself have some memory of reacting to the possibility of mortal danger. Get in touch with the deep driving force that motivates your will to survive.

15:4   Every living thing has this drive to survive, although it manifests in different ways. Imagine an amoeba — a single-celled organism. It has little perceptive ability, but if poked it has some faculty that moves it away from the poke. Why? So it can move away from possible danger. Does it matter that what it perceives is not a clear representation of what's happening? No, not at all. What matters is that it moves away from something that could harm it.

15:5   So now imagine more perceptive faculties being created. The cells divide and some organism evolves over a few million years until it has an ability to see or hear. Now the creature can move away *before* something pokes it. This advanced ability to avoid danger — and also locate food — will increase its evolutionary chances. Does it matter whether the things it sees or hears in its environment are represented as they really are? Not at all. What matters is that the perception somehow compels the creature to act in a manner consistent with self-survival.

15:6 Recall the exercise from Chapter Four (4:37) when you worked to perceive an object without knowing what it was. As you began to sense the object — a book, a table, a tree, the cat — more simply and directly, and then allowed yourself to not-know what it was, you may have noticed something about the nature of your knowing: what you previously perceived or "knew" about the object was *how it related to you.* Inherent in your perception was all sorts of subtle information about the object's meaning, name, use, function, level of threat, whether you liked it or not, and so on. And that was the purpose of the perception — to "position" you in relation to the object.

15:7 Any organism has only its perception to allow it to survive — to find food, to avoid danger, to know when to piss and whether it's pissing, etc. Humans have several sophisticated forms of perception, on top of which we have some even more sophisticated means of interpretation. We know what something is, and we know what to do with it. This knowing, however, is not what we think it is.

15:8 We take it for granted that we perceive the unvarnished truth of any matter, when in reality we have no practical use for the truth. Our perceptions are remarkable, but they don't reflect the truth to us — they evolved to serve a more specific purpose. They're there so we will be compelled to act in a manner consistent with our survival. It's no accident that we like food and sex so much — we're programmed with the need and the means to sustain our bodies and procreate. In fact, perception exists solely for the purpose of survival. I'm saying that all our perceptive faculties and all our interpretations about what we perceive are just an advanced form of whatever allows the amoeba to move away from a poke.

A hen is only an egg's way of making another egg.
—Samuel Butler

Meaning Steers the Self

15:9   In our daily experience, probably the most palpable evidence of our drive to self-persist can be found in the "meaning" we perceive in everything. Our survival-needs demand that the world we perceive be divided into positive and negative, and so every object, person, circumstance, or idea will automatically include a charge of some kind. Of course, we make many other distinctions as well, but one of the first assessments we make is whether something is threatening or benign. After that, it's about determining the specific risk or value the thing has to our particular self, and what we should do about it.

15:10   Our desire to "know" in this way is not a matter of human curiosity, but rather it stems from our need to evaluate everything in terms of its relationship to us. This concern arises so incessantly from our survival drive that if it weren't so automatic it would probably be overwhelming. Whatever we perceive—internally, like thoughts and feelings, or objectively, like objects and actions— this drive fluidly relates each perception to ourselves and quickly provides us with an array of sophisticated meaning and its appropriate charge.

15:11   With our need to survive as a physical self, it's obvious that continually making these flash-judgments can come in very handy for quickly positioning ourselves in relation to whatever comes up. Consider: we hold that the value or threat of any object, person, or circumstance is somehow inherent in its existence, and that we merely "discover" the meaning it has. Once we make this assessment, we're either predisposed toward the thing, or biased against it — one or the other or both. Nothing in our experience is neutral, since anything truly neutral fades away as insignificant. Everything we perceive has some "value-charge" added to it before it is even cognized.

15:12   It makes sense that our drive to discover meaning is a result of our need to survive. Meaning allows us to identify and avoid danger, discern what's valuable, and fulfill our needs — but clearly that's only part of the story. We don't just *discover* meaning. Meaning is *created* specifically for the purpose of our survival. Meaning exists for us because we are in the act of surviving.

15:13   At the risk of oversimplifying, being a self is like living within a machine that sprays your particular blue paint everywhere you look. Of course you know the world is blue — that's the way things are. It doesn't even occur to you to question this. When nothing you see is not-blue, how could you possibly notice the way your own activity colors your every perception? The self that you're surviving generates every interpretation, meaning, and charge that you experience. It does not merely perceive what is there.

15:14   Even if we suspect that it is we ourselves who assign meaning to everything, we prefer not to scrutinize or even acknowledge this fact. It lessens the power of our certainty and interferes with the notion of reality as an absolute. We like to experience reality as a *fact* that exists independent of us. In order to powerfully direct our survival activities, our feelings and other reactions must have the weight of truth, and yet need not be true at all. Besides, the possibility that the meaning we assign to reality is in any way *coming from* us is just too much responsibility.

With great freedom comes great responsibility.

15:15   Recall an instance of spotting a gorgeous woman — a perception that's likely to evoke some meaning and "charge" for anyone. If you're a heterosexual male, then one set of meanings and feelings will arise. If you're a heterosexual female, it's likely that the perception will prompt a very different reaction and charge. How something is perceived is a function of the self doing the perceiving.

15:16   Supplying the meaning to everything encountered is an automatic operation that occurs in the same moment as our perception. A great deal of information is contained within each moment of "meaningful" perception, but the distinctions we make aren't just random conceptual add-ons that we decide to tag onto everything.

15:17   Adding meaning is not a choice; it's a *drive.* All this is just what we do, it is survival *occurring.* As a self, we don't experience our place at the helm of this creating, we only experience being driven by it. We are not conscious that we are generating meaning or charge. It seems as if the resulting emotions and other reactions we experience just rise up out of somewhere hidden within us. That we invest these reactions with an almost sacred validity is survival at work. The "feeling charge" that we experience serves solely to direct the self to adopt an appropriate relationship to whatever is perceived. It's a beautifully efficient mechanism for survival, but it cannot provide an experience of what's simply true or real in itself. Meaning exists to serve the needs of the self.

Whatever the self describes describes the self.
—Jacob Boehme

Two Domains of Survival: Physical and Conceptual

15:18   Of course when we first hear the word *survival* it's likely to evoke images of someone in the forest digging around for grubs just to stay alive. Extreme life or death situations will not often be an immediate concern for most of us, but the same power behind our will to survive still drives everything we do and experience.

15:19   Even at the hectic pace of modern life, handling our physical needs is rather straightforward. Basic acts like breathing are certainly essential for being alive, but we do it regularly and usually without a thought. Having learned what to do from family and culture, we are able to handle the simple tasks of life and "make it through the day." Effort is applied to brushing our teeth, dressing our bodies, eating, walking, communicating, and working. These things we do as part of our survival, but we do them quite naturally. Certainly, whenever our physical needs are challenged — the house burns down or we become ill — these issues move to the very forefront of our attention and efforts, but our course of action is still usually obvious.

15:20   Caring for our intellectual and emotional needs, however, requires a great leap in complexity and intricacy. In fact, the vast majority of our survival concerns are conceptual — even many that appear at first glance to be physical. When we think of such objective aspects as where we live, what we wear, and what we eat, we might hold them as matters of physical survival. Procuring basic food, clothing, and shelter for ourselves is quite straightforward, and if it were just a matter of physical survival, our work would end as soon as these needs were fulfilled in any way. But we're conceptual creatures, so it's inevitable that we add a great many extras to even the simplest physical acts.

15:21 We have associations from our past and hopes and worries about the future, and all the meaning and values that we've inherited from our family and culture. As we consider the issue of shelter, or any other issue for that matter, all manner of "good" and "bad" connotations are interacting with each other, garnering varying degrees of reaction and attention from our conscious minds.

15:22 Whether we live in a shack or a mansion is very significant for us and is a source of strong emotions like embarrassment or pride. In addition to assessing the status of our shelter, we worry about how to pay the rent or mortgage. We compute finances in relation to our budget and plan our future by calculating our likely prospects. We work on creating possibilities for improving whatever we've got. We're apt to fantasize, complain, cajole, make resolutions and promises. We get excited, angry, hopeful, anxious, indignant, embarrassed, triumphant, defensive, and much more. All of this is conceptual.

15:23 So much mental exertion accompanies our management of physical needs that we can easily mistake all of our scheming and dramatics for meaningful action. In other words, we often think that making up excuses, expressing emotional reactions, creating intricate plans, or developing a rationale are the same thing as *taking action*. They are not, and most often just get in the way or even displace the action.

15:24   To pick up a pencil, one picks it up. Deliberating about picking it up, imagining picking it up, worrying about picking it up, vowing to pick it up — none of these mental activities are picking up the pencil. They do not in any way get the pencil up. We can (and when it comes to pencils, usually do) pick things up without any conceptual fuss. A physical act requires only intent and action. In fact, such a bare minimum of conceptual activity is needed to pick up a pencil that we frequently do it "without thinking," which suggests that action can be taken with the merest background intention. The only additional requirement is to do so. Just making this distinction helps us begin to strip away extraneous conceptualizing and free up a great deal of the energy and time that we usually apply to handling life activities.

Just Do It.
—Nike

15:25   Since the human experience is so thoroughly dominated by concept, it's only natural that survival for us includes survival in the conceptual domain. While the ability to think is obviously useful for tending to physical matters, our conceptual concerns also oblige us to address a vast tier of further activities — both conceptual and not — based on what we think and feel about life, about others, and ourselves. On a daily basis, we might engage in interacting with family members, arguing with a coworker, encouraging a friend, reading the paper, complimenting a charmer, picking up the kids, enjoying a hobby, buying a gift for a lover, or any number of acts that make up the business of taking care of ourselves and those close to us. These actions aren't what we commonly think of as "survival," but they're all part of the same basic endeavor — they manage our daily self-subsistence. What we often miss is that many of these activities contribute to our survival on a social level.

Social Survival

15:26 As with just about every aspect of self, the issue of our survival has many layers to it. As "social animals" it's clear that our social concerns take up the greatest portion of our energy, especially with all the machinations that frequently accompany our interactions with other people. Even so, the domain of what I'm calling "social survival" is much broader than you might suppose. It is probably the largest and most continuously attended domain of self-survival.

15:27 You should understand that I'm not talking about the way we behave at parties or how popular we might be, although of course those are included. What I'm calling our "social" experience is active even when there's no one for miles around. The mere existence of another person — whether in front of us or only in our minds — creates an entire world, one that cannot exist without the possibility of interacting with another. Think about it.

15:28 The act of comparing yourself to others, the idea of being a good or bad person can only occur in relation to others. The existence of social interplay generates realms such as judgment, communication, emotion, manipulation, sexuality, empathy, and argument. Without "other," we wouldn't have notions like value, self-worth, individuality, beauty, deceit, honesty, agreement, and accountability; nor would we experience reactions like hurt feelings, intimidation, pride, love, embarrassment, loneliness, hate, and shame. Social survival is the source of language, family, religion, politics, the media, community, culture, entertainment, education, fashion, status, employment, government, subcultures, music, law, and on and on. All of these activities exist solely because the social domain exists. Imagine what it would be like without any of those domains of experience. Our social survival is the source of every concern of self-image, self-consciousness, and self-esteem, and these issues don't pause for us, ever. In fact, most of our thoughts and feelings are socially oriented, since they arise and exist in relationship to other people.

Even when we are quite alone, how often do we think with pleasure or pain of what others think of us.
—Charles Darwin

15:29 We are social, and the majority of our self-identity is designed in relation to the social domain. It's difficult to grasp this because we live so thoroughly ensconced within our identity that it seems merely an aspect of reality. The fact is that our self-identity *exists* because of the social domain. Our overall experience of life is determined in reference to others and the community we inhabit. Even in the life of a hermit, most conceptual "survival" activities are devoted to self-in-relationship. In fact, without others, he could not even be "a hermit." It is very important for us to maintain, promote, and protect ourselves in relation to everyone we encounter, or even imagine. This whole domain is central to our lives, and yet we are rarely able to comprehend the enormity of its effect on our experience.

15:30 The impact of social survival becomes a more grounded idea for us when we examine our emotional reactivity. What and how we feel determines the quality of our lives and motivates our behavior.

Emotional reactions continually arise in relation to how others view and relate to us, or we to them. We can be devastated by another's comment, or exhilarated by their attention. We may suffer a moody depression when feeling inferior to our peers, or delight in witty conversation with our friends. A large part of our efforts in communication and interaction revolve around our emotional states, with our more intimate relationships typically revealing the greatest range and depth of our feelings. We are continually spurred on by how we feel, and our actions are most frequently taken to lead our experience away from negative emotions and toward more positive ones.

15:31 Of course, it can't be as simple as that, since it's obvious that we often fail to avoid negative emotions and sometimes even evoke them or take action that brings them about. Why on earth would we do that? Because there is an even bigger concern than whether or not we feel good.

15:32 The primary concern of your self-survival drive isn't to increase your happiness or status in the world. More important even than that is to "be" in the world. This impulse will include "social" aspects as you promote the continued existence of the person you identify as yourself—your character and personal identity. It is imperative that you survive, and doing so requires a consistent recognizable "you"—the one you've always been. You might like to become all that you imagine you can be, or even make a change to your way of seeing things. Yet whatever you do, you will do it within the boundaries of who you already are in the world.

15:33 "Who we are" in a conventional sense is full of image, history, status, values, character traits, and self-worth. We are largely made up of concerns such as what people think of us, what we want them to think or fear they may think of us, what we think of ourselves, and what we present as ourselves to others. We seem to come by all of these things quite naturally, but upon reflection we can trace much of it to choices we made and struggles we've survived throughout childhood and beyond. These emotional characteristics, behavioral patterns, self-images, personal beliefs, and every other attribute identified as one's self need to persist in order to ensure the survival of that particular self.

15:34   The survival drive protects our conceptual self with the same tenacity that it applies to our bodily persistence. A threat to our identity is a threat to *self*. Since our survival in the conceptual world is largely at stake in our interactions — in other words, "socially" — the way that we think of ourselves and "position" ourselves in relation to other people is seen as very important. Even when there is no one around to challenge our identity, our continuous sense of self-in-relation-to-other remains a nearly inescapable aspect of self-survival.

15:35   Remember the snowball effect? Social survival is the main reason that the snowball dynamic occurs the way it does. The more self attributes we're attached to and the more traits we identify with, the more we have that needs to be protected and managed as "self." This means that every facet of our self-image, every characteristic pattern of our behavior, every emotional nuance that comprises our self-concept and emotional self becomes something to defend, express, and promote — in other words, "be" as a verb.

The ablest man I ever met was the man you think you are.
—FDR

To Be Frank

15:36 Protecting our social status is a primary motive for misrepresentation. We find that what we present and express influences the kinds of reactions we receive. Since we have many social needs, and we want people to have a good image of us, this becomes an almost irresistible trap. We begin altering our expressions, painting a picture of "who we are" that diverges slightly from what's actually true in our experience. This is a misrepresentation. Once we get used to going down that road, it begins to become automatic. By the time most of us are adults, so much of this has taken place and the real and the false have become so blurred that most people honestly believe things about themselves that aren't true. These affectations were only adopted so that we and others would view us in a particular light, but repetition has created a real pattern of misrepresentation. Such patterns then turn into character traits, and become believed as real even by oneself. This is one way a false-self begins to be perceived as real.

15:37 When a false-self determines our expressions, these will not only be inaccurate representations of what's there, they will be purposeful misrepresentations. The consequence of such distortion and misrepresentation provides the bulk of the negative self-concepts, feelings, and experiences that we currently endure.

15:38 For example, say Frank believes himself to be a worthless and uninteresting human being — that these are buried core beliefs to which he has become attached. Finding this condition threatening to his social survival — getting his needs met such as human contact, interaction, partnership, sex, love, company, having a viable self-image, business success, and whatnot — he feels pressed to adopt a different presentation of himself. He pretends to be interesting and valuable.

15:39   Having expressed himself in this way for a long time, he has developed a sophisticated personal "act," and by now thoroughly believes these are character traits of himself. He doesn't understand why he also feels somehow inauthentic and empty. Although he's persuaded even himself that he's interesting, he is still nagged by some unclear sense of self-doubt. He maintains a low-level fear and stress over the notion that he may not actually be interesting, but is unconscious of the foundation for this sense. So he chalks it all up to "life."

15:40   His conversations will always come from the same core that created this misrepresentation in the first place, and his reactions to others will be dominated by this core. When he encounters someone he sees as being a phony, he has a strong reaction and pushes such people away from him. He assumes it's simply because they are being false and so aren't worth relating to, but really it's because it touches a nerve in himself. When he confronts someone interesting, he feels jealous and threatened, but doesn't know why and is careful to couch these reactions in acceptable behavior.

15:41   He might feel good when he seems to have convinced someone that he is worthwhile and interesting, but this will also feel like a shallow accomplishment because of his core beliefs. Regardless how well they work out, these deep feeling-reactions will always be there because he is purposefully misrepresenting himself—he is lying but doesn't consciously realize it. He can in fact have no genuine conversation, nor any genuine sense of himself. But he won't know it, and will pursue this course of action with vigor, since it feels necessary for his very survival.

15:42   This is an extremely simplistic example, but realistic. And of course we're not talking about *you* in any way, are we? But perhaps someone you know? When you discover the myriad of assumptions, beliefs, and misrepresentations you've adopted, many things will become clear about your experience of life that previously eluded you. Unfortunately, as it stands, we've added so many complications and convolutions to life as to make its navigation hazardous and losing our way likely.

The act of persisting as a self is the same act as creating a self.

Surviving as a Self

15:43   We devote our energies and intelligence to whatever we believe to be ourselves. We promote, defend, protect, serve, maintain, advance, care for, and preserve this self. We are genetically and culturally programmed to do whatever it takes to ensure that our selves persist, that we survive any and all ordeals that life metes out. This same motivation permeates every facet of our experience, from escaping mortal danger to a trivial conversation with a friend.

15:44   This impelling force doesn't just relate to some factual or objective self; it is applied to anything that we identify as the self—the entire "snowball" of characteristics that we know as self. We find this self-preservation impulse in everything we do, think, and feel, since we are constantly compelled to maintain our self-identity. When we set out to have a direct experience of "being" through contemplation, we place ourselves in opposition to this relentless drive for self-continuity.

15:45   In the Cheng Hsin consciousness work, we use the word "survive" in an unusual way. When I say *"surviving a self"* I don't mean outlasting or persisting in spite of, as in "I survived an earthquake," but there's no word I know that can do the job as well. The words *maintain* or *persist* are simply not accurate enough since they don't convey the force, magnitude, and complexity of the drive that we're talking about.

15:46   Although to *maintain* something means keeping it in existence, which is what we do with a self, the word suggests both puttering and working on something that already exists. Looking into the matter, we find that self is continually creating as well as maintaining itself, so "surviving a self" is the peculiar phrase I use to indicate the entirety of conceptual survival—the *activity* of generating, sustaining, protecting, promoting, and persisting as a self.

15:47   So "self survival," as I speak of it, should have a sense of someone busy *being* like a verb—like the hamster on his wheel, very active, but not going anywhere. When we are *surviving* a self, we're creating it, living within it, and creating *from* it. We're shaping the world around us in our perceptions, just as we are defining ourselves not only by our reactions in the world but through whatever we identify and cling to as the self. Imagine that *self* is like a "magic dust" that gets on anything we see and reforms it so it becomes part of us, or at least relates to us.

15:48   The way we create and live as a self is quite functional and appropriate for our survival. It's not all that hard; billions of people do it daily. The essential impulse is to "exist," and to exist we need to be something in particular. The drive might be basic and simple, but *surviving* a self is an extremely complex activity, generating the world we perceive as well as the self that we are. The whole process is so all-consuming and so essential to human nature that we are hard-pressed even to recognize it. This is what I want you to find in your own experience.

CHAPTER SIXTEEN
Survival Is Not Being

Three Distinctions in Consciousness

Had we but world enough and time ...
—Andrew Marvell

16:1   At this point, it wouldn't be a bad idea to go back and reread from the first page of the book. I'm not suggesting that you do so right now. It's just that any of the assertions where you've "gotten a hit" in your own experience — a gut-level insight on what's being pointed to — have likely slipped away. What you're left with by now is a concept about that experience.

16:2   Getting another hit on such an insight, you'll find the "trueness" of it still there. You will again need to not-know, and open up to an understanding that is immediate — more experience than idea. It's challenging to truly experience any of these assertions occurring *in one's own case*. And once you manage to recognize something unfolding within your immediate experience, it is further challenging to hang onto this insight. Revisiting past breakthroughs is a way to reassert within your experience the real nature of what is being said, shifting it once again from abstract concept to what's really true. Each time you do this it deepens your level of consciousness in the matter.

16:3   What I want you to get right now is that everything we've been addressing so far isn't just *about* survival, it *is* survival. Your present experience, your very thoughts and feelings, everything you know and how you know it, your actions and expressions, your entire awareness — it's *all* self-survival.

16:4   Recognizing the nature of survival as it occurs in our own experience is difficult because survival *is* our whole experience. Being an ambitious book, our goal lies far beyond even that recognition. What we want is not only to become conscious of self-survival, but to create the possibility of becoming conscious *beyond* it, of getting free of self — to experience transcending it entirely. Many people find that they are unable to do so, and yet will tell you that a lifetime of trying is a worthwhile and deeply satisfying pursuit.

A man may fulfill the object of his existence
by asking a question he cannot answer,
and attempting a task he cannot achieve.
—Oliver Wendell Holmes

16:5   A shift in language can often help us navigate past our intellectual comprehension, so from time to time, I will present material from classic texts of the Cheng Hsin ontology work. The language of these segments may sound a bit different, or may simply reiterate something we've gone over, but don't let this distract you from reading in a mindful and open way. If something is repeated, it bears repeating. Let the implications of what you're reading strike you without having to fully know why. Allow the communication to have a cascading effect in your awareness. Let your consciousness reach into the matter even though it remains somehow beyond reach. Toward that end, adopt a state of mind that is committed only to the truth — beyond what is intellectually or conventionally knowable.

16:6 Let's begin with an overview of what we're going to be talking about here. I'll break it down into three distinctions that are more easily grasped by the intellect, but try not to cling too much to any definitions. Our language is ill-equipped to discuss these matters, so make an effort to recognize what these terms are pointing to rather than getting stuck in merely trying to intellectualize them.

These distinctions are:

- "For-me"

- "For-itself"

- "As-itself"

16:7 Perceiving everything "for-me" is the easiest to recognize. We've been talking about various aspects of this survival dynamic for most of the book, and by now you probably have some awareness of how everything you perceive in this moment is "for-me." "For-itself" and "as-itself" become much more challenging, as these only occur through a shift in consciousness. The first involves overriding the very purpose of perception and interpretation — self-survival — and the second pretty much transcends the human condition altogether. Remember, don't just try to figure out what's being said here. This work must take place in your own experience, and all I or anyone can do is point the way. Let's look at each of these distinctions a bit more closely.

16:8   For-Me:

Surviving a self is the activity of interpreting everything we encounter so that we know what it means "for-me." Although it is not so hard to grasp this dynamic, the enormity of its significance continues to slip away, in part because it doesn't mean anything useful "for-me." Whatever motivates us comes from an intent or impulse that arises from "me." Whatever we do, the action is taken for "me." One might ask, "How could my impulses come from any other place but me, and who else would I take action for?" This is a reasonable question. Clearly, all our actions, reactions, beliefs, thoughts, feelings, and perceptions seem to come *from* and exist *for* one's self. That is their purpose: to serve whatever is identified as one's self. We've covered this extensively already but must continue to strive for a deeper experiential understanding of this dynamic.

16:9   For-Itself:

Since everything we perceive is interpreted within the context of self-survival, nothing is known for itself. It is only known as its relationship to us. To know something for-itself takes a concerted effort, consciously overriding our automatic perceptive processes. Achieving this is just as hard as it sounds, especially if what we want to know for-itself is the self. Remember, even a tree is only a "tree" to the perceiver. Unless I achieve some sort of shift in consciousness, the interpretation of what "tree" is and means for-me will always completely eclipse whatever is there for-itself. This is perfectly appropriate in relation to our survival perceptions, so why would we care to do otherwise? Well, mostly we don't — it depends on whether we want to "survive" or to experience the truth. We'll go more deeply into "for-itself" in the next section.

16:10   As-Itself:

"For-me" and "for-itself" both take place in the domain of perception. By contrast, "as-itself" is a direct consciousness that defies rational understanding.

16:11   Let's begin by looking at "is" versus "surviving:"

> When something "is" it merely is. It is itself in this moment. It occupies the place of itself. When something survives, it is seen as "having survived" or having persisted as itself. It is only as a memory of the past that this persistence arises, and it can only arise in concert with the future possibility of the nonpersistence of that something.

16:12   Survival occurs as a process in time, the process of surviving. This process can only be identified or known from having persisted for at least a moment — as a memory of a past moment of persistence. The concept of something identified as "you" persisting is what is known as the self surviving. When you say "I am" or "I am surviving," you are making a statement that you remember "existing" — the process of identifying with something that is assessed as still occurring. This is all based on the past (even if it is only a moment ago); otherwise what could be identified as "you" or as persistence? The idea of you existing in the future is based solely on the memory of you persisting in the past and extrapolating that out. This provides a "self" experience, not a consciousness of the true nature of this moment. When something "is" it merely is. To become conscious of something as-itself is direct and immediate and takes place outside the realm of perception.

16:13   So what you have now is an idea about three kinds of experience. Of these three distinctions in consciousness, two take place in the perceptual realm, and so are conceivable, while the third is beyond perception, and so remains incomprehensible. You're not designed to easily understand the real nature of these distinctions. The names I've assigned to them may not seem so disparate, but the difference between knowing something for-me, knowing it for-itself, and being conscious of something as-itself could be called infinite.

16:14 Since you're still here reading, you have some interest in getting beyond an experience of mere survival. It hasn't been easy. You have likely had to let go of some cherished fantasies regarding self, spirituality, and enlightenment. If your understanding is not just intellectual and you're getting this on an experiential level, you were probably challenged by the assertion in Chapter Fourteen — that the real self you wanted to find doesn't exist. But you're still here reading. Why? Perhaps you are indeed seeking out the truth.

16:15 For someone setting out to experience the nature of being and reality, the powerful forces of self-survival are blindingly prohibitive. But such characters are rare in any culture, and for most of us, seeking out the truth is no more than a passing interest, or an entertaining debate with some friends. Attention and commitment to such things are usually temporary and minor. For some, they are nonexistent. The very nature of where we need to look precludes the participation of many people, since this kind of inquiry is not conducive to fantasy, and mere fleeting interest yields little understanding. Those who make the effort and find their way to a new depth of consciousness should be prepared to remain alone with even the most mind-altering breakthroughs, since without a lot of work no one is likely to comprehend what you're trying to convey. "When something is, it is *as-itself*." Imagine the looks you'd get if you shared that bit of insight at a family gathering.

What Is "For-Itself"?

16:16 If everything is assessed by us in terms of its value and meaning, then what use do we have for something known only for itself? Without any significance attached, what good does it do us to have such a perception? None. "Is the thing dangerous? Is it useful?" We don't know. "Then let's move on." Our tendency is to overlook what is unknown or is without meaning and value. The only reason we would even attempt to perceive something for-itself is as an exercise, or through placing value on "knowing the truth of things as they are," or any such reason that would make our efforts seem worthwhile. Otherwise, we would never consider trying to perceive anything for-itself — including ourselves.

16:17 Knowing something for-itself without any secondary considerations — such as use, value, meaning, how we feel about it, what we believe about it, or any other "application" — is essential for openly experiencing what's there. To experience self for-itself, what we actually "are" must be experienced in its pure form, directly, as it is, regardless of what we believe, think, or feel about it, and free of any other conceptual activity that we could possibly pile on. This places real self in what appears to be a rather useless, meaningless, valueless category. Being the object of much sincere spiritual seeking, the "real self" or "true self" is assumed to be of ultimate value. If it is indeed actually meaningless, we can see how easily it could go unnoticed.

16:18 Perceiving something for-itself requires eliminating everything in our perceptive-experience that is there "for-me"—all judgment, charge, reaction, preference, use, value, name, and so on. This leaves us with a very immediate perception that something is there, but it is without meaning. We are not relating its presence to the self; instead, it is seen as how it relates to itself. Experiencing things for-themselves is not easy, but it is possible. In such a case, a tree then becomes "that thing" which isn't named "a tree" but is a presence that is experienced as there for-itself. When you get down to the most honest perception of the thing-itself (without *any* of the automatic self-references mentioned above) this is an experience of something "for-itself."

> *Not metaphor*
> *Not standing for*
> *Not sign.*
> —Minor White

16:19 It may be easier to think of perceiving a tree for-itself since it has fewer qualities than a person, and we also have fewer judgments about a tree. But have you ever had occasion to suspend judging a person that you normally judge automatically? I mean to suspend all judgments, good and bad, and therefore the emotional reactions and dispositions that go with them? If you have, you probably noticed that, although the person in front of you hasn't changed, your perception of them has—dramatically.

16:20 You may still see them pretty much looking like they do, but you no longer perceive those qualities and implications that previously filled your experience of them. You no longer see them as good or bad. You don't see what you like or dislike, what you find attractive or threatening, what you approve of or are repulsed by. You no longer see them in the light of your assessments and standards, your judgments and reactions, or what they mean to you. You don't even see what they mean to themselves or what they think of themselves, since they likely don't see themselves for themselves either. You see, to a much greater degree, the "being" that is over there. You see them for-themselves. This significantly alters what you perceive as there, and so the way that you'll interact.

16:21   If you've never done such a thing, the next time you encounter someone you clearly judge—a hero, an asshole, a sniveling coward, a brave and noble person, a slimy con artist, an out-of-touch intellectual, a beauty, a stupid person, a kind and loving soul—suspend every judgment that you have. This may take a few minutes ... OK, probably longer, since you will need to uncover judgments so subtle or taken-for-granted that you overlook them. Once you've managed to eliminate all the judgments you harbor, take a fresh look at the person and see what you perceive.

16:22   Now repeat this whole exercise with the judgments you have about yourself. In fact, consider this a standing invitation to question all your perceptions of self and other.

He who knows much about others may be learned,
but he who understands himself is more intelligent.
He who controls others may be powerful,
but he who has mastered himself is mightier still.
—Lao-tzu

16:23 Because our perceptions work out for the most part and appear consistent and familiar, we imagine that this means they're accurate and that they truly represent what's there. This may indicate some sort of commensurate relationship between our perceptions and reality, but it does not mean that they are one and the same.

16:24 What do you suppose an amoeba envisions as the reality behind being poked? Its "perception" or "interpretation" would probably be extremely simplistic next to our own, but it will be self consistent and make up his perceived reality—it will be exactly what is "known" as reality to this creature. We're told that a fly sees many versions of each object. Of course we know there's only one bottle of soda present, despite the fly's perception of many, but we have to notice how skillfully he manages to taste our drink and evade capture. The fly's perception may be very different from ours, but it works out just as well (and sometimes better). It seems that an accurate reflection of what's true is not necessary for perception to be effective or consistent. How something is related to "for-me" is the only criteria whether or not a perception seems to work. What's there for-itself is actually irrelevant.

16:25 When we experience anything for-itself, we step outside of the automatic self-referential perceptions that are designed strictly for our own survival. This interruption undermines the very capable programming of the survival process, so our minds will always try to resist as a matter of self-preservation. But we're not actually "endangered" by the interruption—we won't forget "who" our self is, or walk our body off a cliff—it simply allows us the freedom to see things for themselves.

Beyond Happiness and Suffering: Perceiving Something For-Itself

16:26   All this talk of perceiving things for themselves without some survival drive overwhelming our perceptions seems mighty abstract.
What is it good for? When we put the book down, who cares?
What's going to occupy our energies and attention then? The same
things that always do. We'll live life trying to get what we want
and achieve our goals. Seeing things for-themselves is just an exercise that will fade away soon enough. Even if we can make this
distinction, how does it influence our lives? It seems merely an
intellectual diversion.

16:27   Our very inability to grasp such distinctions in real terms *is* self-
survival at work. It all seems so unintelligible and useless when
it comes down to real life. When we tire of philosophic entertainment we will get back to business as usual. Our goals and perceptions will remain aligned to the self principle. In general, we'll
continue wanting to be happy and struggling not to suffer. We
might even say that being happy is the most important attainment for us, and suffering our most unwanted condition. They
may be. But what is happiness? What is suffering?

16:28   In order to grasp the truth of anything, whatever is so must be
tackled on its own terms. No matter what our concerns are in the
matter, they can't be allowed to interfere with an open discovery
of what's true — even if the truth turns out to be contradictory
to our needs or beliefs. Still, this work seems so aggravatingly
irrelevant to what's important in our daily lives. But what if we
learn that grasping the distinction of what-is for-itself can tell us

something very significant about both our happiness and our suffering? This should get our attention, shouldn't it?

Getting what you want and avoiding what you don't want is not happiness. It's self-survival.

16:29   Nothing seems to mean more to us than our happiness, but we may once again be confusing one thing for another. Culturally, we share a belief that obtaining what we desire will make us happy. Yet when all is said and done, does it? Obtaining what we desire may indeed temporarily alleviate some fear, tension, or struggle related to our self-concerns. It may even bring the rush of pleasure that accompanies success. None of these is happiness. Contrary to our common assumption, the pleasant emotion associated with accomplishing a goal or avoiding a threat is not an experience of happiness, it is an experience of victory or relief. Perhaps a bit of giddiness or satisfaction arises when we successfully manage some aspect of self-survival, but this is not happiness — and is always only temporary. The next survival issue is sure to arise in due course. Since survival is about persistence, issues will persist.

16:30   Although it may seem like it, happiness never was the goal of our efforts. Self-persistence is our goal. This is an important distinction. Although everyone says in earnest that he or she wants to be happy, this statement really means: "I want to have what I want, and to not have what I don't want." For most of us these seem like the same goal, so what's the problem? The thing is that wanting and not wanting are really a statement of self-survival, not happiness. There is a reason this dynamic goes unnoticed for what it is.

16:31   As a metaphor we could say we are like a mouse running inside its wheel. What keeps us moving is the allure of some tasty cheese — the myth of obtainable "survival-happiness" — just outside the wheel. The "cheese" is only there to get us to run; it is not there for us to obtain. Unfortunately for us, we don't know that. Since we don't seem to be closing the gap, we run all the harder chasing this cheese — the promise of happiness. If we didn't believe we were entitled to the cheese, or we knew we couldn't ever get the cheese, we'd stop running. But our wheel and our running and what we perceive as our particular needs are a large part of what makes us "this particular one." In the overall scheme of surviving as a self, it's imperative that we remain ignorant of what's true and what's only an illusion. If we were to grasp this dynamic for what it is, this self we've become confused with might cease to persist.

16:32   Although we tend to think that attaining all positives and avoiding all negatives would make us happy, this is not actually the purpose of wanting and not wanting. Notice our desire to be happy is not the desire to be happy with whatever happens to be the case, or to be happy whether we get what we want or not, or to be happy regardless of how life turns out. Being happy is confused with being successful, or being comfortable, or having life turn out as desired, or being free from pain and suffering. Believe it or not, all of these last examples are self-survival orientations. They are not the impulse to be happy.

16:33   It's hard for us to recognize the difference between happiness and the sensations associated with successful self-survival. We're hard-wired so that the activities of self-survival take precedence on every level, especially an emotional one. Consider the word *emotion*. Its root word is the Middle English *emove*, which means "to move or incite to action." The emotional promise of happiness keeps us moving on our wheel.

16:34   When we confuse obtaining survival goals — getting what we want, fulfilling needs, winning some battle, protecting ourselves from danger — with being happy, we also assume that realizing these goals is the only way to be happy. This is a false assumption. Using "happiness" as a survival goal puts it out of our reach — it becomes the unobtainable "cheese" that motivates us forward in life. We are stuck moving from one obtainment to another, from one struggle to the next, sometimes feeling good about it and sometimes feeling bad, yet never actually and only being happy with whatever is taking place. The promise of the cheese drives us to persist as the one that we are or want to be, but it doesn't provide a sense of inner freedom or happiness where we stand.

Self-survival is the cause of all suffering.

16:35   As much as we desire happiness, we abhor suffering. Suffering seems to be the antithesis of being happy, and yet they are both based on the same dynamic. As much as we run toward the cheese of happiness, we run away from the pain of suffering. They both keep the wheel spinning in the same direction. It is easy to see suffering as unwanted; it's not so easy to see that it exists solely as a mechanism of self-survival.

16:36   If there were no self, and so no drive to survive, then there would be no suffering. There would be no manipulation, no struggle, no dissatisfaction, no desire, no misrepresentation, no self esteem, no hurt feelings, no worry, etc. There would be no pain, but even if some activity existed fulfilling the role of pain, it would be of little consequence and not a form of suffering. Self-survival is the origin of suffering. Strange as this may sound, "being" and life can take place without a self or the need to survive. It isn't likely, but it is possible.

16:37 Since being without a self is inconceivable and very hard to realize, such freedom remains unknown to virtually everyone. Yet without a self designed for and committed to survival, there is no suffering. To get a handle on this, recall any form of suffering, any distress, worry, upset, fear, misery, stress, longing, or anything else that you suffer, and consider long and hard: if you didn't care about *you* persisting in any way, if it didn't matter to you if you existed or not, got your way or not, or that things turned out in a way consistent with your desires and needs, if you let go of attachment to your self and the survival of your self, would you suffer any of these things? The answer is *no*. You cannot suffer when there is no self trying to survive. You cannot suffer when you have no drive to persist. The desire to survive, to persist as the self that you are, is the cause of suffering.

16:38 Of course, the self can be very convoluted and intricate, involving attachments to any number of things — emotions, perceptions, ideas, memories, character traits, objects, senses, and so on — even objects and concepts outside the jurisdiction of the individual self. But the principle is the same, whatever self "is" or is attached to will engender the persistence and protection of that thing, and the self will also suffer the struggles, and so the fear and pain, that accompany this survival disposition. Freedom from self and self-attachments ends the suffering involved in persisting as a self. No self, no suffering.

16:39 But we needn't reach an absolute state of complete "no self" to reduce suffering. Any movement in the direction of understanding this dynamic will serve to mitigate our suffering. Notice that "no self = no suffering" translates to "no aspect of self = no suffering that aspect." We can see that "being" doesn't mean one has to persist as this *particular* self being this *particular* way. If in the next moment the self is no longer that way, but some other way, then that self didn't survive, but *being* still remains. Letting go of the self-impetus can apply to anything you identify with or are attached to, from the smallest and most insignificant belief or reaction to your life and death.

16:40 Consider: if you were to suddenly let go of one of your beliefs, if you had no motivation to maintain this belief (have it survive), then it wouldn't matter at all to you if it were right or wrong, remained or vanished, would it? You would no longer suffer any of the struggles that formerly accompanied your attachment to the belief — defending it, promoting it, or fearing its loss. This is also true of every emotion, thought, self-image, possession, perception, idea, or anything else you consider you or yours. If "being" is inherently free of any attachments, then it really doesn't matter if any aspect of a self persists or if the entire self fails to survive altogether.

16:41 We assume that if we aren't in immediate pain, if we aren't suffering, we should be happy, but in reality this just isn't so. We may chalk it up to our inherent "human condition," assuming that somehow pain and suffering accompany us just because we exist. In the case of self-survival, this is true. Ultimate happiness seems to elude us no matter how hard we try, and various forms of suffering seem to find us no matter where we hide. Perhaps it is time to seriously reconsider our assumptions in this matter. The assertion here is that both the rarity of happiness and the presence of suffering are based on self-survival.

16:42   Still, we have little interest in challenging what is perhaps the most fundamental presumption upon which we live—our selves. In order to embrace such a practice, we would need to be convinced on an experiential level that the source of our unhappiness is somehow tied to the force of maintaining ourselves. We would have to feel for ourselves that in the very impulse of our struggle to survive, we produce unhappiness. In this way we would be far more inclined to welcome a practice of letting go of the self, and open to becoming conscious of whatever is true about being.

16:43   Strange as it may sound, experiencing things "for-themselves" opens a door to happiness and at the same time reduces or eliminates suffering. This is so because the relentless drive of self-survival is undermined, and this moment of life is accepted for what it is, rather than being eclipsed by references to our self-needs and fears. Pain and relief cease to be the focus of our attention.

16:44   *Consciousness* and *being* are not limited to the way that you currently experience self. But this isn't something that should be taken only on faith; it is something that can be recognized and directly experienced for oneself. You can even go beyond your perceptions to experience what is true as-itself.

A man has no ears for that to which experience
has given him no access.
—Nietzsche

For-Itself versus As-Itself

16:45   So far in this chapter, we have contrasted the domain of self-survival with being able to experience something *for-itself.* We've seen that the survival process necessarily presses our perceptions and experience into a form that relates everything we're aware of to ourselves. Perceiving something for-itself rather than for-me interrupts this otherwise ceaseless activity and opens our minds to further possibilities in consciousness.

16:46   Our main objective in this book is to know self *as*-itself, to experience what being actually is. In other words, whatever is true of self and being, we must become conscious of the "thing-itself," and this must be gotten directly as it is. This experience is literally "inconceivable," and so we start to get some grasp on the distinction by using for-itself as our jumping-off point. But remember, direct consciousness of anything cannot be found in a representation, model, reflection, thought, or image. Nor can it be found in the perception of something for-itself. The truth or reality-itself must be gotten directly "as-itself."

16:47   When we perceive something for-itself we're much closer to grasping its unaltered presence, but it's still a perception, and therefore it's still indirect. When we make a distinction between the awareness of something for-itself and the consciousness of something as-itself, we see that getting something as-itself does not occur in the domain of perception. "As-itself" is the thing. It can't be perceived, since perception by nature is not the thing perceived. Perception is a method, a vehicle, through which to glean practical but indirect information about something. The thing-itself can only be gotten through direct consciousness. With this consideration, we have gone beyond what is immediately intelligible, or even thinkable or imaginable. Yet, pondering what's being said and where it points, we may begin to recognize how the term "as-itself" refers to the true nature of something.

16:48 Unfortunately, the operating principle that founds our entire experience, mind, and understanding is the persistence of the self. Our experience of our whole existence is based on this principle. An awareness that's dominated by self-survival is inconsistent with the consciousness of being-as-itself. Unless we can deeply grasp this, how can we do justice to our attempt to become conscious of Being?

16:49 Taken all together, our perceptive faculties do not amount to consciousness. Beyond what we can perceive physically or mentally, perhaps we sense that there may be a possibility of becoming conscious of what something actually is, what "being" is, without really understanding what that means. Whatever Being actually is as itself cannot be discerned through our perception or mind, if for no other reason than our perception — our experience, our awareness — was never designed for that purpose. Its purpose is survival. Let's continue to consider the way that survival separates our consciousness from the true nature of reality.

Experiencing the Truth Is
Not the Purpose of Self-Survival

16:50 The purpose of self-survival is to maintain and promote the self; therefore all of our perceptions and experience, our thoughts and feelings, our actions, reactions, and interactions are directed toward this effort. Everything that we experience is designed to serve the self that we are. We've covered this. But there is something overlooked here that has a great impact on our efforts to experience the true nature of being.

16:51 We live within the assumption that our sense perceptions endow us with direct information about reality. On the surface this seems reasonable, but as we're beginning to see, the nature of reality isn't graspable on the surface. The true nature of anything must be what-it-is as-it-is, completely and absolutely. It can't be gleaned by bouncing some sensory-perceptive radar off the surface of an encounter and then interpreting what it all means. Yet this is precisely how our perceptions function. They provide only indirect feedback about reality, and no feedback at all about the true nature of reality.

16:52 No matter how many times we hear it, it is still hard to grasp that our perception of what's there is really different from what is there. If we think of our perceptions as various forms of radar, we may better understand this disconnect. A blip on a radar screen represents an object, providing very limited and indirect information about that object. When it comes to radar, it's clear to us that we aren't seeing an airplane and that the blip in no way tells us what the object looks like, or any other information but location. We're merely bouncing radar signals off of some object and seeing the effect this has on our screen. We can grasp the indirect nature of this process because we know that the airplane is so vastly different from the small blip of light we see. It is the same with every perception we have. It is only because our perceptions are so familiar, and the only ones we've got, that they seem to "be" reality.

16:53   An eyeball doesn't actually see the object it perceives. Since the eye functions by picking up light patterns, what the eye sees is only the light that bounces off the object. So we're not seeing the object but the light. We are not even seeing the light that is accepted by the object but what the object itself repels. Since the light hits the eyeball and stimulates nerves that we receive as a pattern that we interpret, we aren't actually seeing the light either. Furthermore, we can only pick up the data that sight as an indirect perceptive process can supply—we don't hear the object, we can't feel weight or texture or temperature, or view inside the object, and so on. Try to get that right now as you see and feel this book.

16:54   We aren't aware of any aspect of the book that can't be represented through these senses. Any aspect of the object that can't be carried within a medium of perception cannot be known via perception. What's most significant about all this, however, no matter what can or can't be carried through some perception, is that we are never directly experiencing anything. We are interpreting the perception of stimulated nerve patterns. This activity is *not* the object. We have no direct contact with or perception of the object itself. This is true for each and every one of our perceptive senses. So, we aren't ever perceiving the thing itself. We never grasp the real nature of the object.

16:55   This is true of hearing, smelling, tasting, feeling, even thinking. Perhaps we grasp that our perceptions of the objective world are indirect, but still take for granted that our thinking and emoting are direct since they are within us. What we perceive within our own minds isn't any more of a direct connection to the true nature of reality than is our perception of an object.

16:56   The content of our imagination and memory has been formed through the "re-creation" of sensory perceptions. Internal dialogue is a conceptual mimic of the sound of our own voice. Our thought patterns and distinctions are based on our particular language and our relationship to a perceived reality. We've already seen many times that concepts are never the thing-itself, and our emotions are manipulations, not feedback about reality. There are other reasons that our thinking, our emotions, and our very awareness are all perceptively indirect, but these will unfold in later chapters. What we need to get now is that we cannot recognize the truth through our perceptions.

16:57   Don't fall into the trap of thinking that what we can't perceive beyond our perceptions would be perceivable with some other organ yet to be invented, or that what is missed is simply more of the same. These examples simply point out the limitations of perception, yet if we could perceive infinite amounts of information, it wouldn't solve our problem. We would still be left with an infinitely indirect experience. What's true is that our consciousness is disconnected from the true nature of reality. The fact that perception is indirect means there is no amount or method of perception that can bridge this gap.

16:58   Even though it is provable in many ways that we don't perceive what is actually there, this means little to us since we live in a world of practicality, not fact. If, however, we dwell on the observation that our perceptions are indirect and set out to experience reality firsthand, it does give us an opening since in our minds we have a harder time writing off the notion that we don't directly experience reality. Still, such a notion will fall to the wayside soon enough, because it seems to have no practical application.

16:59   Whatever we currently perceive is good enough for us — it gets the job done, right? But that's the point. Exactly what job does it get done? If we look into what our likely knee-jerk responses would be to the idea that we don't really experience the truth via perception — "It's good enough, it gets the job done, and who cares?" — we can see that every one of these rebuttals is the product of a mind that's functioning in the domain of self-survival. Are you beginning to recognize what's going on here?

16:60   The implications of this point are very difficult to get, so it bears repeating. Pay attention to the overlooked obvious: our entire field of awareness has been molded around the purpose of self-persistence. Why do we have perception at all? To survive. For what other reason would a creature create any form of perception? Since the beginning, the purpose of *any* perceptive ability has been to serve survival. The truth isn't just secondary; it's unknown and irrelevant to the self, so nothing within our experience or mind is designed to know the truth. We've observed that we don't experience our own true nature, nor that of anything else. This is why. It is also why we cannot find such an experience within our mind or perceptive efforts. It is not possible to use perception to become conscious of the true nature of something.

16:61   Do you really get this? The truth cannot be ascertained through our perceptions or experience. This leaves us in quite a predicament, doesn't it? There is nowhere to look, since everywhere we look is a reflection of this principle. Our perceptions are not up to the task because they weren't ever intended for that purpose. We are perfectly cut off from any direct perception of reality and the true nature of existence. Unless there is another doorway, we're up the creek without a paddle.

16:62 The good news is that there is another possibility. The bad news is that it's not just uncommon and unfamiliar, it's also maddeningly elusive and completely irrational. It lies outside the realm of our conventions and our logic, our cultural assumptions and our willful abilities. Therefore, even when it is talked about, it isn't easy to understand, and when packaged for popular consumption, it is likely to be missed altogether. That's why I'm going to such lengths to lead us to it, setting the stage as best I can for really understanding the relationship between what's going on that we *call* reality, and the possibility of encountering reality directly. We will begin working to realize this possibility later when we address Contemplation and the Nature of Being. Right now we are focusing our attention on the nature of our current experience.

16:63 It requires a great deal of contemplation and immersion into the nature of being and self to recognize the self-principle operating in everything we think, do, and are. Eventually this can reveal the all-encompassing nature of self-survival, as we find that it isn't something simply "behind" or "within" us, it *is* us — as well as our experience of *everything*. Getting free of it, even for only a moment, is as difficult as it is earth-shaking. And yet simply through challenging the human condition in this way, we are on the brink of uncovering what is real but unknown. Even though it seems absurd, the truth of the matter is that if we continue to do this work, at some point we are likely to suddenly become directly conscious of the true nature of being and reality.

Holding up a staff, Shuzan said:
If you call it a staff, you oppose its reality.
If you do not call it a staff, you ignore the fact.
Now what shall you call it?

For-Itself versus As-Itself—
an Ontological Overview

If something is repeated, it bears repeating. Let the implications of what you're reading strike you without having to fully know why. Allow the communication to have a cascading effect in your awareness. Let your consciousness reach into the matter even though it remains somehow beyond reach. Toward that end, adopt a state of mind that is committed only to the truth— beyond what is intellectually or conventionally knowable.

A Thing Is a Thing

16:64   As has already been laid out, I'm defining *Being* as "what-is." Yet not what-is from any point of view, or represented in some fashion. Being is "what-is as itself." But what do we mean when we say "what-is as itself?" Well, certainly that it is no other. It is not there as something it's not.

16:65   At first in our movement toward being, we find that a thing must be a thing, and a thought must be a thought. Once again, what is meant by "a thing must be a thing"? Certainly the thing is already the thing, or at least we assume this to be so. But since we have to admit that we can only assume this to be so, where is it that we are talking about "the thing as a thing"? In our encounter of it. So if our encounter of some thing reveals it or shows it in any way *other* than the-thing-that-it-is-as-itself, then we are indeed not encountering what is being there. In this case it is true that, in our experience, the thing is *not* the thing.

16:66   Completing this first step may put us into a new position with things. Suddenly, an object is merely and only an object. It is not a thought about it, or its usefulness, or our reaction to it. A desire is only desire. It is a conceptual creation that doesn't imply something or mean anything. It is not motivation, and it is not an object. A person is a person and is not our judgment of them. A judgment is an interpretation and not the thing being judged. And so on.

We Don't Know What These Things Are

16:67   The next step that occurs as soon as the first step is taken—and one that most people turn back from immediately, since, coming from survival, it is naturally seen as wrong and/or stupid, and maybe threatening—is that we don't know what these things are. From this observation, it becomes difficult to say where a thing then becomes itself. In our pursuit, this is not a problem or a mistake. It is the next step.

16:68   We practice moving our awareness to the most honest observation of what-is for-itself, and stand facing and looking into not knowing what it is as-itself. As we step toward this unknown—which doesn't look like a step since there is nothing to step on and so nowhere to put your foot down—something may appear more clearly as itself, and then that is what we will experience. No matter what we experience, we remain open by staying in touch with the presence that it is still not known. This practice also applies to ourselves, which may not appear as anything, or may appear as a conviction or a sense or a reference, but mostly as unknown.

Surviving Isn't Being

16:69   When something "is" it merely is; it is as-itself in this moment. When our experience of being is directed by survival, it is directed toward something that *isn't*— something that doesn't presently exist. Being requires no activity or process or purpose to be. Since being already *is,* any activity, process, or purpose that arises is directed toward what is *not.* The pursuit of survival is a continuously active process whose purpose is directed toward the persistence of something that appears to be, rather than toward an experience of reality in this moment. Whenever a process or experience is focused on surviving, it is not turning toward what "is." Therefore, the target for survival must necessarily be something that *can* persist.

Being does not persist. It "is-es."

16:70   Survival demands a constant attempt at fulfillment, and this fulfillment can only take place in the future, and must always and only take place in the future. Recall the metaphor of running on our "wheel" after the happiness-cheese; we must believe it is obtainable. But it cannot take place now. If it did, it would only and completely *be,* and then survival or persistence would no longer be an activity. We can see then that a sense of unfulfillment must accompany and perhaps be necessary for this survival.

16:71   In order to have something that can be and is singled out for persistence persist, another dimension must take place. This is one in which activity and process and experience can all be directed for this purpose. There must be a method in which to accomplish this survival, and the survival of this particular thing. In other words, process, ergo experience, cannot be allowed to arise randomly. It must be directed to serve the persistence of the thing. We've seen that this is the dimension called interpretation. But we still need another dimension to get the job done.

16:72 With the domain of interpretation established, we now have a method in which to channel experience and process so that it will be nonrandom and can be directed toward the job of persistence. However, we still don't have the force or activity that compels these processes toward the objectives that are required for survival. This force is created in the field of "charge" or value, the field of emotional orientation. It is the field of meaning, of good and bad, comfort and discomfort. It is not the mere interpretation of something. It is a reaction to it, a charged field that presses activity, thinking, cognition, emotion, etc. into a particular process.

The experience you are having right now is that.

16:73 I want you to get this going on right now. See how you are in this moment sitting in a charged field, a sensation of value — that survival is the charge and sensation and experience in which you live. Survival shows up in everything, since everything appears as process and charged interpretation, and all this is directed toward maintaining or "surviving" the one you think you are. This perceptive experience and cognition is not in fact directed toward *experiencing* the one that is, and so cannot be an experience of "being." Perhaps it could be called an experience of surviving.

16:74 Your experience is overwhelmed by this nonrandom field of interpretation and emotional orientation. You can see it in your preferences — even in subtly wanting just a little more comfort as you sit. Important things are important because of interpretation and charge. Notice the important things demand strong activity, thinking, and feeling. What things are used for or what they mean or signify is where our attention falls quickly and easily. It is seen in the value or threat that every thing, person, or idea has for you, physically, emotionally, and socially. All of this is charged activity that presses you toward what isn't. Since survival or persistence is directed toward what isn't, it is not directed toward what *is*. It is not an experience of being.

What Does Persist?

16:75 Since being isn't something that can or does persist, it is not possible to pursue it as an objective of survival — nor is it necessary. For survival, we need something that *can* persist. We need something perceived that we can identify with — something to constitute a self. So, what can persist?

- Self-concepts and self-images.
- Personal opinions, convictions, beliefs.
- Memories, having a "life history."
- Convictions and assumptions about the "way that you are," or the "way things are," core beliefs about yourself and your sense of self-worth.
- The notion of objective reality — as if objects remain or persist.
- The memory of fixed "activities" through self-expression, like your personality and character — ways of thinking, emoting, reacting, etc.
- In other words, all that constitutes a self-identity.

16:76 Obviously these are not what is being as itself. Interpretation and emotional orientation are necessary for survival, but are not an experience of what-is-as-itself. Ironically, we claim to pursue survival for being, in order to "be," but self-survival is not being and never "be's."

16:77 A consideration: If something exists to serve a purpose, and you live within an interpretation that this purpose must be realized, and if in fact the purpose *cannot* be realized, then there is no experience of completion or freedom possible here. You will not survive. Even though every effort and struggle pursues that end, you will fail. The pursuit itself is always toward what isn't and what will never be. Think about it.

16:78 Being already *is*. In Being, nothing needs to be pursued or attained. Since our experience is dominated by what is basically an illusion, in order to realize what already "is" we need to free our experience from what isn't.

Besides learning to see,
there is another art to be learned — not to see what is not.
—Maria Mitchell

Entertaining the Possibility of Not Surviving

16:79 In order to be free of something we need to let it be itself — thus becoming fully conscious of what it is and isn't. How can we let survival be itself? In our experience, whenever we let something be for-itself and as-itself, it becomes unknown. This is the freedom of not-knowing. Within this not-knowing is an openness, or infinite possibility. Among other possibilities, what immediately arises is the possibility opposite to whatever our interpretation defines it to be "for-me." In the case of the survival of myself, that would be nonsurvival. So let's use this as a way to open up to the possibility of experiencing "being" by imagining not surviving as a self.

Guided Meditation: Letting Go of Self

Take a moment and contemplate each of the following until you achieve some sense of it:

- In your experience right now, consider and create the possibility of not persisting as anything in particular.

- Create the possibility of not having any of your beliefs or your opinions.

- Experience the possibility of not being the way that you are, or having any history, or relationships.

- Create the possibility of not being attached to any of your emotions, reactions, sensations, feelings, moods, or attitudes.

- Experience not having any self-concept, self-image, self-esteem, or sense of worth or purpose.

- Consider the possibility of not maintaining your sense of who you are, having a "life," or anything else that constitutes you and your experience of your self.

- Create the possibility and experience of not maintaining any of this, anything that you call you.

- In your experience right now create the possibility of not surviving, or of not surviving as anything in particular.

- Experience the possibility of not surviving as your "self."

16:80 This may create an opening so that what's left is a sense of simply being, even though it is still unknown. This is enough. It provides a real and grounded focus for further contemplation.

16:81 Without earnest investigation and study, as well as serious contemplation, we stand little chance of discovering what is actually "being" beyond the self. Freeing ourselves from self-survival to any degree will transform our lives. We simply need to keep moving in the direction of deepening our experience of this as both true and possible.

PART V
Penetrating Experience

CHAPTER SEVENTEEN
Recognizing Self-Survival in Your Own Experience

17:1 Your head is probably swimming from your encounter with Chapter Sixteen, which has a great deal of information directly relating to you and your entire experience of life. But this particular area of the human condition is virtually never addressed anywhere in our culture at any time. Even though what was said is true, it is nevertheless very difficult to understand, let alone experience. I suspect that it will slip easily from your grasp as soon as you return to the job of day-to-day living. It's just too difficult for the mind to retain once the immediate glimmer of understanding has faded.

17:2 To provide a more grounded way for you to comprehend self-survival, I want to shift the focus now to the results or "effects" of the survival principle as it manifests in your current awareness. Grasping how this dynamic operates in your life as you live it will help you begin using your daily experience to work your way back to the source of the principle. In this way, you can make a connection between your experience and what seems to be a very abstract principle, making it easier to recognize and study self-survival — and possibly to transcend it.

Getting from Here to There

17:3 To set out on a journey we need to know a few things. We need to know where we are, and we need to know where we're going, or at least decide on a direction in which to travel. Relative to our work here, where we are is in an experience of a self-surviving. Where we want to go is toward a greater consciousness of the nature of being — free from the influence of self-survival. Understanding the relationship between where we are and where we're going helps us move from one to the other.

17:4 We've read a lot about the major dynamics and forces that presently dominate our experience, so we have an idea of where we are, and since we've talked about "Being" we also have an idea of where we need to go. But for the most part these are probably still just ideas, and perhaps not very clear ones.

17:5 We assume that we're already experiencing where we are, while where we want to go must always remain a *concept* until we get there. This concept might be a memory or just a picture in our imagination. In either case, if we want to go there, this means we don't perceive being there now.

17:6 Before looking into being free of self-survival, we need to fully experience this force in action, dominating our mind and perceptions. But like a fish in water, it is hard for us to isolate and study the matter when everything we think, feel, and perceive is our self surviving. We need a contrast so that we can better appreciate this activity as it takes place, and more clearly see it at work in our everyday experiences. So how can we recognize this core operating principle in the day-to-day minutia that fill our lives? It's easy.

17:7 Recall the deepest sense of inner freedom that you've ever had—some time when you felt at peace and free from any stress, reactions, desires, fears, judgments, or any feeling that you must be some way or do something. Sit for a moment and produce a sense of emptiness, freedom, nonattachment, stillness, and a feeling of inner peace.

17:8 Now, compare this to your daily experience. Throughout your day, what in your experience isn't simply free and at rest? Usually a great deal—actually, it may well be all of it. This should reveal just how forcefully your self-concerns impose themselves on everything you do, think, and feel. Their effect can be subtle, but creating a sense of inner peace will provide a useful contrast with which to more clearly recognize your self-survival at work. In order to recognize self-survival dominating your experience, you simply have to notice that everything you encounter—even your own thoughts and imagination—has an effect on you.

What Is Being at Effect?

17:9 It isn't hard to notice that we're reactive creatures. If Jack calls me an idiot, I may feel hurt and could get angry. If a big spider jumps out of my shoe as I reach for it, I'm likely to be peeling myself off the ceiling. If my lover speaks to me in soothing tones late at night, I might become a puddle at her feet. Whatever we see, hear, think, feel, or in any way recognize, this perception affects us. The hammer hits my toe; I feel pain and yell. I see a beautiful flower, and I'm delighted. I hear fingernails on a blackboard, and I shudder inside. No matter what we perceive, it produces an "effect"—meaning it results in some sort of reaction or condition occurring in our internal state—and this is the work of self-survival.

17:10   The reactions mentioned above are easily seen as reactions, but when you study your moment-to-moment experience, you'll begin to notice many minor effects and even background effects. You will also notice that there is always some sort of mood or "disposition" going on; this too is an effect. Subtle or not, these effects always arrive in the form of a feeling-sense. Although many of your reactions may register just "below the radar," when there is clear evidence of an emotion, this feeling-sense isn't hard to find— it shows up *as* the emotion.

17:11   It may appear as if the circumstances "cause" your reactions, but this just isn't so. Your mind relates the perceived circumstance to the self, and pulls up the appropriate "effect" for the occasion. This process is so automatic and smooth that it seems as if the circumstance is causing the reaction, but with enough consciousness on the matter, you can recognize that the reaction is actually something you "do" rather than something that happens to you. It's the same dynamic as the pouting child in Chapter Fourteen—you're engaged in a game of manipulating self and others to have your needs met, simply on a more all-encompassing scale. It is the unconscious and reflexive nature of this activity that leaves you oblivious to your participation in the process. If you watch your reactions carefully, you can observe the mental actions you generate that produce these effects.

17:12   Within the context of self-survival, mind and perception work together, constantly generating what we call "experience"—all that we recognize within our awareness. While this appears simply as an observation of reality, what we are actually experiencing is the effect or result of this ongoing self-survival process occurring for us at what seems to be the speed of light. In relationship to each interpretation, a self-survival disposition will arise — some feeling activity will occur within your body-mind — this is what we're calling an *effect*.

17:13 But you needn't grasp all of that before noticing how everything perceived has some influence on you. As you become more and more sensitive to the activity of being affected by what you perceive, you begin to notice that effects aren't just evoked in relation to significant circumstances; they are occurring with every circumstance. Each and every perception you have, including everything you perceive occurring within your own mind, affects you. If you perceive it, you are at the effect of that perception.

17:14 In order to create an automatic yet sophisticated response mechanism, self-survival produces an experience, an awareness, that is like a magnetically charged field, constantly polarizing everything that enters this field. It is why we are attracted to or repulsed by anything. The charge and specific orientation to each encounter can be seen as a sort of polarized feeling-reaction. Whenever you are affected by anything (which is always), the effect is manifesting that "magnetically" charged field of self-survival. This is what effects *are*.

17:15 Notice that just in the act of looking at the color yellow some effect or feeling-reaction will occur. It may be hardly noticeable, but it's there. In contrast, looking at blue feels different, doesn't it? How about brown or orange? When you begin to notice that even the mere perception of a color has an affect, you are ready to notice the realm of subtle feeling-reactions that you have to everything perceived.

17:16 Any time we run into a circumstance that we find significant, it will evoke a significant feeling-reaction — love, disgust, anger, joy, delight, irritation, nausea, fear, or what have you. These clearly affect us, as do all of the little reactions or feeling states that occur that are not so clearly defined. It's as though our experience swims in a sea of effects, moved this way or that by the ceaseless sway of diverse currents that we may or may not notice.

17:17 An upsetting emotional reaction is easy to see because it demands so much of our attention, but even the most insignificant perception will produce some effect. Whenever the interpretation is that the matter or object needs little or no attention, the effect is overlooked since it is also seen as insignificant. The effect may occur beneath our notice, but it still occurs because it's necessary for us to determine what is significant and what is not so that we can relate accordingly. Of course, there are many other distinctions made beyond "relevant" or "irrelevant." Each perception we have is infused with these kinds of interpretations plus a whole lot more, and so effects are numerous and constant. This charged field of effects isn't elsewhere or rare. This is it — the experience you are having right now *is* a self surviving.

17:18 It isn't easy to grasp that human experience and human perception are always a function of self-survival. There is nothing outside of it in your perception or mind. This is why directly experiencing the true nature of Being is so uncommon. Entertaining the possibility of being free of effects only emphasizes how difficult it is to be free of them. This is not to suggest that you attempt to suppress your feeling sense. On the contrary, you simply need to notice what fuels it, what the purpose is behind it. If you want to create a realm of feeling that is free of the domination of self-survival, you must first get free of the domination of self-survival.

17:19   By becoming very conscious of this whole mess, and making a distinction between an effect-dominated experience and the possibility of an experience without effects, you begin to recognize in more concrete terms the activity of self-survival—and so, the possibility of freedom from it.

Becoming More Conscious of Effects

17:20   Now, take some time and watch your experience as you move through various circumstances. It makes no difference what you perceive; you will be affected by it. You could be sitting alone in a room. What is the effect? As you sit there, from moment to moment the effects will change because from moment to moment your thinking and perceptions will change. You could have a "theme" of effects, though, like a flow of feeling-reactions that are in the same general category—boredom, moodiness, anger, giddiness, etc. And this could shift to something different at any time depending on what comes into your mind or your sensory perceptions. How many subtle changes in your feeling-experience can you become aware of? How does it feel to be among those people, or in that place, or having these thoughts? With careful attention, you'll start to notice that your internal state exists in a condition of being constantly influenced by whatever fills your awareness—that you are in some way always affected by everything.

17:21   For a moment, stop reading this book and take a look at something around you; when you've done that, come back to the book. What changed in your experience when you did that? If you didn't notice any effect, look again and then look at something else, something clearly different from your first observation. Can you tell some difference in your experience when you look at one and then the other? Do you notice some change in how you feel, even if it's very subtle, or some change in what you think, or your mood or attitude?

17:22   At first, it may take some work to get this, since the effect of the thing is most often confused with the perception of the thing. When you realize that your "experience" of an object always includes a feeling-reaction that tells you what it means and how to relate to it, you can better recognize the effects that occur from simply viewing an object. Whatever shift occurs within your experience when looking at one object or another, this is the effect of that perception. What other effects do you notice? When you look at a chair, how are you drawn to relate to it, what do you "feel" like doing, or what feeling-sense arises in relation to the chair? How about a keyboard or a light switch, a tree or a cat? Notice there is a feeling sense accompanying the mere perception of these objects containing information that determines your relationship to them.

17:23   Try spending much of the day being attentive to everything that affects you, and what those effects actually are. Start with the most obvious, which are usually emotional reactions. For example, if someone says something to you and you get upset, notice this relationship, and call the upset an effect. If you find yourself feeling upset but don't know how it is you came to feel that way, trace it back and try to discover what perception "caused" this upset. Remember, the perception could be a thought, or something barely noticed. It could be an association with something past, or a combination of mental activities and situations. See if you can uncover exactly what it is you're relating to such that a particular effect arose in your experience.

17:24   Keep making these observations over and over. All fear, anger, upset, worry, joy, hurt, boredom, relief, greed, lust, anxiousness, and every other feeling should be clearly observed as effects. For every emotion or feeling of any kind you have throughout the day, become conscious that it is an effect of something perceived by you. Ask yourself what your self-mind is doing or trying to accomplish by generating this effect.

17:25   Once it becomes easy for you to be aware of obvious effects and their "causal" conditions, begin to search out more subtle effects. Effects that can't be called an emotion are still effects. There is always some sort of mood or "disposition" influencing your experience. This "mood" can be very subtle, but it exists as a theme or context for a certain domain of effects. As you become adept at noticing emotional effects, also notice all of the subtle effects even the sight of an object has on you — as you noticed when looking at various colors. Put some time into being aware that your entire experience is an endless stream of effects stimulated by the changing conditions of your surroundings and your mind. Become clear that your experience is at the effect of everything.

17:26   There is a reason for this. We've already touched on it with our look into self-survival and meaning. But this is not always immediately recognizable, and so it will take some more work to draw out. We need to grasp and fully appreciate the depth and scope, not to mention power, of our being at the effect of everything perceived. One way to accomplish this is to create in our experience a distinct perception that provides a vivid contrast to the influence that effects have upon our awareness.

Experiencing Something For-Itself

17:27　It is possible to learn to experience whatever is perceived *prior to* the addition of self-oriented interpretations. As was introduced in the last chapter, this occurs when we perceive whatever is there *for-itself* rather than how it relates to us. Recall trying to interpret something in what appears to be its most basic form — as simply *there*—without any judgments or reactions added to it. Of course, I'm sure it proved very challenging, but we've been moving in this direction all along, and such things take time and effort. Two exercises we did much earlier—trying to see an object while not-knowing what it is (Chapter Four), and trying to stop our thinking altogether (Chapter Six)—helped prepare us to better recognize the nature of mind and perceptions. Now we can ask the question: What is the relationship between experiencing something for-itself and being at effect?

17:28　Let's postulate that an experience of something for-itself is not an effect, it is an experience. Something experienced for-itself stops at itself. Since we aren't relating it to our selves, no self-oriented effects or reactions arise. If we are affected, then that effect is not an experience of the thing for itself, is it? Except for whatever we manage to experience for-itself, everything we experience is an effect. How often do we just experience anything for itself? Not often, since such an experience all by itself goes nowhere, means nothing, and does us no good. Survival dictates that we must know how everything relates to us so that we can relate to it appropriately. Simply being conscious of something for its own sake is meaningless.

17:29   Take care that you don't confuse a neutral or small effect for no effect. No effect has no charge whatsoever, no good or bad — and so no neutral (which is still in relationship to positive and negative) — and such an experience is hard to come by. The very act of becoming aware of something means it has been "preevaluated" as significant enough to register. Much enters our perceptive field that never gets that far in the mental process of recognition. Once something does get noticed, we enter a sophisticated and rapid application of specific values and threats. As we've seen, this is important information in the world of survival, but absolutely irrelevant to experiencing what's actually there.

17:30   If we see someone point a gun our way, we're likely to have an extreme emotional reaction. The gun has a lot of meaning for us, in this case danger. Yet the actual object that it *is* has none of that for itself. All of the things we associate and either like or fear about the gun are what it means to us. Seen for-itself and as-itself it is neither pretty, ugly, dangerous, powerful, threatening, bad, good, neat, repulsive, or any other attribute we might give it. It is simply an object. But who can see it that way?

17:31   Can you see a gun, a pencil, a book, or a dollar bill as simply objects? Try it. Can you perceive each as simply that object, without any reaction, preference, aversion, or judgment? Without name, history, use, value, or association? If you can, and the thing is simply seen as that thing, independent of its relationship to you, then you could say that you are perceiving what-it-is-for-itself.

17:32   This is a very simple interpretation. It is unadulterated, and will be devoid of any effects that arise in relation to our judgments or associations — which, once again, result from perceiving things in terms of their relationship to us and our survival. When our perception of the thing has no connotations of good or bad, no threat or value, it elicits no emotional charge or even subtle feelings of preference or aversion. It is simply a perception of something as it "is" in the most basic sense.

17:33 Having the perceptive ability to get things for-themselves allows you to create a contrast to your normal experience, which is dominated by the effects of survival. This ability is not easily achieved, but practice begins to reveal just how much influence "meaning" has on everything you experience. It's time for you to grasp first-hand that all such meaning is generated by the mind to serve a purpose. This is how the job of managing life gets done. Since meaning is generated, it is possible to *not* generate it. And without meaning, you would not produce any reactive effects.

Changing from Reaction to Experience

17:34 To get free of effects, you need to somehow disengage whatever it is that's generating these effects. Chances are you won't be able to free yourself from this powerful force without consciously and directly experiencing it for what it is. You can begin to move toward such freedom, however, by challenging your own reactive tendencies.

17:35 Challenging your reactions may be difficult in the same way that it's difficult not to eat when you feel hungry. There is a force pushing you to eat, so you need to deny this force any influence on your behavior. When dieting, the direction is clear: simply don't put food in your mouth. In the case of challenging your reactions, however, we aren't concentrating on the behavior resulting from a reaction; we are considering not having the reaction to begin with.

17:36 How can we "preempt" our reactions? Such a change amounts to a transformation in our experience and will not come about through adopting some simple technique or belief. We need to make a fundamental shift in how we hold reality, or all that we'll accomplish is a suppression of these effects rather than freedom from them. So we can't simply adopt an attitude of not reacting; we must change the core principle that has us perceive and react in this way to begin with. This isn't easy, since that principle is the *self*.

17:37 The self principle is the context for our entire experience. It operates on all the content of the mind, viewing all perceived content in terms of a self. As we've learned, the construction of the self is done primarily through creating and identifying with the activities of mind and perception. In particular, this construction occurs through our beliefs and assumptions that form the foundation and define the parameters of the self as we know it. Thoughts and actions are generated within the context of this now formulated self, and reactions occur to manage life events in relation to this self.

17:38 The foundation for our reactions can be eliminated by de-identifying with the self-mind, dismantling our beliefs, and exposing the core assumptions that dictate meaning. In this way it is possible to eliminate or at least change the effects and reactions we have by eliminating or changing the specifics involved in the foundations of the self. In Chapter Fifteen we saw Frank's fundamental beliefs binding him to unnecessary behavior and reactions. In that example, freeing himself from those beliefs would free him from all of those effects. Let's look at some other examples of this kind of possibility.

17:39   Imagine that you believe the world is inherently hostile and that you are basically ineffective at managing your life within it. What could be some results of this perspective? Aren't you likely to carry a constant sense of anxiety and a gloomy mood wherever you go? Wouldn't your sense of confidence be low and suspicions high? Along with this scenario we can imagine that you'd be prone to adopting pretense and underhanded manipulations as ways of getting through life. From this position you're unlikely to ever feel free to be yourself, or let down your guard, or feel authentic in your accomplishments — which would be few since you're likely not to attempt much or risk much. These effects would seem to be a part of your nature, even though they are actually created by your outlook.

17:40   On the other hand, what if you were to shift your perspective, letting go of your current self-view, to see the world as neither hostile nor benign, but whatever you make it? You would perceive that there is nothing inherently wrong with your ability to interact effectively, and that "learning as you go" is a shared phenomenon. We can see that your disposition and outlook would change remarkably, and that your abilities would be free to develop openly. You may not become the most successful or happy person on the planet, but now it isn't out of the question. Regardless of your successes, however, your life and relationships would be much more satisfying. Many of the effects you experience would change significantly.

17:41   Take care not to confuse such a shift for an exercise in positive thinking or a ritual of chanting affirmations. We're talking here about actually perceiving oneself differently, not pretending or even imagining that a thing is true. For this, you need to recognize your own hand in *whatever* is created as your self and your perspective, and realize that there are other possibilities. Consider that what drives you may be your outlook, but this exists for you as what you "are" and not just what you think, and so you must look more deeply than thought alone.

17:42   From such examples it becomes obvious that changing your perspective will change the effects you experience. Now, consider changing on a much deeper level—like transcending some of the most basic assumptions attached to being a self. For example, holding yourself as unique and as the most essential element in existence are likely two unchallenged assumptions you have. (Of course, no one would admit to seeing themselves that way; it's socially unacceptable, and our social survival demands we not admit such a thing too loudly. But we're not talking about what we admit but what we "live.") From such a position it's easy to see you're liable to maintain a reflexive impulse to protect even the pettiest aspects of yourself. As an act of self-persistence you'll tend to dismiss out of hand anything that seems to contradict your views. You will quite naturally be swept away in the struggle to fulfill your needs and realize your "right" to have whatever you want, to preserve and promote your ideas and opinions, and to fear your own dissolution or even transformation.

17:43   On the other hand, what could happen if you stopped assuming you're the unique and essential center of the universe? Once free of this assumption, it's possible you could see yourself as merely a creation, a convenience, a mechanism through which to express Being—completely unnecessary in and of itself. Transformation could well be the norm, and many patterns of effects are likely to be nonexistent, since you're not seriously attached to or identified with anything but "being." You could freely question any and all aspects of yourself since they're not actually necessary, nor are they "you." The truth is not feared since it is seen as already so with or without your self. Such a shift in core perspective would create very different results than the above viewpoint. For one thing, whole domains of effects would be instantly eliminated.

17:44   Of course, this could all be done in one stroke by simply letting go of the self completely. But that isn't likely. We have little desire to give up our selves altogether. Even if we have the desire to give up what's false or negative, we still want to exist. If we intend to persist, at least as a conscious physical entity, we need some form of survival perceptions. This will require that we make distinctions within our perceptions that determine what is safe and what is dangerous, what is useful and what is not. We already make these distinctions, so that isn't the hard part. What's hard is finding a way to experience "life" without our now automatic self-orientation.

17:45   Having access to an experience completely beyond all survival — in other words, a consciousness of Absolute Being — does provide a great deal of insight and freedom, creating an experience of "being" that is outside of self. Still, we don't want to be restricted to such a breakthrough, for it might not be forthcoming any time soon, and more importantly it might not do what we hope it will do. Independent of such conscious insight, we can still make significant changes in our experience of self and survival. It isn't necessary to have an enlightenment experience to realize that having an egoic-self is actually not required for human existence. And most of the effects we experience arise from the persistence of our egoic conceptual existence, and not our simple physical existence.

17:46 When we look at the source of the effects that have the greatest influence in our lives — those that are most dominant and problematic — we find these are generated by the existence of an "egoic" or conceptual self, and a relatively small portion relate to our physical self, and none relate to merely "being." If this is so, then we can see that the elimination of the egoic self would eliminate all of the effects that are generated by mind activities devoted to the survival of this self. Making a distinction between being an "unformed" conscious entity and persisting as a fixed conceptual self, we create the possibility of being alive while freeing ourselves from the most dominant and endarkening illusory aspects of self.

17:47 We can understand how all this works and still be unable to make much headway. Usually this is because our understanding is limited to an intellectual conclusion that does not find its way into the reality of our more primal experience. Whatever we take on, if it is to be permanent and real, it must be based on the truth. This means we need to better understand the true nature of ourselves and our experience. We've noted that the context in which we hold reality and self determines the effects and reactions we will have. It's clear then that if we profoundly change the context we will profoundly change the effects.

Changing Context Changes Effects

17:48 How would we go about making such a change? As I've suggested, we can't depend on experiencing the absolute nature of "being" as a catch-all solution. For even then, the force to identify with past patterns is still likely to be very strong. With or without such consciousness, we can start by tackling what is immediately available. Simply committing our experience and self to principles that are independent of self-survival can have a profound effect.

17:49 By now, we grasp that the personal transformation brought about through adhering to principles such as honesty, letting go of social survival, transcending value or meaning, dismantling cultural assumptions, being free of self-image, and de-identifying with the self-mind will produce very different domains of effects than do our conventional self-survival principles.

The Principle of Honesty

17:50 When I presented honesty as one of the cornerstone principles for discovery, it wasn't arbitrary. The very same reason it serves discovery so well also allows us to use it to dramatically change the effects we experience. This is because honesty doesn't serve the self; it serves the truth. This makes it independent of self-survival — that is, if we're honest about honesty. It wouldn't hurt to review what's said about honesty in Chapter Five before going on, since we're going to take a look at what might happen if we used this principle to govern our experience and mind.

17:51 Adopting honesty as an operating principle for our experience could evolve into a real personal transformation. Remember, the principle of honesty isn't about being a "good" person, it's not what we do as a social pretense or to develop an "honest person" character trait, nor is it just saying what you feel like saying. It goes much deeper than that. Honesty is being committed to what is true. Not to what you think is true, what you agree with, or how you may want things to turn out. Those are all self-oriented. True honesty is committed to the truth, independent of any concern for the self. A shift in one's governing principle to something that is free of a reflexive self-orientation will change the effects that arise.

17:52 For example, honesty as a context for one's self-image and expression would eliminate all of the effects that result from preserving something false. Since whatever is false about one's self is founded on misrepresentations, the main action needed here is to stop misrepresenting oneself. This will take more than simply telling the truth or trying to represent oneself honestly—even though both of these are very necessary.

17:53 We also need to dig out what within the taken-for-granted self is actually false, even though it may not seem that way at first. This can be tricky since anything false that has been absorbed into the makeup of the self is now held as a genuine aspect of this self. So it is not seen as a misrepresentation but as an expression. In order to get free of what has been mistakenly accrued, we must break the hold of such assumptions at their root. As a practice, honesty, along with contemplation, will eventually reveal these assumptions.

17:54 Once recognized and discarded, no more effects will arise from these assumptions or attachments. New effects and challenges may arise, but they will be in a completely different domain. For example, no longer would there be the requisite "hiding" or misrepresenting going on, even subtly, so the effects of doing so will also not arise. The fear and anxiety of being found out or discovered a fraud will disappear. Failing to get others or yourself to validate any role you've assumed would produce no effects because this whole activity wouldn't exist as an expression of yourself. Many other activities and reactions would cease to exist—embarrassment or defensiveness at being caught in a falsehood, the emptiness that accompanies the lack of a genuine self-expression, all the effects that arise from having to limit truly open communication, like loneliness, isolation, inauthenticity, and so on — simply by replacing your attachment to a false identity with the pursuit of an honest experience and expression.

17:55 As you try this out, be clear that your commitment must be to the actual truth and not to new forms of manipulation that can arise in the guise of being honest. Telling someone something hurtful could be an honest statement, but if it is done to hurt their feelings, it is not honesty; it is a manipulation to hurt their feelings. You need to be honest about such things. The commitment must be to get at the truth and to express the truth, especially to yourself. This means that not-knowing plays an active role because even though it may be true that some reactive impulse or thoughts come to mind, you will likely not know what these are really based on, or be clear as to the purpose they serve. This means you need to maintain a pretty constant contemplative attitude as you search deep within to expose what's really true. Since you probably will not be conscious of the whole truth all the time, this will be a direction in which to grow rather than a place upon which to stand. Do you see the important difference here? Such a commitment to honesty is ongoing, and you must be honest about it. Practice will increase your ability to catch yourself subtly using it as a manipulation.

17:56 As the commitment of "self" begins to shift significantly from an attachment to various forms of misrepresentation and clinging to superficial or inauthentic aspects of identity, to being more honest and unadulterated, all of the struggle and reactions caused by the former will disappear. Effects will still occur, given this is all we do, but these will be about whatever else is being maintained and not about the protection or perseverance of something false. In committing oneself to honesty, many new effects will emerge since any remaining self-serving attributes are likely to be challenged or come under siege when the course of honesty diverges from the course of self interest, as it will do. When this happens we will probably undergo many effects as the self writhes in the agony of self-denial. But these effects shall pass, and to the degree we have embraced honesty as essential to our nature, we will end up with a stronger, clearer, and more present sense of ourselves.

17:57   Telling the truth when you'd rather alter the facts slightly or withhold your experience altogether is likely to result in feeling vulnerable and exposed, or suffering the loss of a desired outcome. These can feel like strong unwanted effects, and yet they only exist in that you are still clinging to something other than honesty. They also will be of a different nature than the effects of remaining hidden or lying. Although with the latter it may appear at first that something desirable is obtained or consequences are avoided, other effects will occur, such as a sense of separation and inauthenticity, leading to a dulling of sensitivity. Telling the truth, on the other hand, although scary at times, promotes a sense of aliveness and connection, and empowers communication and consciousness. These effects are clearly different in nature from the alternative.

17:58   As you again work through Chapter Seven, "You Don't Have to Rehearse to Be Yourself," or Eight, "Unknown Origins," or Twelve, "Inventing Self and World," and others, they will contribute to deepening your work on honesty, providing directions in which to look and giving clues about things to watch out for. As you continue with upcoming chapters you'll find many opportunities to clarify and empower this very same effort. The point here is that any time you change the operating context for your thinking and behavior to another context, the reactions and experiences you have will change. Taking on a practice of honesty shifts your experience to one where many effects just don't show up, and those that do will be relating to something more real and transformative. Besides coming from honesty, there are other contextual shifts we can make that can be even more effective at eliminating effects.

Dropping Social Survival

17:59　We find a great deal of our survival efforts are given to the defense of a complex social identity. Building from the work we did in earlier chapters—like Chapter Fourteen, "Creating an Experience of Self," and Chapter Fifteen's section on "Social Survival"—we begin to grasp the convoluted nature of our social-self. For example, our possessiveness of friendships or intimate relationships can lead us into emotions such as jealousy and actions of control, intimidation, and manipulation. We are obsessed with how we look in others' eyes, and suffer anxiety and stress as we try to maintain our self-image. In our social world, we can be embarrassed when we look the fool, or angered when our social "will" is thwarted. We experience victory and defeat in so many subtle ways with every encounter. An endless chain of thoughts and emotions keeps us whirling on the roller-coaster ride we call social interaction.

17:60　We spend a lot of time and effort managing our social world. Our most common and significant reactions arise in our relationships. These reactions are based on our perceived social survival. What would it take to eliminate all of these effects? If we no longer had a self-image and weren't committed to the persistence or attainment of social status, all of the reactions we suffer as a result of those attachments would disappear. If we let go of the many games played in acting out social manipulations, imagine how much effort we would save, and how many reactions would not need to arise. Allowing ourselves to be open and honest and at the same time not taking ourselves so seriously might relieve us of much unnecessary turmoil. Relinquishing our attachment to this social person, or at least letting most of it go, relieves us of the many effects associated with this domain.

17:61 Of course, letting go of your social survival is no easier than being honest. It takes courage and self-reliance, standing on your own — not in spite of social conventions, but simply free of them. Allowing yourself to embrace others, communicate with others, and interact with others, without having any of this based on social games or the survival of your social-self, would generate a different domain of experience. A transcendent feat for sure, but imagine the truckloads of effects and reactions, energy and effort that would be lifted from your shoulders. If a little headway is made by shifting in this direction, your experience will noticeably change. Eliminate the whole realm of social survival, and a huge domain of effects must fall away. Beyond social issues we can also make dramatic changes in our experience by disengaging from the mechanisms necessary for survival reactions to occur.

Letting Go of Value

17:62 As you've learned, one very important ingredient necessary for any kind of survival interpretation is the context of value. The existence of value allows for the creation of positive and negative, good and bad, attraction and repulsion. It produces the domains of evaluation, meaning, and emotional charge. It gives rise to possibilities such as significance, importance, and worth. Can you imagine how many effects and reactions arise in relation to the context of value? Can you sense the depth of influence this domain has on every experience you have?

17:63 Without a framework of value dominating our perceptions and experiences, none of that could occur. It's not that it *wouldn't* occur; it *couldn't* occur. We need value in order for any of the above to exist. Without value we would have none of the effects that come from judgment, opinions, insult, desire, danger, and a huge number of other activities related to our survival. Relating everything to ourselves in order to assess its meaning depends on the key element of value.

17:64 Although such evaluation occurs automatically and seamlessly, value is always an added component: it is *applied* to what is there; it is never *found* in what is there. As such, it can be eliminated. Stop applying value to your perceptions and you will eliminate most of what we call effects. In your emotions the very "juice" of the emotional feeling that tells you to move away from one thing and toward another—whether this is done strictly within your internal state or in your actions—is dependant on value. Without value, one emotion wouldn't mean anything more or less than any other emotion. There would be no positive or negative emotions, and so they wouldn't automatically imply a predetermined reaction toward the perceived "cause" of the emotion.

17:65 You would no longer be embarrassed, arrogant, or humble, fearful, angry, or greedy. You would not be shy, aggressive, or clingy, offended, jealous, or possessive. You wouldn't suffer loss, gain, or disinterest. You couldn't be bored, excited, or annoyed, or experience avarice, selfishness, or hurt. You would no longer have issues about being meaningless, worthwhile, or special, and other people couldn't be better or worse, preferred or disliked, insignif-icant or important. Try to grasp the reality of such a shift. Con-centrate on this possibility until you can have at least a glimpse into a world without the domination of value.

17:66 We can eliminate value in one area and not another, in some ways and not others. But in any domain where we stop applying value, all of the effects, reactions, dispositions, and behavior that were dependent on this value will cease to arise. None of these effects could occur since all of these reactions and dispositions depend on some sort of value in order to make their determination. No value, no value-based effects.

No Assumptions, No Consequences

17:67 In Chapter Three I listed a few basic consequences such as empti-ness, self-doubt, feeling trapped, and so on, which persist, usu-ally in the background, because of particular assumptions that we share as human beings. Although we haven't yet discussed what these assumptions might be (we will in an upcoming chap-ter), I'd like to point out that if we no longer make these assump-tions, then none of these consequences would exist. Can you imagine what your experience might be like without emptiness, self-doubt, feeling trapped, struggle, and suffering?

Being a Simple Entity

17:68 Consider, what effects would occur in simply being an entity with-out attachment to a complex conceptual identity? When we look at animals we imagine feelings and reactions occurring for them. Although we are very likely wrong in our assessment of what is actually taking place within the internal state of an animal, even so we note that they clearly have far fewer disturbances and worries than do we. Identifying oneself as a simple living organism, and not much more than that, eliminates a large number of effects. We can see that many creatures who have almost no conceptual capacity exist just fine, and also seem to have little turmoil or troubles. Whole domains of effects are produced by our conceptual survival. We're not likely to give up our entire range of conceptual abilities, but we might be able to lighten up on our conceptual-self survival. Putting attention and energy into being simply present and grounded in physical life from moment to moment would reduce our woes a great deal. And there are other freedoms available.

Not Taking It Personally

17:69   If someone were to cut your body with a sharp knife, you would probably have a significant reaction. Why? Well, at first you'd say because it hurts. But this isn't the whole story. More than likely, as the blade cuts, you would interpret that it is "you" that is being cut or damaged. It's "my body"; it is "me" that is being damaged. But if it were a piece of tofu being cut, you wouldn't care at all. We figure that's just because we don't "feel" the tofu, but what's also true is that we *aren't* the tofu.

17:70   If someone scratched the paint of your cherished new car, pain could easily be a reaction. Why is there pain in this case and not with the tofu? Because it's "your" car, something that represents you in some way, something to which you are attached. You have no nerves in the car, and it still causes pain.

17:71   Just so, if your body was cut, and you really didn't consider this body as anything *you* or *yours,* what reaction would there be? Even with this sensation present, we can imagine that very little pain would exist, perhaps none. Just sensation. The pain and reaction caused by the knowledge that *your* body is being cut would not exist. Just a feeling that some flesh, insignificant and unimportant to you, was being cut. This is a remarkable difference we rarely appreciate. And yet it clearly demonstrates how attachment to things, and identification with things, amplifies, if not outright creates, effects and reactions — including pain. We can imagine then that without any self-identity or a self at all, there would be no pain.

No Self, No Effects

17:72   If we were to eliminate self or the operating principle of self-survival altogether, we would eliminate all effects. Being has no effects. Since it is not a process, it is also not a process that is trying to maintain itself. There are no "results" that need to occur and so no effects need to arise. Since nothing is trying to persist or remain or exist in some particular way, no reactions are called for. As an entity, it is possible to make distinctions and interact without basing actions on reactions. In this case, the domain of reactive-effects is rendered useless and inoperative.

17:73   Effects arise in relation to what's perceived, and what's perceived is formed by our interpretations. Many domains of interpretation are based on or influenced by what we believe. Eliminate or change what we believe, and we will eliminate or change the effects. In the next chapter we'll look into the domain of belief and the way it contributes to constructing our self experience.

CHAPTER EIGHTEEN
Beyond Belief

18:1 It's hard to come to grips with the fact that our own interpretations determine the effects that anything will have on our internal state. It seems as if merely encountering the world affects us, doesn't it? Yet the truth is more complex than that. Our generation of interpretation is still hard to grasp because this whole process goes on in what's generally an unconscious or unrecognized aspect of mind.

18:2 A quick review of our past work reveals that everything we perceive is processed by the mind in order to ascertain how it relates to us. As a result of this automatic and very rapid process, our cognition is treated to an interpretation. Since this is done so that we can relate to the thing encountered, this "relationship" shows up immediately as an effect in our experience, thus pressing us into a specific self-survival disposition toward whatever is encountered.

18:3 But how is an interpretation formulated in the first place? Obviously a great deal of it comes from our many, many past associations and the meaning these have had for us. It is also constructed in relation to what we believe and assume, how we think of ourselves, how we hold others and life, and so on. A complex "snowballing" of many factors produces the simplest of interpretations.

To this apparently single observation, we react in some way without knowing — or particularly caring — why.

18:4   Even though we've heard it in different forms, it's time to really grasp that every interpretation we make is generated from, and in relation to, the self-mind. All that comprises the self contributes to each interpretation, from our most superficial ideas about things to the most deeply buried and unconscious assumptions and context in which life is held. Clearly we want to get to the bottom of all this — to consciously and directly experience every aspect involved in producing a self, not just directly discovering the real nature of our own existence. This can take some work. Yet, in the end we should have a clear awareness of the entire self-mind, and recognize the connection between this activity, or "entity," and all that we experience. An important stage of this work is to transcend all of our beliefs and assumptions. This provides a truly powerful platform of profound not-knowing from which we might make a huge leap into a more direct consciousness of the nature of Being.

A Quick Review of Belief

18:5   You've seen repeatedly throughout this book that one of the key elements in formulating your interpretations — and so the effects you will experience — is what you believe or assume. There is a relationship between what you believe and what you interpret. Your beliefs — from superficial beliefs you've consciously adopted to deeply programmed assumptions you take for granted — contribute a great deal to how you see things. You've already read much about beliefs; now it's time for you to tackle the specific content of what you believe and why you believe it.

18:6 Throughout our lives, many people have tried to tell us what to believe, what is right and wrong. Yet no one exposed the fact that none of what they said is actually true; it was merely believed. Nor did they clarify that these two domains are totally different. In most cases, an assertion was made rather than a possibility offered. Usually this assertion was made, and accepted, more from the desire to believe it than from a genuine experience of the truth.

How was school today?
Did they teach you how to believe,
or did they teach you how to think?
—Nathra Nader

18:7 It should be clear by now that beliefs are held as an obstacle to our work rather than a benefit. We've seen over and over again that what we believe plays a significant role in determining what we perceive, experience, and know. To take on this domain more directly, let's review a few points we've covered so far about beliefs:

- It is the nature of beliefs that they become the truth for us, since a belief is something we think is true. The operative word here is "think." A belief is not the truth.

- When we confuse a concept for the truth we elevate the concept to a status that it doesn't deserve.

- Since no one believes in something they think is untrue, over time one's beliefs are sure to displace any ignorance that may be felt, and insert themselves much like a malignant growth into the position of the truth. In this way we seal ourselves off from the possibility of discovering the truth.

- Our beliefs both constitute and inform our conclusions, opinions, convictions, assumptions, viewpoints, attitudes, interpretations, values, and assessments. Our beliefs determine the decisions we make, how we interpret what we perceive, how we react, what we pursue, and so on. Therefore, in large measure they create what it is we perceive and experience. This being the case, beliefs play a significant role in determining what affects us, how it affects us, and how we will react to it.

18:8   The domain of beliefs can be broken down into three categories:

- Consciously adopted beliefs
- Programming
- Assumptions

18:9   Your consciously adopted beliefs are your intellectual ideas of what's true, and those representing what you'd like to be true — signifying your chosen "stand" in the world. These could be religious or spiritual beliefs, philosophies, your point of view, "knowledge" accumulated from personal education, beliefs about health systems, and so on. They are what you know *as* your beliefs, those you've consciously taken on as your own.

18:10   Programming refers to all those many beliefs that exist subconsciously: all that's considered true because it's been programmed into your mind — much at a young age — coming about from repetition, intimidation, experience, and just in the act of growing up or living life. These aren't easily seen as beliefs since they're so taken for granted. Generally residing in the background, they often represent your values, sense of morality, self-image, self-esteem, your attitudes towards others and life, and so on.

18:11 Assumptions are another layer down. These aren't known as beliefs, but rather exist in the uncognized aspect of mind, and function as if simply fact. Assumptions are adopted in the same way as programming. However, they may never have been something spoken or even recognized whenever they were first assumed. At this level, such beliefs are as if absorbed into the mind like a sponge absorbing water. No recognizably conscious component needs to accompany such adoption. Both culture and family seem to contribute the most, but this domain also includes everything we've assumed all by ourselves.

18:12 It's useful to focus our consciousness on this whole domain of mind since the self revolves around and is constructed largely from the content of mind that's represented by our beliefs — from the superficially adopted beliefs that serve some social end to the deeply ingrained and unknown assumptions buried within our psyches. Because the number of beliefs we live within is staggering, the "reality" that can be constructed is equally immense.

18:13 Our consciously adopted beliefs are frequently used to try to be the person we'd like to be. Yet these beliefs often war with the programmed beliefs that represent the one we think we are. Both are self-survival. The second set is dedicated to the persistence of the self that "is." The first is a conscious superimposition of a "willful" mind upon a more "unconscious" mind, trying to improve this self by becoming consistent with a desired self-image. We might "believe" in the goodness of humankind, but are slow to leave a purse unattended on the subway. We might as easily believe that we are not our bodies, but there is little danger of knowingly stepping in front of a moving car. Such actions on our part don't take much effort since they're programmed in and seem consistent with our primal survival. These kinds of decisions are automatic, but those that we take up trying to live up to our ideals — like being disciplined, creating loving relationships, acting like a saint, always doing the right thing, or whatever — don't seem to come as naturally.

18:14   Focusing first on the more superficial yet important level of beliefs that you've adopted through hearsay, or reason, or because you like the ideas behind them, consider what lies behind the drive to adopt such beliefs. In spite of all this conscious and unconscious believing, you are still left with the burden of having to make decisions and take actions that influence your ability to live successfully. This may be why most people relish notions of prophecy: they crave some authoritative source of information regarding what's to come, how to act, and the correct choices to make. This explains the popularity of psychic hotlines, astrology blurbs, tarot readings, and advice columns. Who can even resist a fortune cookie? Perhaps most people consider all these as a form of entertainment, a fun thing to do, but certainly there is at least a background belief in their possible legitimacy.

18:15   If a cookie, a psychic, or an astrological blurb suggests a course for the future when there is no overriding idea present, aren't you likely to lean toward the suggested path? After all, what could it hurt? And you never know, they could be right. Doesn't it at least momentarily diminish your apprehension and accountability regarding the unknown future? This is the point. If a fortune cookie can help lighten the burden of not-knowing, imagine what a good set of beliefs could do.

18:16   For the most part, adopting a solid dogma allows you to give up responsibility. What a relief. You can be told what to do, what your destiny is, where you'll end up, what's right and wrong, and believe that everything is known. Damn, don't that beat hell out of a fortune cookie!

The great majority of readers and hearers are the same all over the world. If you speak to them of profound Truths they yawn, and, if they dare, they leave you, but if you tell them absurd fables they are all eyes and ears. They wish the doctrines preached to them, whether religious, philosophic, or social, to be agreeable, to be consistent with their conceptions, to satisfy their inclinations, in fact that they find themselves in them, and that they feel themselves approved by them.
—Unknown Tibetan lama

Getting Free of Our Need to Believe

18:17   There seems to be a drive or insistence within our experience that pushes us into believing, or prevents us from recognizing certain beliefs *as* beliefs. What is this founded on? Why does it exist? Before we consider challenging our beliefs, we should look into why we feel such a need to believe in the first place.

18:18   This impulse should not be overlooked or underestimated. We may be able to transcend many beliefs, but at some point we will run into beliefs not so yielding, or encounter fears or discomfort while trying to look beyond our beliefs. This might drive us to take a stand on *any* seemingly more solid ground. If there's no available ground of genuine experience, then belief will have to do. It is best to prepare ourselves for such a confrontation. Our need to believe in something, or to hold tight to what we already believe, will run contrary to our efforts to dispel these beliefs. This "need" can be seen in two ways:

1. need as in necessary, and

2. need as in emotional dependence.

18:19 First off, our need to believe reveals once again the fact that we don't know. As we saw in Chapter Eight, "Unknown Origins," we are not in touch with what is fundamentally true in the case of our own existence. We are confounded by the fact that we don't know how it is we came to be or why, or what we should do throughout the process of living. This is a great deal of essential information not to know, and yet we ignore the fact by pushing it into some belief — religious, scientific, philosophical — or by engaging in various distractions to avoid or postpone the issue. When the truth is told, we must confess that we just don't know, which leaves us basically with nowhere to stand. Our hardwired aversion to conceptual uncertainty presses us to believe something — anything.

18:20 The other aspect of our "need" to believe is found in the emotional arena. We seem to find psychological and emotional comfort in our beliefs, especially those that can act as a guiding force. This makes sense in light of the shared human condition that shows up in our first point: not knowing what life is really all about. Notice the further potential challenges inherent in the almost universal suspicion that "I may be the only one who got left out of knowing what life is all about or how I'm supposed to conduct myself within it." We are likely to be embarrassed to admit this personal condition to anyone, while feeling desperate to fill that void with something — for our own psychological equilibrium, and to fit into society. If it can't be something "known" then it will have to be something believed.

18:21   Feeling compelled to resolve our ignorance (without letting others know how deep it goes), we're likely to adopt aspects of what others say, especially our parents and culture. Very little of this will be done consciously, yet we can usually find a conscious component to the effort, and if we dig down we'll likely find that our core beliefs match those of family and culture in some way.

18:22   If we're honest, most of us have to admit that deep down our sense of ignorance, vulnerability, or emptiness is still not resolved. Although our beliefs may give us comfort on the surface, we remain deeply aware that we have in no way gotten to the truth for ourselves. We're still in the same condition of having no deep consciousness of the true nature of our existence. This may well leave us with a background sense of being a "pretender" in life, groping for some way to set things right.

18:23   In trying to fulfill this need, we adopt all kinds of different beliefs. Yet the one thing they all have in common is that they've arisen outside of our core experience. Even if we make up a personal doctrine to believe in, it's still only a superimposition on what's already experienced by us fundamentally. Furthermore, the beliefs we use to validate this doctrine will have arisen from elsewhere, and the assumptions on which it's based will likely have come from our culture. This means our beliefs are given, not created. In this case, one succumbs to them, accepts or rejects them, but does not create them.

18:24   It's good to remember that virtually everything we believe was believed before we came along. Our very thinking and interpretations were molded by millennia of the human minds that came before us. When we cease taking for granted what is known, it not only helps free us of assumptions, but also allows us to appreciate what it took to create such knowing.

On the Shoulders of Giants

18:25   Relative to the history of human knowledge, those of us alive today are privileged to be at the forefront. This capacity to see further than previous generations is attributable to the toil of all those people throughout history who have contributed so much to our understanding. Our current level of thought cannot properly be claimed by us. Credit must be given to millennia of evolution, to the trials and errors of our ancestors, and to the occasional visionaries and geniuses who contributed profound leaps in our collective understanding.

18:26   Although we may be "standing on the shoulders of giants," whatever direction they faced is the direction we will be looking. Turning to look elsewhere, we are likely to fall, but it is a risk that we must take. There is much to be said for learning from the people who've made great contributions to our thinking and view of reality, and we should climb up on their shoulders and look in earnest. But an unseen trap is prepared when, in so doing, we stop thinking for ourselves.

18:27   Sifting through the theories and contributions of others to come up with something to "believe" is not having an original idea, nor is it a personal experience. No matter how passionately we cherish a belief, we must remember that it is not the same as having our own experience or understanding. Repeating a profound saying in no way makes us profound. As a matter of fact, we are likely to be expressing our own foolishness, because it is doubtful that we truly understand what is being said, and almost a certainty that we have had no direct experience in the matter.

18:28   The giants of the past had to leap beyond the presumptions of their time to make the strides that they did. Much of the current view they had to surpass came from the giants — and of course the numerous mental pygmies — that came before them. Our collective presumptions are what we've come to accept as real in our time. It is our responsibility to discover the pervasive assumptions that restrict our current thinking and to make the next leap beyond this level of conception.

18:29   Long ago, people undoubtedly took on the beliefs of the tribe or community within which they were born. Being without contrast or alternatives, their ideas of how the universe worked and the particular sets of values that were adopted by the community probably met with few challenges, and so rarely would people suffer the lack of governing beliefs or agonize over the meaning of life and self as we do today. But as various alternative possibilities became known — although probably fiercely resisted at first — doubt arose.

There is no freedom of thought without doubt.
—Bergen Baldwin Evans

18:30   Most of us tend to give greater validity to beliefs that are received from others — especially from an "authoritative" source — than we give to beliefs that we create ourselves. Why is that? Perhaps because one distinction we make about "reality" is that it is objectively outside of whatever we fabricate mentally. Any assertion that comes from an outside source would naturally seem more likely to reflect what's objectively true. Even though another's claims or assertions are probably just as subjective as ours, for us they hold a greater possibility of being true than what we knowingly invent. A personally made-up belief just doesn't have much weight because we're too keenly aware that it is invented.

18:31 Always looking "elsewhere," however — to the past, to authority, to what has been said and thought, or to some fictitious "body of knowledge" where all truths reside — can prevent you from pursuing your own direct experiences. If something within reality is so, then it is discoverable by you. You "are" reality, and so should be able to experience what is real. Such consciousness is never brought about by what you've heard, since, right or wrong, this is someone else's experience.

18:32 Throughout history people have had many, many systems of beliefs — various doctrines or rules to live by. Some come from religion, some are dogma from one ideology or another, codes of behavior, or views about the workings of the universe. Looking back we tend to think of these past beliefs as generally incorrect or not fully formed, and consider what we believe today as the truth. When you think about it, it is rather arrogant and even silly of us to imagine that out of all the beliefs humans have generated over the millennia, our current beliefs are finally the right ones. That we really don't know is a *fact*. Admit this fact and notice the sky doesn't fall and the earth doesn't crumble.

Using Beliefs as a Map

18:33 In our work to get past our own beliefs, we need to remember that belief is not some random mental quirk, but an essential mechanism of our survival. Beliefs are often the "glue" that helps stabilize many levels of society, and, on a personal level, they provide guidelines for our decision-making process. When all else fails, and usually long before, we have our beliefs on which to stand. Just as a map is indispensable in strange territory, our beliefs help point us in a "direction" in unfamiliar circumstances — and since we don't really know anything for certain, we could say that all of life is an unfamiliar circumstance. But unlike a map, a belief rarely represents what's there.

18:34   Useful as they seem, relying solely on your beliefs to guide you will be a self-fulfilling endeavor. No matter where the compass of your beliefs points, it will always relate to your subjective views of reality rather than to what's actually there. You will end up consistently "moving with the map" regardless of its relation to anything on the ground, and your actions will seem appropriate to the given circumstances since these guidelines also determine the behavioral options available. In other words, no matter what you encounter, you will recognize it in relation to what you believe. You will act accordingly and the results will be consistent in some way with your beliefs, thus reinforcing them. No matter what you believe, this is what will be reinforced. What will *not* be occurring is an accurate perception and relationship to what is there.

18:35   For example, if I believe, among other things, that loving my fellow man is the right attitude to take, then my actions must be consistent with this value — unless I fail to live up to my own principles (which is likely now and then, but that's another matter). As I move through unfamiliar territory, my amicable actions will probably be met with commensurate behavior, be it graciousness in response to my disposition, or an attempt to take advantage of me. In either case, my position is clear, and the outcome for me is dictated. My behavior, when met with graciousness or deceit and abuse, is predetermined—I'm thankful for kindness or turn the other cheek to injury. So the ground on which I walk will seem familiar even if it's unknown to me. Adhering to my established belief system as an outlook and way of life will produce a sense of familiarity. It will make an unknown world appear as familiar and known. As long as we're willing to disregard the truth and focus only on what we'd like to experience in life, adopting a set of functional life-enhancing beliefs can be very effective.

18:36　On the other hand, if our objective is to realize the truth, we must confront our dependency on beliefs. As a case in point, people often take up some system of belief that promises a path toward personal transformation. Strange as it may seem, the desire for transformation is not a desire for the truth. Although we might think that gleaning the truth would be a transformative act, our attempts at transformation are almost always based on the particular beliefs of some system, and motivated by our desire to become better in some way. Even though the belief system we adopt may seem to be a tool for getting to the truth, upon closer inspection we find that what we're really up to is trying to adopt behavior and thinking that's consistent with the dogma of that system. This difference frequently slips below the radar, but it is important to keep an eye out for such confusion and to consider why we go down that road.

18:37　Standing on our own without anything genuine to guide us—and although we're reluctant to acknowledge it, we are always in some ways on our own—where can we turn if not to our beliefs? This is always a concern for people whether it is recognized or not, and we tend to take refuge in our beliefs. Genuine understanding, however, only occurs when we consciously experience for ourselves whatever is true, which is an effort best served by deep and honest contemplation. Since we're ignorant of what's true, our pursuit of the truth demands that we stay close to the next best thing: an experience of not-knowing. A state of not-knowing will allow us to resist any impulse to leap into the sanctuary of beliefs, effectively "holding a space open" until genuine insight can arise.

It is impossible to believe your way into the truth!

18:38 Even if we find no solid ground or "answer" to focus our attention on once we let go of a belief, we should recognize that this new state brings us closer to ourselves, not further away. The good news is that once freed from these beliefs, the resultant presence of this moment in our awareness will be far more potent than our clinging to familiar ground ever was.

We don't need an answer to open up;
we need openness.

Radical Openness

18:39 If someone holds a rock in midair and then lets go of it, will it fall down? We believe it will. Is this a certainty? It seems pretty certain. The objective physical world is perhaps our most solid domain of belief, and we seem to have a fairly direct line on such beliefs as experiences. Since we have an abundance of remembered perceptions that consistently appear as valid reflections of reality, we don't imagine that they could be beliefs. This is fine, and challenging such perceptions would not be fruitful at this time.

(Although if we ever run out of beliefs to challenge, then we can push the envelope by going into such considerations.) Instead, we are invited to consider the effect that not-knowing has on even our most solid beliefs — such as: rocks will fall when dropped, or space will remain constant as we move though it, or the sun will appear in the sky tomorrow. It may seem silly to mess with such solid beliefs, yet bear with me for a moment.

18:40 Granting the possibility that even what we "know" is not an absolute certainty creates a new perspective and so a new experience of reality without diminishing what appears as known. Instead, what is experienced becomes more vivid and alive. It takes on a greater depth of presence and at the same time merges with a sense of unknown possibility. We may know the rock will fall down once we let go of it, but do we really experience what's happening as it falls? Do we feel the forces involved? Are we impressed by the fact that it doesn't fall sideways or up? Are we absolutely certain it will fall down when we drop it? Perhaps. But if we were in outer space, it wouldn't fall down — what a surprise! The sense of wonder alone is worth the price of not-knowing.

18:41 Can you see how well not-knowing works to enhance and open up your knowing? It actually creates a more powerful knowing. What is now "known" suddenly becomes open-ended and is neither taken for granted nor pinned down by assumptions. Your perception of what's there doesn't necessarily change, but your perspective does. You get in touch with the possibility that something else could be true rather than your assumptions, and also grasp that it could be different in the next moment. This enhances your perceptions of what's there now, and you are likely to notice qualities overlooked, or sense some possibility missed. As your perception moves closer to getting what it is *for-itself,* a sense of aliveness and clarity arises, and you will tend to be more creative and awake in relation to whatever you perceive.

18:42   In order to step into a greater consciousness of the nature of reality we must be open beyond what we are certain is true about anything. The truth lies outside of what we believe and free of what we assume. It simply may not fit into our most solid assumptions. If this is the case (and it is), how can we become conscious of the absolute nature of existence? If our consciousness stops with the self-mind, we can't. So you can see how such a radical openness is essential to our quest for direct consciousness.

18:43   Taking up a practice of becoming free of all our beliefs is a very powerful and positive step toward such consciousness, and toward finding a way to live without the dominating influence of beliefs. Unfortunately, most "spiritual" practices — or teachings that claim to lead to the truth — are founded on beliefs. Our practice here offers a completely different direction. Instead of believing in something, you're invited to stop believing in anything.

Eliminating Beliefs

18:44   Our culture has yet to discover the power of eliminating beliefs. We certainly have the notion of defending our beliefs. We have the idea of the right to choose our beliefs. We even have the concept of replacing our beliefs with better beliefs. But we don't really entertain the possibility of having no beliefs at all.

18:45   It should be clear now that most of what we "know" was not experienced firsthand but merely adopted through hearsay — from our upbringing, education, the community, and through other more subtle forms of communication. What might not be apparent is that whenever we take on *any* belief we are putting a great deal of faith in what's passed on by others. This faith may be well-founded or not — we don't know. We generally don't recognize beliefs *as* beliefs, so we rarely think to question their source.

18:46   The fact that we haven't experienced firsthand most of what we believe applies to all of us. This means it probably applies to those from whom we picked up our beliefs — be it the hearsay of scientific discovery, social gossip, family programming, political truisms, or religious assertions. Chances are extremely high that the people who passed these beliefs along don't know either. Except in very rare instances, they have not had a direct personal experience of what they are asserting. In most instances, we're merely believing what's believed.

18:47   As we considered in Chapter Thirteen, "Lost in Translation," it is essentially impossible to accurately represent the truth when passing on a belief. Therefore, our faith in another's "knowingness" is moot. Within our own experience, the "correctness" of any belief is unknown. Our own made-up beliefs are no more valid than those collected from others. Regardless of the source, even if some belief we have happens to be correct, the belief still doesn't provide us with an experience of what's true. It remains a concept, a representation, an illusion. It is to this world that we have become bound. It is the illusion of this world that needs to be dispelled.

18:48   "To dispel" means "to drive away," or "to rid one's mind of." If we want to stretch it here, we can consider the word in light of the "spells" in folklore that were thought to have power over someone's experience, behavior, or fate. In fairy tales, the people under a spell are often unaware that their mind and body are controlled by someone else. Once they realize a spell has been put on them, however, they devote all their efforts to eliminating it and getting free of its influence. I may be taking liberties with word association here, but the point is made.

18:49 Beliefs are very much like the spells and superstitions of old, which worked only because people believed they did. We all fall under the spell of beliefs. We become entranced, succumbing to an illusory world in which we act out our lives. This is true of both positive and negative beliefs. When we think that what we believe is true and right, we think it is *reality,* and so we leave no room for the possibility of directly encountering what is real. We live in an "illusion" of which we are unaware. Sounds like a spell to me.

18:50 Awakening from a spell is not accomplished by falling under yet another spell. If we replace one belief with another, we may be more likely to acknowledge that our particular beliefs are not etched in stone, but we won't be freed from believing. The impulse to grasp for something to hang onto will remain, and we will still be inclined to overlook the way that our "beliefs" create an illusory world that is mistaken for reality.

18:51 Of course the moment you try to perceive a reality that is not subject to the illusion of beliefs, you will likely fail. Whatever you come up with will simply be another perspective or imagination, and not what's true as an absolute. This is what makes our task so difficult. Even when you earnestly attempt a direct consciousness of this moment of existence, that doesn't mean it's forthcoming. You may remain without any image at all, without any alternative to whatever you believed or imagined about self and reality heretofore. This is an important aspect to grasp about the matter. We've banged into it repeatedly and perhaps have come to understand its significance, but may still wait for an answer, some conceptually graspable description of the "real" reality. We're after the openness inherent in not-knowing, not something new in which to believe. Destroying all that we believe helps move our consciousness into the open state from which it becomes possible to grasp what is real.

The Practice of Dispelling Beliefs

18:52   It's time to take up a practice of eliminating everything you believe. You started this practice in Chapter Two when you did the "Emptying Your Cup" exercise. But such a practice won't be done in one sitting. It's likely that you can continue fruitfully for years. Discovering and eliminating beliefs is best done as an ongoing practice throughout the course of your life. It's also very useful from time to time to focus your attention on this practice as an intense contemplation, deliberately conjuring up everything you believe, on whatever level you believe it, and working to get free of it.

18:53   Using one simple distinction, you can begin to uncover what are beliefs and what are not. You've already encountered this distinction in the form of this simple question: Have you experienced whatever you're referring to firsthand or not? With this notion, you can start to sort out all that is believed from what is experienced. If you yourself have not had a direct experience of the matter, it must be a belief. If you have experienced it for yourself, firsthand, then don't call it a belief.

18:54   As a contemplation, ask yourself: What do I think is true? This will not only produce a lot of material to ponder, it will push you into challenging all three levels of beliefs that we talked about earlier. Your consciously adopted beliefs are easiest to notice, but you will also begin to run into your own programming and assumptions — beliefs about yourself, others, or life so entrenched or taken for granted they just seem like fact. When you bring to mind what you believe, one thing after another will come up.

18:55   As you consider this matter, one of the first things you need to challenge are your consciously adopted beliefs. In particular, turn a critical eye onto the systems of beliefs that you use as guidelines for living, or as practices for personal improvement — all those beliefs coming from religions, New Age notions, philosophies of various kinds, practices for growth, or simply ideas about the cosmos, health, or human behavior. These "consciously" adopted beliefs or philosophical precepts are appropriated as one's own from an external source. This means that by definition they are not directly experienced.

18:56   Have you personally and directly experienced God, or that there is no God? No? Then whatever you believe about that is a belief. Do you really know that there is an afterlife, that all religions are essentially the same at their source, or that yours is the only true one? Who said so? Do you really know that health food is good for you, all cults are bad, reason can solve all problems, or whatever it is you personally consider true? Discover and acknowledge everything you've consciously adopted as a belief and get free of it.

18:57   At some point in this effort, you'll touch on beliefs you have about yourself. This will certainly push you into the level of programming. Tackling this level of belief will take a concerted effort and focused attention. Merely challenging anything you hold to be true about yourself will open the door to further contemplation. In upcoming chapters we will put more attention on addressing deeper assumptions, but it doesn't hurt to start working on it now.

18:58   Even those beliefs that seem more factually based should be challenged. You might not consider some idea as hearsay at first glance, but after looking into it further you'll realize that it is. For example, you might ask yourself: have I directly experienced a molecule? No? Then what you believe about molecules is a belief. For most of us it is complete hearsay, something we've read in books or heard from professors. But even those of us who have done experiments that validate the existence and theories of molecules must confess to never having perceived a molecule firsthand. It is hearsay, no matter how valid or certain we are of its correctness. Have you yourself seen that the earth is round? You've seen pictures, you say? This might seem to count as an experience, but if we are sticking with the "firsthand" rule, then it is not an experience of a round planet, it is a picture of something claimed to be the planet — and besides, you have no experience of how big it is, whether it is in fact three-dimensional, and so on. Close, but no cigar. It is a belief. We can make a distinction between beliefs that seem factually based, and those that have no real basis in fact. Yet for our work here, we must still call them all beliefs, and realize the implications of this fact.

18:59   Are you getting the idea of how to do this practice? Working with the distinction between hearsay and firsthand experience might be easier if you imagine dividing all that you think is true into two separate piles. As you concentrate on this task, you will have one pile of hearsay, and another much smaller pile of what you've experienced for yourself. The latter may or may not turn out to be beliefs in the end, but you don't need to decide everything about that right now. What's most important is to recognize all that is hearsay, since these will clearly be beliefs, and you will find they will far outweigh what you come up with as experience.

Eliminating Beliefs Exercise

Now, take some time and seriously practice going through everything you think is true. As you do, distinguish all that is hearsay from what you consider personally experienced. If you aren't certain about whether you've actually experienced something or not, then you can toss it on the to-be-considered-later pile and move on. Most of what you think is true, however, is one or the other. Out of all that you believe or hold to be true, clearly acknowledge what must end up in the pile of not-experienced-firsthand.

18:60   Once you've discovered that certain "truths" you've held are clearly beliefs, you must recognize and acknowledge them *as* beliefs. This is the same as perceiving them as not the truth, and so destroying them as being true. A significant shift will occur in your experience by doing so — even if you don't really stop "believing" them — because they will no longer be held as "true," simply as believed. Letting go of a belief altogether provides an even more significant shift in your experience. Once you eliminate all that you acknowledge as hearsay, then you can re-create the exercise by challenging all that you designated as "personally experienced." You will find there is much you originally thought of as experience that turns out to be belief or assumption. Make an ongoing practice of discovering beliefs tucked away within your experience. The more conscious you become of this domain, the more beliefs you will discover and the deeper you can go. Just keep working on it.

A New Experience in Consciousness

18:61 Every time we recognize and eliminate a belief, a new experience arises. The moment we are free of a belief, we experience a sense of aliveness, openness, and freedom — a little bit or a lot depending on the depth of effect the belief had on our lives. This act may be preceded by resistance, or a fear of loss or possible pain, but once done, a sense of freedom replaces any sense of trepidation. The belief is instantly seen as a belief and so obviously not the truth — since we just stopped believing it. This leaves us with a sense of open possibility.

18:62 For example, if I believe that people are hostile, or that the moon is made of green cheese, by confronting the fact that these are beliefs and may not actually be the case, I can let them go. I can stop believing them, and hold in their place a willingness to discover whatever's true. In that moment my experience will change. People are no longer hostile — they might be any number of ways, one of which could be hostile, but since I no longer hold as a fact that they are inherently hostile, this perspective no longer fills my entire perception of people or the world. Suddenly there is room for other possibilities. The moon is not made of green cheese — once again, it could be, it could be made of an infinite number of things, but since I no longer *believe* it is made of green cheese, the matter is wide open. Infinite possibilities arise within the presence of not-knowing.

18:63 In the exercise above, what happened when you recognized something you thought was true was a belief, and stopped believing it? Simply dropping that belief changed your experience of reality, at least a little bit, didn't it? Something disappeared, and in its place you were left with nothing and openness. Now, imagine what might be the case if you dropped many beliefs, or all of your beliefs. Your experience of openness and possibility would be huge, as would your sense of not-knowing.

18:64 Normally we try to fill such an opening as quickly as possible — being unaccustomed as we are to this experience of openness, and being programmed to believe that the state of not-knowing is to be avoided. Usually the openness is filled right away because we only dispense with a belief when swapping it out for another — when we've been convinced for some reason that some new view is the correct one. As soon as we get past our habitual resistance to the new idea, the transition is often rather smooth, and so any sense of openness is quickly replaced with a sense of certainty and newness. We don't like spending time on the "wrong" side of things. Whenever we're open enough to find out we've been mistaken about something, we quickly jump to the newly perceived "correct" view by adopting a new belief.

18:65 Aside from any embarrassment (or razzing by friends) that might have accompanied such a switch in the past, when you look back you may notice a sense of aliveness or openness that occurred whenever you managed to let go of something you believed. No matter how short the time span, this happened just before you assimilated the new belief. Now instead of grasping onto a replacement as you consciously disassociate from some current belief, you can simply settle into the open space that ensues. If you can be comfortable with not-knowing, you have no need to rush on. Coincidentally, in this space, your attention is immediately drawn to a more genuine sense of yourself — that is, until you move on to the next distraction.

18:66   With each belief we eliminate, we get a little closer to a genuine experience of something real, since our realness lies prior to as well as beyond our beliefs. The conceptual overlay that clouds our perception of real "being" begins to lift a little. The more beliefs that are removed, the more present and clear our sense of this "beingness" becomes—having an increasingly large crack through which to shine. The deeper and more dominating the beliefs, the larger the opening.

18:67   I suspect that deep down, everyone is aware of this to some degree, even if it's thoroughly overlooked. If we strip away every belief, perhaps nothing will stand in the way of becoming conscious of what is genuine and real. Certainly our experience would be more immediate and genuine because we'd be left with a sense of what *is* rather than what is *believed*—even if "what-is" is unknown. We may not have an insight or direct experience of the truth of this moment, but that possibility suddenly becomes real and present. Since our experience is currently conceptually dominated, whenever we make such a shift, these concepts will lose much of their power. Breaking free of the inherent illusion caused by our conceptual self-introversion creates a huge openness and a greater sense of realness.

18:68   As this process unfolds, we may suffer a feeling of disorientation from time to time. Practice will increase our ability to tolerate the openness of not-knowing, and a genuine experience will begin to emerge. In order to take such a practice to completion, we need to unearth every assumption and destroy all of our beliefs. This will reveal where we stand as a self, and create an opening for the truth. Through this opening, "being" can emerge, and from this new depth of consciousness a greater sense of wonder and a more joyful, fulfilled experience of being alive is possible.

18:69 In the next two chapters, we will turn our attention once again to our shared assumptions and their consequences. Emptiness, self-doubt, feeling trapped, suffering, and struggle persist as core elements of our self-experience. It seems that our assumptions not only make it possible, but inevitable that some variation of this set of negative consequences remains pinned to our experience and buried deep in our psyches. What are these assumptions? Let's take a look.

CHAPTER NINETEEN
Freedom from Assumptions—Part One

19:1 As we work to become free of the self-mind, we realize that the depth and scope of this endeavor are staggering. We can readily recognize the operating principle of survival as it dominates our experience through effects, and we've touched on the world of beliefs that frame our particular perspective. Now, we turn our attention to the deeper aspects of belief—in particular the way in which our unrecognized assumptions act as a foundation for self and our perception of reality. It's difficult to make every aspect of mind accessible in one book. We can, however, create new doorways into the deeper domains, and in time the diligent reader can use these to move to greater consciousness.

19:2 Earlier we touched on five consequences that result from shared cultural and human assumptions. Our personal experience of these consequences can lead us into a new depth of mind as we investigate the assumptions that create them. In so doing, we will tackle far more than these particular assumptions and consequences. That's the point. As we become increasingly conscious of this domain we'll begin to touch the core of the self-mind.

19:3 Normally when we speak of assumption we mean something that is taken for granted to be true without reflection or proof. The domain of assumption that I'm talking about is an unusually obscure domain. This is an aspect of mind that is the source of so much of the activity that we recognize *as* mind—thinking, perceiving, reacting, emoting, behavior, and so on—and yet this source remains hidden from view. We don't cognize these assumptions, but we live from them.

19:4 This doesn't mean they are elsewhere. They exist within and as the whole mind activity. They simply aren't recognized. We might say it is a bit like a bush where we see all the leaves but not the branches and stems that generate and support them. These branches aren't elsewhere; they're just different in nature from the leaves and also hidden from view. We could also think of these assumptions as the system that runs our computer. It remains hidden from view and always in the background, while all that we see and do on the computer is dependent on this framework—it allows and also dictates what we can and can't do.

19:5 We might call this domain of mind "contextual assumptions," or perhaps we could call it source assumptions, or foundation assumptions. In any case, regardless what we call it, this domain is a deep aspect of mind taking place right now in your awareness, determining what you will be aware of and how you will think about and interact with what's perceived. It is this domain of mind that we will attempt to bring to consciousness.

19:6 Our goal is to increase consciousness. While it is appropriate to improve our ability to discern the cause of personal challenges, our work here should not be construed as simply making a list of possible causes, nor should it be seen as some kind of psychotherapy. The five consequences are representative of what ails us just in the act of sharing "human" assumptions. They represent facets of the same basic human condition, and so, insight into one will necessarily provide clues about the others. As we uncover the founding pillars of our self-mind, much of the remaining structure will become clear and, in the face of this clarity, begin to crumble.

Making Connections

19:7 One of our more difficult tasks in this work is making a connection between newly discovered assumptions and the effects these assumptions have on our lives. Too often it remains an intellectual connection, and this does very little. Only through grasping that something assumed really does cause distressful consequences will we be motivated to let go of the assumption. Unless we can link these consequences to our own impulses, and witness them resulting from our decisions and thinking, reactions and behavior—all based on contextual assumptions—we will not gain the clarity needed to achieve any real freedom from them. We will continue to hold fast to these survival impulses much like a monkey who grasps a piece of fruit inside a narrow-neck bottle remains imprisoned because he won't let go of the fruit. It's not that he's so greedy or stupid, it's that he doesn't make the connection between holding onto the fruit and his inability to escape the bottle. We are very much like that. Once we realize within our own experience the relationship between something to which we cling and our own suffering, we are sure to let it go. Prior to realizing this relationship, however, we will remain "monkeys trapped by a bottle."

19:8 The first thing we need to do is become conscious of what we are assuming. This has to be done through personal contemplation, but taking a look at possible candidates can warm us up to this task and provide some directions in which to look. Be clear these five consequences don't represent everything that goes on with us. They act only as a sampling of the human condition. Actually, suffering and struggling are primary, these are fundamental aspects of a self trying to survive. Emptiness, self-doubt, and feeling trapped are really just specific forms of suffering that are usually insidious and background in nature, involving their own kinds of internal struggles that also affect one's reactivity and behavior. Yet, they are found so frequently in the human condition that they contribute something useful and specific to our investigations. We'll focus our work on assumption by looking into the origins and components of these five consequences:

- emptiness
- self-doubt
- feeling trapped
- suffering
- struggle

19:9   What are the core cultural assumptions that produce these common effects? Whatever they are, they won't appear as mere ideas, but will seem to be perceptions of reality. They won't offer themselves up easily to scrutiny. Our first encounter with possible assumptions would have to be seen as unconventional, since they'll likely go against the grain of accepted truisms. Given this, they may also be difficult to understand, and so we should be patient in our consideration.

19:10   Intellectual attempts to conjure up possible assumptions can provide material for further contemplation, but is not likely to lead to insight. A conscious experience of the assumption at its source will always be different from the thought about what it might be. Though we may use intellect to search out probable candidates, if we want to make a difference in our lives, we need a real experiential recognition of these assumptions actively operating in our own minds.

19:11 Beyond shared assumptions, personal programming also contributes to these effects, but such programming must be discovered individually. Our foundation assumptions create the base that generates the likelihood that certain consequences will arise. Yet an individual may suffer similar effects that relate to his or her particular programming, and this isn't necessarily a direct result of shared assumptions. This has to be sorted out within the mind of the individual in his or her own contemplations and investigations. Individual and cultural contributions, however, cannot truly be separated, and so awakening one will affect the other.

19:12 An open and contemplative listening needs to take place as I mention probable assumptions for the above consequences, since the communication might too quickly be clouded by a reaction from the assumption itself. Also, since these effects are background or general in nature, the assumptions may well seem very abstract or hard to pin down. They act in a place of the mind that is not readily accessed. Generally, this depth of thought is only discussed in such environs as a philosophy class, and is taken seriously only as long as our fascination for interesting ideas lasts. Yet assumptions that are at the root of such effects as emptiness or suffering are not merely a matter for metaphysical discussion. They are a serious part of the foundation for our daily thinking and perceptions.

19:13   We must be careful not to let any form of cultural programming or accepted ways of thinking influence our exploration. The very standards for being "socially correct" are based on what we as a culture want to be so in our thinking at this time in history. Being "proper" or "good" or "correct" in one's thinking precludes any real investigation of what's "true" about one's thinking.

19:14   We must be willing to discover and confess ideas and beliefs that run contrary to social acceptance, and even contrary to what we may personally want or believe. The only thing it needs to be is true—whether we like it or not is irrelevant. This doesn't mean "true" in an ultimate sense, but actually occurring—such as something found to be in fact assumed, although we were unaware of this condition and perhaps even believed it to be otherwise. It may be that we believe the emperor has clothes, but once it's pointed out that he does not, we mustn't insist that he does regardless of our fear of disfavor. If we consider the spirit of this adventure on a par with deep psychoanalysis, fearless contemplation, honest spiritual investigations, or committed philosophical or scientific research, we can see that personal beliefs can only get in the way. It is the truth we are after.

19:15   Regardless of any individual assumptions we may dig out, the overriding assertion here is that all of these five consequences, and many more, are a result of believing ourselves to be a self. In simple terms: once we've mistaken ourselves for something not real, shit happens. The particular twists and turns aren't nearly as important as the fact we are sent racing down a slope of being controlled by effects because we are trying to survive as a self.

19:16   In this work, we shouldn't lose sight of the fact that none of this would be necessary if we weren't set in motion in the first place.

What sets us in motion, what knocks us off course, is mistaking a self for the act of "being." Keeping this in mind assists us in not getting lost in the maze through which we may enter as we try to sort out some of these assumptions. The connection between the assumption and its influence on our lives needs to be clearly seen. But, like being in a maze, it may be more easily seen by backing up far enough to see it as part of a whole pattern.

19:17   Simply put, emptiness, self-doubt, and feeling trapped are all forms of suffering, and struggle is what we do to deal with these effects. Each has its own story, however, the discovery of which helps us unveil the particular assumptions that produce much of our self-induced distress. We will look briefly into these consequences of "selfdom," but remember, such considerations are simply a sampling provided to assist you in discovering for yourself the foundation of the human condition.

19:18   Many of the conditions and assumptions that produce one effect will also contribute to producing other effects. Much of what we discover at the root of emptiness will be true for self-doubt, and this will also connect up with suffering and so on. They are parts of a whole, and so we shouldn't see them as isolated causes and effects. As the story unfolds, the relationship between various beliefs, cultural assumptions, and the effects and challenges these produce in our lives should begin to become clear. The complexity and obscured nature of this subject requires a much greater depth of contemplation about what's discussed, but we can begin to sort out these assumptions and feelings right now. Although we'll briefly look at some possibilities, the real work will continue to rely solely on your own contemplation. To start us off and set down some groundwork, let's take a look into emptiness.

Emptiness

19:19   When you consider various kinds of emptiness, you might come up with feeling as though you are personally isolated, incomplete or not whole, as if something is missing, or simply having a sense that your life or self is without meaning. In whatever form it shows itself, this sense seems to occur in the neighborhood of feeling empty, alone, or lacking. What could this sense of emptiness be founded on?

19:20   Every negative exists in contrast to a positive alternative. If these negative feelings are occurring, we must believe that some other, more positive feelings should be true instead. Certainly we must presume that our experience and selves could and should be some other way. It's likely we assume we're not as we should be, if for no other reason than that we confuse our selves with false notions. Observing the way we identify ourselves as something other than our true condition is a start, but what else do we assume to be true of ourselves or reality that leads to feelings of emptiness or meaninglessness?

19:21   Emptiness occurs in relation to two possibilities, fact and fiction. In simple terms, we feel empty in relation to the fact that we *are* empty, which is to say, we are missing an experience of our real-selves. We also feel empty in relation to cultural misunderstand-ings — or fiction. This "fictitious" emptiness may feel like a real condition but is founded on false notions, on the belief that some-thing should be present that is not or that something shouldn't be present that is. Both fact and fiction feed each other, and the result is a powerful background sense that we're calling emptiness. If we can eliminate the presumptions that cause it, our sense of emptiness will lift.

Generating a Sense of Disconnection

19:22   If our integrity is broken, we will suffer a lack of cohesion and authenticity within our experience, creating a sense of being disconnected from others and from ourselves. When it becomes the norm or an accepted behavior to lie or misrepresent in some manner, a lack of integrity within one's own experience must occur. This means that what is expressed to others, and even to ourselves, doesn't match what is actually true of ourselves. We've seen that misrepresentation occurs on many levels, and even to those not consciously trying to mislead. Intentional or not, however, once our integrity is broken we will suffer the consequences. A lack of integrity here simply means that there is a split or crack in our self-experience.

19:23   A cracked china bowl may leak and can very easily be broken because it lacks the integrity of a unified bowl, which is cohesive and self-consistent. Just like the bowl, when the integrity of our personal experience is broken up, we will suffer the consequences. When misrepresentation is adopted, a split in our integrity is unavoidable. We tell ourselves that it doesn't matter, or that we can get around it or put up with it, or share with each other the acceptance of "little white lies," but we fail to share the fact that we are misrepresenting ourselves in very subtle and sometimes overt ways. No matter how much we try to convince ourselves that this "forbidden fruit" is harmless to eat, or an old-fashioned notion that no longer applies, we still suffer the consequences of breaking up our integrity.

19:24   Even as we attempt to be an honest person, misrepresentation still slips through the back door. In our culture and with our assumptions, this is unavoidable. Let's look at an example of how this could happen using one specific case. If a shared assumption in my particular subculture is that personal worth determines acceptability in the community, then I need to appear worthwhile in order to obtain the good judgments of others and the status assessed as requisite for my success, ergo survival. Consistent with such an orientation, if knowledge is a valued commodity in my culture, I would then strive to appear knowledgeable. A split in my self-experience is now at hand, because at the core of my being I am not originally knowledgeable. I'll go about trying to accumulate knowledge so that I appear to be "one who knows," even though fundamentally I am not.

19:25   Let's be clear that what's important to me is the acceptance of others. *Being* one who knows is not really the objective and is actually a side effect if it does occur. What's important is that I am *perceived* as one who knows. In this case I will tend to misrepresent myself and so create a split in my integrity. I will adopt affectations attributed to "knowers" in our culture. I may present a "superior" demeanor, and act as if I know far more than I really do. When confronted by disagreement, the important thing for me is to "win" the argument, which frequently means to discount or discredit the other's ideas regardless of their validity. Given such a disposition, not-knowing would have me quaking in my boots. Unless, of course, I could quickly make it into a form of "knowing that I don't know." Believe it or not, all of this is a form of misrepresentation — even if I don't know I'm doing it.

19:26   There are many, many such possibilities, and they are all founded on various assumptions and misrepresentations that lead to a fundamental lack of integrity. This is not a moral issue; it is a practical one. Once misrepresentation has taken over, it is not possible to feel genuine because the fact is we are not. This provides us with a feeling of inauthenticity—no matter how much we try to ignore it, or convince ourselves it doesn't matter. In our culture, chances are high that such an inauthentic sense has permeated our bones. Inauthenticity isn't found merely in the musings of the mind or the struggles of our emotions; it lies in a taken-for-granted background sense inherent in our very experience of self.

19:27   So this inauthenticity arises from an activity—we actually generate a sense of being disconnected from a genuine experience of ourselves, which contributes to our sense of emptiness. If an honest self-experience is buried and unacknowledged, a very crucial component to our wholeness will appear to be missing. If we assume that misrepresenting or manipulating our experience will get us what we want, we will live within an inauthenticity that provides us with something we don't want—but we are likely to remain unconscious of the connection between the two.

Chasing After Fulfillment

19:28   Another assumption that exists in our culture is the presumption of fulfillment. We presume that we should be fulfilled, even deserve to be fulfilled. We also assume we know how this should take place, and that attaining one's desires will provide a sense of fulfillment and happiness. When asked, however, most people really have no concrete idea how they could attain fulfillment beyond a fuzzy notion of obtaining everything they desire. Anyone who has gotten past the initial delight at attaining some desire can attest that deep fulfillment and happiness are not forthcoming, or at least not for long. We can observe that after fulfilling any number of desires, the need for fulfillment remains an issue.

19:29 Still we assume, especially in our culture, that somehow we deserve to obtain what we want — that we deserve to feel good, to get our way, to have our every desire realized. Since we assume that getting what we want should naturally come about, we can see the many ways in which struggling would become a constant activity, and a lack of fulfillment, both shallow and deep, couldn't help but work its way into our ongoing experience. Chasing unattainable fulfillment is but one of the ingredients in the cheese that our mouse so diligently runs after. Another one is our set of ideals.

Pursuing Ideals

19:30 Our stories and fables, our cultural myths and allegories, help provide us with important cohesive standards for behavior and benchmarks for finding meaning and attaining fulfillment. Dependence on them, however, leaves us vulnerable in an unexpected way. Our relationship to these ideals — which represent the shoulds and shouldn'ts of our community, family, and selves — can actually be quite damaging.

19:31 Since we were very young we have been inundated with stories and ideas of destiny, romantic notions of being a hero or heroine, of being someone special, fulfilling our potential for greatness, or realizing a dream. From such culturally promoted ideals we are likely to assume that something awaits us in our lives, that our individual existence has a particular purpose and meaning. Of course, this purpose and meaning is frequently obscure. Realizing this destiny, fulfilling a life plan, is supposed to give meaning to life, without which we would likely feel something is missing or that our life is not living up to its potential.

19:32 In the background everyone has images of what their lives and selves should be like. These can be quite subtle and buried, or very obvious and openly touted, perhaps presenting a standard impossible to reach. Although almost no one would admit to the more outrageous ideals—being a superman in ability, the wisest human on earth, or a saint in spirit—they nevertheless tend to have such ideas in some form or another and can be quite dominated by them.

19:33 How could anyone possibly be dominated by such outrageous fantasies? First, they don't exist as a fantasy, they exist as what's expected, as that which would make a person worthwhile, special, and loved. Yet it isn't just the impossible ideals that run us. We are chock-full of all sorts of images of who we should be, and who we shouldn't be. These are both personal and cultural. But the bottom line is always the same: we don't perceive ourselves to be that way. By presuming that we should be some way that we are not, we are setting ourselves up for disappointment.

Some dictionary definitions of ideal:

Ideal, n.

   1. A conception of something in its absolute perfection.

   2. One that is regarded as a standard or model of perfection or excellence.

   3. An ultimate object of endeavor; a goal.

Ideal, adj.

   1. Conforming to an ultimate form or standard of perfection or excellence.

2. a. Existing only in the mind; imaginary. b. Lacking practicality or the possibility of realization.

3. *Philosophy*. a. Existing as an archetype or pattern, especially as a Platonic idea or perception.

19:34   We see that, as a noun, *ideal* is described as perfect, ultimate, worthy. These sound good and we'd all like to be considered perfect, to attain the ultimate in human existence, and certainly to be found worthy. Yet is this our experience? Not likely. We often hear the phrase "no one is perfect," and yet we are still filled to the brim with what a perfect self should be like. If both are true — no one is perfect, and yet we should be perfect — it is clear we can't avoid a strong internal conflict.

19:35   We do not experience, and perhaps cannot attain, an ultimate status in anything. The thing is, these are concepts, mere ideas. They are not supposed to be occurring as a human life. Another way to say that is: the life lived consciously and genuinely as itself *is* the perfect life; it is exactly what it is without distortion or deceit, without pretense or fraud. This makes it perfectly what it is. But this is not our case. We are always relating to a battery of ideals that form the world of what we're not, but should be.

19:36   What if ideals never were meant to be attained? Sounds silly, doesn't it? Of course they are meant to be attained; it is only ourselves that are lacking. Perhaps not. Perhaps, in fact, there is nothing lacking within ourselves at all. If an ideal was not meant to be attained, in other words, "lacked the possibility of realization," then what good is it, and why does it exist? An ideal may have been created to serve the function of providing a direction in which to develop, or it may have been instilled as a form of control, a way to standardize values, or to humble the recipient. All manner of possibilities could explain the presence of our many ideals, none of which require personal realization. We can see once again that the analogy of chasing an unattainable cheese fits here perfectly.

19:37 For the most part, we fail to notice how numerous and unconscious many of our ideals are. Most of them aren't what we consciously call our ideals. They're unnoticed and often unglamorous shoulds and shouldn'ts that we live as accepted failings or as personal aspirations. We are like fish in water, and find it difficult to make out the ideals that run us because they are always present and constantly running us. The mass of beliefs and images we have that act as "ideals" are wired into our thinking, our self-images and self-concepts. They act on us without any conscious effort on our part. When a phrase such as "existing as an archetype or pattern" is included in the definition of ideal, we understand this better by recognizing that many patterns in our thinking are devoted to what we are not. These are usually not even patterns observed to be so of us — such as observable patterns that characterize the self's identity. What an ideal archetype or pattern represents is something not so observed, but something imagined and idealized.

19:38 Being programmed with so many nonoccurring images and ideals, we can't help but experience a huge emptiness. We can't help but compare and contrast what isn't — fantasies of our future destiny, images of how we should be or how things should turn out, beliefs about what life should be like, standards to which we should measure up — with what "is," or at least "is perceived," and find the "is" lacking. By extension, we find ourselves lacking.

19:39 To make matters worse, we have as many "anti-ideals" that drive our experience as well. This form of ideal consists of what shouldn't be true of us, or what we fear may be true of us. Running away from something is ultimately the same dynamic as running toward something. These shape us as much as any perfection ideal. Pursing our ideals, both subtle and gross, drives us in the same direction as fleeing from our anti-ideals. Altogether this world of images and ideas contributes a great deal to the particular cheese we run toward — or in the case of anti-ideals, away from — and molds our experience to a large extent by forming the parameters of how we should be. But we remain separated from this cheese that was never meant to be attained. We suffer in our ignorance and struggle.

19:40 Normally we presume that ideals are a good thing, that they represent what we should strive for, and indicate admirable qualities in a human being. Yet we overlook the damaging effects of ideals. We fail to recognize the fact that many of the images to which we aspire, including our programs of shoulds and shouldn'ts, are not so idyllic. We also don't notice that binding ourselves to these mostly unattainable and unlikely self-images, and fleeing from our feared self-images, keeps us perpetually in motion. This motion is unhealthy, shaming, and provides a lot of fuel for our sense of emptiness, since we don't exist within our ideals. Ideals are never focused on what "is" and so are never about what we are; therefore they can't lead to a genuine and honest sense of being.

19:41 In any case, we are stuck in a relationship with these beliefs that leaves us bereft of the qualities that suggest we are already what we should be. An "ideal" is largely used as something to indicate what we are not. At best it provides a direction in which to go. At worst, it is something we use to beat ourselves up with because we find ourselves and our lives continuously lacking.

19:42   It will take some contemplative efforts to discover all of your ideals and anti-ideals. The doorway to such a practice is a nonjudgmental feeling-sensitivity to your innermost notions about yourself. (You will have an opportunity to work on increasing your contemplative skills in upcoming chapters.) The point here is that cultural assumptions regarding ideals can't help but contribute to your nagging background sense of emptiness. Inherent in the drive for attaining ideals is a need for meaning. It's not hard to see how this need might be another contributor to emptiness.

A Need for Meaning

19:43   If we presume that we should inherently have meaning, we would naturally expect meaning to fill our experience of self and life. But how would this happen? What makes us meaningful? This may vary depending on the individual and culture, but don't we generally expect a degree of significance, of personal value and worth, to accompany our existence? There is no question that we are supposed to have meaning—it is a hallmark of self-survival. Without meaning, what could it all possibly *mean*? What is life *for*? A life or self devoid of meaning is regarded as depressing, something to be avoided at all costs. Let's look anyway.

19:44   Imagine that your existence is itself—that your actual "being" exists for itself. This might be said like "you are because you are," or "you exist that you exist." The only way something has meaning or value is in relation to something else. If we ask, "What does an apple mean?" what are we asking? We find we are stopped short. We need to ask what we mean by "What does an apple mean?" Unless we are referring to something other than the existence of the apple, the question doesn't make any sense. This is because an apple doesn't "mean" anything just "being" an apple. What does a person mean? What do you mean? Just like the apple, these questions have no relevance. We don't mean anything in just being. In order to determine our meaning, we have to look at our relationship to our community, or our value or usefulness in relation to something else.

19:45 For example, an apple is valuable to us as a food item. It is valuable to the apple tree as a reproductive organ, and if we used the apple as a ball, it would be useful for playing catch. What does the apple mean? Unless we apply some meaning to the apple's existence, we cannot really determine such a thing. If we can't say what kind of tool it could be used for, what function it might serve, or what destiny we can imagine for it — all of which are relations of the apple to something else, such as to ourselves, the tree, a game, or an ideal — we can find no meaning whatsoever. The apple simply exists. This means that without relationship or comparison, without ascribing a use, there is no inherent meaning in the apple all by itself. It is simply being an apple — it has no meaning.

Meaning, n.

    1. An interpreted goal, intent, or end.

    2. Significance.

    3. The sense in which something is understood: import.

To mean, v.

    1. To act as a symbol of; signify or represent.

    2. To design, intend, or destine for a certain purpose or end.

    3. To have as a consequence; bring about.

    4. To have the importance or value of.

Meaningless

1. Having no significance.

2. Having no assigned function.

3. Not formed according to the rules.

4. Not being a genuine element.

19:46　Whenever we apply meaning to the apple, we will miss the experience of the apple just being an apple. Instead we are concerned with its use or its future. Meaning is a secondary application. Does the apple deserve "apple rights?" Does it deserve fulfillment, or to feel good, or to have its way? Obviously it would be impossible to tell what that could possibly be, but even if we could, it would be ridiculous to assume that apples deserve anything beyond being an apple. It is equally absurd to presume that we deserve anything, or require value just in the course of "being." "Being" has no meaning. It just "is." Therefore, we have no inherent meaning; we simply are.

19:47　To our cultural ears this might sound like a negative, but it isn't negative at all. As a matter of fact, there is some very good news in all this. "Meaninglessness" here doesn't mean "less meaning" or "negative meaning." Meaningless means "without meaning." It is "no" meaning. Therefore, we are inherently free of meaning. Realizing this should immediately end our struggle for meaning. Do you see how this works? Although it might sound depressing to hear that you have no meaning, the good news is that you absolutely cannot be worthless. Since value is a function of use, it is artificially applied to things; it is secondary and not inherent in anything. This indicates that it is impossible for anyone to be inherently worthless.

19:48   It also means that one cannot have value. The whole issue of value and worth, of meaning and significance, is a social issue. It is not applicable to "being." One simply is what one is; this cannot be measured, valued, or made to be in any way better or worse than it is. As a matter of fact, better or worse cannot apply to "is." Would you cease to exist if everyone thought you were worthless? Would you begin to exist if everyone thought you were great? Of course not. Did you exist before you had any notion of good or bad, self-consciousness, knowledge, worth, or any judgments whatsoever? Of course you did. So obviously you *aren't* any of it. Your "being" exists as itself, for itself. The rest is secondary.

19:49   We *create* any meaning that our selves or lives have. This is actually the only place a "meaningful" life can occur. Knowing this empowers us to take responsibility for any meaning or lack of meaning we might experience. The significance of our lives is an assessment that we make. It is determined by whatever goals, ends, or usefulness we assess as meaningful, and how we act in relation to this assessment. Yet no matter how much meaning we apply, as a "being" we are still unchanged—we have no meaning.

19:50   The point is that feeling empty because we can't find meaning is a mistake. If there is no meaning to "being," then no meaning can ever be found. This is not cause for depression, it is simply the truth. Instead of a negative relationship to this condition, we can find reason to celebrate our state of openness and revel in the freedom it affords. It is the same dynamic we've seen occurring with not-knowing. Whenever we designate some inherent condition of our own *being* as a negative, we are compelled to deny and resist that condition, creating a fundamental separation from a genuine experience of ourselves. Suffering this condition is completely unnecessary and inappropriate.

Being — Without Knowing

19:51   We've seen that whenever we look deep within, we can always find a sense of not-knowing in one form or another. It may show up as a feeling of ignorance, or as just not having desired information. It may show as an absence of understanding, or as not knowing who or what we really are. It may manifest as the suspicion that unknown aspects exist within ourselves that nevertheless influence our reactions and behavior, or it may simply be a sense that something is missing or inauthentic. However it appears, the bottom line is that we simply don't know. Given our cultural assumption that this somehow points to a defect, we naturally feel discomfort and perhaps even a bit of panic.

19:52   As is obvious by now, not-knowing is a normal and healthy aspect of being human. Whenever we set up antagonistic relationships to our own attributes, we will continue to run into problems. One of the more central and yet overlooked areas in which not-knowing has a distressing effect was addressed early on — this is the possible origins or foundation upon which we create a self.

19:53   I've suggested that because we actually don't know how we came to be, or what existence is, we are drawn into a game of pretending to be something and calling that "who we are." This probably goes on subconsciously for most people, and since we are so filled with beliefs, it may be difficult to recognize. It is quite obvious, however, once the first glimmer is seen. Having this condition (in which we are without a direct conscious experience of the nature of self, reality, or existence) will necessarily produce an experience of somehow being separate from those things. Doesn't it seem strange that our everyday experience seems separated from the deepest aspects of ourselves and reality?

19:54 We are clear that we exist, and that we exist within reality. We just don't know how we came to exist or the ultimate nature of existence. Given that these questions remain, we are bound to sense a very profound ignorance at the deepest levels of our consciousness. Not-knowing occurs as a lack of conscious experience, and therefore will evoke a sense of disconnection from the very roots of our existence. This experience may well be at the heart of our sense of isolation and separation, our sense of emptiness.

19:55 Contrary to our culturally popular assumption that asserting an opinion or taking on a particular belief about these ultimate matters will somehow resolve one's place in the universe, actually the opposite is true. Standing on the artificial ground of hearsay or opinion — no matter how seriously or reverently it is done — actually places us in a position of pretense. It forces us to ignore our ignorance, and binds us to a conceptual overlay that might seem like a ship come to our rescue, but is no such thing.

19:56 As long as we can get our minds to believe some given answer in all seriousness, we might be able to fool our sensibilities and psychology into perceiving reality as being consistent with such beliefs. But if we question the truth in any way, our lack of personal and authentic experience of the roots of self and reality will emerge, and we are likely to feel lacking or defective. In truth we are neither lacking nor defective; we are simply not-knowing.

Existential Loneliness

19:57 Have you ever felt alone even in a crowd? This is an example of being existentially alone. What does that mean? It means that this aloneness exists simply because self exists. You exist as a distinction that is set off from all that it is not—which is what makes a self a discrete entity—and this creates a core sense of being separate and isolated. Because a self is conceptual in nature, it also lacks any objective solidity, and this adds to your sense of unreality. You tend to overlook the source of this universal human condition and suffer as if it is an undeserved affliction that perhaps you alone endure.

19:58 Since we seem to live within our own internal world, a sense of isolation is to be expected. We may share ourselves with others and value their company, but some deep aspect of our being never seems to be touched by them, or rarely in any case. This may owe its origins to two conditions. The first we've already discussed: the sense of disconnection created by our lack of direct personal experience when it comes to the basic origins and nature of our own existence. The second might be best understood through the use of the Lucifer myth.

19:59 A myth of long ago tells us of a fallen angel, Lucifer, whose statement to God went something like: "I'd rather rule in hell than serve in heaven." My understanding of this myth is that Lucifer is the self—that it points to an illusion within, an activity to which our original being falls prey, separating us from what's real and true. The hell in which we rule is our own self-mind. The heaven we refuse to serve is the real nature of being, the absolute truth.

19:60 It is within our own minds that we seem to have free reign. There we can adulterate or distort whatever we wish. We can choose what to accept and what to reject, what to believe and what to disbelieve. It is within our own minds that we can lie, pretend, misrepresent, affect, ignore, and more. It is here that we have our opinions and pass our judgments. We can reorient data, rearrange facts, and disregard the truth if we so desire. We can alter our perceptions and recreate our memories. It is here that we reside as a self overlord. This is where it appears as though we rule.

19:61 We can do all this, but we can't create a sense of being connected. Our "rule" requires a separation between what we experience in our own cognizant mind, and our experience of others and reality — as well as a separation between us and the absolute truth. Although we seem to be the self-overlord, in truth we suffer the consequences of this illusion, and so our little fiefdom also becomes our prison, and we spend our time serving a false master, and struggling against meaningless foes. This is the world of the self.

19:62 On the other hand, if we were to be dominated by whatever's true, if absolute reality impinged upon our awareness in no uncertain terms without allowing for distortion or alteration in any way, or ignorance of any kind, then we would have no choice but to succumb to an experience of being at one with the truth and reality. Another way to look at it is: without self there is no separation. We could call this "serving" Absolute Consciousness.

19:63 Regardless of how this illusion of self-rule came to pass or what we may be able to do about it, the fact remains that we find ourselves within an awareness that is separate and introverted. At our core we suffer a sense of "existential aloneness" — an experience that we are alone simply in the act of existing. This is a result of existing as a separate self-awareness, and this awareness is, by definition, isolated.

The Assumptions of Emptiness

19:64   Our sense of emptiness can take many forms and be generated by various sources. In the end, each is in essence based on mistaken notions or dispositions to life or the human condition. We assume many things that lead us to feelings such as being inadequate, disconnected, or empty. Let's review some of what we've looked at that contributes to this consequence:

- Misrepresentation leads to a lack of integrity, the consequence of which is a deep sense of inauthenticity.

- The idea that we deserve fulfillment sets us up for endless disappointments.

- Both conscious and unconscious ideals tend to create an unnecessary loop of comparing what "is" to fantasies about what "isn't," and finding "is" lacking.

- Much of our childhood programming leaves us infused with shoulds and shouldn'ts that we take for granted and are driven by without creating satisfaction.

- Our self-survival assumption that we *must* have meaning condemns us to an endless struggle with the fact that we have no inherent meaning or value.

- Our core ignorance of the true nature of reality draws us into believing claims regarding ultimate matters that are in fact simply unknown.

- Merely being a self provides an existential loneliness that we can easily mistake for a very distressing effect.

19:65 Other influences can contribute to our sense of emptiness, as we will see when more connections are made and assumptions addressed, but they all boil down to one basic fact: they are founded on assumptions, and they are unnecessary. These assumptions exist within the context of the self, and whether culturally assumed or not, their importance lies in their relation to your self. Let go of the self and all of these assumptions lose their power.

19:66 Don't forget, however, that simply because something is a concept doesn't mean it is without power. Our core concepts have great power and influence in our lives. They can very easily be perceived as real and solid aspects of life, since, for us, they are. We can't deny the pain and suffering we experience from time to time. We clearly struggle with life and our self-image on occasion, and we have overwhelming emotions that press us toward unwanted behavior now and then. All of these are rooted in the conceptual realm, yet their force in our lives is undeniable. They simply aren't necessary, and they aren't etched in stone.

19:67 Since the domain of emptiness is based on mistaken shared assumptions, the feelings associated with emptiness can be used to track down those assumptions and eliminate them. Using some form of contemplative effort, set out to embrace the empty feelings, intending to fully feel and deeply experience what they are really about and so discover the assumptions that generate them. This allows you to begin freeing yourself of the assumptions. Of course this is easier said than done, but a few chapters ahead we'll take a pragmatic look into contemplation as a functional practice. First we will address the four remaining consequences in greater detail.

CHAPTER TWENTY
Freedom from Assumptions—Part Two

20:1   Addressing the four remaining consequences will bring to light some interesting dynamics that are frequently overlooked, and will also take us much deeper into our search for assumptions. Self-doubt has a significant contribution to make here, as does feeling trapped, but when we tackle the heart of all negative experience in suffering, we are taking on the very primal and core assumptions of the human condition. Such assumptions will take deep contemplation to experience since they definitely run counter to our conventional views, and certainly to the force of self-survival. Without suffering, no struggle would be necessary, but glancing at the domain of struggle helps us realize more clearly the foundation for many of our actions—both in our internal state and our behavior. Let's continue our work on assumptions with a look at self-doubt.

Self-Doubt

20:2   The effects of self-doubt are more prevalent than most people realize. The form and depth of this doubt, however, aren't limited to low self-esteem. At its root, we've seen that we doubt our very existence—we have reason to suspect that somehow we may not be real, that in some way we may not even exist. At first glance, this assertion seems absurd, doesn't it? Such a notion seems contradicted by our very experience — which confirms our existence from moment to moment. But it's not the *having* of experience that we doubt; it's the authenticity and realness of our selves that are in question. We quickly see that self-doubt is closely linked to the origins and effects of emptiness.

20:3   Once again, popular beliefs and family programming about who we are and who we should be provide many of our personal doubts. Struggling to be what is expected — for ourselves and others — becomes an almost full-time job. It rarely dawns on us that this might be a foolish occupation. If we didn't doubt ourselves in some way, if we didn't think that what we are — or are not — should be some other way, then our efforts to live up to expectations would be unnecessary. Yet, at its heart, the presumption of self-doubt isn't about whether we are a "good" person or not, it is whether we are a "real" person or not.

Doubting Our Own Reality

20:4   The sort of challenge to our thinking that I'm proposing here is not common. In self-survival we see that our attention is driven toward the ways we need to manifest in order to get what we want — by appearing worthy or good, or useless or "bad" — whatever gets the job done or is valued by self, family, or a particular subculture. In such a context, we are rarely invited to openly consider how real or authentic we are, except in a philosophy class or spiritual quest of some kind. Whether openly confessed or not, the question of our realness is the source of much of our personal distress.

20:5   Since we are not aware of ultimate truths—nor are we absolutely certain about the most appropriate way to accomplish our continued survival or even deal with all the complexities of social interactions—we feel unsure. Our sense of disconnection from what we presume "should be known" leaves us open to uncertainty and insecurity. Living without knowing who we are, or what life is, we are sure to sense some doubt in the matter, regardless how many beliefs we've piled on top of it. We've seen again and again how, in a very deep way, our not-knowing is perceived as a grave personal defect. This sense of defect is suppressed for the most part, but is cause for embarrassment and self-doubt nevertheless.

20:6   When we begin to be honest about it, refusing to be bullied by cultural embarrassments and assertions, we start to see that no one knows everything. Everyone shares this state of not-knowing, yet no one is willing to admit it. Once enough social games are mastered, or beliefs obtained, most would rather pretend a greater degree of understanding and capability than is true of them. This adds fuel to the tendency of adopting attributes that altogether we've called a false-self. Such misrepresentation can't help but lead to feeling in some way a fraud. Feeling like a secret charlatan is sure to exacerbate the doubt we have about our own realness.

20:7   Turning inward, it is not hard to find a sense that an essential aspect of ourselves is without a substantial character or a precise mind. This aspect of our being is usually ignored, but felt nevertheless. Socially, our tendency is to hide this unformed beingness, to cover it up, and present something else in its place. Having no substance or definite form, such a state of beingness doesn't appear capable of handling the job of social interaction. The tendency to cover up, however, turns into a vicious cycle. The act of creating a persona or adopting a way to be that appears socially viable and acceptable suggests that we doubt ourselves, that we don't trust what is already naturally there. By pursuing affectations in order to bolster our self-image and disguise our self-doubt, we are confessing to ourselves that we don't trust our own reality, that whatever is genuine isn't good enough to be presented, and so must be submerged. This reinforces self-doubt.

20:8   It also reveals to us an aspect of our own manipulative mind. No matter how we try to justify or ignore it, if being genuine means not knowing what to do, where to stand, or how to present oneself, we will tend to choose a path of inauthenticity instead. Since everything within the domain of self-survival is evaluated, we see that "real" and "authentic" have a different value than unreal and fake. A lack of realness implies a lack of substance and therefore a lack of worth. Self as unreal would have no value, and so the idea can't be taken seriously. The mere notion that self is not real is unacceptable for us since it represents a real threat to the self. Therefore, suspicion of our possible unreality must be hidden away from others to preserve the perception of our value and meaning, and must also be kept hidden from ourselves for the same reason.

20:9   As we've seen with the snowball effect, once such manipulative behavior and identification begin, they grow. Yet how can so much struggle be attributed to whether we are real or not? "Of course we are real; we have to be. It is a matter of fact, isn't it?" It's hard to buy into all this fuss about realness.

Proof of Our Own Existence?

20:10   Everyone has heard the phrase from Descartes: *Cogito, ergo sum,* or "I think; therefore I am." But few have a clue as to his real meaning or how he came to such an assertion. The most common interpretation is that it asserts "beingness," the proof of which is our thinking: if I think, I must exist. And yet few people have any idea what it took for Descartes to arrive at such a simple statement. Perhaps a quick second look might be useful.

20:11   His real work in this area related to doubt. He began a long and difficult practice of doubting everything. He doubted what was believed by his culture and religion. He doubted what he had been taught or had learned. He doubted what he thought and believed, what he perceived, and so on. As he approached a state where he could doubt everything, he was still left with the observation that he couldn't doubt that he was doubting. Realizing that the action of doubt is beyond doubt (since if it is doubted, doubt would no longer exist) leaves us with what is simply occurring—the act of doubting. It is itself, so to speak. So his original notion might have been more like: I doubt; therefore I doubt.

20:12   Being unable to doubt the very act of doubting reveals something beyond doubt. In such a realization you become aware of the existence of the source condition that is doing the negating or doubting. In other words, the first thing is always what is occurring as itself. It is simply what "is"; in this case, the act of doubting. An assessment is always secondary. You can doubt your belief that something is true; you can doubt that your experience means what you think it means; you can doubt any assertion about the nature of things, even the realness of things. These are all about something other than the action of doubting. They are once removed from the thing being doubted, as well as the action of doubting and the source of the doubting. Yet the act itself is itself.

The thought of an apple is not an apple, but it is a thought.

20:13 Descartes' insight may have sprung from a direct experience of the "doubter," the one that doubts. Perception may not be accurate or even real, but the act of perceiving is difficult to deny. What we think may be completely false, but *that* we think seems self-evident. Perhaps another statement he could have made would be: I cognize therefore I am (cognizing).

20:14 What's most intriguing about this subject, however, is the speed at which people grab onto a statement that is rarely understood but seems to confirm one's existence. Why do you think we adopt and assert such a thing so readily? "I think; therefore I am." It is frequently said with a certain degree of pride in the background — right next to the doubt that presses such an assertion to the fore. Could it be that we aren't so certain?

20:15 Yes, it absolutely could. We're not certain. Strange thing to say, isn't it? But true nevertheless. "I think; therefore I *am*." Why do we feel so drawn to such a statement? Why is it so well-known and popular? Could it be because it is one of the few assertions that flat-out suggests proof of our own existence? For most of us it is completely superficial, and in no way suggests a direct experience or insight. Yet it still seems to validate the fact that we must exist, that we are real. After all, we do think. Is this proof that we indeed exist? What a close one! We were almost caught doubting whether we are real or not.

20:16 The depth of our "self" doubt is not something fully acknowledged. All sorts of beliefs can divert us from such a discomforting and unconventional notion. We'll take anything! Yet somewhere deep inside and rarely visited, we doubt. At some point, everyone confesses some sense of inauthenticity or doubt. After all, for all you know, you may be the only one that doesn't really know who you are or what life is all about. This generates a feeling of insecurity and uncertainty. Riding on the crest of this doubt are our tendencies to pretend, misrepresent, embellish, fake, and so on—no matter how sophisticated is their presentation. In simple terms, we doubt our own existence, we doubt our "selves." This doubt can be rectified by simply allowing not-knowing to be a fully acknowledged aspect of being alive, or by becoming directly conscious of your own true nature.

Feeling Trapped

20:17   Assumptions that lead to emptiness or self-doubt can easily contribute to feelings such as being dominated, stuck, impotent, restricted, limited, imprisoned, helpless, and whatnot. We've seen that feeling trapped is found in our inability to change or be free of things unwanted—our own weaknesses, the influence of others, or circumstances. In essence, the fundamental root of this consequence is a sense of being incapable.

20:18   If we felt truly capable in the area in which we felt trapped, certainly we would feel free to eliminate such circumstances. Therefore, we can see that an assumption of "incapacity" exists in our relationship to life. Since we are in doubt regarding ourselves and our realness, and since our experience is disconnected from directly knowing what life is all about or what the ultimate nature of reality is, it is not hard to see that we have cause to question our capacity to deal with it all. Yet we assume we should be able to deal with it all, that as a self we should be capable of life.

20:19   No one was given the authoritative manual regarding life and how to live it. We are personally quite blank on that important subject. We may have learned a great deal, and have had instilled within us many beliefs and viewpoints, but this does not diminish our ability to notice that originally we ourselves don't know; that everything that gets us through life began as external to us — as not-us. This isn't a very comforting observation. It suggests that we don't inherently have what it takes to handle the tasks of life, or know what life is all about. We seem to have to get these crucial skills and knowledge elsewhere — they don't come with the package. Given this condition, it is easy to feel walled off from any inherent capacity to manage life in the ways that we would like.

20:20   Maybe we are given the ability to learn these things and the will to do so, and perhaps it is true that this condition applies to everyone. But we aren't dealing with a reasonable explanation; we are dealing with a deep psychological impact. It might be true for me that my life is in the hands of the pilot whenever I'm flying in an aircraft. Not being a pilot I may have no choice in the matter, but that doesn't stop me from noticing that my life is not in my own hands. In a similar way, this is our fate throughout our entire life. As such it is likely to generate a deep and frequently overlooked sense of incapacity.

20:21   Clearly the self is charged with the responsibility of being capable, but this doesn't match our deep-seated experience. Seeing that our simple "beingness" doesn't appear to have what it takes to survive in life, something else seems called for. The activity that is called into action to serve this need is the "self." But all of the struggles and machinations we engage to deal with life or free ourselves from perceived limitations don't change our inherent nature. Our feelings of limitation may simply be a result of ignorance and mistaken assumptions.

20:22 Whenever we experience a limitation, it appears as though we are thwarted from getting what we want. Limitation, however, may not be the problem. Confronting some sort of limitation in our capacity, knowledge, or skill, or our inability to break free of some influence or obstacle, may have us feeling trapped, but this disposition is of our own making. We want all things to be possible and we struggle against any obstruction. We don't notice that limitation and possibility are the same thing. We assume that one provides access, the other restriction, and overlook the fact they both exist as sides of the same coin.

20:23 Possibility is open-ended. When we consider that something is possible, we have already limited this openness to a particular idea or form in which it can "be" possible. Without this "formation" of the possibility, it would not actually be possible, since infinite possibility doesn't manifest as anything in particular. By limiting possibility to a particular form it becomes possible to actualize it in reality. The existence of something means it is possible for it to exist, and also that it is limited to that exact way of existing. They are the same event. So whenever we confront a limitation, we are confronting a particular possibility. Whenever we want to realize a possibility, we can only do so in the domain of limitation — that is what makes it real in the objective world in which we live.

20:24 What's frequently the case in our disposition of being trapped is that there may be no real problem whatsoever, except in the assumption that there is. It's a bit like the conundrum of asking someone posing as *The Thinker* why his fist is stuck to his chin.

One could meditate this for a long time, but the truth is that his fist is not stuck to his chin, so we can never discover why it is. Another good example of this is seen in that monkey caught with his hand in a bottle. He can't pull his hand back out, because he won't let go of the fruit. Is the monkey trapped? Only by his own action, his own desire, and his ignorance of the relationship between his impulse and being trapped. In so many ways this applies to our own condition. Often the solution to being trapped is to recognize that you are indeed not trapped at all.

Suffering

20:25 It's obvious that self-doubt, emptiness, and feeling trapped are all forms of suffering, as are pain, loss, fear, despair, and count-less other states visited with unceasing regularity within the human condition. We've heard that the key to suffering is found in the mechanisms of self-survival. The real truth of this, how-ever, continues to be harder to grasp experientially than it is to understand intellectually. This core dynamic needs to be reviewed frequently just to make a dent in the very mind whose operating principle is self-survival even as it's trying to grasp self-survival. It takes time and repeated exposure.

20:26 Right now try not just hearing "about" it, but get that it is hap-pening "as" your experience. The experience of a self surviving is the experience you are having in this very moment. It is already that way; nothing has to change to get it. You live with a constant background sensation of a self surviving. Your instinctive and powerful devotion to your persistence and self-concerns provides the fuel for everything you perceive and do — and "are." This includes all that you call positive as well as negative. Although you struggle to avoid the negative and attain the positive, you are stuck in unconscious cycles designed to provide a never-ending flow of both. In the end this is called suffering.

20:27 In our work in earlier chapters I asserted that self-survival is the cause of all suffering. Although we have already addressed this argument, it is wise to hear it again and to dig a little more deeply into it in the process. Looking again at some of the basic but over-looked axioms of self-survival helps set the stage.

- Within the fact of "being," there is no need to pursue something that's not present. Yet, whenever we are serving our self-interests, we are in fact pursuing what isn't rather than what simply is. Survival is an activity directed toward the pursuit of things that are not.

- When something pursued is attained, survival demands the protection and maintenance of that thing, continuing to pursue what isn't. Most of our attention proceeds to whatever "isn't" that's deemed necessary to maintain or further our selves and our survival.

- This is not an experience of "being." It is an experience of a self struggling to survive.

- Suffering is an inherent aspect of self-survival.

Self-Survival Causes Suffering—Revisited

20:28 We can readily recognize the kinds of suffering inflicted upon our lives by unfortunate and unavoidable circumstances — the death of a loved one, the loss of our fortune, being left by someone we love, losing a leg in an auto accident, and so on. Even though these incidents are traumatic, and often have effects long after the events have passed, we maintain many more frequent forms of suffering that are not so dramatic but just as influential. We might be bothered by an overly chatty friend, be irritated because someone took our favorite parking place at work, feel unheard in conversations with our mate. These and many more daily incidents that are quite common and too subtle to stand out are more often the events that compose the greater portion of our suffering. Regardless of the circumstances that invite our suffering, none of it would arise if we had no commitment to assert and defend the self—and so pursue what isn't. If we could free ourselves from self-survival, we would free ourselves from suffering.

20:29 Such a statement might still sound far-fetched or nonsensical. After all, the most important and cherished impulse of being alive is the desire to persist as oneself. Without such an impulse, we assume that we would not live very long, since the forces of nature would soon overwhelm and destroy us. This might be true, but regardless, our reflexive drive to survive as a self is the source of our suffering, and so we need to do more work to understand how this is so.

20:30 It is clear in the most obvious forms of physical danger, such as being attacked by a grizzly bear, that our suffering is directly related to our concerns for self-survival. We can see that all of our suffering just prior to the attack exists within our own minds— seeing this monstrous creature charging our way will likely evoke great fear and anxiety. Yet if we didn't give a fig about whether we lived or died, this fear would not exist.

20:31 When the bear comes chomping down on our body, certainly we can expect a degree of pain, and yet without any fear being provided by imagining the dismal forecast of the end of our lives, there is only pain. Although this might well be very uncomfortable, we are not suffering our "death," only some pain. Most people don't realize how much more painful physical pain becomes when we add our emotional and mental suffering to it.

20:32   Even this physical pain, viewed deeply enough as a preference for certain sensations over others, would disappear if we could manage to achieve a state of having no preference for or aversion to any sensation or experience whatsoever. Because this preference or aversion only exists as a mechanism for our need to survive, it is possible to *not* create the painful mental and emotional reactions evoked by the circumstance of being mauled, and it is also possible to *not* create pain in relation to the physical sensations of being mauled. So we can see that it may be possible to not "suffer" even the most brutal form of physical death. Such a possibility depends on giving up the desire and attachment to persist in any way at all.

20:33   Few of us are ready for such extreme detachment. We're unlikely to take on or even want to take on a state of mind so detached that we would give up caring about our own destruction. The good news is that we don't have to go to such an extreme, and we can still end virtually all of our suffering. We can't do it, however, without fully grasping and embracing the very same principle that frees us from suffering even when being eaten alive by a bear. If we can't imagine experiencing this principle in such an extreme circumstance, it is because we are still stuck in a context of self-survival and remain blind to any reality outside of that context.

20:34   Most of our suffering is not about physical danger at all, but arises from danger that is entirely conceptual. Taking effective action to avoid danger requires no upset, anguish, fear, or any other painful reaction. As a matter of fact, it turns out that our ability to respond effectively to a physical encounter is enhanced when these forms of suffering are absent. Whether danger is physical or conceptual, the very same freeing principle applies. If freedom from concern for our physical death would end suffering related to physical danger, then freedom from concerns over conceptual or "egoic" threats should do the same. It does.

20:35   Where does suffering arise? In our experience of something, which means it is created by the mind. There is no suffering in an object. If suffering is not inherent within the existence of anything, then experiencing something as-itself and for-itself cannot produce suffering. It is only within the interpretive mind that suffering takes place.

20:36   My internal state can only interact with the objective world through physical actions. Any suffering that's created is a result of this mind both producing actions and perceiving reality in relation to self's survival. For example, say I am a very "macho" guy and would rather die than be seen as a coward. If my courage is challenged or threatened, I might enter into some deadly physical dare — perhaps wrestle a grizzly bear — to prove my courage and "defend" my self-image. Give it some thought and you'll see that this is not a physical survival issue but a social one.

20:37   Likewise, if I hold myself to be a woman of great taste and refinement, I could spend a fortune I don't have on the most tasteful dress to wear to the ball in order to maintain my self-image in the eyes of others and myself. Yet, even though in these two examples the focus is on a strictly physical event — wrestling a grizzly or obtaining a dress — the expression is an act of social survival. In each case, both the "danger" and the response are conceptually produced and serve a conceptual purpose. Take away the devoted commitment to the persistence of a self-image and they would not occur, and so neither would the physical challenges or any pain that results from them.

20:38   Still, it's not the *having* of a self-image that creates suffering, it's that we *identify* with it. Those may seem like the same act, since for us the mere having of an image of self is the same as identifying oneself via conceptual imagery. But this doesn't need to be the case. It is possible not to identify with the images we have about ourselves. We can allow it to be just an image, separate from the reality of the self. No matter what form the self-identity takes, the same principle applies. The very act of *identifying* one's self occurs through "having" or "being" any number of perceived phenomena. If we don't identify with any of it, we can't suffer in our struggle to maintain or defend or to persist as any of it.

20:39   Imagine walking in the forest. You pick up a stick. You *have* the stick; it is in your hand. You toss it away. No problem. There is no suffering the loss of the stick unless you're attached to it. Once you pick it up, however, there might arise a sense of ownership, or you might use it as a symbol of your personal domain of influence, and these acts will link it to your self. But one can have a stick and not identify with the stick at all. You have it. You don't have it. It doesn't matter. Such an idea is more easily seen with sticks since it is possible to imagine not getting attached to a stick. But even this is a bit of a challenge since *you* picked it up, *you* hold it, it is *yours* . . . and bingo, self is confused with the stick, at least just a little.

20:40   When we can see all that we cling to—all that we call our "selves"—on a par with sticks, it may be possible to have these experiences, perceive them for what they are, and not confuse our selves with their presence. "That's my opinion, this is how I see myself, here's my gut sense of personal worth, there's a thought that looks like it's coming from me, here is a character trait I've held to be an aspect of myself for a long time, there's some more useless internal chatter." All sticks. Here they are, there they go. Who cares? The forest is full of sticks.

20:41 We can start working toward this freedom in small ways, such as being willing to give up defending an opinion — especially one that we don't really care about, but find ourselves defending out of an automatic impulse to identify with our ideas. The instant we let go of it, we will experience an end to our struggle, and a freedom from having to have this opinion persist. The opinion, as a notion, may not disappear, but we don't have to carry on with the burden of defending it. Besides, when we can do this, we begin to discover that many of our opinions are not so terribly profound or important to us anyway. We simply assume they are because they are "ours."

Chasing the Cheese Is a Form of Suffering

20:42 In order to recognize that the force of suffering is self-created, we need to understand that the forms in which we create suffering are commonplace. Suffering is actually produced by such familiar actions as judging others, trying to control life, clinging to ideals, and resisting or conforming to what's happening, and it is even produced in the activity of wanting. Believe it or not, these are all forms of suffering — and in case you didn't get it then, they are all activities included in that sweeping generalization made earlier using the metaphor of "chasing the cheese." We have looked at how ideals can produce a negative result, and we've looked into the pain of desire and fear, but how do activities like judging or trying to control life create suffering?

20:43   We know that generating a survival experience demands a field of charged value judgments about everything — is it good or bad, is it threatening or useful, does it meet with my approval or not, can I accept it or should I reject it, and so forth. Remember, these aren't restricted to just those judgments taking place within our internal chatter. They occur in the very act of perception, as part of the experience of the thing judged. This goes on constantly, but we don't usually notice we're doing it until an outstanding judgment pops up, like "he is disgusting, and I don't want him in my presence." We suffer this negative judgment since we've already assessed the event is an unwanted encounter that has been thrust upon us, but feel the judgment is warranted because we really do feel that way, and the feeling itself justifies our actions and relationship. If we happen to have a moral value against judging other people, then we may also feel bad about doing it, and so suffer in two ways. If we have no such value and simply feel superior or better or more correct than this person, we still suffer, but we attribute the cause of our suffering to the presence of the person rather than to our judgment. All of this is a mistake.

20:44   In so doing we are contributing greatly to the persistence of an endless loop of suffering. The cheese we are chasing in the case of judging and controlling life is trying to make the world conform to our preferences while eliminating our aversions — thinking that these exist in the world rather than in our own minds. Since preference and aversion cannot exist without our value judgments, clearly they are applied, not perceived. But we mistakenly view them as perceived — as *caused* by the world around us — and so enter into a war of sorts, trying to dominate our world enough to make it turn out the way we want.

20:45 This seems like it should work, yet we don't see the overall cyclic nature that keeps the futility of our efforts undisclosed. We work hard to make things turn out, but what is it that we are trying so hard to make come to pass? We have many conscious and subconscious images of how we and life should be or become. This multilayered and complex program of goals produces a field of decreed objectives that collectively provide a purposeful but obscure sense that we can accomplish some final resolution (the cheese). We can see that through our need to realize this particular notion of destiny, we are restricted to that objective, and will reject or struggle with all that doesn't appear consistent with it. Anything we experience that does not match those images — which is most of it — will be viewed, in both small and large ways, as threats or failures to the goal of attaining our self-agenda objectives. We suffer within the struggle itself, and we suffer that it endlessly fails to work out. We suffer this condition no matter which way things turn out.

20:46 Clearly we can see that not only must we suffer when things aren't to our liking, we must suffer the potential loss when they are. Regardless of our particular assessments, we are called to enter into an endless struggle with events, others, and circumstances, trying to realize something that will never happen. We are desperately trying to make everything in life conform to ourselves. Although we think this is the way to achieve happiness, what's wrong with this picture?

20:47 It isn't getting what we want that makes us happy. It's being happy with whatever we experience — or perhaps I should say, being happy regardless what we experience. To some people this will sound like a defeatist attitude, settling for mediocrity rather than striving for more. Yet nothing in the statement says that we can't strive, or create any number of activities or experiences. Simply that we are happy with whatever we experience, even the striving. But one of the traps we tend to fall into is to confuse being happy with being "finished."

20:48 Since we assume that happiness is our goal, and that achieving what we want will make us happy, it follows that when we are happy we must be finished, we must have attained all that we want. Now, who can see the flaws in this thinking? Obviously, the chances of being happy must by definition be reduced to moments of achieving something we want, and to be completely happy we would have to have achieved all that we want — which is very unlikely since our wanting never ends. Given that wanting is a function of self-survival, this drive won't end until we do.

20:49 The endless desire to get what we want isn't restricted to major life-altering events. It can be found in everyday activities, like attaining just a little more comfort as we sit, scratching an itch on our foot, winning an argument with our mate, finding a good program to watch on TV, or getting something good to eat. These things bring us pleasure or relief, but not happiness. Happiness is based on being happy, not on circumstance.

20:50 It's clear that if our happiness is circumstantially derived, whenever we fail to avoid unpleasant circumstances, we must be unhappy. Striving to make circumstances conform to our personal desires not only puts us in a position of endless struggle, it seduces us into a mental frame of judgment and opinion, reaction and manipulation. By their very nature these will always lead to some form of suffering — even if it's so taken for granted that we assume it's simply a natural aspect of life. The bottom line is that this dynamic produces an endless stream of reactions that appear as inflicted and unwanted. Since getting what we want seems the opposite of suffering, it follows that if we aren't getting what we want, we must be suffering. If both are an illusion, however, then neither needs to be the case.

Neither happiness nor suffering
are circumstantially derived.

Pain and Suffering

20:51   At the root of all suffering is some sort of pain. Something we would call unpleasant, irritating, annoying, hurtful, unwanted. Put simply: painful. Pain is readily classified as suffering. Without pain in some form or other, how could we suffer?

20:52   When we are in pain, we assume that we are suffering. Yet suffering is actually "being forced to put up with something unwanted." Certainly pain is unwanted, isn't it? It could be the most basic unwanted thing. Ouch! Pain! But it might be that we are not forced to put up with it. It might be that we generate it — on purpose. There, I've done it again. Said something stupid. Well, you must be getting used to that by now.

20:53   If pain, which is the heart and soul of suffering, is generated rather than merely perceived, then what must be true of all suffering? We experience pain regularly, and are strongly drawn to experience it. Pain and pleasure clearly exist to provide information regarding our relationship to everything. As a self, we need to classify everything in positively and negatively charged fields. Pain is part of this activity. But we can see by now that such classification exists solely for the purpose of self-survival. The charged assessments are additions to our experience rather than an experience of what's there. We need to get that they are not what's true—they don't even provide an accurate perception of what's true. That's not their job. We can see that if personal survival were in no way an issue, we would have no need for pain. But we don't want to give it up, because deep down we know that pain provides a real service to our survival, and we all want to survive.

20:54 It becomes increasingly clear that in the domain of self-survival we need pain to occur. It isn't so difficult to consider that as a result of that same function, we need suffering to occur. We need it to occur in order to continue to generate the particular activities of the self that we have become identified with. It is simply an overall by-product of the complex of activities that depend on pain and pleasure, value and threat, good and bad, to determine survival. Since we want to survive, we want to suffer.

20:55 Of course, we say we want pleasure and don't want pain, and that we don't want to suffer. It just seems to happen to us, try as we might to avoid it. But we're missing the big picture. It isn't happening to us; we are actually producing it. Since it is not acceptable that the self dissolves, or that anything associated with or serving the self is surrendered, we do not care to let go of the activities that allow us to hang onto these things. It is unacceptable not to have a way to navigate this complex self through our field of experiences. We need a positive or negative charge on everything to do so—and this field is generated, not merely perceived.

20:56   When we are clear that our suffering is occurring within our own internal state—our own thinking and emotions, judgments and reactions, perceptions and interpretations—we can better recognize this suffering in its many forms as an activity that we create. It becomes evident that to a large degree, it is a by-product of activities we ourselves are doing. If we can locate in our awareness the activity that creates pain, no pain needs to be experienced as simply occurring. If pain need not occur, suffering need not either.

20:57   It is difficult to see all of these familiar and taken-for-granted activities—desire, judgment, ideals, beliefs, opinions, clinging, self-image, fear, self-identity, upsets, needs, and concerns—as creating our own suffering, but with contemplation and observation it is possible. I know this isn't easy to grasp at first glance, and especially hard to grasp when we're confronted by life's activities. But if we contemplate the matter, getting past the knee-jerk assumptions that emanate from self-survival and our adherence to cultural dogma, we begin to see that it is true. We do in fact generate our own suffering because we cling so much to our self-interests on so many levels.

20:58   Even if you're unwilling to give up the basic sense of being a self—and are willing to suffer the consequences—you might be willing to give up the complexity of your conceptual-self and false-self, and so need not suffer the preservation of these. The vast majority of your suffering is caused by clinging to the conceptual world of self. By far the best thing to do is to experience what your self really is. This would clear up so much. Until then, profoundly observe what the self "does" and grasp how you *generate* suffering rather than *endure* it.

20:59 Were we to recognize that such suffering isn't necessary, we imagine we wouldn't endure it. Yet we do. Clearly, it requires a much deeper experiential recognition of the activities that cause the suffering. Beyond simply hearing about it, we need to be willing to challenge assumptions that are as close to our hearts as our very selves. Moreover, we suffer the ignored knowledge that in our struggle to survive we will, in the end, fail. The main assumption that results in the consequence of suffering is the assumption of self. We presume that we need self to exist. We do not. Let go of self and we let go of suffering.

In ancient China a terrible and ferocious warlord
was ransacking the countryside.
Coming upon a Zen monastery his army
began killing and pillaging.
When the warlord entered the inner courtyard
he found the abbot of the monastery sitting in a chair.
The abbot said firmly, "Get out of my monastery."
The powerful warlord walked up to the abbot, sword in hand,
and said, "You don't understand. I could kill you
without blinking an eye."
The abbot replied, "No, you don't understand.
I could die without blinking an eye."
After this, the warlord became a devotee of the abbot.

Struggle

20:60 Whenever suffering is even remotely possible, struggle will not be far behind. Since suffering can take many forms, our methods of struggle will also vary widely. Many struggles are so taken for granted as to be unnoticeable. The root of our sense of struggle, however, is the same as that of our suffering. It is survival. We feel a need to persist, defend, promote, control, cling, attain, etc., and we readily enter into all manner of efforts to do so. One of the problems here is that much of what we struggle to maintain is not only unnecessary, it is itself a source of problems. We don't merely struggle to exist, we struggle to persist in a very particular way. This particular way is called "ourselves."

20:61 Struggling to survive the demands of life is a constant activity — avoiding bad things, overcoming personal defects, or resolving unwanted feelings. Even when all seems well, we can often still sense a background unease or an inner struggle that is never fully pacified. Usually we need look no further than our interpersonal relationships to get a sense of our tendency to struggle. Simple acts such as worrying about what clothes to wear or trying to sound smart at a party are actually struggles. If we scrutinize our every thought, feeling, and action in terms of effort, we will find a great deal that we might call struggle. Why is that?

20:62 We struggle to stay alive, to keep our relationships operating smoothly, to maintain a satisfactory self-image, to live up to our ideals, overcome self-doubts, and free ourselves from limitations and unwanted circumstances that are common and endless. Our relationship to these matters is not only founded on the basic assumptions that have already been discussed, but on the assumption that some form of struggle is necessary to help us fix what's wrong and maintain what's right. We also assume that there is something that needs fixing, and that there is something that needs to be maintained. The nature of self-persistence requires no real resolution, only activity. As two sides of the same coin, this activity takes the form of struggling either to obtain something or to avoid something.

20:63 So much of our lives is lived within the social arena because we assume that social survival in its many forms somehow reflects and empowers us. We take care to avoid any expressions that would produce embarrassment, guilt, shame, disapproval, dislike, and other feelings that might reflect a negative self-image. We all know this produces a lot of internal effort and social toil, which shows up both in the minutia of life and in the dramas. For most of us, merely reflecting back on our teen years reveals how much struggle is involved in trying to create and maintain some social status and self-image. Even those of us who are well past that stage of life still continue to engage in endless struggles on much the same issues, although we're likely to be more adept at it and have also established a more solid collection of tried and true images and expressions. Not unlike any teenager, however, we still assume all this effort is necessary and that it is accomplishing what we suppose it is accomplishing. Perhaps that isn't so.

20:64 Let's look at an example of a goal that seems attainable but is actually not, spurring a person to enter into a futile lifelong struggle. Say a child grows up with parents who don't love him. Being loved and cared for by parents is very important for the survival of any child, since without it he is not likely to survive. Sensing this on a deep core level, the child would work very hard to achieve the love of his parents. Throughout his entire life he might unknowingly engage in all sorts of activities aimed at achieving the love of the parents. He might try to be a "good" boy, be helpful, become successful at a worthwhile career, obtain prized possessions, try to mold himself into a person with admirable values and qualities, and so on.

20:65 All this would probably appear to him simply as "life." Along with others in his circle, he might view his accomplishments as personal growth (which is not necessarily untrue), while in his core he remains locked in that same futile struggle to demonstrate his "worthiness" and so receive love. We can see that none of these activities would actually work, since if it's true that his parents didn't love him, no activity after the fact can change that.

20:66 What he's left with is a big unfulfilled hole in his psyche that he strongly feels he must mend. He will attempt this by trying to get someone who doesn't love him (originally his parents) to love him. Since it originated very early in life and is so deeply linked with his survival, this may be an unconscious but consuming mission of his life. Is he going to be attracted to someone who loves him? Of course not. He will only be attracted to someone who doesn't love him. Someone who loves him doesn't count, since he must get someone who *doesn't* love him to love him. This is what drives him — the issue that's unfinished and needs mending. This need is what his perceptions will relate to when assessing the value and attractiveness of another.

20:67 Let's say he finally does find someone who doesn't love him, and pursues her and gets her to love him. An uphill climb for sure. But now he should feel fulfilled. He has what was missing, and he can be at peace after achieving the all-important feat of mending the gaping hole in his psyche. Right? Not a chance. Because the moment she loves him, she no longer counts. He needs to get someone who does *not* love him to love him. This is the issue. If she loves him, he will suddenly find himself disinterested and have to move on. Resolution in this matter can never happen. He can't get someone who doesn't love him to love him, because she *doesn't* love him. This irresolvable drive behind his struggle will continue to operate unseen.

20:68　This is a clear example of the kind of endless struggle that many people get caught up in all their lives. To a greater or lesser degree, such struggles exist for all of us, and far more than we know. The main drawback of using such a well-defined case of personal dysfunction is that we might get carried away with the psychological implications and forget the bigger picture—ultimate consciousness, which is our main objective. It's true that long-term psychoanalysis might help the unloved boy discover the original source of his drive. In time, he might achieve a healthier way of acting out his struggle to be loved or become free of the drive to do so. But that's not what we're after here. What we want is to get free of the entire mechanism and assumptions that allow for any such mistake to dictate our existence.

20:69　Without being fully conscious of what we're doing or why, we continue to engage in many forms of struggle to obtain what we want. It is not so far-fetched to consider that we might equate struggle with success, or even with staying alive. It follows that we would assume that should we give up our struggles we might die, or that at least something bad will happen. Such assumptions would put a lot of pressure on us to continue to struggle, wouldn't they? Struggle exists in our constant busy-ness with life, our efforts to make things turn out, the reactions and emotions that drive us to take care of business, and we take it all very seriously, even the manipulative dramas we engage in, or the internal gut-twisting feelings we are loath to share with others. But let's not confuse merely taking action or even accomplishing something with engaging in a struggle.

20:70　In a comedy we might see a man walk into traffic with his face buried in a newspaper. Oblivious to his surroundings, he almost gets hit by a bus, but it misses him and he never even notices.

What strikes us as comical is that the man is completely undisturbed by the potential danger. This is attributed to his lack of perception regarding the danger, and so an absence of reaction. Yet it also shows that getting out of the way of the bus doesn't require all of the emotional upheaval that we normally attribute to such an effort. The point here is that the vast amount of struggle — whether internal reaction or physical action — is added; it is not inherent or necessary.

20:71 More than being unnecessary, we find that our reactivity debilitates and confuses us; it detracts and deflates. It causes even more reactivity and clouds our clarity. By contrast, when we simply take appropriate action without the normal upsets and fears, worries and doubts, manipulation and hope, or any of the many other forms of internal struggle that we feel are necessary to get our way, life is always easier and our goals take far less time and effort to achieve. What's more, we can usually act with greater clarity since our perception is on what counts rather than on our reactions.

20:72 Struggle is always based on resistance to what is perceived or imagined. When self-survival is the operating principle, struggle of some kind will determine the nature of our involvement with life, even if it is very subtle or taken for granted. The forms in which struggle can take place are infinite; some can even be pleasant or exciting. These are usually found when our struggles seem to be working out, when things are going well for us. But the nature of the struggle is the same whether we are winning or losing. All in all, it takes work and effort to try to make the world match up with what we want. To let things be the way they are takes no effort at all.

20:73 Recognizing just how much we struggle can be difficult. It's so taken for granted that we merely consider it part of the sensation of being alive. But it isn't—it's the struggle to persist *as a self*. The self principle may be the most fundamentally mistaken assumption we have regarding the nature of existence and life— especially easy to overlook given the complexity of our conceptually dominated lives. Once we become directly conscious of the nature of "being," the freedom from the background sensation of a self struggling merely to exist reveals just how much overlooked struggle naturally occurs for us. But don't take my word for it; directly experience the true nature of your own existence and see.

20:74 "Being" as a real and genuine event does not require a lot of conceptual complexity, or the pursuit of self-survival. The whole issue of the survival of a particular self is a nonessential affair, produced by our identification with so many aspects that we are not. Awakening consciousness to the true nature of being helps free us from emptiness, self-doubt, and feeling trapped, and can possibly eliminate or reduce the suffering and the struggles we engage. As a culture, we seem completely alienated from such a possibility. This may speak more about our focus on mistaken assumptions, deep as they are, than it does about our capacity to make such change.

20:75 When we realize that something as basic and primal as pain and as complex and intricate as ourselves are both products of our own minds, our understanding of these activities becomes profound. Realizing that the basis for our emotions, our interpretations, our perspectives, and our selves is conceptual, we must also realize that these are activities that we do, not things that we *are*. This suggests that we can "not" do them. But in order to not do them, we need to experience this fact in the very place that we do them. Such not-doing brings real freedom, and since a prerequisite for eliminating so much of this activity — which we heretofore thought of as inflicted, or found, or put up with — is the direct experience of the activity itself, then we are also given a degree of wisdom as well. To pursue this freedom and wisdom requires contemplation.

20:76   There is more to contemplate than what is buried in our psyche, or the assumptions that found the human condition. Our ultimate goal is a direct consciousness of the nature of our own existence — in essence, but also in the many forms or activities or confusions that may be still occurring. Understanding the nature of our perception and experience provides a very different relationship to what we call life and reality. Becoming directly conscious of our own nature provides the best view from which to look into anything else, and yet even with such enlightenment, there is more work to be done. We are after the truth, no matter what it is or where it is found.

20:77   Contemplation is an indispensable tool for becoming conscious of the truth of anything, and in the next chapter we will work in a practical way to clarify our understanding and increase our ability in this area. It is actually quite a tricky subject and endeavor. Although extremely straightforward in itself, we are apt to become derailed in ways that we cannot yet imagine.

CHAPTER TWENTY-ONE
Contemplation

To arrive at the simplest truth, as Newton knew and practiced, requires years of contemplation. Not activity. Not reasoning. Not calculating. Not busy behavior of any kind. Not reading. Not talking. Not thinking. Simply bearing in mind what it is that one needs to know.

—George Spencer Brown, on Sir Isaac Newton

Creating a Place to Stand

21:1　The ultimate purpose of our work is to experience the truth—the true nature of our own existence. This is done primarily through the use of contemplation, although if we have no real desire to know for ourselves whatever is true, then we won't contemplate in earnest. If our desire is slight then we will be stopped early on when some other motivation or distraction arises. A desire to know the truth is the first requirement for its pursuit, but the desire alone is not enough. No matter what path we take in pursuit of the truth, we will find there are many obstacles along the way.

21:2   When we speak about pursuing the truth it is hard to know what we are talking about, since if we aren't conscious of what's true, we don't know what our goal really is. What's more, the word *truth* can seem ill-defined because we often confuse a *statement* about what is true for whatever is actually so. Any statement can be wrong or misunderstood, and then it is indeed not true. Claiming something as true is just that, a claim or assertion, a way of speaking. What is "so" is whatever it is — whatever exists as itself. When referring to our own nature or our own "being," we could say we are seeking to become conscious of who and what we actually *are*. This is what we are calling the truth. Personally becoming conscious is our goal, not making an assertion or believing a claim. We need to become conscious of *what-is-as-itself*.

21:3   The truth must stand on its own, independent of anything it may or may not do for us. Our path toward consciousness may take many forms, yet in the end it must always be an honest intent to grasp whatever's true whether we like it or not, whether it fits with what we believe or not, and whether it does us any good or not. Of course, sacrificing our own self-serving ends in this way flies in the face of our self's constant pursuit of survival. So we should be prepared to find that such an undertaking can be difficult and sometimes threatening.

21:4   Since our commitment to "self" seems to interfere with our pursuit of the truth, at first it may seem like we should work to eliminate the self. Certainly we could take on any number of ideas that suggest self-dissolution is a good thing, or take on various romantic notions of winning some internal struggle of good over evil. We already operate with a sense of warring against our unwanted attributes. We could simply expand this notion to make the entire self an unwanted attribute. We *could* do these things, but it would be better to recognize these activities as more of the same self-survival dynamic. They simply represent versions of self-persistence in other, albeit unusual, forms.

21:5 For example, if we take hold of the idea that self-dissolution is good — if we adopt it and believe in it — we begin to identify with it and add it to "self." Soon we're no longer allowing self-dissolution; what we're engaged in is self-promotion with a twist. The "idea" — and any action that manifests from the idea — is itself not self-dissolution. It is just self-mind generating more new ideas to pursue what's seen as a self-serving end — to get rid of the "self" so that "I" can become more conscious.

21:6 We're simply adding to the snowball effect by putting another layer (although an unconventional one) onto the self-identity because it's our habit to do so. Well, actually it's more than a habit. In such an activity we are driven by the very core dynamics that drive everything we do. We want to be special and unique, and we're willing to take on all sorts of outlooks, including the drama of a "noble fight against the self." But in the matter of consciousness it's not "being" versus "self." It's possible to enter into a struggle or war with ourselves, but this is just a circular battle that leaves us stuck with *ourselves* no matter who wins.

21:7 Instead of entering into a fruitless battle, we can distinguish between what's genuine and what's false within ourselves. This is something we can do to make progress toward our original goal of getting at the truth without engaging in a battle with the self. Then our desire to discover what's true can be supported by the intent to find whatever in our experience or in ourselves is untrue. If something is recognized as false and is no longer called ourselves, it becomes natural for us to let go of it. In this way we aren't focusing on destroying the self, but on finding the truth of ourselves — and this is easier for a self to accept and align with. If everything that isn't true is let go, then what remains must be true. If it turns out that there is no self in what remains, then that will be discovered when we get there, but then it will be clearly an experience of what's true, and not an application of something believed.

21:8   How do we know when we've reached "the end" so all that remains is true? We don't. During this process, we won't necessarily recognize an ending point, but this is irrelevant. The distinction itself — letting go of anything that's false — provides us with a direction with which we can continue to pursue the truth in each moment. In this way the overwhelming drive of self-persistence is redirected toward supporting this endeavor, even though our ultimate goal may be unknown. We turn our attention to discovering all that is not really ourselves but with which we have become confused and by which we have become dominated. Our "will" in the matter is given a place to stand, so to speak, and so we can incorporate the self-survival drive, and redirect it rather than fight it.

21:9   Devoting ourselves to what is true rather than to maintaining the self is a very uncommon use of survival. The unstoppable flow of our tendency to persist as a self can be channeled in such a way that it becomes congruent with the pursuit of a direct consciousness of our own existence. Since the true nature of Being doesn't need to persist or be maintained (since it already *is*), in the end the survival principle will be undermined. Allowing ourselves to identify with the truth, and pursue it even though it is unknown, helps press our survival tendency into serving the truth rather than self. Certainly we can't completely identify with the truth because we don't ultimately know what it is, but we can give self-survival something to do that is consistent with the pursuit of the truth. While seeking this consciousness we can at least point ourselves in the right direction. Achieving this consciousness is the job of contemplation.

The purpose of discipline is to promote freedom.
But freedom leads to infinity and infinity is terrifying.
—Henry Miller

Being as Unknown

21:10 In contemplation, focus on what truly exists in this moment. Extracting your beliefs and concepts from your experience of "being" leaves you with a real and present sense of what is more immediate. This points your consciousness toward what *is*. Still, moving in this direction can be scary. Giving up all your beliefs so that you can press your experience into this moment might feel like standing naked without anything to buffer what's exposed. Yet without belief, opinion, conjecture, judgment, assumption, or interpretation there is still something there: your consciousness of this moment.

21:11 This raw and immediate experience of yourself or of life comes as a presently felt awareness of the moment, even though what you experience in this way is also unknown. The mind will immediately try to interpret what's there, engaging assumptions, history, programs, fears, needs, and whatnot. But if you allow yourself the time to soak in this unknown experience without trying to resolve it, and without allowing the mind to rush ahead and conceptually pin everything down into a knowable form, a new awareness will begin to arise. This awareness will be at the same time both known and unknown.

21:12   What's known of this moment is our experience of the circumstances that happen to appear at this time via our immediate sense perceptions. But even this is dominated by and received as an interpretation, which is a process, and so not totally now. Mostly what I'm referring to as an awareness of the moment is the always present yet unknown experience of "now." The very moment of now-as-itself seems somehow known even though there is always something unknown about it.

21:13   This unknown quality manifests in at least two ways. On the one hand, it occurs from the lack of identification or certainty—which usually takes place automatically. Placing our attention on the immediacy of the moment prior to any thought or interpretation, we might feel as if something is undecided or unclear, or like some vital information is missing. On the other hand, we will have a sense that even what is known in our present experience is itself unknown in the very same place and moment. We might perceive a body, yet realize that this "body" is also unknown. We might sense ourselves or our awareness, but perceive that this self and awareness is itself unknown, or not fully known. Everything we perceive will be infused with this unknown quality. It is important to allow ourselves to remain aware of what is unknown as well as known. The moment the unknown quality is shut off, the mind will take over and dominate our entire experience.

21:14   Living as an unknown is a very unusual thing to do in our culture. Very few people have the courage to enter such a confrontation with themselves and to allow it to remain to some degree unknown. It would not even occur to most people to approach life without their beliefs and interpretations. It's likely to seem an absurd thing to do since it comes with a sense of vulnerability, away from which the mind automatically turns. Yet the more comfortable and familiar we become with this sense of unknown-being, the easier it becomes to find and live within such an experience. After all, it is already true and always true.

21:15 Strange as it might sound, a genuine not-knowing can hold the place of a direct experience of the true nature of being. It seems that if you look into who or what you are in this moment and the feedback you get is that you "don't know," then at least that is the truth. Still, you experience being present and being aware, so this unknown place of being seems to be right here in the very place where you are. You need not know what you are for the moment; you simply have to have a sense of what is most genuinely you-in-this-moment, even if that appears as pure not-knowing.

21:16 Once we're clear that this unknown place of being is where we really *are*, we strengthen our ability to let go of every concept and belief that we have confused with ourselves. Of course, many traps remain, and it can still be a challenging task. The trick here lies in recognizing where to put our attention. We'd like to simply be conscious of the true nature of our own existence. The best way to do that is to experience what *is* ourselves, and this is where contemplation comes in. It is this very unknown but genuine and immediate place of "being" that we contemplate, setting out to become directly conscious of what it is.

Contemplation

21:17   In our culture we often think of contemplation as a relaxation technique, a mystical exercise, or a strange practice done on occasion either by disciplined people or weird ones. In this work, contemplation is not meant to be mysterious or even particularly "spiritual." I want you to be able to contemplate as naturally as you breathe. Contemplation is a deep and focused questioning, and an essential tool for increasing consciousness.

21:18   Contemplation is creating the possibility that something can be known outside of what is already known or knowable. Since our pursuit of the truth demands we step beyond the limitations of what we "know," this is an essential possibility to have. Contemplation begins at the limit of our observations. We use it to push out past what we can readily or immediately observe and into the unconscious regions of our minds. As well, contemplation is our only means to pursue a direct consciousness of the true nature of things.

21:19   When we contemplate, since our goal isn't to interpret what we perceive, or stop with what is immediately accessible to our understanding, there is no need to give meaning to whatever comes up, or to figure out what something is within our intellect. Our goal is not one of having good ideas or drawing new conclusions. Our goal is to have a direct conscious recognition of what's true.

21:20   Standing at the brink of the present experience of being is the place where contemplation steps out. We learn to keep our attention on the very threshold of this moment for the purpose of actually experiencing what something is.

21:21 Traditionally, contemplation is done sitting quietly and focusing on a question without distraction. But if you are in any way attempting to be conscious of the true nature of something, you are contemplating. Contemplation can be taking place throughout the day as a natural event of questioning and openness. Such contemplation can be found in questioning what is perceived, seeking out a deeper understanding rather than accepting a surface encounter. Questioning what anything is, attempting to grasp its real nature, can be an ongoing and fundamental aspect of human awareness.

21:22 Although true contemplation is not about the posture you take, how you breathe, or where you put your hands, it is quite useful to take some time to do nothing but contemplate silently. This takes discipline. Eliminating unnecessary distractions and keeping your mind focused on one question without break helps empower your focus. There is much to contemplate in this book, and for true understanding it all must be experienced directly. Your contemplations should not be seen, however, as trying to experience hearsay or intellectual observations *as* the case. It should be a complete abandonment and commitment to experience whatever is true, whether it fits in with what's been heard or believed or not.

Pre-contemplation

21:23 In order to go deeper with this work, at some point you need to embrace a serious and focused period of contemplation devoted to doing nothing but contemplating a particular subject — most frequently your self. The real essence of contemplation is very simple, and yet this work can be difficult to undertake. Although an extremely direct and straightforward activity, effective contemplation includes several components all occurring in the same moment. Below, I've divided these into Pre-contemplation Components—which outline the best state to enter into a period of contemplation—and Contemplation Components—which will help you understand what needs to occur as you contemplate.

21:24 Prior to entering into a period of focused contemplation, adopting a particular state of mind is beneficial. No matter what the subject of contemplation is, greater success will come about when three things are actively occurring: You're grounded in the present, clear about what you're up to, and create the possibility that you will succeed.

Pre-contemplation Components:

- Presence: Put your attention on the present moment.

- Clarity: Clarify what you are going to contemplate.

- Possibility: Hold that it is possible to become conscious of whatever it is you are contemplating.

Being Present

21:25 When beginning a round of contemplation, it is useful to make sure your attention is in the present moment. Contemplation is not an intellectual endeavor, and if you are occupied too much with fantasy or memory or intellectual musings, you are in the wrong place. Contemplation is about this very moment. It is about what "is," and what *is* exists only in this moment. Contemplation is not thinking about things, pondering the past, or imagining an outcome. The best way to begin your contemplation is by allowing your mind to let go of distractions, and devoting your full attention to this moment of existence.

*As long as we have some definite idea or hope about the future,
we cannot really be serious with the moment that exists right now.*
—Suzuki Roshi

Being Clear

21:26　Once you feel fully present, consider the matter you intend to contemplate. Establish what it is you want to know. Be specific and clear. If your subject matter is vague and you set out to experience some general notion or open-ended idea, your mind will wander endlessly, and progress is unlikely. For example, you'd be ill-served to ask a question such as *What is true?* since there is nothing to really focus on there. It is better to ask a more specific question such as *Who am I?* or *What is life?* But even then it's not clear enough. What do you consider self or life to be? What are you referring to as "I?" Find this "I" in your experience and nail it down as best you can. What exactly do you want to know about life? What do you mean when you say "life"? It isn't just a matter of creating a phrase for a question; you need to be clear what you are actually asking, to clarify the subject of your contemplation.

21:27　Hone in on the true subject — what is your best sense of what it really is? Don't confuse your contemplation with the intellectual activity of trying to figure out what something is. This will go on in any case, but the more explicit you are to start with, the more powerful your questioning will be. You don't want your contemplation to degrade into an intellectual exercise. You want it to remain a constant attempt to have a breakthrough in consciousness about the subject in question. This may seem obvious, but trust me, even though you have said the name to yourself and have an idea of the subject — even a very specific idea — that doesn't mean you are on top of it yet. In fact, this process of clarifying your question is the beginning of contemplation. Tell the truth about it as best you can. This helps clarify what it is you are after.

21:28 The more you can pin down what it is you are asking—what you want to know and about what subject—the better you can focus and stay on track. Getting clear on your subject saves a lot of time, since you can more easily focus your attention and efforts on that subject, and more readily bring it back when your attention wanders. You can contemplate anything, but whether your subject is an apple, communication, the nature of life, or a number 2 Mongol pencil, you need to clarify your real experience of this subject. Isolate it in your experience as the subject upon which to hold steady concentration. Since the goal of contemplation is to directly experience the true nature of something, in one way or another whatever subject you choose or question you ask, in essence it will be: What is the true nature of that matter? It is important to be clear what the matter is specifically.

21:29 So if you want to experience the true nature of yourself, you could ask *Who am I?* Your subject is you, yet we've seen that the notion of self can refer to quite a lot. If it's about your true nature, then the question is not about self-image, or history, or any concept of self. At the same time, if any of these are what you honestly consider to be your real self, then that is your best direction. Of course, when you put your attention on your being, ideas will come up. You may look here or there for yourself, or settle on something you've been told is true of the "real you." But what in your experience is honest-to-God *you*? No kidding, what are you for real? Even though the true nature of you may be unknown, you must locate the most honest sense of you that you can—that is your starting point. This clarification will have to be ongoing throughout your contemplation, since what you most honestly experience as yourself might change, but it should also begin your contemplation. Once you've gotten clear on your best sense of you, then you can contemplate what that is.

Creating Possibility

21:30   Throughout the "spiritual history" of humans, so many people claim to have become conscious of the true nature of things that the possibility of such consciousness does seem likely. There is no reason to suspect that you can't become conscious of the very place and one that you are, since, after all, you are in the very place of yourself. And since you are alive and you do exist, there is no reason you can't become conscious of what life is or what existence is. Standing on the possibility that you can become directly conscious of what you or anything really is creates the space for contemplation to exist.

21:31   That may all sound reasonable and true, and it is. But for you it is still only hearsay. There's a pivotal question you need to ask yourself prior to contemplating, and even in the middle of contemplating: Is it possible for me to become conscious of the true nature of this matter? In the case of contemplating your self, do you hold that it's really possible for you to know who you are, to directly experience the true nature of yourself? If not, then why are you contemplating? It is either possible or it is not possible. If it isn't possible, then contemplation cannot occur, and you might as well just go have a beer. You have no choice in the matter. If you are going to contemplate, it needs to be possible — and it must be possible for *you* in this moment.

21:32   If you do not hold that it's possible to become conscious of the true nature of yourself, existence, or any matter, you will be severely restricted in your contemplation. I've watched participants in Contemplation Intensives work diligently for days, without creating the possibility that they themselves could actually get it. This seems strange, and it is, but somehow people can unconsciously overlook the necessity for personally grasping that they can become conscious of the truth. Sometimes without even noticing, you may be operating under the assumption that it isn't really possible for you to experience something directly. This is a reasonable position to have, since all perception is indirect, and no recognition or interpretation is the thing being interpreted. In fact, there's no rational reason to assume that it's possible to actually get something directly as-itself. This is why it has to be created. You need to make sure that you hold it is possible for *you*—not just generally possible for some unnamed person, but for *you* personally—to become directly conscious.

21:33   These three components comprise a lucid and unimpeded state that is ideal for contemplation. You are present in this moment and not given to distraction by any concerns, thoughts, or fantasies. The subject of your contemplation is clear so that you can readily locate it within your experience. And you stand squarely on the possibility that you yourself can directly experience what's true. All of these are necessary throughout your contemplation. They are ongoing components. It is best, however, to begin with them in place and simply keep them present while contemplating.

The unknown presence of "being"
is the best place to begin a search for true wisdom.

Contemplating

21:34 Now I want to describe—actually, to create with you—the essential components for powerful contemplation. It's useful for contemplation to be broken down into four components. The above pre-contemplation components of presence, clarity, and possibility start us off in the right state of mind, and four more—intention, openness, focus, and questioning—complete the list.

21:35 Throughout our contemplation, we need a clear intent to grasp the truth of whatever we are contemplating, remaining open to whatever that might be, and keeping our attention focused on asking a question that drives us into wondering what this subject really is. These are all aspects of a powerful contemplation.

> **Contemplation Components:**
>
> - Intention: Intend, right now, to become conscious of the truth.
> - Openness: Allow yourself to deeply not-know, and be open to whatever may be true.
> - Focus: Keep all your attention on your subject; when you wander off, immediately bring your attention back.
> - Question: Truly wonder; keep a steady questioning that's related to your intent.

Intent

21:36 For contemplation aimed at awakening a deep consciousness, or "direct experience," the primary ingredient is the intent to do so — to experience, beyond doubt or belief, whatever you set out to grasp. If you don't really want to know, if your intention isn't actually to become conscious of the truth, then you are unlikely to discover it. A casual motivation is rarely enough. A serious no-nonsense intention and commitment to personally get to the heart of the matter are required. This is what creates contemplation. Really want to know. Make it your business to find out. Now that you've created for yourself the possibility that you can become conscious of the truth, you must intend to realize that possibility. For our work here, it is appropriate to begin with the intention to become fully conscious of who you really are.

Want to know.

Openness

21:37   If the first ingredient is intent, the next ingredient has to be openness. While being open is essentially simple, it is also difficult to convey. Even though there's a dictionary list of meanings for the word *open* in Chapter Five, no definitions seem to adequately characterize the state I'm referring to with the word *open*. Openness is a spirit and condition of mind that is ready to accept whatever is true, without alteration or prediction. It is being willing to experience what can't be thought or imagined, what may be paradoxical or seemingly nonsensical, so long as it is true.

21:38   To increase and support a spirit of openness you need to allow not-knowing to fully enter your awareness while you're contemplating. This state of open wonder may seem at odds with the mind's grasping drive for an answer — which is why it is so necessary. Remember, the mind's job is to continually provide information, not to enter into a state of not-knowing. Such a state appears to the mind like shutting down, or "no-mind." This is antithetical to self-survival and so will be resisted. Even though not-knowing is already a fact, an experience of not-knowing must be created, or the activity of mind will simply overwhelm the unknown truth and your openness to experiencing it.

21:39   What's being said here can be helpful, but it is not the same as experiencing the state for yourself. Recall the one-way ladder: you are to climb up to a new view and then get off. When you can get past the "closed-ness" of your own knowing, you are free to deeply experience that in this moment you in fact do not know the true nature of who you are. Once this deep, personal, and essential not-knowing enters the picture, you can be open, creating a real willingness to experience the truth no matter what it is. This openness is one of the most important aspects of contemplation.

Open up to not-knowing.

Focus

21:40   Of course, you also need to focus. Much of the discipline that contemplation requires is in the relentless focus with which you must train your attention to stay on both the subject and your intent to experience it. If your subject is you, put all of your attention on yourself and keep it there. Whatever the duration of your contemplation, you must keep your attention on yourself without letting up. Your mind is likely to wander. When it does, the discipline is to bring attention back to the subject immediately upon discovering it has wandered. Don't spend any time berating yourself for your lapse — that is just more distraction. Simply get back on track and remain steadily focused on your contemplation. The intent to experience your subject provides the driving force, but focus provides the subject, without which, where would you place your intent?

Don't goof off.
—Suzuki Roshi

Question

21:41   Finally, since this focused intent refers to something currently unknown, besides openness, you need to use your ability to wonder, to question, to pursue awakening to the "answer" or consciousness. Really wondering, or holding a question — such as "What is existence?" — helps you focus on your aim to directly experience the subject in the question. For a contemplation directed toward yourself, you might ask "Who am I?" Repeating this question helps channel your mind's activities into wondering about your own nature. After a time, verbalizing the question becomes unnecessary, but the wonder must still remain.

21:42   The essence of having a question is found in the wondering, which leads to a wanting to know and the intent to know. It also helps provide the openness needed to find out. Yet you need to get that the question isn't in the words. Real questioning occurs in pushing out past your present experience and wondering beyond what is obvious.

21:43   For example, let's say you want to become conscious of the table, so you set out to experience it directly — the table as-itself. "What is the nature of this thing?" If merely perceiving the table was all you needed in order to become conscious of its nature, then there would be no need for contemplation. The job would be done simply at perception: it is a table. Obviously then, you're not just asking what you perceive and interpret as there, but what's *really* there. You're trying to become one with the table, so to speak, and realize what the table actually is — what is the absolute nature of the existence of that? You can ask the same question of yourself or anything else. If merely perceiving yourself was all that was possible, there would be no wonder and so no contemplation. This is what asking a question provides. You must create a wonder about what is obvious, suggesting there is more to become conscious of than what you perceive.

Wonder.

21:44   It is not a mistake that some of the ingredients seem a bit mutually exclusive in nature. Having both openness and focus, intent and questioning is necessary to keep your awareness committed to your task and at the same time create the possibility for your consciousness to go where it has never gone before.

Developing a Steady Practice

21:45   To contemplate, you might sit quietly for a period of time, or if you feel capable, you could contemplate while doing a mindless task such as digging in the garden or walking to the store. At first, however, it is best to contemplate without distraction and in a quiet time that doesn't require attention to be diverted for anything else.

21:46 How long should you contemplate? That really depends on you. You can contemplate for a few minutes or hours, or as a background questioning you keep as a steady or repeated activity throughout your day. You can also take on a serious commitment for a set period of time, for instance, three or four days of intense and frequent contemplation. If you intend to set aside some time to contemplate steadily for consecutive days, then it's best to set up a schedule of individual sessions, each lasting more or less an hour, depending on what works for you. Such a commitment is intense, however, and needs to be taken on after sober consideration, and is best done with others and a staff skilled in such work, such as participating in a Contemplation Intensive. Contemplation Intensives are designed to remove distractions and support you in staying on purpose. Such a setting maximizes your chances of making a breakthrough. To take up contemplation as a daily or lifetime practice is another matter.

21:47 As a steady practice, I recommend doing at least fifteen minutes a day. In this way it is hard to build up excuses for not contemplating, and makes it an easy thing to accomplish. If you want to do more, then do more. But avoid setting yourself up by trying to take on so much that it begins to conflict with other life demands and your discipline starts to erode. To prevent this, start with what is easy yet still requires a modicum of discipline, developing good habits and a positive track record in your own mind. Establishing a sense of success is valuable for staying enthused about your undertaking. From time to time you can always enter into an intense period of serious contemplation to help boost your efforts.

21:48 If contemplation is relatively new to you, it could be useful to do a more meditative practice or two before stepping into contemplation. Let me suggest three practices that can assist you in learning how to contemplate. There should be no rush to proceed to the next practice since only a natural development will bring real insight. When you feel comfortable with one and ready to proceed, then begin the next practice. If at any time you feel like you are losing track or your practice is becoming too abstract, simply go back to a previous stage for awhile.

I. Attention Practice—Stage I

21:49 The first practice is to observe your mind. Sit quietly and be present. Notice whatever your mind is doing. Simply keep your attention steadily on your thoughts and feelings as they arise and pass. Don't take them seriously, and don't fight with them—just watch them arise. Watch them come and go, or fade and shift into other thoughts and feelings. Sit quietly and be attentive to what comes up for you moment after moment, without attachment to any of it. Do this for fifteen minutes.

21:50 The Attention Practice may sound too easy, but you'll find that after awhile you begin to be easily distracted or become involved with your thinking or feelings and lose track of your observation of them. The key is to remain conscious of your mind activities without getting caught up in these activities. Remember to keep attention on what comes and goes in your mind. Stay dispassionate about it as best you can without interfering. Simply stay aware of you and your mind.

21:51 Another practice that will empower and clarify the Attention Practice, as well as help you train to focus your mind, is a practice I call "Waiting with an Object."

> **Waiting with an Object:**
>
> In this practice, find a small object such as a stone, or perhaps a marble — something fairly plain. Place it in front of you, and simply put all of your attention on this object. Don't think about it, wonder about it, or talk to yourself about it. Just *be* with it. Wait there, keeping all of your attention focused on this object. It's best to set a timer for a short period, just a minute or two is plenty at first, so that you don't even have to be distracted with time passing.

21:52 The Waiting with an Object practice, like the Stop Thinking exercise we did early on, will clearly reveal how much your mind is driven to think, chat, and engage in all sorts of distractions, some very subtle. It's good to be sensitive to this drive and how it manifests. This practice also gives you an opportunity to work on quieting your mind and keeping it focused. The more you practice, the better you get.

21:53 After working with the Waiting with an Object exercise enough to clarify your mind's tendencies, and make some progress, go back to Stage I of the Attention Practice. You should be more sensitive and better able to keep your attention on your mind's activities. When you feel comfortable staying attentive and observing your shifting mental and emotional awareness, and can stay with it for at least a full fifteen minutes, then go on to Stage II below. How long should this take? In some courses, I suggest students stay in each practice for a week, devoting at least fifteen minutes each day. But it's up to you. It could take weeks, or months, possibly even longer if this is all new. Then again, perhaps you feel ready to move on sooner. You can always come back to any practice as often as you like. The important thing is that you progress naturally and notice some shift in your consciousness or ability to do the exercises before moving on.

Attention Practice—Stage II

21:54 With Stage II of this practice, you'll still be watching your thoughts and feelings as they arise, but now you will be actively letting go of them. Remain calm and undistracted by this effort — simply try to let go of your thoughts and feelings sooner rather than later. Don't resist them coming up at all, but as soon as you notice you are thinking or feeling something, rather than following it out — completing the line of thought or dwelling on the feeling — calmly detach from it and let it go. When it is replaced by another thought or feeling, let that go too. Watch them come, let them go. Again, don't worry that they come up, nor try to stop them from arising. Just let them go as soon as you notice they are there.

When you feel ready, try doing this for a little longer than 15 minutes.

II. Awareness Practice

21:55 This practice continues from Stage II of the Attention Practice. Here, let go of any attachment to the thoughts or feelings that pass through your awareness, and remain attentive to the moment. In this practice, however, put your awareness on your "awareness" of thoughts, feelings, or anything else of which you might be aware. The key here is to keep your attention on your awareness itself. As you are aware of anything — a thought, feeling, or something perceived objectively — be aware that you are aware; focus on your awareness of these things rather than the things themselves.

21:56 Begin to note that your awareness itself is not any thought or feeling or perception that you have. Don't begin to think about awareness or try to feel this awareness, since that would just lead to more of the same. Instead, be aware of whatever enters your awareness, and simply notice you are aware of it. As best you can, keep your attention on this awareness steadfastly for the full fifteen minutes.

21:57 The more you do this, the more sensitive you will become to simply being aware. Mental-emotional states start to have less dominance over your experience — both while you are doing this practice and at other times as well. Also, your mental activity will begin to slow down and won't seem as strongly influential. When this occurs, and you feel comfortable with your ability to stay sensitively "aware of your awareness" for fifteen minutes, try doing it a little longer.

21:58 To assist in the transition from these meditative practices to contemplation, let's do a guided contemplation in which you will move through the various contemplation components using the subject of awareness as your focus. Since you have to read and then contemplate, I recommend reading each sentence and then working on it until you have an experience of whatever is suggested in that sentence. Then move on to the next. When you've gone through the whole exercise enough to do it all at once, then sit and go through this exercise as a steady contemplation on awareness, making sure all of the components are occurring. When you're able to do that, then proceed to the third practice.

Contemplating Awareness Exercise

- Get into present time, and be aware of this moment.

- Locate this awareness and clarify what it is.

- Create the possibility of becoming conscious of the true nature of awareness.

- Right now, intend to become conscious of the true nature of awareness.

- Allow yourself to not-know what awareness really is, and open up to the possibility of experiencing something beyond what you are experiencing right now, or something different in what you are experiencing right now.

- Keep your attention focused on awareness without distraction or break. If you lose your focus, continually return your attention to the presence of awareness.

- Truly wonder as you ask the question: "What is awareness?"

III. Contemplation Practice

21:59 This final practice is an actual contemplation. Put the focus on yourself with the intent of directly experiencing the source of your awareness — you. Once your mind activity isn't the only feature in your awareness, and your ability to focus on your sense of self-awareness is pretty solid throughout your contemplation, then begin to ask, *Who am I?* in order to direct your intent toward becoming conscious of the nature of yourself. *Who am I?* is a good question to ask for this purpose.

21:60 Remember, you are not seeking an answer but an experience, an insight. You are wondering where awareness comes from, or goes to (depending on how you look at it). Having established a steady sense of yourself, set out to become directly conscious of who is being aware. Keep your attention on this goal, even if it seems to go nowhere at times. When your attention wanders, and it will, bring it back to an awareness of *you.*

21:61 This is a true contemplation, but will be weak without including all of the components mentioned earlier. *Intend* to become conscious of who you are in this moment. At the same time, be *open* to whatever it may be. Allow yourself to soak in not-knowing who you are so that real openness can occur. Even though you may be setting out to directly experience yourself, and so tacitly admitting that you don't know, the overwhelming assumptions about yourself will interfere with a full-blown state of not-knowing who you really are. Being open is essential, as is keeping your attention *focused* on yourself, and *wondering: Who am I?*

21:62 If it becomes difficult to stay focused and your mind wanders, a technique that helps put you back on track is to ask who is doing whatever you are doing. You can easily ask this question in many forms, such as: *Who is thinking this thought? Who is walking down the street? Who is eating? Who is upset? Who is confused? Who is being aware of whatever you are aware of in this moment?* This pushes you back toward the origins of your awareness. It can be done no matter what is occurring for you, or how distracted, confused, or emotional you are. This keeps moving you back to an immediate sense of yourself and wondering who you are. *You* are the focus of your contemplation. See if you can steadily contemplate who you are for at least fifteen minutes daily.

21:63 There are often misunderstandings about what's needed for successful contemplation. Sure it's nice to have a quiet setting and feel very calm and "spiritual" for your contemplation. But don't confuse "setting" or "mind-state" for consciousness. You are not looking for a "perception" or an "experience"; you are looking for *you*. Who you really are is *who you really are* even when you are upset, angry, distracted, intellectual, sleepy, or any other experience that "you" may be having or aware of. You don't need to force the world to stop or create the exact circumstances for you to become conscious of what's already so. You *are* you! Simply become conscious of what's true. The circumstances or even your internal state are not the issue, or all that significant to this effort. Remember, the job of contemplation is to become conscious of the truth.

21:64 Once you've become directly conscious of who you are, you can go on to more difficult contemplations such as what is Being, what is the nature of another, what is life, or what is existence or reality. You can also contemplate any aspect of your self or life to obtain insight into such activities as communication, emotion, perception, space, interaction, or whatever else you want to be conscious of directly. Your contemplation can be intense or casual, long or short, frequent or occasional. In any case, it is best if it is ongoing and regular.

21:65   When contemplating, don't try to find or invent some method to make it work other than the direct one: become conscious. Don't try to apply what you've read throughout this book (or anything else you've ever heard) as a method to be used to circumvent direct contemplation. If anything is true, it will be discovered as you discover the truth, not through trying to realize it *as* true. Do you see the difference here? Go for whatever is true — not what you believe is true, or have heard is true. The truth must always stand on its own.

21:66   Whenever you've taken time to contemplate during your day, even if it is only for fifteen minutes, its influence will touch the rest of your day. If you keep up a daily routine, gradually the repeated stimulation will begin to seep into the flow of your life. Contemplate at any convenient time throughout the day. The accumulated effect is an increase in your sensitivity and awareness, and this will enhance your ability to penetrate through obscure fogs of mental activities and emotions to reach a clarity of insight. Take the opportunity to contemplate in the shower, on a drive or a walk, gardening, or at any other time when activity allows. If you pay attention, you will find far more of these occasions than you might suspect. Through persistent contemplation, the experience of Being should begin to surface.

21:67   Earlier I made an analogy between the drive of self-survival and a mouse running inside his wheel. This is very much like our selves trying to survive in the world. Shifting our commitment from surviving as an individual ego to becoming conscious of the truth will transform our experience of self and life. Even so, regardless what our energy and attention is on, we are still running on the wheel no matter which direction we go. What would it take to step off the wheel entirely?

21:68 Since Being is "what is as itself," it is already off the wheel. So what's needed here is to become conscious of what's already the case. Although direct consciousness might seem like another "cheese" to pursue—one that will make things all better or finally resolve our inner disquiet—it isn't. The truth is already so—there is nowhere to get to, and no reason to run. There is nothing to attain. The "mouse" is already "being" whether he is conscious of it or not. Experiencing what he "is" has nothing to do with attaining another cheese. Running after it is only a promise and a distraction. Instead, he must experience himself in the very place that he already "is." Even so, it appears the only activity that can get us to where we already are is contemplation.

Looking Both Ways

21:69 There seem to be two directions in which to look in contemplation. One is into the true nature of existence. The other is into the foundation of our minds, such as deep personal and cultural assumptions, or any other aspect of the uncognized mind that dominates our experience. Given that we don't presently grasp the true nature of our own existence, then what are we experiencing and why? This is like contemplating the nature of mind, or perception, or the true nature of self-survival. No matter which direction we look, we don't want to leave any stone unturned.

21:70 Now, it may turn out that these two directions are ultimately the same, or it may turn out that they are not. At our current level of consciousness we're left with either not-knowing or just believing what we hear about such things, and so we can't really say how it will turn out. Our focus above was generally directed toward contemplating to achieve a direct experience of the true nature of something. In the upcoming chapter, we'll find that contemplation is also quite useful to bring us insight into the uncognized aspects of mind.

CHAPTER TWENTY-TWO
Awakening the Uncognized Mind

Contemplation directed at becoming conscious of the true nature of what "is" points us toward the absolute truth.
Contemplation directed at the foundations of the self-experience points us toward awakening the uncognized mind.

22:1   In the previous chapter I suggested that fighting the dynamic of self-survival is a fruitless battle. Our goal isn't to fight self-survival but to transcend it. This sets us on a different path because in order to transcend something we first need to let it be, and we can't let it be until we become fully conscious of what it is. This isn't done through battle but through acceptance and comprehension. I also postulated that perhaps we could redirect the survival force toward pursuing the truth. This would produce a significant change in how the self is conceived and goes about handling its needs. Yet we should be clear that the survival mechanism remains, and is still the foundation for our experience.

22:2   We need to come to grips with, and to some degree "master," what we express and how we manifest. Since we don't live in the world of "absolutes" we will continue to relate and manifest in a domain of relative perceptions. We will engage in what is in the end an illusion, but this is the world in which we must live and act. If we aren't conscious of what we're doing, we can't break free of it, or if we do get free, we are likely to become confused with it once again.

22:3 We can't free ourselves of anything of which we are not conscious, so our task must include discovering the unconscious structures that found the self-experience. Becoming conscious of this level of the self-mind reveals what runs us. Once this is done, we can become free of it. But for the most part we need to tackle this domain one piece at a time. We need to contemplate our self-mind until we are fully conscious of how it works and why it works that way.

22:4 As with Zen, becoming conscious of the true nature of ourselves and reality is always our central goal. In Zen disciplines, however, there is no time spent looking into the mechanisms of mind and self, as we've been doing in this book. Even the possibility of direct experience — the whole point of Zen — is generally expressed only through enigmatic or poetic means, if at all. This makes sense, because direct consciousness cannot be accurately conveyed. A wise Zen master keeps quiet on this subject most of the time and lets his students wrestle with the questioning for themselves. But over the years, I've found that contemplation is useful not only for pursuing a direct consciousness of the true nature of things, but also to bring to light what's hidden in the unconscious mind.

22:5 Since Zen existed long before modern psychology, nowhere in the old teachings will you find references to the unconscious aspect of mind. Still, the old Zen masters likely recognized that there is a danger of sliding into a morass of endlessly sifting through the concepts that the self-mechanism creates, rather than transcending the mechanism itself. There is still that danger. But we need to boldly face all that constitutes our experience and see it for what it is before we can truly be free of it.

22:6   We could say that attempting to get free before we're conscious of every unconscious aspect of mind is a bit like trying to pull up a tent when some of the stakes are still firmly stuck in the ground. We can't completely free the tent because something holds it in place. The unconscious aspects of the self-mind will keep us attached in some way to a self surviving. We might become free of some things, but could still be snagged on others, keeping us attached to whatever we identify as ourselves—even if we're not fully conscious of all that's involved in our makeup.

If everything that isn't true is let go,
what remains must be true.

22:7   In order to distinguish what is true from all that is false, we need to become conscious of everything that constitutes our mind and experience, including the uncognized aspects. Although we may strive to become conscious of the true nature of ourselves and reality, we shouldn't deny the fact that our mind and perceptions do not currently share in that consciousness. Our mind is structured to provide information that serves the self, but this same mind's "need to know" policy keeps us unconscious of its supporting structures. We must find a way to penetrate into what we don't currently cognize. We can use our newly developed skills in contemplation to trace what we observe *in* and *as* ourselves back to the very source of our identity and behavior.

Finding Our Way into the Unconscious

22:8   We've seen that much of our perceptive experience is founded on a framework of uncognized concepts in the form of convictions, conclusions, beliefs, and assumptions. These in turn govern our behavior. As a whole, what we habitually generate within our internal state and how we characteristically interact with whatever we encounter could be called our self-agenda. It is what each one of us is up to as an individual self. This agenda will show up most clearly in our desires and fears, our beliefs and opinions, our emotional reactions and patterns of behavior. Yet such expressions are just the tip of the iceberg.

22:9   Since we don't have an immediately discernable access to what's uncognized within us, we have to find a way to get there. Be clear that the uncognized aspects of mind are not elsewhere or in some other place; they exist right in our experience. We simply aren't conscious of them. Since the experience we have right now includes what's not recognized, we can use our most familiar internal states and behavior patterns to lead us into this unconscious structure of self. By putting attention on specific patterns of action and reaction, we can contemplate this experience and become conscious of what's driving it. Action and source are already connected. Through contemplation we simply follow this line of connection to its source.

Contemplating the Uncognized Mind

22:10   It may seem like a leap to go from observing thoughts, emotions, and behavior to discovering what is behind these activities, but it is possible. There is a technique that involves isolating an emotional reaction, belief, impulse, or characteristic behavior and focusing on it. We then contemplate this experience by feeling it fully and asking: what is it really about? What is the core motivating feeling-concept that incites this reaction?

22:11   Obviously, the reactions and behaviors that mark your character or self-identity are revealed by how you relate to life circumstances. It could be how you typically react when something hurtful is said to you, or how you feel and behave at a party. It could be the way you argue with your mate, or feelings that arise when your boss walks into the room. It could be what goes through your mind sitting alone in the park or passing a stranger in the street. It could be how you deal with waiting in traffic or forgetting your umbrella on the subway. In other words, it could be anything.

22:12   Any characteristic reactivity or behavior can be the subject for such contemplation. For example, if I notice an uncomfortable shyness around others, I could concentrate on the feeling that produces such shyness — a form of fear. As I do, I might notice certain ideas or beliefs that fuel that feeling. Everyone goes this far from time to time, but we usually turn away before realizing that there is much more behind the reaction. Continuing to dwell on the feeling and the concepts that generate it, I can become increasingly clear about the source of my shyness.

22:13   It is not enough to have an idea about why I'm so shy. Even if my idea is correct, it won't make any difference simply for me to "know" about it. I must experience within my own self the "bottom line" or real source of my shyness, and in such a deep way that the shyness will wither away like a weed cut at the root. By deliberately contemplating my shyness, I can uncover the personal programming and cultural presumptions that produce it. When I've consciously experienced them for myself, disengaging from them will dissipate my shyness. If it does not, then I must assume that either they are not what is really responsible for my shyness, or I haven't actually experienced the source of them within my own mind. In either case, more contemplation is appropriate.

22:14   In most cases, emotional reactions are the best link to what is stimulating our behavior or familiar internal states. It is important not to deny how we feel. We are motivated largely by our emotional states, beneath which lie our dominant programming and unconscious beliefs. Our relationship to such feelings should be to feel them fully, and yet not be swept away by them or take them too seriously. Once we acknowledge the presence of these feeling reactions, our task is to experience them completely and to consciously get to the bottom of what generates them.

22:15   Clearly this can't always be done while the reaction is occurring. As much as possible, however, addressing the issue when the mind is set in motion is best, since this allows the most tangible access to the core beliefs and assumptions that are activated. It is also the hardest time to get to the bottom of these feelings, because the motivation to react is strongly assertive.

22:16   Our emotions are engaged, of course, because our self "survival" is active and trying to do its job. With negative reactions, we feel at risk in some manner, and we are trying to handle that risk. We are responding with programs designed to relate to the perceived circumstances in such a way as to eliminate the risk. Normally this immediate need to pursue a reaction demands our attention more strongly than our will to investigate it.

22:17   Because our reactions are so automatic, our most direct access to their origins is when the reactions are fresh, and they can't be any fresher than when they are occurring. This might be during a conversation, an argument, or any other kind of interaction, or even when we are confronted by circumstances that involve only ourselves. Still, it is difficult to "contemplate" while a characteristic feeling or behavior is being stimulated. That's all right; such contemplation can be done afterward in a quiet moment.

22:18 In undertaking this kind of contemplation it's useful to make some distinctions in your experience. Increasing clarity about your "recognized-experience" helps in becoming conscious of parts of your experience that aren't normally recognized. One reason people fail to be more conscious of what runs them is that they blur too much of what's going on for them into an indistinct mass of generalized experience and reaction, and so remain insensitive to what is really taking place. Remember, self-survival only requires interpretation and effect—finer distinctions and facts are unimportant. If you start with the obvious and clarify each aspect of your experience—grasping it as independent but related to other aspects of your experience—this rigorous attentiveness can carry over into becoming conscious of what isn't obvious. In the next section, as I attempt to clarify the elements involved in this kind of contemplation, see if you can make the distinctions I mention in your own experience.

The Process of Contemplating Uncognized Mind

22:19 First you need to sort out and ballpark what it is you are to work on. The subject matter for investigation could be anger, fearfulness, cruelty, guilt, overintellectualizing, sadness, giddiness, shyness, hurt, or any other human reaction—whatever the self-mind reflexively identifies as familiar reactions to life. Our goal is to uncover the assumptions or programs that have been dominating our perceptions and behavior in some way, forming a "characteristic" self. The idea here is that if the reaction is unwanted, we can become free of it. If it is not, then perhaps we can enjoy it but still not consider it to be oneself or necessary.

22:20 To begin to get to the bottom of some aspect of the reactive self-mind, start with a characteristic reaction and expression. Once you encounter a life circumstance, you will react internally in some way, but often you will also react with an expression or behavior of some sort—such as yelling, crying, speaking, winking, jumping up and down, frowning, smiling, trembling, or some other external manifestation. The first thing to do is notice that these two activities—your internal state and your expression—are distinct. They may be related, but they are not the same event and exist in completely different domains. Usually this distinction is blurred, and you relate to your feelings and behavior as if they're one thing. Clarity here helps create that rigor I was talking about above, assisting in sorting out your experience and what it is really up to. Make a distinction between your internal reaction and your expression.

22:21 Many of your expressions are very subtle and not animated at all, yet they are still expressions, which simply means that the body takes some sort of action, be it a gross movement or an almost imperceptible change in one's face or posture. Behind that expression is your experience, what you might call your internal state. Your actions arise from this experience. For example, if you're happy, your action could be to smile. If you're angry, you might yell or scowl.

22:22 Most of the time when we see someone yelling with a particular tone and volume and accompanying facial expression and gesticulation, we say he is angry. We don't say he is having an internal state which we call the emotion anger and expressing this state with the activity of yelling. But it is easy to make this distinction: he is yelling because he's angry, or he is happy and so he's smiling.

22:23 Looking into one of your characteristic behaviors, get in touch with the internal state that evokes such behavior, making a distinction between this emotion or internal reaction and the behavior or actions you use to express it. Then ask why you are having that experience. What is pushing those feelings or thoughts to the surface? If you're feeling angry, why are you angry? This is not asked as a general question, like why are humans angry, but specifically: why are you angry in this case? You will probably attribute the "cause" of your anger to the circumstance—she said I'm stupid, or Fred got the promotion instead of me, or whatever. But this is only a starting point. You're looking for a specific reason that those incidents produce anger in you. What do you believe or assume such that you get angry when these events occur? What is true for you that you feel a need to react in this way?

22:24 In our culture we rarely go past assuming the circumstance is the cause. When we do go deeper, it frequently takes the form of a psychological assessment pointing to some aspect of our personal history. Here, we're not concerned with anything but the truth. It may appear in a psychological form, an ontological one, or in some other form; it doesn't matter. What matters is that it is actually experienced as true, and is recognized as the source of our reaction and behavior.

22:25 Underneath or behind your reaction is what this circumstance means to you. Your reaction is created from the associations you make in relation to a particular circumstance. It arises the way it does to manifest your form of manipulating the circumstances, compelling you to behave as you do. Clarify the associations you're making and you will experience that these interpretations arise from programs and assumptions. Experiencing this process deeply enough will allow you to recognize and acknowledge that your behavior *is* a manipulation. Recognizing what this manipulation is trying to accomplish will bring the whole activity home and put it into a much clearer light. This puts you on the threshold of discovering the source of your reaction.

22:26 This form of contemplation helps you get to the foundation of your reactions. Once you've isolated a characteristic behavior, look into the experience that drives you to act that way. Become analytical about it, but take care to delve into the experience rather than the intellect. Begin to notice that there is more going on than what you cognize on the surface. If you keep feeling underneath this experience, you will get to the deeper source of it, something that might have you say, "Oh, that's what it's all about!" Have you ever done that? Some connection is made, some experiential realization pops up as obviously truer and more deeply honest than your initial reaction. It is what you unconsciously identify with that produces your particular experience. I call this motivating source the "bottom line."

Explaining the Process

22:27 Such a discovery tends to free you from your attachment to the reaction in question — at least for the time being. One reason you are moved out of your reactive state is that such a realization puts you into a different part of the mind than the place where reactions occur. What your emotional reaction or characteristic behavior is based upon is in a different domain of experience than is the reactivity itself. For example, the bottom-line source of being angry might be a deep belief that one is personally incapable. This recognition of personal weakness is not itself a reaction, nor does it evoke a reaction when realized at its source as it would if perceived within the reactive sphere of the mind. It is a belief or assumption revealed. The connection between this assumption and one's anger is suddenly made conscious, and the assumption is experienced as the source of the anger. When you become conscious of the source of the program that stimulates the reaction — as a way to deal with some circumstance — there's no longer a reason to react.

22:28   Just as a core belief is different from the reaction it produces, the realization of a core belief is also different in nature. At this point your consciousness is in a nonreactive state because it is not engaged within the domain of mind that produces the automatic drama of self-survival. Observing the framework that is being maintained reveals the "rationale" behind the strategy for your survival that is emerging as a way to deal with a particular circumstance. Since this process of association and reaction happens very quickly, it usually goes unrecognized until it appears as a reactive emotional impulse.

22:29   As we've seen, the process of self-survival is twofold, demanding not only the activity of maintaining and protecting, but also providing the "something" that it maintains and protects. The self's accumulation of automatic programs guarantees consistency in reaction to all similar circumstances. These are the roots of our characteristic approach to personal survival.

22:30   Thoughts, emotions, and behavior are easy to recognize in our experience. What's far more difficult to see is the source of these — the buried conceptual framework that spurs and dictates our thinking, emotions, and actions. Self-survival has no reason to go there, and every reason to stay away, but with some concentration and sensitivity, the conceptual framework that drives us becomes increasingly recognizable.

22:31   Such consciousness, however, tends to undermine our exclusive and solid sense of self, because it reveals the foundations of this self-sense, and this interferes with blindly fulfilling the needs that stem from this foundation. Taken as a whole, the entire structure of uncognized mind is the origin of our sense that we are somehow a self existing within, at the source of our reactivity and action — like the Wizard of Oz hiding behind the curtain and pulling levers to maintain the illusion of self. Discovering such a thing just doesn't help in keeping up the illusion.

A Sample Bottom-Line Contemplation

22:32   Let me run through a sample contemplation of getting to the bottom of a characteristic experience, just to give you an idea of how it might work. Remember, for you it could go very differently, and probably will. This sample represents only one possible pattern of discovery for someone who has these particular associations, presumptions, and programming.

22:33   Let's say I start contemplating an unwanted behavior. This behavior is yelling at my wife. I recall as vividly as I can the experience of this behavior and sit for awhile and try to "soak" in the experience, orienting myself to the subject matter. I'm yelling. Why am I yelling? I notice very quickly that I am yelling because I am angry at her. This is my immediate experience behind the yelling, I am angry. So I soak in this feeling — like soaking in a hot tub,

I let the experience permeate my consciousness. Trying not to make any judgments about it or leap to any conclusions, I just "feel" into this experience.

22:34   When my emotional reaction is clear and fully felt, I ask, *What is underneath that?* Perhaps what comes up is: "I am pissed!" This feels like more of the same, but perhaps a little more raw and unaltered. So I continue: *Well, what's underneath that?* It's important that I don't rush ahead, but keep immersing myself in what feels most real. I might consider: *What am I "communicating" or getting across by being angry?* As I sit and feel into the anger, I attempt to discern what motivates it, what my mind and emotions are up to by generating such a feeling. It's important that I don't dwell on trying to manipulate the feeling or engage in any manipulation of my experience. I just let it be as it is. Of course, the feeling itself is a manipulation, but I'm not trying to justify or explain it, which are simply more manipulations. Instead, it's as if I'm reaching into the emotion itself with my sensitivity and consciousness, trying to notice something about it that is in the feeling but beneath the surface.

22:35   As I contemplate my reaction, at some point I realize that even more fundamental than my anger is that I am hurt—*Oh, yeah, it's true, I'm hurt.* She hurt my feelings—that's why I'm angry. I didn't notice that I was hurt, only that I was angry. Now it becomes clear that the motivation behind my anger is this hurt feeling. Feeling hurt seems somehow more real, more honest or to the point than what I started with. So I now contemplate the experience of feeling hurt. *What is the hurt about? What is this experience standing on such that I could be hurt in the first place?*

22:36   Each time I look into my feeling-experience I stay with what seems most real and honest, what is really there. Yet at the same time I continue to probe more deeply into it. I set out to discover what lies at the root of this chain reaction that's occurring within my experience. I ask: *What motivates the hurt?* At some point it becomes clear to me that I believe she doesn't like me. As I try to get to the bottom of that, I realize what is actually more true is that I fear she might not love me.

22:37   What's important is that I do this as an actual experience and not just as an intellectual exercise. This process is not one of thinking it through or figuring it out. I must be willing to "feel into" each emotion that arises and follow it to its root bottom.

22:38   So perhaps I get stuck on this fear for awhile. It might be a new concept for me that my anger could somehow be related to fear. The realization that I feel vulnerable may be difficult to fully confront at first, but I persist and continue to contemplate my experience. I might want to "escape" the more vulnerable feelings and again take refuge in thoughts and feelings that are more familiar and "safe." Whenever I become distracted I work to bring myself back to the deepest realization I've come to. It's important that I avoid jumping around to all sorts of other feelings or thoughts that pop into my mind as I contemplate. Some of them seem associated with what I'm contemplating but may also be distractions. I can save them for another time, since right now I need to stay on track and limit my contemplation to this particular subject.

22:39   As I focus my feeling and attention on the most genuine sense of this experience — which at this point is a fear that my wife might not love me — I start to awaken to the sense that I have this overwhelming sense of needing to be loved by someone. This feels real to me, but it is not the whole story. Then it hits me, and I suddenly realize in a flash the bottom of this whole reaction. The realization comes all at once but can't be expressed all at once. I uncover an assumption that if I'm not loved, then I'm not a good or authentic person, and if I'm not good and authentic, then I am not real and I don't deserve to live. These are connections between two programmed presumptions, the bottom line of which is that somehow my wife's behavior threatens my life, or at least the continuation and safety of my self-identity.

22:40   That would be the bottom line: I assume I will die without love. We can see how this might relate to my manipulations of yelling, although it is a long and winding route. We also notice a great difference between the anger and the need for love, or the presumption of something bad happening to my self without it. The fear and need are primary motivations that will automatically produce the hurt and anger. The hurt is produced to stimulate a reaction, and the anger is produced to stimulate a mode of behavior or action that is designed to protect my self. None of this has to be logical or rational; it only has to be true. The structure has its own rationale based on my assumptions and history. Someone else could have the same assumptions but react in a different way since they identify with different characteristics that need to be maintained, and this governs how they will go about manipulating both self and environment. In either case, a specific reaction will arise in the face of any threat to the emotional self-identity, motivating behavior to deal with the threat.

22:41   Of course, none of this is actually true in the sense that I will die or that yelling will prevent it. And my perception of my wife's expression may have absolutely no bearing in reality. But it is true in the sense that I really experience it that way, and at my core somewhere I actually believe it is a threat to my existence.

22:42 Frequently what we find as the real origin of our reactive behavior doesn't seem logically connected even to ourselves. In fact, it might be so far-fetched that a logical approach would never find its way to the bottom line. We don't really need to believe it intellectually, and it may be a "socially incorrect" disposition to have. None of that matters. The only thing that matters is that it is what's so — it's what the reaction is truly and deeply based on. Once this "bottom line" is discovered, we can begin to disassociate from our dysfunctional core beliefs. When that is done, the reaction will cease to arise.

Guidelines for Your Bottom-Line Contemplation

22:43 How your contemplation might go is unknown. It is an "organic" process and will proceed as the truth and your consciousness dictate. The following are some guidelines, questions, and points that can be used to help your contemplation stay on track and penetrate into your mind's unconscious construction.

22:44 Be open to experiencing whatever is behind what you're feeling or experiencing. See if there is anything more basic or more true for you than what you presently experience. Whenever you get in touch with something more fundamental, then move deeper to contemplate that. If not, then continue to contemplate the experience that feels most genuine. This keeps you on track and fresh with the experience you're working with.

22:45   Continue to wonder: *What's underneath this experience? Is there anything sourcing or motivating it? Anything more real? More honest?* Stay with the whole experience, and keep in alignment with your original reaction or behavior. Is there any feeling or sense that is underneath, behind, inside of, or in any way more basic, fundamental, true, or honest? Remember to do this experientially. Look, or "feel" into it; don't just think about it. Is there anything that "hits home"?

22:46   When you get to the origin of your experience, it is the real "heart of the matter," the source of what is going on for you relative to that experience. It may not appear logically connected to the surface reaction and expression; it's just what's true. When you get to the bottom line or origins of your reaction, there is nothing underneath, sourcing, or motivating it. Dispelling this core belief or assumption will dissolve your reactions and unwanted behavior.

22:47   Remember, it is important to understand that this domain of "uncognized" mind is not elsewhere or separate from what is called the conscious mind. It is simply what is not conscious in the very same place as what you experience. For example, the core beliefs and assumptions that source what you recognize as emotions and expressions are inherent in the emotions and expressions themselves. They are not somewhere else; they are simply an uncognized aspect of what is occurring in your experience. Since you don't *need to know* in order to survive, you remain unaware of them. As you contemplate a bottom line, keep a vigil on the tendency to think of this domain as elsewhere and so not within the experience you are contemplating.

Five Points of Reference

22:48   Although we shouldn't confuse our attempts to organize our efforts with anything etched in stone, or as complete, we can use some points of reference to assist in pursuing this particular contemplative process. The foundation principles of contemplation all still apply to this effort and are the same, but here they manifest a bit differently. Rather than working to become conscious of something independent of our experience, the task with bottom-line contemplation is to uncover what is already in our experience but simply unseen.

> Five Points of Reference:
> - Be honest
> - Be focused
> - Be open
> - Be patient
> - Be persistent

22:49   The main thing to do, and to continue doing, is to be honest. By now you understand that this depth of honesty goes beyond convention. Really tell the truth to yourself about your experience. Start with what's there; admit what is really the case in your feeling and action and thought. This is not an opportunity to shore up your self-image; just be willing to let the truth of what you're really up to come forward. Don't take for granted that you immediately know everything about what you're experiencing. Leave room for the fact that people inevitably and automatically distort their view of what's true for them. Spend time and be critical. You aren't trying to establish an ultimate truth here; you are simply attempting to strip away any distortion or ignorance, and acknowledge what your actions and reactions really are.

22:50 Once you've gotten as honest as you can about your experience, then you must focus on this experience as it is. Set out to penetrate into it, to discern what you've yet to discern. Look or "feel" directly into what's there, without turning away. Maintain your intent to discover what this experience is all about, what's there that you aren't cognizing. Keep your feeling-attention focused on the experience, trying to get to the bottom of it.

22:51 As you focus on this experience, develop openness and courage. Allow not-knowing to bring you to a place of genuine openness. Generate the courage to challenge what you assume to be real but don't directly experience as such — which, by the way, is *everything.* This will take some work, and as you go deeper and deeper into it, you will be confronted with the need to recognize core assumptions that exist as a framework for your beliefs but of which you have been unconscious. These assumptions include what has been absorbed through your culture as well as the core beliefs and programming that form the foundation of your personal conceptual identity. Clarifying the core beliefs and assumptions that comprise the brick and mortar of your self-mind, you are better able to step into the unconventional and transformative work of dissolving the self-identity — taking it apart brick by brick. Even though you may be attending to this stage throughout your work on yourself, you will have more success at being able to recognize and disassociate from your self-identity as you awaken your deeper assumptions.

22:52 You may not grasp the source of your experience right away, so be patient and persistent. Wait with it; don't rush or leap around trying to satisfy some need to find a quick answer. Only the truth will do, and you must be able to make an experiential connection between this source and your reactions and behavior. Stay with it until you can discern what's most real or honest; press on until you reach the rock bottom. It may take quite a while before you reach the source of your mind and character—why it is that way, what it is founded on or based upon. You may realize something quickly, but something else could take repeated contemplations over a longer period of time. Don't let up; keep your attention on this experience until you grasp what it is all about.

22:53　These points are not a linear progression, but more like a cycle that requires much repeating. Each aspect assists and enhances the others. The more honest you are, the more capable you are of engaging and focusing on what is really going on in your experience. The more open you are, the easier it is to challenge your beliefs and assumptions. The more assumptions you recognize, the more you are able to dissolve aspects of your self-identity, and thus become even more open. And so on. Due to the complex nature and well-worn grooves of your viewpoints, using these few distinctions will assist you in the beginning. In time and with repeated contemplation, you will realize that these distinctions are all simply facets of a single effort to reach the truth of your experience.

22:54　As you become adept in this domain of contemplation, your self-identity will begin to change, since once you recognize something for what it is, you will tend to let it go. The more detached you become from self, the greater will be your capacity to contemplate what is true. If you directly experience the true nature of your own being, you will have an immediate increase in freedom from self and greater wisdom in your contemplation. Depending on the depth of this consciousness, however, you will still be left with many habits of mind and tendencies of culture that must be challenged directly in order to get free of them. Further contemplation in both of these modes will assist in deepening your consciousness of both Being and self.

22:55 We can also use such contemplative skills to discover what is true about human emotions in general. Discovering the underpinnings of our emotions and drives gives us clues about the nature of the human condition. Transcending the human condition is a matter best addressed through contemplation. In the last chapters, we take a look into the very elusive domain of the nature of things.

PART VI

The Nature of Reality

CHAPTER TWENTY-THREE

The Nature of Emotion

23:1   Assumptions don't just exist beneath the surface of our consciousness; they also occur in the form of shared ignorance. In our bottom-line work, it becomes more real for us that our self-mind is composed of unrecognized personal assumptions and core beliefs. But it is also composed of collective human assumptions that no one questions or even thinks to question.

23:2   Since our cognition seems limited to what we "need to know," we generally take whatever comes to mind at face value. When we experience something, we assume that's all there is to know about it. Digging into these experiences, however, we find it's possible to make many new distinctions. We've been making new distinctions all along in our work to reveal unconscious aspects of mind. But new discoveries can also be made that aren't buried in the unconscious; they are simply unknown to humans in general. We're ignorant, but don't know that we are ignorant.

23:3   For example, the strongest forces that dominate our experience are found in our emotional states, and yet we know little about what these are. As a culture, we usually relegate the status of emotional impulses to what we think of as our more primal or animal nature. We've been taught that our emotions are fixed and simplistic activities — that our role in the matter is one of feeling the emotion and reacting to it. This is a small and limited view, making emotions very misunderstood. Because our relationship to emotions is limited to reacting to whatever they motivate us to do, we are off taking action or adopting dispositions rather than understanding what any of these feeling-states are really about.

23:4   It can be challenging to experientially grasp the activity of an emotion. What we experience as an emotion is the end product of a complex but lightning-quick process. We're simply provided with the motivation or impulse to orient ourselves in a particular way, and take action accordingly. Just as in any other survival impulse, the whole of our experience — what we perceive, believe, value, and assume, as well as our memory, programming, self-image, and so on — is weighed against the current circumstance or perceived issue, and the "self-survival disposition" needed to relate to those conditions is summarized in a feeling. This is an emotion.

23:5   We can't tackle every human emotion and impulse here, nor do we need to. Using a sampling of the most central feelings that drive us, we open the door to understand all of the rest — either because they are merely variations or combinations of the same dynamics, or because we are now equipped with the tools to investigate different emotions along similar lines.

23:6   Here we will study the two most central negative emotions we have, fear and anger, and the two most central driving forces of the self-mind, desire and pain. These four are the basis for far more than people realize. They are a bit like the primary colors, which combine to make up all colors. With these four we may not be tackling every primary color, but certainly most of them.

23:7 When we study the composition of what drives us, we discover some startling facts. The first surprising notion is that there are components to be discovered within emotions. When an emotion arises we seem to know what it is, and leave it at that. We can recognize it and label it, and assume that's all there is to know about it. It isn't. As we'll see, there is more to this activity than we acknowledge. Just by calling emotion an activity I'm already challenging the assumption that an emotion is something like a feeling "object." We seem to "have" fear, anger, love, or sadness. They appear to reside in the body and we perceive and react to them. Yet, as we study each of these four primary feeling-states, we see there is much more to them.

Fear

23:8 What constitutes fear? I don't mean what generates fear, but what is necessary in order to create a state of fear? What are the components of fear? The mere presence of fear is usually enough information for us, and we act on it, trying to make it go away. This is where our consciousness stops in the matter. We don't know what fear is, nor its makeup. We don't even know that it's possible to know such things. We know a car has wheels, a source of power, steering capabilities, and so on. We know an atom is made up of a nucleus and electrons. Without these components we wouldn't have a car or an atom. So, what constitutes fear? Discovering the components of fear requires making new distinctions, perceiving something in fear we haven't consciously experienced thus far.

23:9 When we look at fear we see something unwanted, an uncomfortable feeling we'd rather not have. We find fear in many different forms — being worried, anxious, shy, startled, frightened,

493

timid, scared, cowardly, terrorized, and so on. We imagine that fear is necessary because it keeps us from doing something harmful to ourselves like walking off a cliff, right? Hogwash. Fear doesn't keep us from walking off the cliff. Knowing we would die keeps us from walking off the cliff. If we can't be trusted to keep our attention on this fact and so arrange our actions accordingly — and strangely enough, frequently we can't — then perhaps we need the cattle prod of fear. But this only confesses our irresponsible and mechanical relation to the matter.

23:10   Since our cognition lives so much in the "need to know" level of consciousness, we simply accept that we are dependent on forces and impulses to push us around. All we "need to know" in the case of the cliff is that we are afraid, which provides the impulse of avoidance so that we don't walk off it. Yet it's clear that merely being aware of the potential danger makes us capable of not walking off the cliff, and we need not be afraid.

23:11   The more secure we are in our ability to handle any given circumstance, the less we are afraid. Most of us aren't afraid to drive a car, even though if we swerve into oncoming traffic, we could be killed. Why not be afraid? Because we are pretty confident we won't do it, and we feel capable of steering the car properly. Someone who walks along cliff edges every day isn't fearful of stepping off the cliff. He might one day, as we might have a car accident, but we can do that without maintaining fear as a preventative measure, and we can be killed even if we are afraid all the time. Fear isn't the deciding factor. So, what is fear?

23:12   Well, take a look — or a "feel" in this case. When you are fearful, what's there? What does the fear consist of? Circumstances are usually cited as the "cause" of fear. Is fear the circumstance? As

we've seen, the circumstance is independent of fear being produced or not produced. Some people are afraid of a certain object
or circumstance — heights, snakes, public speaking — that others are not, so it's not the circumstance that causes the fear. What
does?

23:13   If we could take fear apart, what would we find? This is a tricky
investigation since normally we see fear as a single "unit" of emotion. If we were to dismantle such a feeling, we would simply have
pieces of feeling. But fear is not just a feeling. Emotion is not simply an interpreted sensation like feeling cold, or feeling pressure
on your fingertips. An emotion is more than the feeling-reaction
we receive in our awareness at the level of "need to know." Beneath
our awareness, concept and time play indispensable roles in creating emotion.

23:14   All emotions are conceptually based. They are complex rather than
simplistic impulses. In the case of fear, we find four major components, three of which are conceptual.

- An unwillingness to have a particular experience

- The possibility of a future

- Conceiving an unwanted scenario involving a particular
  experience

- A physiological feeling-reaction

23:15   The first is an unwillingness or resistance to having a particular
experience. When we imagine the consequences of falling from
the cliff, for example, or smashing into an oncoming car, we see
they are experiences most of us would rather not have. Actually,
they are experiences we would try very hard to avoid. We resist

495

having these experiences. We don't want them. We are unwilling to have them.

23:16   In simple terms, we don't want to experience pain or death. We've seen in the principle of self-survival that resistance can take on many forms. A threat to the self may not look like physical pain or death, but still be experienced as seriously unwanted, or painfully threatening. Speaking in front of a crowd is so threatening for many that it is considered a risk closely matching death, and yet we find no physical danger whatsoever. No matter how it arises, there is always a component of conceiving something painful that we are unwilling to experience.

23:17   This doesn't mean fear is an intellectual matter. This resistance, or unwillingness, is itself an action, not just a thought — even though it is conceptually produced. This activity is inside of the emotion itself. It makes up, in part, the emotion of fear.

23:18   Unwillingness is not a separate activity, or a causal activity. It is fear — or, I should say, one component of fear. This means that when we are afraid, it's possible to recognize this unwillingness taking place, in whatever form it occurs. Once we make this distinction, if we can eliminate it — in other words, be completely willing to experience whatever we're resisting — no fear can take place.

23:19   Sounds suspicious, doesn't it? Maybe, but it's true. If this unwillingness is actually a component of fear, then fear cannot occur without it (it also makes it easier to see fear as an activity). Test it out. If you become completely willing to experience falling from the cliff, dying, being injured, being ridiculed by the crowd, looking like a fool, or whatever it is you're afraid of, then you cannot be afraid. It says nothing about your safety — that's a self-survival issue — it only says you won't be afraid. This is true of all components. A component is part of the structure of the thing itself; therefore eliminating any component will eliminate the thing.

23:20 The second component of fear is the possibility of a future. A future has to exist in order for fear to take place. Fear doesn't take place in relation to the present, only in relation the future. Yet, we seem to experience fear in the present, so what's this future business all about? The future component is frequently misunderstood at first, so hang in there for a moment. If we observe closely enough, we will notice that whatever is occurring as fear in the present is in relation to the possibility or notion of the future. Most of the time, it is clear that you are afraid of what you think is going to happen or might happen. This means it has not yet happened. Without the future (or the past, which has already passed safely) there would be no possibility other than what *is* happening, so fear could not arise.

23:21 I first made this distinction while engaged in several days of intense contemplation. I was standing on an upper floor of a house that had a fireman's pole in the middle of a rather large hole in the floor. As I looked down through the hole, the danger of falling and getting hurt occurred to me. At this time, being a little afraid and also deep in a contemplative state, I suddenly realized the nature of fear and its relation to the future. So I decided to do a little experiment. Putting my hands behind my back so I couldn't grab onto the pole, I watched my mind as I let my body fall forward. Staying completely in the present moment, I was unable to be afraid. There was no experience I could have other than the one I was having, and so nothing to be afraid of. My body stopped moving when my head hit the pole. I stayed there for awhile, with my hands still behind my back, staring down below, impressed with the total lack of fear and excited by this new discovery. I don't recommend such physical experiments —I was a bit obsessive with my investigations. It works just as well with the countless number of social fears that don't put you in harm's way. The point is that without a future, fear is not possible. The future is a component of fear.

23:22 "But when I'm afraid of a spider, I'm afraid right now and the spider is right there." That may be so, but it isn't the presence of the spider that you're afraid of. It is the potential that the spider's presence seems to represent. In other words, it is what could happen in the future. In some cases it may seem like the mere presence is causing the fear and so there's no need for the future component. Yet, if the spider were in a glass cage at the zoo, would you still be afraid? Most people wouldn't. This demonstrates the future component, since now the spider is safely behind glass and so it can't hurt you —and this hurt must take place in the future. Still, some may be afraid even if the spider is behind glass. We call this an irrational fear because the evidence of safety isn't enough to eliminate the fear. Irrational or not, the future component still applies, since what is related to isn't the spider being there but that somehow, even behind the glass, it will hurt you. Obviously this hurt can only occur in the future since it's not taking place now.

23:23 Sometimes people say they fear the unknown, but this isn't accurate. It isn't the unknown that's feared. You may not know the ultimate nature of the universe, or who dinged your car, but you're not afraid of these things, are you? It is the potential for harm lurking in some unsuspected place that is feared. But that's not exactly true either, is it? Some type of harm *is* suspected, and it is suspected in some particular place. You simply don't know exactly what it's going to be or when it's going to show up. But that's a far cry from fearing the unknown. If you're about to step into a dark room and you're afraid, it isn't because you don't know what's in there; it's the fact that you think something bad might be in there.

23:24   Whether perceived as present or not, the experience you're unwilling to have is always in the future. You fear experiencing pain of some sort, but it hasn't happened yet. If it has, you're not afraid; you're in pain. And the only way you can be afraid of what you're in pain about — what you're experiencing that you didn't want to experience — is to imagine more of it continuing in the future, or it getting worse, or the consequences of having gone through it. All of these are future events. You might say you are afraid of a tiger, but once again it isn't the tiger you're afraid of; it's what the tiger could do to you. If the tiger is gnawing on your skull, then you aren't afraid of it eating you — you are afraid it might finish, or continue to eat you, or you might be afraid of having to live with half a head, but you aren't afraid of what the tiger is *doing*. You're in pain about what it is doing. Fear is a function of the future. Having made this distinction, if you eliminate the future, you will eliminate fear. Have no possibility of a future occur in your consciousness, and you cannot be afraid. Interesting, huh?

23:25   So, let's look at the third component, conceiving an unwanted scenario. It's somewhat of a combination of the first two, but a new element is introduced. This component is generating a scenario that something unwanted will occur in the future. It is not simply unwillingness, nor is it just the future. It is the conception that whatever you are unwilling to experience will happen in the future. Frequently this takes the form of picturing a negative outcome—a mate leaving you, losing your fortune, breaking a leg, falling off a cliff—and imagining it happening to you. If you are willing to experience whatever it is, you won't be afraid. If there is no future in which it can occur, you will not be afraid. And if you don't conceive of something bad happening, then you won't be afraid. Without the "scenario"—the particular thought, image, notion, sense, or whatever form it may take—occurring for you, you won't be afraid, even if you would be unwilling for such a thing to happen, and you do imagine a future.

23:26   When we put these major components for fear together, we have fear, the sensation or physiological reaction of which manifests as a specific negative "feeling." This could be called the fourth component. These components altogether are experienced or "known" to us as an emotion, an activity that is felt and called fear. Almost no one has even wondered what the activity of fear is all about. Contemplating these distinctions of the composition of fear allows us a very different experience of this activity. By making these distinctions we can eliminate fear simply by eliminating any or all of the elements that compose it. This is so with any emotion.

23:27   Our next stop is anger. Anger also takes many forms—being enraged, pissed off, irritated, upset, annoyed, irked, fed up, furious, exasperated, irate, riled, mad, and so forth. Spend a moment to grasp how many emotions you experience that are a form of anger or have anger as a component. Like fear, anger constitutes a large domain of emotions.

Anger

23:28   Recall some time when you were clearly angry. Concentrate on this feeling. What is necessary for the anger to be there, what is it doing, what is it accomplishing? Dissect this emotion for yourself and see if you can come up with the components of anger.

23:29   Following the same investigative techniques used for fear, we discover that in contrast to fear's relationship with the future, anger exists in relation to the past. It is historically based. Just as fear can be relating to the next millisecond or days from now, anger can relate to something that occurred a fraction of a second ago, or many years ago. But it is always about the past. Someone keyed your new car, leaving a scratch. It has already happened, and now you're angry. Your boss admonished you in front of coworkers, and you're seething inside. It happened already. You're not afraid, because it's not something that might happen. You're angry, because it did happen. And it hurt.

23:30   Anger is always based on hurt. Some form of hurt or pain is a component of anger. As with fear, in anger there is always something resisted, not accepted. Given that this experience has already taken place, its rejection shows up as hurt. Conventionally this is rarely noticed. People go right to anger and never get that it is based on the fact that they are feeling hurt. Perhaps one of the main functions of an anger-reaction involves ignoring or avoiding the hurt. Try an experiment: find something to be angry about. Now stop being angry and feel the hurt that the activity of anger wants to correct or eliminate. See if you can feel the hurt and yet still be angry. Why would you be angry? You are already feeling the hurt; what good would anger do? It seems that one of the functions of the anger is to avoid acknowledging the feeling of hurt. What is the hurt about?

23:31 Once again, recall a time when you were angry. Try to feel the anger presently. Now, what thoughts preceded and accompanied this anger? What is the thought or statement that the anger is expressing? What underlies that? See if you can use your skills at contemplation to unearth the bottom line of this anger. What is it?

23:32 Beneath the hurt, you will find some sense of feeling incapable or unworthy in a very fundamental way. This component is not always easy to grasp, but a sense of something I'm calling incapacity is taking place. Imagine that you are completely capable in relation to what's happened. Someone dents your car and you can magically remove the dent and restore it to its former beauty. Angry? Probably not. If you could correct what went wrong, without pain, why be angry? Of course, sometimes things go wrong, or bad things happen, and we aren't angry. We might be depressed, or sad, or flippant, or embarrassed, but not angry. So why are we angry when we are angry?

23:33 Anger, like all emotions, serves self-survival. How does it serve our survival in this case? Obviously something has occurred that you don't want to be the case, and you feel incapable of having it simply or easily be the way you want. Something or someone has impeded your will, your plans, your self. And somewhere in there you feel incapable of having reality be the way that you want — whatever is seen as serving your self. A personal deficiency has been demonstrated to you by some action or event that has brought to the fore a sense of incapacity that's normally buried deep within your psyche.

23:34 Deep down you are unsure of your capacity to live life. How could it be any other way? You don't know what life is, how you came to be, or that your survival is guaranteed. This deep sense of incapacity is drawn to the surface to some degree by a given circumstance. You want this circumstance to be another way, and you feel incapable of having it be that way — especially since it has already happened. This event can be about what someone has said or done, what you have said or done, or a circumstance that has occurred — it simply needs to bring up a sense of incapacity, which is resisted and so is painful. You'd like to set things right. You want to get rid of this sense of incapacity and the resultant hurt produced by the event that has occurred.

23:35 So how does anger help? Where are the feelings of anger directed? What would they like to bring about? With anger we feel we are now taking some sort of action, at least internally. What is the purpose of this action? Anger is an attempt to feel capable, to restore a sense of capacity to one's self. At least the sense of being fundamentally incapable of life can be returned to its buried place in one's psyche.

23:36 Usually we harbor some thoughts and feelings about proving ourselves to be capable — like beating up a bully, doing damage to the boss, or hurting ourselves. The component needed is simply action that demonstrates capability, and what is the easiest way to demonstrate capability? Destroy something. Creating something would work, of course, but creating is much too hard and usually takes too long, and also holds the possibility of failure (revealing our incapacity once again) way too much. Destruction can be immediate, and is the easiest thing to do. It's negatively based, like the feeling of hurt, but produces a result that feels positive: the sense of capacity. Obviously these destructive thoughts, feelings, or actions are often directed at a particular reality that you don't want, but are also frequently directed elsewhere. The drive is to restore a sense of capacity.

23:37 Everyone knows how to destroy and feels capable of doing it. Crush a flower, kick over a chair, toss the chess game from the table, throw mud at a clean dress, create pain in your or someone else's body, take something of value from someone, say something hurtful, and so forth. There are many ways to express anger, some extremely devious and subtle, but they all have in common trying to salvage the self's sense of capacity, and the most common avenue by far is a destructive course. It could simply be giving someone an angry look, or having destructive thoughts or fantasies, yet the immediate effect is feeling capable of something, feeling or imagining oneself as having some power. Of course if these attempts fail, one is likely to be sent into frustration and despair. But destroying is easy, so failure isn't likely—especially if it is only acted out in your imagination.

23:38 As with fear, four components seem to compose anger. Remember, these elements need to be seen as occurring in the anger itself, not as causing or contributing to the anger.

> Anger is
> - About something that has passed
> - Based on a feeling of hurt
> - Revealing a core sense of incapacity
> - Regenerating a sense of capacity through a destructive intent or feeling-reaction

23:39   Once again, eliminating any component of anger will eliminate the anger. If there is no concept of the past, there is no anger. If your experience is totally in the present, anger cannot exist. But remember, this means being present moment to moment, and the possibility of conceptualizing the past can include mind activity not easily recognized, so anger can be fuming in some form beneath the surface. In such a case, the "bottom-line" work we did earlier is necessary to uncover and let go of the uncognized aspect of mind that remains locked in repeating past pain. Completely let go of whatever has passed, and you can't generate anger.

23:40   Likewise, if you do not create hurt or pain about something, you cannot be angry. Hurt can be difficult to avoid, but it doesn't have to lead to anger. Turn your attention fully onto the presence of the pain rather than trying to avoid it or do something about it, and you will interrupt the activity of anger. When the pain is fully experienced without resistance, there is no need to create anger. Further, if you can become conscious of the core feeling of incapacity that founds the anger and transcend this self-mind disposition, you won't need action (internal or external) to restore a sense of capacity, and so there will be no anger. However you go about it, if you interrupt or eliminate any of the components that make up the activity of anger, you will free yourself from anger.

23:41   You can do this kind of investigation on all emotions, but I'll leave that to your personal contemplation. What's most important, however, isn't just learning how to interrupt an emotion, but to understand experientially what emotions are and how they are created, thus changing your relationship to this dominating feature of self. By increasing the depth of your consciousness and sensitivity to what your self-mind is doing in this area —

automatically but subliminally—you develop a clearer and more responsible experience of the activity of your own self.

23:42   Now let's look at two very deep core impulses that are the foundation for most of our emotional reactions and survival perceptions. These are desire and pain. Certainly the opposite of desire is repulsion, or perhaps indifference, and the opposite of pain is pleasure. But these opposites are tacitly included in the activity itself and share the same nature. So by uncovering the composition of these two important impulses we uncover so much more. I want to focus on the most primary feeling states that drive us, and we are clearly driven by desire and pain.

23:43   The impulse or drive to pursue pleasure, comfort, or good experiences is called desire, while pain is what provides the impulse to move away from anything deemed a bad experience. These are fundamental elements for self-survival. Attraction and repulsion, positive and negative, are key to determining value and threat, and so are essential for determining how to "be" in relation to what's perceived.

23:44   We know that as a circumstance is being interpreted, the self requires from the interpretation some type of directed motivation regarding which actions will be appropriate to take. This direction arises in the form of feeling impulses that steer our mental, emotional, and physical activities along the proper paths for self-survival. They exist to serve that purpose. Understanding their nature should bring us closer to understanding the nature of the self principle.

Desire

23:45 What does it mean to have desire? It seems that the domain of desire is one of being moved to have or obtain something, being attracted toward or wanting a particular experience. Desire and fear have a few fundamental elements in common. Whereas with fear we resist an experience, with desire we crave or embrace an experience. We tend to overlook the implications of this fact. If we crave or want something to be so, clearly we are apt to have a negative disposition to the observation that it is not so. Which brings us to the next thing that fear and desire have in common: they both relate to the future.

23:46 One of the components of desire is that it is an assessment of what is missing now. Desire, like fear, is not about the present moment; it's about what is *not* occurring presently. Desire cannot be about now, because desire requires an assessment of what is missing now—ergo it can only take place in relation to the future.

23:47 With fear, we imagine something unwanted may come to pass that is not presently so. With desire, we imagine something we want to occur that doesn't exist now. Certainly, sometimes we perceive something and say that we desire it in this moment, but what we're actually relating to is something not occurring now. Think about it. If it were occurring already we would be enjoying it, not desiring it. And if we are enjoying something and still have desire about it, then clearly what we desire is that the enjoyment continue on into the future.

23:48 If we find nothing missing in our experience right now—nothing that should be experienced that isn't being experienced—then we can have no desire. If we have no future as a possibility, we will also have no desire, no craving, no wanting. If we don't imagine any possibility other than what is already so, we will have no desire. We can see how desire and fear are polar opposites of the same impulse.

23:49   In fear we are pushed to take action, such as flee or freeze. In desire we are also moved to take action. This impulse to action is implied by desiring, since desire suggests something isn't as it should be, and so implies that we need to bring it about somehow. Action is not necessary for desire; it is simply implied. Sometimes we have confusion between feeling a desire and taking some action suggested by the desire. These are two different things. They only seem like one because the action is charged with relieving the pain of the desire.

23:50   Now there's another odd thing to say. The pain of desire? Generally, we think of desire as a good thing or a pleasant feeling. This seems reasonable, since it is relating to something we want, some experience we want to have, to enjoy. Isn't that pleasant? Imagining the enjoyable experience can seem enjoyable, and any fantasy about having that experience would include imagining the pleasure or good feelings that we crave. Yet what is also true is that we are in fact not having it. If this absent experience is contrasted with what we are having now, and we find our present experience lacking, this will tend to elicit a form of suffering. From this suffering — putting up with an unwanted experience — be it a dramatic suffering or a buried, almost unnoticed "itch to scratch," we are moved to take some form of action to turn the not-so-enjoyable present into the enjoyable future.

23:51   So we can see that some form of pain actually accompanies all desire; it's just difficult to perceive because it's always buried

508

underneath the anticipated pleasure. Pain provides an even stronger motivation to take action than simply acquiring something you don't have. We can imagine that if we were fully and completely enjoying the present moment, had pleasure coming out our ears, we would be less likely to desire anything — except possibly that this experience doesn't end. When we long for someone, however, and the relationship we desire doesn't come to pass, it's not hard to see that we will likely suffer in this longing. We could easily experience outright pain over this unrequited attraction. When we are very sensitive to every form of desire we have, we might indeed find that pain is always a component of desire. This makes desire a form of suffering rather than a form of enjoyment as we conventionally tend to presume.

23:52 To exacerbate this unseen problem, we rarely make the distinction between the thing we desire and the concept of the thing we desire. We assume that our fantasy of the experience — imagining whatever happiness or pleasure the object of desire will provide — is the same as the actual experience or encounter. Of course, this is not true. When we get what was desired, it often turns out to be quite different from what we anticipated. Furthermore, since our "beingness" lives only in the present or actual moment, all conceptual activity that is directed toward the future is not directed toward now. The activity of desire contrasts what "is" to some preferred experience that "isn't," and so in some way makes our present experience into a negative one. This subtle diminishing of the present is accompanied by another unnoticed existential consequence of desire.

23:53 We fail to notice the inherent unseen barrier that is created between our feeling of desire and whatever is desired. Simply the fact that we desire implies a separation between us and the object of desire, and between our present experience and the desired experience. If there were no such separation, we can see there would be no place or need for desire. We would not be desirous; we'd be enjoying or experiencing what is otherwise only a concept. This suggests that the very act of desire separates us from the thing we desire. To bridge this gap we are drawn to take action.

23:54 Sometimes we take objective action—we go and get that tasty food, buy the new car, call someone for a date, or meditate for peace of mind. In this way, desire is associated with consumption, gratification, possession, and achievement. Since desire implies there is something wanted that we don't have now, taking action to get it seems the logical choice. Still, many times the first and only action taken is within the mind. We imagine, or fantasize, or make plans, and although this is often as far as we go with our desires, it may not be as harmless as we presume. It might produce a kind of suffering that is not immediately apparent.

Confusing Desire for Intent

23:55 We frequently get our desires mixed up with what we actually want or intend to have happen. Doing something—anything—suggests wanting to do it. Every act you generate is something that you want to undertake for whatever reason, even though it may not seem like you truly desire the action or outcome. It may even seem that you hate doing it, but you do it anyway. For instance, imagine you find yourself stuck in a smelly outhouse—an unpleasant experience that you would say you don't want to have. But when you consider the fact that just outside is a pack of wild dogs that chased you in there, it becomes clear that you want to be in that outhouse. By the same logic, it's easy to guess that you do not desire to experience the pain of grabbing onto a hot poker, but seeing that it is otherwise going to fall on the baby, you clearly want to grab it.

23:56   Those examples may be extreme, but they are clear and useful for helping us work out a distinction between what we intend and what we desire. The word *want* is often used as either *intend* or *desire*. Intention is committing to take a course of action — it is what we actually end up doing, and so in this way we can say it is what we *want* to do. Desire is imagining something we'd like to experience in the future. It is indulging a conceptual possibility, recognizable as the pleasure-charged effect evoked by imagining that experience coming to pass. This is different from what we intend to do. Although there may be an urge or impulse to have a desired experience come about, desire doesn't demand action. Intent does. We might intend to act on our desires, or we might not. If say we want to bring about our desires, or we want to do something else, we are talking about what we intend to do rather than what we merely desire.

23:57   When we fail to make this distinction, we can easily fall into resisting what we're doing. This may be quite subtle, or we may feel clearly unhappy and stuck — either way it's still another form of suffering. I might say to myself, *I want to go out and play, but I'm stuck here forced to work*. Not only is that a very sloppy statement, but my viewpoint — especially if it's habitual — creates misery that is entirely unnecessary. Actually, when I look into the matter, I see that what I truly want is to accomplish something useful and to make a living, so I intend to work. I *want* to work.

23:58   At any given time, we can probably think up some experience that's better than the one we're having. I can imagine other things to do right now, but I don't actually want to be doing them since they won't provide me with what I indeed want to have happen in life. Besides, even if I were to go out and play, I could still probably imagine something *more* fun than whatever I would be doing. I intend to work — end of story. Complaining about my choice and generating images of more exciting activities only creates pain. Enjoying my work while I work and my play while I play produces no separation and so no suffering.

23:59   The struggle to get what we want seems endless. But what exactly is "getting what we want"? Why do we need to get what we want? Why are we so driven toward wanting and obtaining? Culturally, we just take "wanting" for granted. It seems a natural human function, and so we either position ourselves to be unquestioningly dominated by this force or we resist it in its raw form, usually through some sort of discipline, morality, or religious stance. Whichever direction we might go with it, the root activity is the same. It is the self chasing the "cheese."

23:60   Remember, the survival of self and self-concept is at the core of all desire. Clearly the self is so confused with complex agendas regarding what should survive — in other words, what should constitute self and life, and what ought to provide a sense of worth and value — that our multiple and varied desires just seem like natural activities. They may often appear benign, but they are still a central aspect of self-survival and self-concern. As such, our desires contribute to our suffering.

The Components of Desire

23:61   On every level and dimension in which self-survival exists, there is a forceful and irresistible core activity — one far-reaching aspect of which is desire. Although we tend to think of desire quite simplistically, it is not simplistic at all. As with fear and anger, desire is an activity that is founded on several components. One component of desire is the possibility of a future, since desire does not relate to the present moment of experience but instead involves imagining an experience that is not occurring (something enjoyable that we tell ourselves we want or deserve). This coveted experience is assessed as "missing now."

23:62 Another overlooked component of desire is pain, and the possibility that the very activity of desire produces much of our suffering. Desire is conceptually based, and it implies a separation between our current experience and the experience we crave. Although desire does not demand action, it tends to imply, motivate, or suggest action. This can get us into trouble when we don't make the proper distinctions regarding what desire is and is not.

23:63 Below are the components found in relation to desire. As with all the emotional states we've examined so far, eliminating any one or all of the components that comprise the activity of desire will eliminate the desire itself.

- The possibility of a future
- An assessment that something is missing now
- Concept of a preferred experience
- Separation between object-of-desire and self
- Feeling-sensation of imagined pleasure, masking overlooked pain

23:64 In this chapter we've been making some new distinctions within distinctions that we've already made as a culture. Normally the distinction of emotions like fear, anger, or desire doesn't occur for us as a set of components; they occur like the distinction of the emotion itself. Recognizing them as activities that are com-posed of several contributing factors allows us to have a very dif-ferent relationship to all emotions.

23:65 Usually we relate to any emotion as some simplistic force that is "caused" by circumstances. Frequently it seems as though an emo-tional reaction is somehow "inflicted" upon us. With such a per-spective, our options appear to be limited: we can suffer its presence, we can struggle to suppress or control it, or we can sim-ply give in and act out whatever it suggests. Making these new distinctions, however, allows us choices that we did not recognize before. We see that we don't have to suffer, struggle, or be swept away by emotions. Since they are activities we ourselves are gen-erating, we can let them be, change them, or eliminate them. This new way of relating to our emotions creates a new perspective that leads us to a deeper experiential understanding of what emo-tions are all about, and why they exist.

23:66 So we see how emotions that appear as a single experience can be broken down into various elements — like molecules, which are made up of atoms. Making such new distinctions is extremely useful, but we also want to move toward understanding experi-ence itself. To complete our look into the nature of feeling-states and to further our consideration of the nature of experience, we're going to investigate *pain*. Pain and pleasure are very basic aspects of our experience. They can't be broken down into components the way we did with fear, anger, and desire. To investigate pain requires the more difficult task of directly discerning its nature, and this will provide us with an opportunity to better recognize the nature of experience itself. Pain is a good one to work with because it is so basic and primal, and perhaps the most central motivat-ing force behind self-survival.

Pain

23:67 Pain itself is misunderstood. We most often think of pain as a particular sensation in the body, and we assume that it is simply a physiological phenomenon. But we also acknowledge all sorts of mental anguish and emotional pain, both of which are obviously conceptual activities. How is it possible that we can feel so much pain — such as the loss of a loved one — arising simply from an activity of the mind? If we can see that pain is always generated as an activity of the mind, then this is not such a great leap.

23:68 As I asserted earlier, pain is a concept. Such a statement clearly takes our concept of *concept* into a domain beyond our common understanding. Saying that all concept is produced by the mind, and that pain is a concept, suggests that pain is not what we've assumed it to be. I'm not saying that pain is intellectually produced. Pain is not just an idea. It is the very thing that hurts! *That,* the very experience that we call a painful feeling, is conceptually produced. It is not a thought — although we can generate pain through what we think. It is a specific form of interpretation. This is what makes something painful. The thing to get is that the very hurtful experience that we call pain is what I'm asserting is a product of the mind.

23:69 When it comes to emotional pain, we can readily recognize that the pain in our heart is conceptually produced, but what about physical pain? We seem hard-pressed to grasp that physical pain is conceptual. This is because we don't distinguish the experience of pain from the *sensation* provided by the nerve tissue acting as pain receptors. The sensation produced by the nervous system is only the circumstance or opportunity for physical pain. Pain as

an *experience* is actually an interpretation created by the mind—
we confronted this fact when imagining a bear chomping on our
bodies in Chapter Twenty. Pain-interpretation can be applied to all
sorts of input—physical or emotional—and wherever it is applied,
pain is perceived.

23:70 Pain doesn't exist in and of itself. It is created. Perhaps we can
measure the nerve activity that is likely to be interpreted as physical pain, or note circumstances that are likely to be perceived as
emotionally painful, but these don't actually cause pain. It depends
on the interpretation given to whatever is perceived, the meaning that is added conceptually to whatever is objectively or sub-
jectively there. If the conceptual activity that creates pain is not
applied, no pain will exist.

23:71 Sounds fantastic, doesn't it? Pain is a concept? Ridiculous. Still,
it's true. In order to get this, we must acknowledge that such a
concept is not a mere thought or intellectual musing. It is reflexive and automatic for the most part—and it hurts! That very feeling of *pain* is itself a concept. Stop generating the concept and no
pain will be there. A physical sensation might be there, but this
is objective. A circumstance might be there, and this too is objective. Neither of these is necessarily painful. Without the ingredient that perceives such conditions as painful, there is no pain.

23:72 Understanding this is grasping the essence of pain, what pain *is*.
This brings us a lot closer to grasping the nature of emotion and of
experience (which we will look into more in the next chapter). If
we ask, "What are the components that make up pain?" we find
that there aren't any components, which is why pain is more like an
atom than a molecule. So we might ask: what kind of distinctions
can we make within pain? We can make all sorts of distinctions in

types of pain and degrees of pain and so forth, but the very distinction of pain itself is simply the distinction "pain."

23:73 No matter how many times I assert that pain is a concept, the idea is likely to continue to be resisted and misunderstood. Looking directly into the nature of pain isn't easy since we have no conventional consciousness about it; we simply take it at face value. It's true that when we're in pain, it doesn't look at all like a thought. It is painful. That *is* the distinction "pain." And that distinction hurts! This is what pain "is." We can't say that it's an object, but we could argue that it can be objectively produced through the nervous system. Yet, as we've seen, we don't find pain there. We find an activity to which we apply the "stuff" we call pain. We can in fact have that activity without the pain — we can feel the sensation of nerve stimulation without having it be painful.

23:74 If something does not exist in the objective domain, what domain does that leave us? The most likely candidate is concept. Of course pain is a distinction, but so is everything else (even objects, but that's another chapter). Pain is produced by the mind. It is not an intellectual notion, but its nature is conceptual, which covers a much broader scope than people realize. If we're going to consider pain as conceptual, mind would have to cover a pretty broad scope, wouldn't it?

Pain and Now

23:75 We know that a memory of the past and an image of the future both acquire their existence through concept — as mental constructs of something that is not so in this moment. They must be conceptual because such experience is not of the present, and so does not exist as something that "is" but only as a representation of something that is not. But pain seems to occur *in this moment,* so let's look more closely at what we experience as "pain in this moment."

23:76 When we recall pain that has just passed and also fear pain that is to come, we greatly increase the level of pain in our current experience. While pain itself does not consist of divisible components, we can see how memory and fear are superimposed on top of what would otherwise be simply this moment of pain. In fact, a great deal of what we know as pain is this amplification that we ourselves create through concepts regarding past experience and future possibilities. Since the conceptual amplification exists in a domain other than *this* moment of pain, eliminating past and future considerations may not eliminate the pain, but it will reduce it a great deal.

23:77 Beyond reducing the pain we create by dwelling on past and future, it's also possible to eliminate the distinction of pain altogether. Since pain occurs as a process—granted a very, very quick one—we may be able to interrupt that process. I can say from personal experience that, because I recognize pain for what it is, I can also make the pain disappear. It's not that I suddenly become ignorant about the distinction pain, or that I suppress it. Anyone who's willing to recognize and fully experience the true nature of pain will realize that it is without substance. It's unnecessary—it doesn't need to exist. Another way to say that is we can locate the activity of creating pain and simply stop creating it.

23:78 I have tested this no-pain distinction at the dentist by refusing novocaine. As he drilled, sometimes right into a nerve, I would be completely sensitive to the sensations, and yet they were not painful as long as I refused to add to them the activity of pain.

This takes some understanding of what pain is and is not, but I can honestly say that it was not a painful experience. Be clear that it is not a matter of ignoring the pain, or pretending it isn't there, or calling it "sensation" rather than pain. There was no pain! Were I to make the distinction of pain, it would hurt. Since I did not, it didn't hurt.

23:79   Once I had a crown put onto a pretty badly damaged tooth. I was told it was going to take at least an hour to grind down the tooth and shape it for the crown. The dentist also needed to drill a hole into the middle of the tooth and insert a pin to add strength. I admit I found myself a bit nervous while I was imagining the future possibility of an unwanted experience. I'd never done this for such a long time; I wondered if I might get distracted or be unable to focus for so long. Still, I went forward and declined novocaine.

23:80   What I found was that not only was I able to experience the whole procedure without pain, I had the opportunity to play around a bit. As I sat there (not much else to do in the dentist's chair) I noticed that I felt I had to remain serious and control my mind. It occurred to me to ask myself: why? If I can keep myself from creating pain, why do I have to be serious and controlling about it? I can also stop creating the distinctions "serious" or "controlling." So I dropped that disposition, relaxed, and began flirting with the nurse. (This is hard to do with your mouth full of fist.) Still no pain.

23:81   I tell this story to help demonstrate what I'm talking about and also to reveal that it is not a matter of "suppression." It is simply not creating pain. Granted, a degree of sensitivity and direct experience is necessary to realize what pain is — or, for that matter, the true nature of any distinction — but freedom from pain is simply the ability to stop making a distinction that is usually made automatically.

23:82   One might think then that I go around in a painless state. Not so. I have easy access to pain just like everyone else. The programmed function of pain is active, and it pushes and pulls my body into paths beneficial (hopefully) to its well-being. Yet, the distinction of pain is recognized for what it is — an activity and impulse the purpose of which is to govern action so as to be consistent with personal survival — and so my relationship to pain is transformed, and I don't take it so seriously. Pain may be "so," but it's not "true."

23:83   An analogy might help clarify my unusual use of the word *true* above. If we saw something as an illusion or hallucination, we would still see and relate to it, but we would relate to it differently than we would if we saw it as objectively real. If we felt something and thought it was a spider crawling up our leg, we'd relate to it differently than if we knew it was simply some grass brushing our skin. And yet the sensation could be identical in both cases. When we see something as harmless or insubstantial, we're likely to take it far less seriously. Even if we continue to have certain domains of pain, understanding that we don't *need* to have any of them lessens the impact of the pain. It makes a difference to know that any pain can be eliminated simply by not creating it.

23:84   There are many painful experiences and reactions that simply need not exist and serve no useful purpose, except for the survival of a conceptual-self. We can do away with those. There are many opportunities to eliminate the distinction of pain — as well as other distinctions, including many assumptions and beliefs. We can free ourselves from much suffering that we thought unavoidable, and at the same time get closer to a sense of real-being. I invite you to look into it for yourself to see whether it does indeed work that way.

23:85   In this chapter, we've made some new distinctions in our experience of the feeling states that drive us. Most of the distinctions came about by becoming aware of the components that make up fear, anger, and desire. This allows us to recognize some things about our feeling-reactions that we didn't see before, which in turn makes it possible for us to experience emotion in a new way. In previous chapters we looked at pain in the context of "suffering," which told us something about the purpose of pain. Now we see that the nature of pain is another matter.

23:86   Our look at pain indicates a direction for discovering the true nature of experience. If we can recognize pain in such a way that it is seen as created and otherwise nonexistent, then we are on top of getting the nature of what we experience as reality itself. The main reason I used pain as a subject here is that it is so undeniable, so primary, and so respected as a real experience that it is just beyond belief that it could actually be insubstantial. Experiencing pain as a created activity of mind is truly a solid insight. And there is even more to get. In the next chapter we will turn our attention more thoroughly onto the essential nature of all experience.

CHAPTER TWENTY-FOUR

The Nature of Everything

24:1   Our work in uncovering uncognized aspects of mind helps us to experience more clearly what drives us, and discovering the unseen components of our emotions puts us one step closer to understanding how these impulses come to pass. As we move toward grasping the nature of experience itself, however — as we did with our investigation into pain — we start to see that things may not be what they seem. If things aren't what they seem, then what are they? What is the essence of our experience of anything? How does "reality" exist for us?

24:2   These are pretty big questions, and trying to tackle such questions can be tricky on many levels. Moving toward a realization of the essence of anything requires an unconventional openness and a willingness to instantaneously leap both into the center of the obvious as well as beyond it. So if it seems like what I'm about to say is too simplistic at first, bear with me, and imagine there is more to get than meets the eye. Remember, you are reading for an insight, not just for more information or an explanation.

What Is Everything?

24:3　Our world consists of many things. A "thing," in this case, might be a rock or an apple, a thought or speed, self-worth or the sky, philosophy or sound — everything and anything we encounter or perceive. Within this world there are differences. Yet regardless of the differences, "things" are what determine our world. Perhaps more accurately we might say it is our perception of these things that determines our world. All together these things are what we live within and are aware of, and so they constitute our experience of life and reality.

24:4　Sometimes we encounter a beautiful thing — the thought of a loved one, a magnificent vista, a flower — and sometimes a horrible one — the death of a friend, a monster in our dreams, a painful injury. As we've seen, when we encounter something, be it beautiful or horrible, this influences or dominates our experience — at least until we encounter the next thing. We've heard the idea that we can relate to each of these things in various ways, and that perhaps we can free ourselves from unwanted reactions that are bound to follow our encounters.

24:5　Is there something more we've yet to discover about our world beyond what we already perceive? Let's begin by laying a simple historical foundation for this question, to set the stage for further investigation. If we assume, as common sense tells us, that everything is simply what we perceive it to be — a rock, an idea, a feeling — and that our experience is caused by its presence, then we are stuck with whatever seems to be there. In such a case, it seems that our only option for changing our experience is to somehow manipulate the things. But three other possibilities arise in relation to the possibility of experiencing beyond our immediate perception of things. Two of them — psychology and philosophy — are generally known, if not generally practiced, and one is virtually unknown and so not named or considered by us at all.

24:6   Our first possibility arises from the world of psychology, which proposes that our experience of things relates to a personal history, and further asserts that certain unwanted reactions can be eliminated by uncovering the foundation trauma or program that determines our reactions. Our work on contemplating the "unconscious" aspects of mind seems to touch down in this domain of thought, suggesting that at least some of what we are experiencing isn't actually what is so. We acknowledge that our perception of the thing may be too heavily influenced by the past to be considered accurate, and could sometimes even be untrue.

24:7   Although the psychological domain is useful, the bulk of our reality in this possibility is still considered to be as we perceive it to be. Psychological thought also seems to relate primarily to our emotional relationships with people or things. This still doesn't tell us what anything is, just that it can be confused (and unconfused) with what once was. We don't want to limit ourselves to a psychological paradigm to search out what's overlooked in the obvious.

24:8   The second possibility is one that arises from a more philosophical investigation, or from the work of certain schools of "personal transformation." This possibility arises from the observation that none of the things we encounter actually "cause" our experience of them at all. Our experience and our reactions are determined by our interpretation of what's there and not from an experience of what's actually there. We touched on this possibility in our work on experiencing things "for-themselves," which eliminates almost all survival interpretations and so almost all effects, thus radically changing our experience of what's there.

24:9   As we consider along this "philosophical" vein, we can find our way to a greater degree of freedom in our relation to things. Unlike psychoanalysis, we aren't required to unearth every historical foundation for our experience. We simply perceive the thing as independent of our perceptions and interpretations, so we are freed from needing to react in any particular way. We can be "unaffected" by the presence of the thing by merely seeing it for-itself rather than reacting to the way it affects us. But the things perceived will generally remain as if they are still those things, since our assertion is that they do not cause our experience of them, not that we know what they are.

24:10   Beyond common sense, the domains I'm calling psychology and philosophy might offer directions in which to look to discover something about the obvious that's unseen, but they don't really tell us what something is — just that whatever it is, it is separate from our history or perception of it. So, what about the third possibility? You're probably on the edge of your seat waiting for me to get to the point. But this possibility isn't so easily understood.

24:11   Consider: what if we could see that which is real and solid, seemingly immutably so, as essentially illusory? Certainly this might change our relationship to life a bit. What if, without changing a thing, there is a possibility to change how we perceive what everything is such that it is of a truly different nature than what we have always believed? In this book we've touched on the very foundations of our self-mind and our motivations in life. We've looked into some of our assumptions about it all. We've considered a few methods for approaching discovery and insight. Yet all of this remains in the domain of process and construct. This is reasonable since the world in which we live is full of processes and constructs. That, however, is not all there is.

24:12 One possibility allows, without process, for pain to be unpainful, for meaning to be meaningless, for import to be without significance. It allows, in one instant, for the most horrendous or overwhelming thing to be nothing at all, and the most beautiful thing to be what it is, without fear of loss or distortion. What's more, it's easier done than said. Sounds good, doesn't it? It is. There's nothing like it.

24:13 Of course, we expect there's got to be a monkey wrench in the works here somewhere, and there is. But the monkey wrench lies in our own hands. For one thing, like the philosophical possibility, this third possibility is not particularly useful when it comes to self's survival, so the impulse to create and maintain such a disposition will not have self's support for long. Also, the third possibility is a challenge to understand because it stands outside of all that is conventional in our beliefs and experience, and therefore it is not easily graspable by the mind.

24:14 What is the third possibility? It is grasping firsthand the very nature of our experience of reality. No sweat, huh? Actually, don't despair. We can walk through this together, but it needs your participation beyond merely hearing about it. As with other things we've tackled, the words are only pointers, springboards from which to jump into a new consciousness. And this *is* a new consciousness for almost everyone. As I lay some groundwork, keep moving in the direction of directly experiencing the very nature of what you are perceiving. This demands insight, and you are capable of insight.

The Distinction "Distinction"

24:15   Let's begin by tackling the nature of "distinction." Our experience of absolutely everything, and in every way, is a matter of distinction. Making a distinction in our experience means we can now isolate and "know" something in our field of awareness. A distinction can be anything, any thought, feeling, object, class, category, level, measure, etc. If it is distinct from what it is not, it is a distinction.

24:16   For example, fear is a distinction we already make as a particular experience within the domain of emotions. In other words, we know the difference between fear and anger, joy and any other emotion — these are "distinctions" in emotions. We also make distinctions in kinds of fear, such as feeling worried, anxious, startled, frightened, timid, horrified, and so forth. In the last chapter we looked into fear, anger, and desire, and made some new distinctions within those familiar distinctions that we probably hadn't previously made and so did not perceive or experience before. This suggests a direction to look for the nature of distinction. But the nature of distinction isn't understood merely through examples. So we first need to know what a distinction is, and then work to become directly conscious of the true nature of what's there.

24:17   Distinction is everything. It makes up our entire world and everything in it. A rock is a distinction. What distinction is it? It is the distinction "rock." And since we said "a" rock, it is the distinction of that particular rock. We may also make a distinction regarding the color of the rock, the weight of the rock, the size and shape of the rock, the substance of the rock, the temperature of the rock, and any other "piece" of information or perception about the rock. Anything else we are aware of in relation to the rock is another distinction. All together, these are what constitute our awareness of the rock.

24:18   It might sound like I'm saying that distinction is concept. But I'm not. (Imagine that!) The thought of the rock is a distinction also. We observe that the object rock is not the thought of the rock, that these are distinct. They exist as two different experiences, even though they refer to the same thing. They are "distinctions" in our experience.

24:19   When we make the distinction "object," and get the rock as an object, we see that the air or ground around the rock is distinct from the rock (air and ground are not-the-rock), and so we can locate and identify the rock. But distinction isn't just noticing differences between one object and another — the rock versus the air — or discerning various objective qualities — weight, shape, temperature.

24:20   Although we say the weight of the rock is distinct from its shape, they are not separate from each other. The weight exists in the very same place as the shape, and yet we say they are distinct. Weight isn't shape. This is true. We are making a distinction. In other words, we are aware of something we call "weight" and something we call "shape." We see in this that we are also making a distinction between the object and any quality that we say the object might "possess." Making a distinction doesn't mean any separation has occurred between one distinction and another. Separation itself is a distinction.

24:21   Further, there are domains of distinctions such as concept, emotion, physics, sex, rules, fruit, and all manner of genera or classification. We can make distinctions of context such as space, self, value, language, objective reality, and within these we experience many distinctions of content such as distance, esteem, good and bad, words, or a number 2 Mongol pencil. We make distinctions in directions, stages, hierarchy, and more. Absolutely everything is a distinction.

24:22   How do you "make" a distinction? If you are aware of something in any way, if you can think about it, perceive it, imagine it, or know it in any way, you have already "made" the distinction. If not, then you cannot think about it, perceive it, imagine it, or know it in any way. It does not exist at all in your experience. This is why in our work you cannot understand anything that you do not create for yourself, and much of it must be created. Making a distinction is simply creating in your consciousness a particular awareness or experience — this is then that distinction.

24:23   When you smell the freshly baked lasagna in the kitchen, you make a particular distinction: the smell of lasagna. As you approach the lasagna sitting so invitingly on the table, you bend down and take a good whiff. Ah, *this* is lasagna! But, being a gourmet yourself, and maybe slightly jealous of your friend's ability to cook great lasagna, you also search out the ingredients with your nose. What cheese is that? What spice is this? Isn't that a premade sauce? You start to smell many distinctive aromas within what was at first a "single" smell of lasagna. All of these are distinctions — the smells, the appetizing appeal, the jealousy, the lasagna. We make distinctions all the time. They are what constitute our reality, our experiences, our perceptions.

24:24   We can also bring to the fore distinctions made but generally ignored as unimportant. For example, most people have had the experience of becoming interested in something, like a new car, and then seeing that car all over the place where it seemed virtually nonexistent before. Or being able to notice details in the workmanship of some craft once you learn to do it yourself. We can also make new distinctions not yet made. We do this every time we learn something; we then perceive something we hadn't before. There are even distinctions such as *vague, unknown, indistinct,* and *paradox*—so a distinction itself needn't be "distinct" as in the conventional use of that word.

24:25   Whenever we make new distinctions, we have new experiences and new perceptions. And since our interactions are determined by what we experience, we can also create new abilities. Every ability to interact effectively with the world around us — or within us — is determined by the distinctions we make. This would be seen as what we know and how we know it.

24:26   How we perceive events, what we perceive in the event, and how clearly we perceive it are all functions of the distinctions we make. If we make fine distinctions in balance, for example, we are able to balance our bodies much better than if we made gross distinctions in balance. It is the same with space, distance, movement, forces, thinking, feeling, communication, and so on. It is the prime ingredient of all perception, and therefore of all interaction, and so determines the interaction. This determination governs what can and what will occur in the interaction, and so determines the level of ability anyone will have within an interaction.

24:27   When we realize the prime place distinctions play in our lives, we realize that nothing can occur or proceed without them — they constitute our entire experience and every element of it. And although all power and ability arise from the distinctions we make, we should not ignore the fact that real personal freedom can only be had through eliminating distinctions.

Power lies in making distinctions.
Freedom lies in destroying them.

24:28 So, are you starting to get what a distinction is? If you are aware of something in any way at all, it is a distinction. It is what something *is*. The mere "is-ness" of anything makes it a distinction. When we ask the question "What is the nature of distinction?" we're not asking for a definition or explanation, or even an example. We already have those. The question is, "What is the true substance of everything that exists?" When we ask this question, we're also asking what is the true nature of *anything,* since it is only as a distinction that a thing can be experienced.

24:29 The nature of distinction, and so the foundation of our experience, becomes even more mysterious when we realize that distinction is something that we create. Remember, in this question we're asking: What is the nature of experience? What is the nature of existence? Where does "reality" exist? Becoming clear about the most basic experience of everything puts us right on top of what "is." Being on top of this "is-ness," we can now better ask: What is it? What is the true nature of existence?

Distinctions and Existence

24:30   One new distinction we can make is to realize the nature of every-thing itself. That's Everything. Itself. This is difficult to grasp since it is not a common level of consciousness. It can only occur with a sudden increase in the depth of your consciousness regarding the true nature of anything. To communicate about this degree of consciousness is a challenge. I wish I could make it easier, more accessible. But there are no gentle steps that can be taken — it exists in a domain of paradox and is not subject to thought or per-ception. You just can't get there from here. So I will simply say it outright, attempting to be as clear as I can. Hang on to your hat; here goes.

24:31   Consider the possibility that there is no difference between what you experience for-itself and as-itself and what is there, that the substance of its existence is of the same nature as the distinction of its existence. Distinction is a function of consciousness, or to say it another way, distinction constitutes all that is, and in every way that it is, and yet the nature of distinction itself is not something that is. Its nature is nothing. Hearing this doesn't do much for us, except perhaps confuse us. What we need to do is realize it.

24:32   This "nature" I'm speaking of is not what is thought when we hear the word *nothing*. We cannot grasp with the intellect, nor with feeling, or even intuition what is meant by "Nothing." Grasping would be *making* a distinction, which is not the same as distinc-tion itself. Said again, straight out: the very nature of conscious-ness and Being is Nothing. Nothing is the "substance" that Being is, and also the substance of any distinction made in the domain of awareness. Realizing this nature turns anything encountered into something nonconventional, yet also places it in the very place of itself.

24:33 Our experience of the distinction of an object for-itself exists exactly in the place of the object. Otherwise it is not an experience of that object but an experience of another distinction such as the memory of the object, or a judgment concerning the object. These can be conjured up anywhere, without the object present or existent, because they are concepts. Since concepts are not the object, they occur in the place where they arise — what we call the mind. But the distinction of an object is exactly where the object "is." This distinction we call the "object-as-itself." This is distinct — but not separate from — the perception of the object. It is not different or elsewhere; it is what that object is, and what the experience of the object *is*. The distinction of an object is its "is-ness" itself.

24:34 This doesn't suggest that the real object is somehow outside of or apart from the experience of it. If the distinction "object" is truly an experience of the object as-itself and for-itself, then it must *be* itself. Object is a distinction. The true nature of an object is a distinction. It does not exist really, or one could say its nature is nothing, yet this is not separate from the existence of the object. The object is just *that,* the distinction object, which is the same as nothing. The true nature of absolute existence is a distinction usually not made, so this is challenging to consider.

24:35 None of this is to be believed. It is in fact unbelievable. It is beyond belief and must be made directly conscious; otherwise it will always remain a mere rumor. It is best not to believe it, since believing such a thing does you no good and distances you from what seems an obvious contradiction in your experience. To say that nothing is real, or that reality is nothing, when in your perceptions the opposite is glaringly apparent, only creates a split between your common sense perceptions and something you've merely heard about and believe. Such belief is only a step backwards.

24:36 As long as the distinction "objectively real" is made about things encountered, then that is what will exist in your perceptions. This "real" distinction — or the distinction "real" — must be grasped for what it is, as it is, despite conventional presumptions to the contrary. This can only be done with direct insight. Believing doesn't help. As a matter of fact, if you superimpose a belief onto such an obviously contradictory perception, how can you draw your attention to the true nature of the distinction being denied? You can't.

24:37 We need to create the possibility — perhaps backed by some personal breakthroughs made in this matter — that the fundamental nature of things is different from what is normally presumed and taken for granted. This possibility can then provide some genuine fuel for contemplation. There is no inconsistency, however, between the distinction of what is and what simply is. What is perceived as this or that — a tree, pain, laughter — is indeed *that*; it exists as that distinction. When the distinction is being made — or, as we would normally say it, being observed — we are perceiving its existence, since that is what it is. Hot *is* hot. Real *is* real. Pain *is* pain. Joy *is* joy. The very experience *that* they are is *what* they are.

Pai-chang wished to send a monk to open a new monastery.
He told his pupils that whoever answered a question most ably
would be appointed.
Placing a water jug on the ground, he asked, "Who can say
what this is without calling its name?"
The head monk said, "No one can call it a wooden sandal."
Kuei-shan, the cooking monk, tipped over the jug
with his foot and went out.
Pai-chang laughed and said, "The head monk loses."
And Kuei-shan became the Master of the new monastery.

24:38   I know all this may sound like nonsense. That's probably why truly wise people don't talk too much. Not being truly wise myself, I gab a great deal. But you can make use of this chatter if you use it to dive into your own contemplation and have genuine insights. As was true from the beginning, this work can only be done personally and honestly in your own consciousness.

24:39   This communication about Being and Nothing may elicit various reactions, from interest to frustration or objection. Yet if what's true is that it seems to be some other way than what I'm claiming, then that's where you stand at present. It shouldn't be denied. I sympathize with the challenges of tackling such seemingly ridiculous assertions, especially when the only conventional tools you have at your disposal are intellect, emotion, intuition, and instinct. None of these are up to the task, nor can I explain the matter. I only bring it up to provide a springboard from which to consider a radical possibility. A possibility that provides real freedom. But as I've mentioned a few times, it's okay to not know.

24:40   We need to have something take place here other than what we can figure out with our usual methods. There is really only one communication in this book, and yet it will never be said. This is not because it's withheld — it's left unsaid because it cannot be said. The usefulness of this book must be extracted through the process of doing the work. It starts to be grasped by using what is said and by figuring, thinking, feeling, observing, and confronting what we are really up to here, but also by having something else take place that is beyond all of this mental activity. Ultimately, the only way to really understand it is to have a direct experience of the nature of all this for yourself.

> *Whereof one cannot speak, thereof one must be silent.*
> —Ludwig Wittgenstein

24:41   But making use of this new domain of distinction doesn't demand a direct consciousness of the nature of Being, or grasping the true nature that is Nothing. We can still make a great deal of progress simply by realizing that we don't know what anything is. This sets us on a similar ground — although not as solidly as does grasping the nature of Being itself.

24:42   A deep and genuine willingness to not-know provides us with "some nothing from which to come." This can transform our experience without changing anything perceived, because standing on "nothing" we view everything from a different perspective. We're not drawn to presume that the mere presence of something demands we react to it, since we can recognize the possibility that it is empty and arbitrary. From this perspective, we are also empowered to drop any distinction or create new ones, bringing us closer to truly getting that our experience is of our own making. Consider once again this quote:

> *Power lies in making distinctions.*
> *Freedom lies in destroying them.*

24:43   In the next chapter we will continue our look into the nature of being and consciousness. Is it possible to have consciousness without knowledge or sense perceptions? If so, we must imagine that this form of consciousness is different from what we usually speak of as our conscious experience. It would have to be more fundamental than whatever occurs within our minds or perception, and yet not separate from it. It couldn't look like anything, or appear to be some way, since the nature of such consciousness is absolutely nothing and infinitely everything.

CHAPTER TWENTY-FIVE
The Nature of Being

Meaning Doesn't Mean Anything

25:1   What is the meaning of life? Such a question might provoke discussion and debate for awhile, or maybe cause us to ponder the significance of our lives, but we will soon return to the job of living life rather than questioning it. Do we really care what it's supposed to mean? When we go to work or relate to our families and friends, the meaning of life seems implicit in the goals we've set and in the emotions we feel. Next to the real concerns of our lives, questioning the meaning of it all seems like merely an indulgence in philosophy.

25:2   Earlier we touched on the idea that we are inherently meaningless, and that's likely one of several ideas that doesn't sit well. We are troubled by such questions whenever they come up — the meaning of life, the significance or worth of ourselves, what existence is all about. Our desire for answers might lead us to some doctrine or personal conclusions, and these might suffice for a time, but the real questions will continue unabated in the background despite any viable sounding "ideas" that come our way.

25:3   What if we just sat with an experience of having *no* ideas? Forsaking all ready-made conclusions reveals our discomfort with confronting the reality that inherently we have no genuine answers and find no intrinsic meaning. Our inability to assert from our core the meaning of self and life suggests that we might be looking in the wrong place and for the wrong thing. Perhaps this occurs because where we need to look is not only unacceptable to the human mind but also very difficult to grasp.

25:4   Since self is the center of as well as the context for the human mind, meaning is an essential aspect of all our interpretations. Without meaning there can be no preference or charge, nothing to tell us the import of the thing interpreted—and this is a necessary function for self-survival. In relation to oneself or life, when meaninglessness is encountered, it is often a source of much suffering and depression. Meaninglessness is intolerable to the self-mind. It is resisted, ignored, suppressed, overcome, and denied. Rather than confront this meaninglessness head-on, we're apt to seek some kind of consoling beliefs that will help us "find meaning" again.

25:5   Life, self, and the universe are all absolutely meaningless. And the fact that it doesn't mean anything *doesn't mean anything!* Notice that, despite the word within the word, "meaninglessness" does not denote *less* meaning. It refers instead to *no* meaning. Meaninglessness is not a negative or bad thing, since that connotation would itself be meaningful. It is simply what it *is, as* it is. So "meaningless" simply indicates a condition of being *without meaning*. We ourselves are meaningless. If we believe our purpose in life is to pursue meaning — to discern and exist within life's inherent meaning — even an honest and intelligent effort to fulfill this purpose will lead to disappointment.

25:6   We've seen that "being" cannot be either inauthentic or worthless, since to "be" is itself and has no meaning. It is an authentic event because it is the first event, it is the mere existence of something. The truth is you cannot be worthless because you have no worth to begin with. Being exists prior to worth or value, which are always applied to things; they are never inherent. Understanding this might help in overcoming resistance to the idea of being without meaning. But merely hearing about it isn't enough; what's needed is a direct conscious experience.

25:7   Meaninglessness needs to be grasped as a fundamental truth of Being, and this can only be done directly. Perhaps we could say that truth transcends meaning. At least that sounds better, doesn't it? A deep and direct conscious experience of this kind may still not seem possible in our search for the truth about our own existence. This could be because, as a culture, we've restricted such a search to the domain of hearsay. In other words, we assume that the only possibility open to us is to believe something about it, which rules out the possibility of a personal direct consciousness or even profound insight. Such a perspective owes its origins to a long history of attempts to understand our own condition.

In Search of Absolute Knowledge

25:8   From the time of the ancient Greeks through the era of the Renaissance, many debates and earnest efforts were undertaken by great minds to discover — or to prove impossible to discover — a genuine *direct* knowledge of reality. From this struggle various philosophies emerged, as did the basic doctrine of science.

25:9 Even though religious and metaphysical concerns dominated much of the ancient thinking and perception, a group of thinkers known as the Skeptics arose as a viable and undeniable force of reasoning dating back to the early Greeks. The Skeptics' argument had such strong validity that even reasonable men of faith were compelled to respect and consider it. What the Skeptics pointed out is that knowledge cannot be trusted. They asserted that true knowledge (direct consciousness of the true nature of reality) could not be ascertained through the senses or reason, that all such perceived phenomena are always separate from the truth they purport to be or to convey. The extreme Academic Skeptics concluded that all true knowledge is impossible.

25:10 Throughout the following millennia of Western culture, knowledge of God, or some comparable metaphysical component, was considered of utmost value, and most people believed it necessary for defining what it is to be and live as a human being. In any culture where such beliefs were dominant, the stance of the ancient Skeptics was seen as very negative. As faith replaced reason in the centuries to come, knowledge of God was taken for granted, and questioning or doubting the validity of this knowledge was heresy. When reason began to take hold once again with the emergence of the Renaissance, many arguments were proposed by those stuck between faith and reason, trying to reconcile doubt with belief. They desired to provide a solid ground upon which the possibility of true knowledge could stand, beyond the barren, unmanageable quagmire presented by absolute skepticism.

25:11   Emerging from centuries of such debate came a book by Marin Mersenne, *La Vérité des Sciences* (*Truth of Sciences,* 1625), in which he provides an argument for scientific thought and methodology by sidestepping the irrefutable observations of the Skeptics. He suggests that the use of science is limited to the appearances of things and does not deal with the metaphysical or yield knowledge about any transcendent reality. He proposes that our senses do not inform us about the real nature of anything, but that this does not prevent the formulation of theories to account for observed events.

25:12   This was a turning point in the evolution of the debate, and it is perhaps what allowed for the flourishing of the world of science as we know it. Unfortunately, another conclusion that Mersenne drew, mimicking the Skeptics, was that knowledge of absolute truths is not possible. The space or context created for scientific pursuit still follows the same assumption today. These conclusions, however, are based on a reaction to powerful observations made by the ancient Greeks. The initial proposition appears to rest on the assumption that consciousness is limited to knowledge, and it was in that form that it passed through many centuries of intellectual debate. But it's clear that this assumption regarding knowledge did not come about through direct consciousness.

25:13   Now that's sort of a funny thing to say, since direct consciousness is what is in question, and what has been asserted as impossible. Yet we must consider: the stance that asserts the impossibility of direct consciousness is the same one that made a distinction between the world of appearances — or an ordinary and useful world — and the world of absolute truth. It seems this was done to appease both blind faith and the arguments of the Skeptics, thus providing a "place" in which science could be seen as a viable pursuit. Today we see science as a most formidable pursuit, probably the most valued and respected source of knowledge currently available. Yet we also have fallen into the very assumption handed down from the seventeenth century when arguing the merits for the existence of science. As a culture we have taken on the assumption that direct consciousness is not possible.

25:14   In Asia the question regarding the possibility of direct consciousness took a different direction. Gaining great strength from the communications of Gautama Buddha, it became almost universally accepted that direct consciousness *is* clearly possible. As a matter of fact, for the people within the cultures that embraced this possibility, working toward what became known as "enlightenment" became the most honored and revered pursuit. But as is true of all human endeavors, most of this possibility became wrapped up in dogma and forms of knowledge and hearsay. We shouldn't confuse any system of belief — any traditionally religious notions or beliefs — as accurately representing this possibility. By its very nature, no system or method can be the same as direct consciousness. Direct consciousness stands on its own as a possibility that can only be realized, not systematized.

25:15   Whether conclusions are reached through lengthy debates by powerful minds, or simply through beliefs adopted by the faithful of some system of thought or dogma, in the end it is all really just indirect chatter or hearsay. None of it is a firsthand consciousness of the truth.

By all means, climb the ladder of argument for a new perspective, but where the ladder ends, you must step off.

The Possibility of Direct Consciousness

25:16 But is direct experience possible? Well, it is either possible or it isn't. If it is not possible, then we are stuck with not knowing the true nature of existence as an immutable and universal truth, and equally stuck with beliefs and perhaps viable theories and formulas as our only avenue for knowledge. If it is possible, then we can personally become conscious of some or all of the absolute truth.

25:17 Over and over again in this book, we've confronted the fact that we do not directly perceive what anything is: not a chair, not a self, and not consciousness. Try as we might, it seems there is some impenetrable wall between our consciousness and anything of which we are indirectly aware. At this point, we are not — and it looks like we probably can't be — directly conscious of what something is. But it is possible.

25:18 This possibility doesn't occur through believing that something is true, or as a fantasy, or a conviction. It exists in the exact same place as its impossibility. That very impossibility that we confront every time we set out to experience the truth *is* where the possibility lives. If not, we wouldn't notice that it is impossible. If we didn't already hold that such a possibility can exist, then our attempts to realize it couldn't be frustrated. It's not necessary to look elsewhere. It is right here within this impossible task of knowing the true nature of existence.

25:19   It may seem like this possibility is destined to stay within the impossible forever. Even though I say it is possible because I have become directly conscious of the true nature of Being, I could be lying, or mistaken, or hallucinating. How would you know? It's hard for me to tell you why I am certain, since within the world we share everything is known only in relative terms. Absolutes are not part of our shared world. In any case, it is hearsay for you and so not a direct experience. The fact that for thousands of years people have occasionally made the same or similar claims, asserting that direct consciousness has occurred for them, still does nothing to enlighten *you*. It remains hearsay, although it does empower the notion that direct consciousness is possible. Others say they have done it, and for the most part, isn't that the reason we would venture down such a road for ourselves?

25:20   The people who claim to have had direct experience generally seem to be honest and sincere sorts. Their candor is such that they are believable. But this doesn't offer any proof. The only way to prove this one is to do it yourself. And the proof cannot be shared since it is only experienced directly.

> *Whereof one cannot speak,*
> *thereof one must remain silent.*
> —Ludwig Wittgenstein

The Nature of Being

25:21   The more often we set out to become conscious of our own present existence "for-itself and as-itself," the closer we get to a different kind of awareness. Our awareness becomes extremely simplified, and the content of our experience seems to disappear or become unknown. We don't seem to be able to say anything intelligent about this experience or to pin it down in our minds. At the same time, something remains in our consciousness.

25:22   When you were a child, did you ever ponder the infinity of space? Perhaps you asked, How is it possible for space to go on forever? Certainly it must end somewhere. Yet, if it ends, what is on the other side of the end of the universe? So you come to see that it must go on forever, without end, infinitely. Unimaginable! And inconceivable.

25:23   We cannot conceive of something without end because it has no boundaries. We conceive of space only because of the distinctions we make, such as "from here to there," or "this and not that." Without any end we cannot in any way perceive infinity, and so we cannot conceive it. There is no picture or image we can conjure up, no idea or notion that can match it, nor any sense or feeling that is big enough to encompass it. Yet we are pressed to admit that space must be infinite.

25:24   What's overlooked here is that infinity, like any absolute, is not itself limited to our intellect or cognition; only we are. Infinity is the same as Nothing. How can that be? How can it not be, is more like it. Since we conceive of nothing as the absence of anything, not filled, emptiness, or whatnot, and we conceive of infinity as larger than imaginable, going on without end, and so on, they seem to be different, even opposites. Yet this is neither Nothing nor Infinity. As absolutes, both nothing and infinity are not different at all. How can you place them in different places or separate them in any way? Nothing has no end and no beginning, just like infinity. Infinity itself actually has no size or amount, and so is just like nothing. Absolute nothing and absolute infinity are the same.

25:25   One reason we have such a hard time coming to grips with the true nature of things is that it does not fit into our ability of conception and perception. The nature of Absolutes is "absolute," and so paradox here is not a problem or a mistake. An absolute includes all possibilities, which is why we call it Absolute. So although Nothing is indeed nothing, it is not elsewhere or separate from anything. I know this kind of talk can be irritating, but it's true nevertheless.

25:26   Nothing is not the same as no thing, or the absence of things. It is no more possible to conceive of what I mean by Nothing than it is to perceive infinity. But let's have a crack at it anyway. When we consider the essence of nothing, we might imagine space without anything in it, or the absence of objects or light, or perhaps an infinitely small point. None of these are nothing. Nothing really isn't anything at all, absolutely. Try this just for fun: notice what you are thinking right now. Relative to a word you are about to read shortly, notice that you have nothing there in mind. Now read the word *giraffe*. Prior to reading it, what did you have relative to giraffe? Nothing. Not a giraffe-shaped hole, or the absence of giraffe. There was really nothing there. I'm just trying to point to nothing instead of the different kinds of "somethings" that are mistaken for nothing.

25:27   Nothing is in no way a negative, or a positive. As we saw with the words "not-knowing," any negation depends on something first existing so that we can negate it. Prior to knowledge is not a negation of knowledge, it is what's so, or the "being" of whatever is true, before knowledge. In this way, not-knowing functions as a doorway to a greater consciousness or "knowing," yet this consciousness doesn't exist in a "known" form. This is a domain accessed only through direct consciousness. Just so, Nothing is not in relation to "things." It is existence prior to anything, including space, objects, distance, thought, beingness, or beings of any kind at all. But it's even trickier than that since Nothing is not separate from or different from any thing that is. The very object of a cup is exactly in the same place as Nothing. But that's impossible to communicate in any way since we have no shared experience that can relate to it.

25:28   Nothing is the nature of existence before there is existence. It is also the nature of existence after there is existence. Just like not-knowing is the nature of consciousness before consciousness is filled with knowing, yet this not-knowing doesn't disappear in the presence of knowing. We miss that this is so, and that it is so right now and will always be so. The not-knowing and "nothing" natures of consciousness and existence didn't go away. It is that way right now.

25:29   Just as objects cannot exist without the space in which to be, something cannot exist without nothing. And yet the moment you imagine space without objects, space itself becomes an object. If you can hold space as not just a big empty area — and so an object — then you will have a new perspective on space. If it isn't like a big object or vast area in which objects reside, then it isn't located anywhere either. We can see how this relates to nothing, which is also not an object and not located. This "place" of no-space or nothing is the "original" place, or "being" without content. It is the location of existence prior to anything "being," and so is the very same "place" as Being, and of you and I. It is what and where we really are right now. Interesting, isn't it?

25:30   One of the challenges we face in trying to understand this stuff is a little like mistaking a model of a molecule for the reality of a molecule. When we hear the argument or "logic" presented for these apparent metaphysical concepts — and to be clear, they are not meta-physical, they are as much physical as they are non-physical; it's what's simply true even if difficult to grasp — we get caught up in intellectual attempts to conceive of what's being said. These attempts to construct mental "models" of understanding are abstracted from the reality that's being addressed. You have to think what you *cannot* think.

25:31   In school, when the science teacher was discussing molecules, he'd bring out a wooden model of various colored spheres connected by dowels. We could see shapes and distinctions in a carbon molecule or a glucose molecule and speak about them intelligently. Yet we might fail to notice that the model isn't in any way like a molecule. This might seem a dumb thing to say since the model is supposed to represent the molecule. Yet, there are no balls in a molecule, no mass or structure similar to the model, and certainly no wooden dowels connecting them. Fixating on the accessible model, as humans are apt to do, we might fail to make the leap away from the model and into a more direct or authentic "experience" of what a molecule actually is, or at least is likely to be.

25:32   With these assertions about Nothing and Infinity and Being, your job is that much harder since there are no models that can be used successfully to illustrate such consciousness, much less help you make a leap to a genuine understanding. You'll just have to do it anyway.

25:33   Infinity, Nothing, Consciousness, Absolute existence, and Being are all of the same nature, and in the same place, so to speak. The essence of Being and Consciousness is Nothing, which is the same as the Absolute nature of existence. It is prior to anything, and so it is the first "truth." It is beingness without beings, existence without space or objects. It is also beingness with beings, and existence with space and objects. It is also present and now.

25:34 Consciousness is not some thing or object, and it is not an activity of mind, nor is it mind. In the place of its nature or essence, consciousness occupies no place. It is not located within what we are conscious of or in the act of being conscious. These are functions of mind and perception, and they are cognition. Consciousness in and of itself is an absolute. It is the true nature of this moment. When we include time within our consideration it is the same. It seems that now exists as a point in time, but when we recognize that time always and only exists now, we can see that Now is an absolute, and so it is of the same nature as the others. It is all Absolute Being.

25:35 When we think of the existence of something, what comes to mind is the distinction that it *is* and allows for it to be perceived or brought to mind. Yet the true nature of existence isn't dependent on anything that exists. It just is. *Is* is. *Is* never changes or comes or goes; it is what *is*. There is no persistence of *is*, since *is* never remains nor can it not-be. Persistence only applies to what can *not* exist, and what *will* not exist, and so must persist or perish — this is not the nature of Being. Being *is*. Absolutely.

25:36 This place, this moment, this existence are all based on and a function of what is absolute — Infinity, Now, and Being. It is all the same. It is this. And none of it exists. This doesn't negate existence; it just points out its true nature. Do you get it? Perhaps you can see why Not-Knowing is such an important aspect of mind, since for the most part it is the human mind's only window into such matters.

25:37 Of course, all of this is simply an attempt to get at this matter using our intelligence, and so cannot actually create the conscious experience that a direct insight into the matter can. I am working backwards, so to speak, from the direct consciousness that now tries to find a way to lead the mind into understanding. This of course will fail. It is not possible via the intellect, but it is an interesting attempt, don't you think? You can have a direct consciousness of the matter in any moment, including this one. At least this kind of discussion creates an opening and basis from which to confront the truth on its own terms through contemplation. When contemplating, however, go for the truth and keep none of this chatter in mind.

> *Form is not different from emptiness.*
> *Emptiness is not different from form.*
> *Form is precisely emptiness, and*
> *emptiness is precisely form.*
> —The Heart Sutra

The Paradox of Being

25:38 Although it may seem like we're talking of Absolute Being as though it's nonobjective, we cannot separate consciousness from object or separate nothing from something. Absolute Nothing is not anywhere or elsewhere and so is not different from anything, nor is it anything. Nothing is an absolute. If it were different from anything or different from something, then it would be a something, wouldn't it? It would be the "thing" that is not whatever it is different from.

25:39   We've seen that distinction doesn't mean separation. That's true even of Being and self. Simply because we're conscious of what "being" *is* doesn't mean it is separate from self or somewhere else other than the self. If our true nature is an absolute and isn't located, then it is also not elsewhere, since "elsewhere" refers to some other location. This means that Being is also self; they are not separate. This doesn't mean, however, that as a self we are conscious of the nature of Being, or that our experience is a reflection of this nature. Self is a distinction of mind, not a direct experience of the truth.

25:40   I've used the phrases conceptual-self and false-self to reveal distinctions that we are "doing," and in this way "being," and yet it doesn't mean that the very place of such activity is in another location from Being. We are simply ignorant of what we are really doing and what we really are. You can't *do* Being. Being just *is*. You can only become conscious of what Being is, and this changes what you will identify with and so what you tend to do, but Being is only what you "are" and not something you can do. What you *can* do, along the lines of trying to experience Being, is be "real"—be honest, and straightforward—and you can contemplate.

Being and Self

25:41   As a self, our purpose is to pursue our survival, in whatever form that takes. We can change what it is we maintain or "be" by changing what it is we identify with and preserve. The more conscious we become, the more we can identify with what's true. This is called transformation. Relative to the self, our job is to become conscious of what's real and what's false, to uncover everything that dominates our personal experience and awareness, and to transform our identity, piece by piece, into what is real and true. But this doesn't change the truth or the nature of "being" in any way. Being doesn't require any action or maintenance or "doing" to be.

25:42   Relative to Being, our job is to become conscious of our true nature — to directly experience what the truth is, what we are. This in itself will create instant clarity since it is a direct consciousness of the truth, and within such consciousness the mind will relate to reflections of the truth, rather than inventions of the self. Again, this is impossible to describe or understand intellectually.

25:43   Self is never far away, however, even after such profound realization. The very same impulses and drives that created the self in the first place will likely still be in operation after any direct conscious experience, since our entire mind and system of awareness and cognition have been designed around self principles. Even following a profound "enlightenment" experience, it is unlikely that this whole system disappears completely. It is possible, but very unlikely.

25:44   For a period of time after realizing the true nature of being, the self-mind fades into the background. It is without import and engenders no pressing survival activity. It becomes just a tool to use rather than to be used by. Still, as long as any self remains, regardless of its attributes, survival in some form will in time reassert itself. We will once again become attached to and identified with something: either old habits and patterns, or new ones.

The dynamics of survival will be the same, even if the experience is different.

25:45   Until we can consciously realize that self doesn't really exist, it will remain the central feature of our lives. Once a charged field of perception has been created—enabling the self to relate to and manage its environment (internally and objectively)—this becomes and remains the reality in which we live. Judgments and emotions, reason and "instinct" rule the day. All this exists to serve the self, and so our very thinking, behavior, and awareness are dominated by the context of self-survival. Consciousness, on the other hand, is a matter of the Truth—what something really is. It is not subject to perceptions stuck in the context of the self principle. It is free of any filter or perspective, any belief or purpose. It exists only for itself, and as itself. It is about what is true, on any level.

25:46   Becoming more and more conscious is the goal here. Becoming more conscious is not about acquiring more beliefs, or education, or knowledge, or intellectual understanding, or even becoming aware of something. It is consciously grasping the real nature of something—anything—from a habit, an emotion, or relational dynamic, to an object, existence, or reality. Repeated enlightenments, or "direct experiences," generally become deeper and more inclusive each time they occur, and begin to produce greater wisdom and consciousness, and so continue to transform anyone who remains committed to this work.

25:47   This work shows up as becoming more conscious of personal traits and their origins, becoming more conscious of the nature of the forces that run you, patterns of thinking, assumptions, and core beliefs. It shows up as becoming more conscious of behavior patterns and why they exist, internal states and what they are, and so on. It shows up as becoming more conscious of relationships and what is really going on, of one's agenda in relation to others and life, grasping the design of the body and movement, the principles of effective interaction, the nature of manipulation, the nature of social survival, the consequences of lying, the nature of maturity and honesty, the nature of communication, etc. It shows up as becoming more and more conscious of the nature of self, the operating principle of self, the nature of life and existence, the true nature of being and reality. It shows up as becoming conscious of everything.

25:48   As conscious attention is placed on one's own experience and self — on every level and in every domain — this experience and self gradually become seen for what they are. Direct consciousness is always sudden, but human transformation is almost always gradual. The insights and enlightenments that create an increase in consciousness greatly empower the work of becoming more conscious of the mind and the subconscious, of self and life. As any aspect of the self-mind becomes conscious — seen and experienced for what it is — some transformation in the person will take place, a little or a lot depending on the depth of the consciousness and how much it changes one's awareness. The work feeds the work. Commitment is rewarded with greater insight, and with occasional leaps in conscious awareness that make even further leaps and insights possible.

25:49   Over time, the path of increasing Consciousness moves one's identity from a false self toward an honest conceptual self, and from this conceptual self toward the true nature of being a self, and from being a self toward the true nature of being, and from being toward absolute consciousness. Sudden insights may occur, and are necessary for transformation, but a very grounded and experiential understanding of the nature of every aspect of existence is necessary in order for true transformation to occur, and the immensity of this task usually requires time and commitment. But what else are you going to do? Until you die you've got nothing but time. You may as well use it to become conscious of the truth. It's what *is* right now.

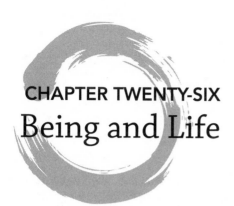

CHAPTER TWENTY-SIX
Being and Life

Neither a lofty degree of intelligence nor imagination
nor both together go into the making of genius.
Love, love, love, that is the soul of genius.
—Wolfgang Amadeus Mozart

What Now?

26:1 After such a barrage of in-depth information about almost every aspect of yourself and your experience, you may be a little confused about what to do with it all. The first thing to do is to read the book again. I know that may not sound like much fun. You just managed to get through an entire book that admittedly isn't easy reading. Do it again? I'm sure you realize by now that this communication isn't easy to grasp or hold within your daily experience. It will not be fully understood with one reading.

26:2 We're attempting to crack the shell of the human condition, to get at the heart of a matter that has not offered itself up for easy comprehension for as long as humans have pondered their own existence. This material needs to be studied, revisited, contemplated, and experienced by you. As we used to say at the Center, "You need to do the work in order to do the work." You need to read the book in order to understand how to more powerfully read the book. Still, back to the question: what to do with it all? Where do you go from here?

26:3 Become more conscious. There is no shortage of questions to ask about your self and life. So ask them, ask again, and then ask even more deeply than you did the last time. No matter what you are experiencing or what circumstances are present, you can always ask: What *is* this? This puts you in an appropriate frame of mind for creating a deeper and more conscious relationship to whatever seems to be so. The matters addressed in this book require a great deal of study and insight before they become truly clear. The good news is that, since these matters are about you and your experience, there is always something at hand to work on. Simply commit yourself to becoming more conscious, period.

26:4 Be ready to take on confusion and paradox, and remember that increasing consciousness rarely follows a linear progression. This work, and even great insights, can sometimes appear incongruous at first. Once you become conscious of the true nature of the matter, however, you're not likely to be confused. But if you happen to fall short of a deep direct consciousness, yet still get a hit on something genuine, the truth may seem inconsistent at times. Like trying to recall a dream, your insight may fade from view even as you grasp for it. Keep going for the truth, regardless of consistency, or whether it matches your picture of how things should go. In the end it will all work out. Just keep your attention on what's true—and then, on what's even truer.

26:5 Take care that you don't harbor a background conviction that becoming more conscious is somehow "elsewhere" or beyond your reach. It's not. It is right there in your present experience. You, just as you are, can become conscious in this very moment of what you are. You can, without doubt, grasp who you are, what mind is, and what life is really all about. Right now. Enlightenment and deep conscious insights usually occur through leaps of consciousness, or breakthroughs. But personal transformational progress is most often made in stages, increasing the depth of your consciousness step by step as you go. In either case, just hold that it's possible to become conscious, and keep pushing for an experience of what's true.

26:6   It is to be expected that, at some point, you will run into challenges or seem to hit a wall beyond which you find it difficult to proceed. So stay there awhile; it's all right. Become as conscious of yourself as you can, tell the truth, and keep contemplating. When you hit a wall, simply keep "staring" into it. Eventually it will crack open and you will realize what it is that your mind failed to grasp. Continue in this way even when it seems you can make no more progress.

> *Have good trust in yourself—*
> *not in the One that you think you should be,*
> *but in the One that you are.*
> —Maezumi Roshi

26:7   Let me offer a story that might confuse things further, but then again it could also provide a new perspective in which to hold your efforts. Gautama Buddha was someone who is said to have had "complete" enlightenment, meaning there was no more left for him to become conscious of regarding self, life, or the nature of reality. This is difficult to imagine, and we have only hearsay to go on, but let's consider it might be true.

26:8   Gautama was said to be truly compassionate, and yet after having attained complete consciousness, his first impulse was to wander into the mountains to finish out his life. It was not to teach or help others. When one of his future disciples asked him to share his enlightenment, his response went something like, "Why? No one will get it." But the disciple said, "Someone will." Gautama replied, "True, someone will." And so took up his teaching. Gautama gave his life completely to teaching what he had learned to others simply because "someone might get it."

26:9   Now, since his first position was that people just won't grasp this depth of consciousness, we can imagine it's probably not easy to grasp. Not only that, but throughout his first years of "teaching," he was silent. So what was he communicating? Further, one of the people said to have deeply "gotten it" did so during this silent period. So what was going on with all this? Obviously, we're not dealing with a logical subject matter that is readily understood with conventional thinking. But it is "get-able."

26:10   There's something worth noticing about Gautama's teaching and the teaching of other historical founders of participatory consciousness work. Consider the evolution of their work during their lifetimes. After great insight, such teachers are usually very clear and direct in their facilitation, attempting to convey the source of their understanding. Yet gradually, over time, they seem to become more and more structured, directing more of their communications to what amounts to "rules to live by." My guess is this is done out of compassion for the majority of people who just won't grasp the deepest aspects of the communication, and so is an attempt to provide these people with something to improve their lives — or "rules to live by" (which essentially boil down to something like "be good").

26:11   Another benefit to these rules, however, is that they put one into a more propitious state from which to recognize and really do the work of increasing consciousness. There are powerful principles to live by that empower personal growth and assist in creating a ground from which to more clearly see what's really going on in one's life. I recommend studying and adopting these principles. Yet ultimately my work is to facilitate those willing to grasp for themselves some of the deepest levels of consciousness about life and reality — what anyone does with this consciousness is up to them.

Our life is shaped by our mind;
we become what we think.
—Gautama Buddha

Life Principles

26:12   There are any number of intriguing belief systems — spiritual, philosophical, even scientific viewpoints — that we can adopt to change the way we experience life. But for the most part, after our initial infatuation subsides, the fact that they are externally obtained and require a belief in what others say begins to erode any deep sense of validity. We don't feel completely authentic in the matter since we have not experienced for ourselves the truth of that matter.

26:13   In contrast, notice that we are completely and undeniably certain that we don't know. This not-knowing is *ours*, and it's deeply personal. It is valid and requires no belief or hearsay. We can stand in Not-Knowing fully and without doubt. Strange as it may seem, from here we can more genuinely take on any other principle upon which to live.

26:14 Direct consciousness of who and what you are is possible, but as long as a self is the dominant factor in your experience, the operating principle of this self will remain self-survival. Yet the principles upon which this self stands, or that one is committed to in being a self, can vary widely.

26:15 Even within the domain of self there is a vast array of possibilities. The one most of us are stuck within is a self that is personal, individual, highly conceptual, and sometimes false. This is a very closed and limited system to maintain. By nature, it is exclusive rather than inclusive. But is this the only way to hold "self"? No— a self could be identified as almost anything. Through programming and custom, we certainly identify with the cultural norm—the internal and separate ego, and the body within which this ego seems to reside. This is only convention, however, and although it may be a difficult shift to make, it is possible to "re-identify" what self is, or at least commit whatever self seems to be to something other than the cultural norm.

26:16 For example, instead of identifying self as an exclusive, individual body-mind, we could identify self as all of humanity, or as life itself, or even as Absolute Consciousness. Such a shift from the individual to a larger context radically changes what we experience. The petty struggles of the individual become insignificant and are replaced by a much broader struggle far outside one's exclusive mind. Our actions become aligned to principles of an inclusive self-sense, without the pressure or demand that anything work out for us as an individual. When we consider a shift from the exclusive to the inclusive, very different principles become the foundation for our awareness, mind, and actions.

26:17   By contrast, as self-serving individuals our survival often involves such activities as misrepresenting ourselves to get what we want, taking care of our needs even though it may hurt someone else or the environment we share, competing with others for resources, and so on. We're likely to view things relative to our own small world and exclusive needs, but these self-serving activities may in some ways be even more detrimental than we comprehend. Because we identify with such an exclusive self-sense, our efforts can be misdirected relative to the whole, and in this way limit our own health and well-being. A more inclusive self-sense would offer a different view and so a different relationship to all that we encounter — cooperation would naturally replace competition.

26:18   Shifting the context in which we hold ourselves evokes a different domain of experience and will produce different actions. For example, if our "self" were to identify with consciousness, and our objective was to promote the growth of this consciousness — survival in a broader sense — our focus would change remarkably. We would find such principles as honesty, communication, learning, teaching, and cooperation to be indispensable. They would still be actions taken to support what we identify with — only the self-identity would change, not the basic dominance of the impulse to persist — but this impulse would be turned toward very different pursuits, perhaps even some that are inconsistent with self's needs.

26:19   There are empowering principles that are inclusive of a self but not limited to or completely centered around the individual — principles such as compassion, integrity, authenticity, communication, learning, and peace. The reason these are not exclusive by nature is that they require the inclusion of and openness to concerns of others, ideas, and actions that are not just self-serving. Such principles frequently demand that self serves something outside its own needs and mind. For example, real communication is clearly not limited to oneself.

26:20   Communication requires the inclusion of another person, and listening to truly get his or her experience as it is and for-itself, without reacting to it or turning it into something it's not. Communicating your experience to someone necessitates honestly presenting what you actually experience, without serving some other agenda or manipulation. So we can see that real and honest communication isn't exclusive to the individual, and from time to time may even interfere with self's desires or needs. It facilitates a true understanding and connection with another consciousness, and this may or may not be consistent with one's exclusive agenda. It is the same with all inclusive principles. Committing oneself to any such principle creates a different context for the self, which will show up rather differently than the introverted self-constriction usually slotted for the job.

Before we can become who we really are, we must become conscious of the fact that the person who we think we are, here and now, is at best an imposter and a stranger.
—Thomas Merton

26:21   There are also principles that are independent of the self and self-survival. Such principles as real inner freedom, deep questioning for the truth, committing oneself to enlightenment, and taking on an ever-deepening honesty are all non-self-oriented.

For example, we've seen that honesty doesn't support the self; it supports the truth, and such a pursuit can readily diverge from what a self wants. A commitment to honesty can often be inconsistent with a commitment to the needs of an individual self, whose complex matrix of attachments can easily undertake various courses of action and communication that are designed to misrepresent. We can see that "honesty" as a character trait could be an aspect of a self, and to the degree that one genuinely attempts to conform to this quality, the self will be bound by the limits of honesty. In other words, we will have to give up any action or communication that would require dishonesty or misrepresentation, and forgo any results that we might desire if they are inconsistent with being honest.

26:22 Yet, as merely a character trait, the depth of honesty will only go as far as the image of honesty—whatever that particular person imagines is meant by "being honest." Honesty beyond self, or honesty as a *principle*, is a practice of getting to and representing the truth. All communication and even all thoughts undergo the demand to be absolutely truthful. We are also charged with being open and not assuming that we know what the truth is. This becomes an ongoing practice, since when the truth is unclear or unknown, then the commitment is to discover what the truth is. When the truth is known, or to the degree it is known, then that is what the self must serve—compelling one's actions, thoughts, communications, and relations. We can see how this commitment would interfere on many occasions with the normal activities and drives of an individual ego-self.

26:23 We should be clear that all of this can still exist within the context of the self principle; it simply won't be self as we know it. Although such a new self-experience may seem transcendent and beyond survival, it is not. It is simply beyond the survival of what we conventionally are — an exclusive ego-self. Shifting from exclusive to inclusive will shift experience and relations to a greater context. It may destroy the particular self that was, but it does not eliminate the principle of survival altogether. Getting beyond survival is another story.

No matter how massive and detailed and complex and real
your "house" of self-concept seems, it is and never will be you!
You can walk out of the house at any moment.
And you know what? You won't miss it at all.

26:24   Independent of any self exists a Consciousness that is in no way bound to perception, mind, or survival. This is the stuff known only through direct realization or enlightenment, becoming conscious of the absolute or true nature of reality. Realizing that one's self — no matter what is identified as that self — *is this very Consciousness* reveals that the self, and therefore survival, is already nonexistent and unnecessary. This transcends survival since there is no self to survive. There is only Being.

26:25   Self-survival is not wrong. It is not right. It just *is*. So in this way, even self-survival is Being. At the same time, our experience within the context of self-survival is so dominated by right and wrong that we're unable to recognize this principle for-itself and as-itself. Although the self principle is necessary for a self to survive, when we consider that self is whatever is interpreted *as* self, then we also see that self can be almost anything. Self is a *distinction* within consciousness.

26:26   When the distinction of self is applied to particular aspects within the field of perception, those aspects are then identified as the self, and the impulse to maintain them arises. If "self" is wrapped around a specified number of cells, then that will be what must persist. If self is wrapped around a set of ideas or characteristic behavior patterns, then those are what need to survive. Within the context of the self principle, a distinction is made that categorizes everything as either me or not-me, and then goes to work to make sure "me" survives. If self includes absolutely everything, then no self-distinction can exist. Self, everything, and nothing are all one and the same.

26:27   But as long as you are identified with a self, you need to tell the truth about that. To move in the direction of freedom from this self-constriction you can take up disciplines toward that end, but your participation in these should not be mistaken for being outside the survival impulse. When self-survival is no longer the operating principle, then the act of "being" is no longer restricted to the concept of a self or the concerns of self-persistence. Attention is elsewhere, so to speak, and "being" resides nowhere at all. But such realization needs to be had by you; merely hearing about it does no good and will be misunderstood. Instead, what will do some good is to contemplate, and take up the discipline required by principles and practices that are not self-oriented.

Life may be found in the little things,
but it's how these circumstances are "held"
that determines our sense of satisfaction.

26:28   Committing to any nonself principle always empowers your life, and it also becomes an extremely powerful tool for discovering everything about yourself. But it's very challenging to stay with such principles because — even though taken on intentionally — they rip the shit out of the self. As you follow them and delve into them, you find they go deeper and deeper and continue to overturn previously unseen rocks of ignorance, revealing aspects of yourself that you never knew were there. Your goal should be to increase your consciousness of the truth, no matter what it is you're looking into. Committing to a powerful principle outside and independent of the self allows this course to be taken, and for your contemplation to be more fruitful.

26:29   As Leonardo said, "Among the great things which are to be found among us, the Being of Nothingness is the greatest." Said another way, this Consciousness work is the best thing to do. But will such work make us happy? Since life is lived within the ordinary day-to-day activities we engage in, no matter what our goals or aspirations, we all want to be happy. So let's take another look at this business of being happy.

Many persons have a wrong idea of what constitutes true happiness.
It is not attained through self-gratification
but through fidelity to a worthy purpose.
—Helen Keller

Happiness: Don't Want It

26:30   Once again, let's address one of the assumptions that keep us confused in a deep way. Even now it may still sound strange to hear that our purpose in life is *not* to be happy. Life as a goal of persistence demands that our commitment and attention be devoted to survival, and our perception be designed toward this end. Since mind serves and is generally considered to *be* the self, this self-mind is where all experience arises from and relates to. Our constant thinking and chatter, our emotions and reactions, our underlying drives and instincts, are all designed for and committed to the persistence of this self. Nowhere in any of this is happiness the purpose.

26:31 The devotion of mind and body to the persistence of ourselves is not a devotion to happiness. As a matter of fact, for reasons other than the simple fact that it is not, survival cannot be directed toward happiness. Happiness is not found in the pursuit of happiness. Strange as it may sound, *wanting* happiness is itself unhappiness.

26:32 We've addressed this contradiction before, and have seen that *wanting* implies a separation from the thing desired. So wanting to be happy suggests we are not happy. The very act of wanting happiness is an act of suffering. Happiness on the other hand is only found in *being* happy. Although we looked at the relation between survival and happiness in Chapter Sixteen, we were bombarded with so much information that this important point may have slipped through the cracks (another reason to read and study the book again). A quick review of some of the cultural assumptions related to happiness helps bring it back to mind.

26:33 Since we've noticed that getting something we want frequently brings a sense of pleasure, we reason that attaining everything we want should take pleasure to some ultimate, permanent level. If we think that an abundance of fulfilled desires indeed brings happiness, it makes sense that one of our culturally accepted goals is to get a lot of everything we want — an abundance of love, success, wealth, or even enlightenment. Without investigating it too much, we naturally assume that making everything work out and obtaining all that we want will bring the happiness we seek.

26:34 But we've seen that the fundamental operating principle of self—which dominates our every perception, thought, reaction, emotion, and action—makes this reasoning incomplete and happiness unattainable. Getting or maintaining what we want is a function of survival. It is not the pursuit of happiness even though it seems like it is. Remember the mouse is never meant to get the cheese, only to persist by running after it.

26:35 Ordinarily we tend to focus on acquiring whatever will fulfill our needs. With experience, we notice that our needs are never finally or ultimately fulfilled no matter what we accomplish. We begin to suspect that our activities and impulses may be cyclical—that they may even somehow cause our distress. This awakening suggests a high degree of sensitivity and alertness on our part, but still we find ourselves unable to step off of the mouse's wheel.

26:36 Unfortunately, our attempt to handle our many needs doesn't come to us like a cheese-chasing metaphor; it comes to us like life. Yet no accumulation of wealth, knowledge, status, or obtained desires will create happiness. We may be happy to have those things, but without being free within, we won't actually be happy. Happiness is as much about being free *from* ourselves as it is about being free to *be* ourselves. Try as we might, we still struggle with this as a possibility rather than live within it as a reality.

26:37 By now we know that navigating through the ups and downs of circumstance and the good and bad of our internal states is self-survival in action. If we're upset when something doesn't go our way, how can we be happy? We imagine it is a temporary glitch, and once we fix this problem we can then be happy. Usually the problem is seen as standing in the way of our happiness and so must be overcome in order for us to be happy. Yet it does not stand in the way of happiness; it stands in the way of self. This is a big difference. We've confused accomplishing survival—which shows up as getting what we want—with being happy.

26:38 Survival doesn't make us happy. It keeps us alive and persisting as ourselves. In the realm of survival, happiness is an illusion—it's some of the cheese that keeps us running on the wheel and so is just a tool of survival. Actual happiness is not something to pursue for itself. Happiness is better seen as being happy with whatever you are experiencing. This obviously is not the goal of survival, which must divide experiences into good and bad. Imagine being happy even though your experience is sad, or upset, or afraid. Imagine being happy without desiring happiness. Imagine being happy regardless of how you feel. This is true happiness. Doesn't sound like what we're used to as "happiness," does it? We aren't used to happiness; we're used to "victory" (or defeat), and victory is always temporary.

26:39 Earlier I pointed out that no matter what is accomplished throughout life, no matter how successfully you meet all of life's challenges, the end of the story is that you will fail. You will not survive. All goals accomplished and ordeals overcome will fall away. That may be a depressing and unacceptable fact for a self. But to Being it doesn't matter. If happiness is dependent on successfully realizing your goals, then ultimately there can be no satisfaction. On the other hand, if you are happy working toward your goals, then your happiness is not reserved for attaining them. If you are happy with whatever you experience, then you are happy. Being happy is a matter of being happy, period. As far as being happy goes, your true nature is already happy; simply let it "be." Realize that this is true, and then it is true. It doesn't matter what comes or goes.

26:40   It's an odd thing to say that life is already complete, and that at our source we are already happy. Perhaps happiness is an inherent aspect of Being, just as suffering and struggle are inherent aspects of self-survival. Don't fall into the trap, however, of thinking it is either one or the other—happiness versus suffering—but rather as being happy in the struggle and with suffering, and being happy without them as well.

26:41   Strange as it may sound, I love to work with people on the nature of suffering. I experience such joy when I do. I am often laughing and thoroughly delighted, not as a cruel joke and not from a lack of empathy, but because the matter is so obviously nonexistent that such work focuses my attention on this and puts me in the place where there is only joy. My experience of this seems to arise freshly when sharing it with others. Suffering isn't something to be resisted; it is to be fully experienced and understood. Just as happiness isn't something to be desired, it is also to be fully experienced and understood. Being conscious of the true nature of things elicits joy and humor. I don't know why. Perhaps the miraculousness of it all always blows away the human mind, and freedom within shows whatever is there as unnecessary, and so our long suffering then appears—although not without affection—as rather humorous.

Someone may be able to take your life away,
but they can't keep you from enjoying it as it is.

Discipline and Freedom

26:42 In our culture we often think of freedom as being able to do exactly what we want whenever we want. This is not freedom. Are we free from the drive to want? Are we free to be happy, whether or not we get what we want? When we realize that doing what we want is a programmed impulse, we see that we are not actually free; we are limited to and imprisoned by impulses, reactions, fears, desires, etc., that push us through life. These forces and activities simply "befall" us, seeming to occur naturally and reflexively without any choice, creativity, or consciousness on our part. This is why discipline is frequently an aspect of any work directed toward growth or transformation. Discipline has an integral relationship to freedom. Without discipline we can't tackle anything other than what befalls us. Discipline is taking on an activity outside of what would naturally arise for us without such a discipline. Think about it.

26:43 If you are driven to eat but also want to be thin, then you take on a discipline of not succumbing to the impulse to eat. In this way you are free to eat or not eat and can choose what to do in the matter. If you want to know who you are, you may wonder for a moment, but if this produces no results, then you'll move on to other things — ask someone, or just go have lunch. If you discipline yourself to contemplate the question, you aren't stopped by the wall of not knowing. You are free to pursue a direct consciousness of who you are rather than be controlled by the forces of boredom, distraction, frustration, and the like.

26:44 If you choose to master some art, how could this be done if you were constantly subjected to the momentary whims of your desires? Clearly, you'd need to discipline yourself to engage in activities other than your whims or succumbing to your fears and resistances. In this way you are free to take on mastery, to create something that wouldn't just befall you in the course of answering the call of whatever impulses or fears enter your mind from moment to moment. This ability to create a discipline is what allows you to get free of your own immediate self drives. Without discipline we find no access to freedom. When truly free, we don't need discipline, and yet are free to create any discipline.

Genius is eternal patience.
—Michelangelo

The Lava Syndrome

26:45   Even among those who have had genuine enlightenments or deep insights, most overlook a very important relationship between consciousness and mind. Consciousness is actually not a function of the mind, but the mind is profoundly influenced by any leap or increase in consciousness. Because the mind—what appears within one's experience via perception, thought, feeling, and the senses—is what is "known" in a conventional sense, it appears to be reality. I've seen person after person have an "enlightenment," or increase in consciousness, and then promptly confuse the actual consciousness with the impact this consciousness has on his or her mind. It can be difficult to discern the difference between becoming conscious and the effects that such consciousness may bring. This confusion occurs because nothing's there that *is* consciousness, and so the mind's attention readily falls onto what is there.

26:46 You may have heard that absolute Consciousness is not anything perceived. It's not something seen, or felt, or thought, or intuited. This is true. Consciousness has no quality, and is not ascertained through the senses. And yet how many times do you hear "notables" refer to the truth or the absolute as some sort of perceived experience, like seeing a bright light, or feeling some great ecstasy, or even something silly like grasping a blue pearl? Repeatedly, gurus and teachers of "spirituality" speak of all sorts of phenomena as if it's the truth. It's not. I'm not doubting they may have experienced these things; I'm just saying they are confused. These are all "experiences"—they have shape and location, or sense and distinction. They have form! Consciousness is not an experience. It has no form—and is not separate from form. So when you hear of someone speaking of absolute consciousness as if it is perceived, formed, or has a quality to it, they are wrong. Of course, you need to make a distinction between assertions of what *is* and metaphors used to make a point. But be wary of those who say consciousness is this or that.

26:47 The relationship between Consciousness and mind is perhaps best gleaned through using a metaphor I call the Lava Syndrome— which is applicable to enlightenment or to any kind of insight or breakthrough you may have. Our experience could be likened to a mountain of rock forming the perceived reality of the moment. In this metaphor, a breakthrough is seen as a volcanic eruption, breaking through the known rock that shapes current perception and opening it up to a new possibility. But what happens to a volcano after an eruption? The lava that came with the breakthrough—often confused with the breakthrough itself—forms a new layer and simply reshapes the rock that was there. It becomes the newly formed mountain of rock.

26:48 What's almost universally overlooked is that every breakthrough or insight will itself form new rock that will need to be broken through. This always happens. An actual insight or increase in consciousness isn't formed, and so cannot be held or known in a conventional way. What we can cling to is the "lava"—the new concepts or experiences that arose as a result of or in concert with the insight. In this way we say we "know" something. It is wise, however, not to confuse what has become known through a formulation of mind with the consciousness that evokes such formulations.

> *The fundamental delusion of humanity is to suppose*
> *that I am here and you are out there.*
> —Yasutani Roshi

A Final Word

26:49 The most basic truths about being a self may be hard to understand and experience, but not acknowledging them puts us in discord with our own nature and gets us into trouble. Simply because absolutes are difficult for the mind to grasp doesn't make them untrue or elsewhere. Who should be closer to an experience of our own being than we ourselves? Who could possibly have more authority in the matter of experiencing our own true nature than we do?

26:50 Experience for yourself the true nature of your existence. Whenever you look to others for assistance in this pursuit, make a distinction between what only sounds good and what actually makes a difference. There is a lot of fantasy surrounding these issues, and a great deal of opinionating and storytelling. Many people fall into the trap of thinking that if similar sounding words are used, or ideas proffered, one is the same as another. Rarely is this true. When you strip away all the fantasy and take out all the good sounding ideas, ask yourself: what is the real communication, what's its purpose, and does it deliver?

26:51   It isn't the information that you need; it's a personal understanding, a personal experience of what's so regarding this information. In the end, it is always up to you. It is your own awareness and experience that must become conscious, and only you can do that. This book adheres to the principles and spirit of real self-discovery. It's not meant to be taken as a new dogma to be believed but instead as an invaluable hand offered to you in your own efforts.

What has been shown to be possible by one of us
means that it is possible for all of us.
Our task is not to assess whether it is possible or not.
If it has been done, it "is" possible,
and most of what people want in life
has already been done at some time by at least one of us.
Our task is to determine first what we want to accomplish,
and second how it can be done.

26:52   Imagine that a "secret" is held within these pages that will only be revealed through personal investigation, experiential experimentation, and lots of contemplation. The book's communications must be seen as real in your own experience and as taking place in this moment, or they can't be truly understood. Become conscious of what is so about your own existence, and remember, the ultimate goal is freedom from all of it. Such freedom can't be had without grasping at the root bottom what all of this *is*. So at this point you have a choice. Having read through the book you have an idea of the work and what's involved. Now you have to decide: do you really want to take on this work, or just toss the book aside and go on as you always have? I recommend doing the work. It is really worth the effort.

26:53   This work is devoted to penetrating the human condition. Make sure not to confuse the many challenges of this endeavor with some new struggle and suffering. Granted, consciousness work can be daunting, and at times difficult to the point of being overwhelming. But even in the midst of such challenges, the mere possibility of the freedom that's available is cause for celebration. You can't transcend anything that you don't acknowledge and face head-on. The objective is to become conscious of what's so. Confronting what's true may not always be easy or reveal what you want to find, but it is still the truth. The good news is that in the end, it will set you free, and this is joyful beyond any fantasy.

If you understand, things are just as they are . . .
If you do not understand, things are just as they are. . . .
— Zen saying

26:54   There are many doorways through which to pass to reach the depths of your own consciousness. In one way or another they are all opened by some form of contemplation. Although contemplation shouldn't stand on its own, it is the key to this kind of consciousness work. When the purpose of your contemplation is to discover your true nature, remember, if you can't find your being directly, then the most genuine experience of *you* is found in not knowing who you are, and at the same time in the experience of you *being* in this moment. Don't jump to conclusions or try to fill in the blank. Simply be with the present experience of you in this moment and not knowing what it is. In this way, you remain closest to your most genuine experience: you don't know who or what you are—and it's OK. This is the place that is most genuine and true; and it is also in this very place that you can find out. But whether you do or not, be happy.

You are Being.
Being and self are not separate.

For more information about the work of Peter Ralston,
visit the Web site:
www.ChengHsin.com
or
www.PeterRalston.com